THE CONTEMPORARY GLOBAL
ECONOMY

A HISTORY OF THE CONTEMPORARY WORLD

General Editor: Keith Robbins

This series offers an historical perspective on the development of the contemporary world. Each of the books examines a particular region or a global theme as it has evolved in the recent past. The focus is primarily on the period since the 1980s but authors provide deeper context wherever necessary. While all the volumes offer an historical framework for analysis, the books are written for an interdisciplinary audience and assume no prior knowledge on the part of readers.

Published

Contemporary Japan
Jeff Kingston

Contemporary America
M. J. Heale

The Contemporary Global Economy
Alfred E. Eckes Jr.

In Preparation

Contemporary Latin America
Robert H Holden & Rina Villars

Contemporary South Asia
David Hall Matthews

Contemporary Africa
Tom Lodge

Contemporary China
Yongnian Zheng

THE CONTEMPORARY GLOBAL

ECONOMY

A HISTORY SINCE 1980

ALFRED E. ECKES, JR.

WILEY-BLACKWELL

A John Wiley & Sons, Ltd., Publication

This edition first published 2011

Blackwell Publishing was acquired by John Wiley & Sons in February 2007. Blackwell's publishing program has been merged with Wiley's global Scientific, Technical, and Medical business to form Wiley-Blackwell.

Registered Office
John Wiley & Sons Ltd, The Atrium, Southern Gate, Chichester, West Sussex, PO19 8SQ, United Kingdom

Editorial Offices
350 Main Street, Malden, MA 02148-5020, USA
9600 Garsington Road, Oxford, OX4 2DQ, UK
The Atrium, Southern Gate, Chichester, West Sussex, PO19 8SQ, UK

For details of our global editorial offices, for customer services, and for information about how to apply for permission to reuse the copyright material in this book please see our website at www.wiley.com/wiley-blackwell.

Library of Congress Cataloging-in-Publication Data

Eckes, Alfred E., 1942–
   The contemporary global economy : a history since 1980 / Alfred E. Eckes.
      p. cm. – (History of the contemporary world)
   Includes bibliographical references and index.
ISBN 978-1-4051-8344-4 (hardback) – ISBN 978-1-4051-8343-7 (pbk.)   1. International economic relations.   2. Economic history.   3. Globalization.   I. Title.
   HF1359.E23 2011
   337–dc22
                          2011001494

A catalogue record for this book is available from the British Library.
This book is published in the following electronic formats: ePDFs [9781444396843]; ePub [9781444396850]

Set in 10.5/13pt Minion by Toppam Best-set Premedia Limited
Printed in Malaysia by Ho Printing (M) Sdn Bhd

1   2011

Contents

Series Editor's Preface

The contemporary world frequently presents a baffling spectacle: "New world orders" come and go; "clashes of civilizations" seem imminent if not actual; "peace dividends" appear easily lost in the post; terrorism and "wars on terror" occupy the headlines. "Mature" states live alongside "failed" states in mutual apprehension. The "rules" of the international game, in these circumstances, are difficult to discern. What "international law" is, or is not, remains enduringly problematic. Certainly it is a world in which there are still frontiers, borders, and boundaries but both metaphorically and in reality they are difficult to patrol and maintain. "Asylum" occupies the headlines as populations shift across continents, driven by fear. Other migrants simply seek a better standard of living. The organs of the "international community," though frequently invoked, look inadequate to deal with the myriad problems confronting the world. Climate change, however induced, is not susceptible to national control. Famine seems endemic in certain countries. Population pressures threaten finite resources. It is in this context that globalization, however understood, is both demonized and lauded.

Such a list of contemporary problems could be amplified in detail and almost indefinitely extended. It is a complex world, ripe for investigation in this ambitious new series of books. "Contemporary," of course, is always difficult to define. The focus in this series is on the evolution of the world since the 1980s. As time passes, and as the volumes appear, it no longer seems sensible to equate "the world since 1945" with "contemporary history." The legacy of the "Cold War" lingers on but it is emphatically "in the background." The fuzziness about "the 1980s" is deliberate. No single year ever carries the same significance across the globe. Authors are therefore establishing their own precise starting points, within the overall "contemporary" framework.

The series treats the history of particular regions, countries, or continents but does so in full awareness that such histories, for all their continuing distinctiveness, can only rarely be considered apart from the history of the world as a whole. Economic, demographic, environmental, and religious issues transcend state, regional, or continental boundaries. Just as the world itself struggles to reconcile diversity and individuality with unity and common purpose, so do the authors of these volumes. The concept is challenging. Authors have been selected who sit loosely on their disciplinary identity – whether that be as historians, political scientists, or students of international relations. The task is to integrate as many aspects of contemporary life as possible in an accessible manner.

Most volumes in this series have a focus on particular countries, regions, or continents but this book "thinks globally" in expounding and explaining the dynamics of the "world economy." It is the intensity of contemporary "globalization" which gives the period under review its special character. The scale of exchange, in one form or another, exceeds that in any other era. So too do the speed of international communication and the size of capital flows. In these circumstances, classical expositions of the "terms of trade," conceived in earlier centuries, can seem archaic. "Free Trade," however, continues both to have its enthusiastic champions and committed opponents. If the "world economy" can be thought of as a "system," it appears volatile and unpredictable. It can sometimes be subjected to some degree of regulation of trade and tariffs through protracted and fraught negotiation, but only with great difficulty and fluctuating success. The economies of particular countries emerge, contract, or stagnate and upset assumptions of global hegemony (for politics is never far away). Charting a confident path through the complexity, this book distils the essence of the world economy and its workings with admirable lucidity.

Keith Robbins

Preface

In the generation after 1980, the world economy experienced both vast changes and enormous volatility. Technological advances in transportation, communications, and information-processing erased traditional barriers of time and distance. With the collapse of the Soviet bloc and the integration of China into the global trading system, four to five billion people entered the global market economy. These events opened the door to a new era of deregulated capitalism, led by the world's only remaining superpower. The United States pushed its neo-liberal economic model involving free trade and open-markets. As a result, people and nations became better connected. Flows of trade, capital, migrants, and information accelerated. Trade agreements knocked down barriers to market access. Multinational enterprises began to treat the world as a single economy for purposes of producing and selling goods.

In this radically-transformed environment, many bulls foresaw a long boom with expanding growth and rising incomes. They envisaged billions of new capitalists and middle-class consumers. Nation-states would fade into insignificance.

As it turned out, the post-Cold War global economy was flawed. Lax lending, easy credit, untested financial instruments, inattentive regulators, and free-market ideology all combined to fuel a world-wide boom in real estate and equity markets. When the bubble burst in 2007–8, housing prices collapsed, borrowers defaulted on mortgages, hastily-made fortunes vanished in collapsing stock and bond markets, and enthusiasm for deregulation and trade expansion dampened. As had occurred in the 1930s, governments stepped in to reform and resuscitate markets, and attempted to rescue enterprises deemed too important to fail.

The collapse left most developed countries in bad shape, facing massive adjustments. It shook faith in the Washington consensus of free markets and lightly regulated capitalism. It appeared to bolster emerging market advocates of state-owned enterprises and vigorous government regulation. While Britain led the nineteenth-century world economy, and America the late twentieth-century world, many thought the 2007–10 economic crisis signaled another leadership transition. Developing countries, such as China, India, and other emerging giants, would play enhanced roles in the twenty-first-century order and become the new engines of global growth.

This book on the contemporary global economy endeavors to provide an historical perspective on important developments. Chapters examine broad trends, key regions and countries, the evolution of thought about the international economy, international trade and finance, the rise of transnational business, and the economic crisis of 2007–10. The book also explores the underside of globalization – including issues relating to human trafficking and sweatshops, crime and terrorism, health, and the environment. Finally, the epilogue reviews initial efforts to regulate and rebalance the global economy, and to achieve sustainable growth, at a time when emerging powers aspire to a leadership role in international economic affairs.

Abbreviations

ATA	Air Transport Association
BIS	Bank for International Settlement
ECB	European Central Bank
ICC	International Chamber of Commerce
ICFTU	International Confederation of Free Trade Unions
IFSL	International Financial Services London
ILO	International Labor Organization
IMF	International Monetary Fund
IOM	International Organization for Migration
ITU	International Telecommunication Union
MPI	Migration Policy Institute
OECD	Organization for Economic Cooperation and Development
TI	Transparency International
UNCTAD	United Nations Conference on Trade and Development
UNDESA	United Nations Department of Economic and Social Affairs
UNODC	United Nations Office on Drugs and Crime
UNWTO	United Nations World Tourism Organization
USBEA	US Department of Commerce, Bureau of Economic Analysis
USBoC	US Department of Commerce, Bureau of the Census
USCIA	US Central Intelligence Agency
USDoS	US Department of State
USEIA	US Energy Information Administration
USFRBG	US Federal Reserve, Board of Governors
USFRBSF	US Federal Reserve Bank, San Francisco
USGAO	US Government Accountability Office
USNIC	US National Intelligence Council
USTR	US Trade Representative
WEF	World Economic Forum
WFE	World Federation of Exchanges
WTO	World Trade Organization

Chapter 1

Introduction

At the beginning of the twenty-first century the typical resident of Western Europe, North America, or Oceania was increasingly cosmopolitan in consumption and outlook. He or she drove an imported car (perhaps German or Japanese), wore Chinese-made clothing, ate food products from various corners of the world as part of a daily diet, and communicated with an Asian-assembled computer or cell phone to friends or relatives all over the world. Internet e-mail, innovations like Skype, and Facebook, eased the way for exchanging information and images, and keeping up with a global network of friends and contacts. Those fortunate enough to have investment portfolios often diversified with foreign stocks or bonds. And residents of affluent nations thought little of vacationing abroad (France, Spain, North America, and China were popular destinations). Retirees opted for more leisurely travel, perhaps on one of the giant cruise ships that frequented Alaska or the Baltic in summer, or the Caribbean and Mediterranean in winter.

Four to five billion people joined the global market during the last quarter century. While local political and economic elites opted to hobnob with other elites, skiing at Davos in winter or yachting at St. Barts or Monaco in summer, many of the poor intersected the global economy differently. Some 500 million new factory workers – many of them young women – produced t-shirts, sneakers, iPhones and other products for export to consumers in other countries. Frequently, they labored 12-hour days, or longer, for low wages (perhaps the equivalent of $2 per day, or less), and had little leisure time. Many spent a portion of their meager earnings

The Contemporary Global Economy: A History Since 1980, First Edition. Alfred E. Eckes, Jr.
© 2011 Alfred E. Eckes, Jr. Published 2011 by Blackwell Publishing Ltd.

to enhance their mobility and connections to family and friends. Even in the most desolate locations, basic products like motor scooters, cell phones, and televisions expanded knowledge and widened opportunities. Hearing of better jobs in high-income countries, some entrusted their lives to professional smugglers who locked them in shipping containers, or led them on desert treks in the middle of the night, to cross borders. As millions of migrants had done in centuries past, they risked their lives to improve prospects for their families and themselves.[1]

While millions of people have benefitted from the contemporary global economy – particularly high-income and professional elites – not everyone has shared its prosperity. OECD studies show an increasingly skewed distribution of wealth in some countries.[2] Jobless data indicate that factory workers, and their families, in high-income countries have experienced disruptions to their lives, as plants closed and jobs moved to countries with cheaper labor. In the Soviet Union, the collapse of state planning produced widespread hardship for pensioners and those unable to adapt to new circumstances. Others over-estimated their circumstances. They splurged, and took on risk and debt far in excess of their resources. As it turned out some of the greatest excesses were in government, where elected officials in many countries made fiscally irresponsible promises to win votes, and budget deficits soared.

In some ways the period from 1980 to 2010 was reminiscent of the late Victorian and Edwardian years before World War I. From about 1870 to 1914, the United Kingdom was the center of a similar world economy. It too was open to trade and finance, and imposed few restrictions on migration. As a result of submarine cables, news and information traveled rapidly. British-owned cables linked the world to London, and the Royal Navy protected maritime routes. Residents of the United Kingdom consumed the world's products and invested their savings abroad in mines, ranches, railroads, and utilities. John Maynard Keynes, the famous British economist, recalled this extraordinary period nostalgically in *The Economic Consequences of the Peace* (1920). Keynes marveled at the "internationalization" of economic life, noting in a famous passage from his writings how an inhabitant of London could order by telephone, while sipping his morning tea, the various products of the whole world. He could invest his wealth in natural resources and new enterprises overseas, or buy the bonds of any substantial municipality on any continent that his fancy or information might recommend.[3]

But, alas, the open world economy that preceded World War I vanished in that conflict, as governments imposed controls to regulate economic affairs. For some 65 years until about 1980 national governments restricted trade and finance, controlled migration, and managed communications through government-owned or regulated monopolies. During this period two world wars, a great depression, and intense Cold War competition disrupted earlier economic patterns. But, late in the twentieth century when Cold War tensions subsided and enthusiasm for market forces revived, a new era of open markets and deregulation dawned.

Scope

This introductory chapter provides an overview of the extraordinary economic, political, and technological developments that shaped the contemporary global economy over the last generation. It considers the overarching themes, while the second chapter offers a short historical perspective on the early- and mid-twentieth-century international economy. The next two chapters examine how the broad themes of growth, integration, and volatility impacted the rich countries and the developing world. The fifth chapter discusses how ideas and individuals shaped the contemporary economy. Here we review the thoughts of Adam Smith and David Ricardo in the eighteenth century, and more recent business and economic thinkers like John Maynard Keynes, Milton Friedman, and Peter Drucker. Subsequent chapters consider how these themes apply to international trade, global business, and finance. Then the book revisits the recent global financial crisis, and examines the interplay of darker forces, including organized crime, trafficking, sweatshops, health and safety, and environmental issues. A concluding chapter surveys recent efforts to regulate and rebalance the global economy, and to engage rising powers.

The Contemporary Age of Globalization, 1980–2010

During the period from 1980 to 2008 the international economy experienced a second golden era, reminiscent of the peaceful prosperity before World War I. Despite a number of local and regional conflicts in the Falklands, the Balkans, Afghanistan, the Middle East, South Asia, and Africa, there were no overt hostilities among the great powers. Governments gradually cut taxes, deregulated markets, sold off state-owned enterprises, and dismantled trade barriers. During the 1990s they reduced arms spending sharply as the Cold War ended. The pace of change accelerated and transformed the political, social, and economic landscape. A variety of long-term trends and short-term conditions produced new opportunities for humankind, but also brought greater uncertainty, dislocations, and anxiety about modernization. On the one hand, there was greater integration of people and nations (globalization). On the other, there was resurgent localization (as ethnic groups sought greater self-determination and devolution of power) and protectionism, as afflicted groups challenged international efforts to knock down barriers and integrate markets. The meaning and implications of these terms will be addressed in subsequent chapters.

On the political front, the fall of the Berlin Wall in 1989 and the dissolution of the Soviet Union in late 1991 introduced an era of relatively peaceful co-existence among the great powers. Responding to new circumstances and ideas, governments around the world deregulated economies, privatized industries, and permitted market forces to revive. In encouraging deregulation and privatization Prime Minister Margaret Thatcher and President Ronald Reagan led the way. Meanwhile, new technologies of transportation (wide-bodied jet aircraft and container ships), communications (cell phones, optic-fiber line, satellites), and information processing (personal computers), integrated national markets and dissolved border barriers.

For the global economy, these changes accelerated flows of information, goods, services, and money – and produced volatility as market forces responded to events. The world of the late twentieth century was no longer one in which ordinary people and communities were loosely connected by trade, occasional visitors, and sporadic information flows (an occasional telephone call or letter). The new world was immediate, interactive, and integrated. In the digital age information and ideas flowed at the push of a button. Retailers in one area of the world communicated electronically, and instantaneously, with suppliers thousands of miles away. Changes in commodity markets, exchange rates, stock prices, and interest rates impacted investors and producers in far corners of the world immediately. And large sums of private capital flowed easily and quickly from one region to another, challenging local authorities and regulators.

Life expectancy and literacy

During this period of economic restructuring, millions of people improved their own lives and living conditions. In most areas of the world, life expectancy increased. In 1960, a person born in a high-income country could expect to live to 69 years, 29 years more than a person born in one of the

Table 1.1 Life expectancy at birth (total years), 1960–2008

Region or country	1960	1980	2000	2008
World	52	63	67	69
High income countries	69	73	78	80
Australia	71	74	79	81
Canada	71	75	79	81
Euro area	70	74	78	81
France	70	74	79	82
Germany	70	73	78	80
Japan	68	76	81	83
New Zealand	71	73	79	80
United Kingdom	71	74	78	80
United States	70	74	77	78
Low and middle income countries	47	60	65	67
Least developed countries	40	47	54	57
East Asia and Pacific	46	64	70	72
China	47	66	71	73
Hong Kong	66	75	81	82
Indonesia	41	54	67	71
Malaysia	54	67	73	74
Philippines	53	61	69	72
Singapore	64	71	78	81
South Korea	54	66	76	80
Thailand	54	66	68	69
Vietnam	44	57	72	74
Latin America and Caribbean	51	64	72	73
Argentina	65	70	74	75
Brazil	54	62	70	72
Chile	57	69	77	79
Mexico	57	67	74	75
Middle East/North Africa	47	58	69	71
Egypt	46	57	68	70
Israel	72	72	79	81
Saudi Arabia	44	61	71	73
Turkey	50	60	70	72
South Asia	43	54	61	64
Bangladesh	40	48	61	66
India	42	55	61	64
Pakistan	49	58	64	67

(*Continued*)

Introduction

Table 1.1 (*Continued*)

Region or country	1960	1980	2000	2008
Sub-Saharan Africa	41	48	50	52
Ghana	46	53	58	57
Liberia	40	57	72	74
Mauritius	59	66	72	73
Nigeria	38	45	46	48
South Africa	NA	57	56	51
Zimbabwe	51	59	43	44
Eastern and Central Europe				
Czech Republic	70	70	75	77
Poland	68	70	74	76
Russian Federation	NA	67	65	68
Ukraine	69	69	68	68

Source: World Bank, *World Development Indicators Database*, http://data.worldbank.org/data-catalog (accessed August 2010).

least-developed countries. By 1980, the gap had fallen to 26 years, the high-income country resident living 73 years, the least-developed country resident 47. Twenty-eight years later (2008), the last year for which data was available, the gap remained large at 23 years. Those born in a high-income country could look forward to 80 years of life; those in a least-developed country to 57 years. While an enormous gap remained, life expectations had expanded both in rich and poor countries with only a few exceptions. In sub-Saharan Africa, where AIDS took a heavy toll, nine countries had declining life expectations. They were Botswana, the Central African Republic, the Democratic Republic of the Congo, Kenya, Lesotho, South Africa, Swaziland, Zambia, and Zimbabwe. Zimbabwe, one of the world's most mismanaged economies, experienced a decline of 15 years (from 59 to 44). In a few countries outside Africa, there were also declines in life expectancy: Kazakhstan, and the Ukraine, and North Korea.

In the developing world of low- and middle-income countries, the literacy rate for adults ages 15 and above rose from 69.9 percent to 80.2 percent between 1990 and 2008.[4]

Improving living standards

Economic growth offered other evidence of improving conditions. During the late twentieth century, economic growth dramatically elevated living standards in many markets. Since 1980, the world's gross domestic product (GDP) in constant dollars increased at a compounded rate of 2.8 percent annually. In developing economies GDP growth averaged an impressive 6.7 percent, but in older high-income countries the rate was closer to 2.5 percent.*

One of the better indicators of individual incomes is GDP per capita measured in constant dollars and using purchasing power parities to adjust for costs in different economies. For the world during the period 1980 to 2009 GDP per capita rose 60% from $5,949 in 1980 to $9,514 in 2009. The UK (74%) and the US (62%), had per capita GDP growth rate above the world average. But developing countries set the pace. In East Asia and the Pacific per capita GDP soared, rising 594% from 1980 to 2009. China enjoyed a 1,083% increase, followed by South Korea with 360%. India's per capita GDP rose 230%. Such meteoric growth turned millions of peasants into consumers with cash to buy cell phones, televisions, and motorized transport, and to connect with the outside world. Rapid growth also created many new Asian millionaires. In 2009 it is estimated that individuals with at least $1 million of investable assets in Asia equaled the number in Europe and approached North America's 3.1 million.[5]

In some areas of the world, per capita GDP growth was less spectacular. Remnants of the former Soviet Empire, undergoing the difficult transition from state-controlled to market-oriented economies, experienced uneven growth. Countries such as Poland and Slovakia, which attracted

---

* GDP is the gross value of all goods and services produced within an economy during a year. When divided by a country's population it becomes GDP per capita. Because price and currency fluctuations complicate comparisons, we rely on GDP per capita in constant dollars using purchasing power parities. Purchasing power parities enable economists to more accurately calculate comparative living standards and to compensate for exchange rate fluctuations.

GDP per capita is widely used as a proxy for the standard of living in an economy, because living conditions tend to improve when GDP per capita rises. It is not a measure of personal income and does not take into account the distribution of wealth or non-market transactions.

GDP data is widely available and is collected regularly, permitting international comparisons. Because it is the best available indicator of relative economic performance, we use it extensively in this study. In our country comparisons of per capita GDP, we have relied on World Bank data based on purchasing power parity (PPP) in constant 2005 international dollars. For more information, see World Bank, *WDI*. According to the World Bank, an international dollar has the same GDP purchasing power as the US dollar has in the United States.

considerable foreign investment, did better than more remote locations. Russia managed a small gain – up 7 percent from 1990 to 2009. In the Middle East Turkey and Egypt experienced solid gains, as did the countries of South Asia. Latin America had uneven and sub-par growth, except for market-oriented Chile which turned in a superior performance. Sub-Saharan Africa was the laggard with GDP per capita climbing only 8 percent, but this region generated strong growth after 2000. A number of countries in that region experienced declining incomes. Some of them had unstable governments, wars and internal conflicts, and high-levels of corruption in the public sector.[6]

Accelerating international migration

People move across borders, as goods, money, and information do. During the period from 1980 to 2010, the flow of migrants accelerated. In 1980, nearly 100 million people lived outside their country of birth, 30 years later 214 million (3.1 percent of the world's population) did. The trend was reminiscent of the first golden era of globalization (1870–1914) when governments imposed few barriers to migration and people moved freely. But two world wars, a great depression, and increasing immigration restrictions discouraged large-scale migration until the 1960s when governments began to relax restrictions. Some European governments began to recruit low-skilled labor in Turkey and North Africa. Over time former colonial powers – Belgium, the Netherlands, France, and the United Kingdom – admitted substantial numbers of immigrants from foreign colonies. Also, Australia, Canada, New Zealand, and the US relaxed immigration restrictions that benefited immigrants from Northern and Western Europe. Then during the early 1990s members of the European Union gradually loosened restrictions on migration, opening up opportunities for emigration among the member states.[7]

The dominant trend over the full 30-year period has been the growing movement of persons from low-income to high-income countries. Flows from Europe to traditional countries of emigration, like the US, Canada, and Australia, waned. Political events also influenced migration statistics in the 1990s. Among the big events were the collapse of the Soviet Union and its satellite regimes in Eastern Europe, the reunification of Germany, conflicts in the Balkans, and the opening up of China. Russia absorbed 4.4 million immigrants, more than double the previous decade. In part this was a statistical issue, the result of reclassifying internal migrants as international migrants when the Soviet Union disintegrated, and 15 independ-

Table 1.2 Gross domestic product per capita (purchasing power parity, constant 2005 international $)

Country or region	1980	1990	2007	2008	2009	2009/1980
World	5,949	6,814	9,529	9,688	9,514	160%
High income countries	19,495	24,505	33,873	33,870	32 ,600	167.2%
Australia	20,042	23,979	33,848	34,522	34,259	171.0%
Canada	22,569	26,355	36,074	35,895	34,567	153.2%
Euro area	18,961	23,393	30,966	30,993	29,603	156.1%
France	20,253	24,315	30,651	30,546	29,578	146.0%
Germany	20,688	25,672	33,236	33,719	32,144	153.4%
Japan	18,647	25,946	31,660	31,296	29,688	159.2%
New Zealand	16,952	18,434	25,649	25,270	24,873	146.7%
United Kingdom	18,461	23,743	34,099	34,048	32,147	174.1%
United States	25,931	32,474	43,745	43,533	42,107	162.4%
Low and middle income countries	2,435	2,786	4,684	4,902	4,968	204%
Least developed countries	–	812	1,184	1,238	1,259	155% (1990)
East Asia and the Pacific (developing)	793	1,393	4,800	5,167	5,507	694%
China	524	1,101	5,239	5,712	6,200	1,183%
Hong Kong	13,945	23,697	39,958	40,599	–	291.1% to 2008
Indonesia	1,361	2,087	3,521	3,689	3,813	280.2%
Malaysia	4,891	6,646	12,752	13,117	12,678	259.2%
Philippines	2,618	2,385	3,182	3,244	3,216	122.8%
Singapore	14,454	23,429	49,739	48,002	45,978	318.1%
South Korea	5,544	11,383	25,021	25,517	25,493	460%
Thailand	2,231	3,961	7,333	7,469	7,258	325.3%
Vietnam	–	902	2,455	2,574	2,681	297.2% (1990)
Latin America and the Caribbean (developing)	7,482	6,975	9,489	9,781	9,496	127%

(*Continued*)

Table 1.2 (*Continued*)

Country or region	1980	1990	2007	2008	2009	2009/1980
Argentina	10,067	7,492	12,506	13,220	13,202	131.1%
Brazil	7,572	7,179	9,181	9,559	9,455	124.9%
Chile	5,366	6,583	13,045	13,391	13,057	243.3%
Mexico	10,422	10,121	13,371	13,434	12,429	119.3%
Middle East and North Africa (developing)	4,357	4,311	6,144	6,298	6,379	146.4%
Egypt	2,432	3,184	4,762	5,011	5,151	211.8%
Israel	15,028	17,864	25,005	25,548	25,268	168.1%
Saudi Arabia	34,599	19,162	21,302	21,713	21,245	−38.6%
Turkey	5,694	7,806	11,973	11,904	11,202	196.7%
South Asia (developing)	892	1,222	2,458	2,540	2,679	300.3%
Bangladesh	604	680	1,178	1,233	1,288	213.2%
India	899	1,249	2,695	2,796	2,970	330.4%
Pakistan	1,191	1,678	2,348	2,345	2,381	200%
Sub-Saharan Africa (developing)	1,760	1,585	1,859	1,914	1,899	108%
Ghana	983	897	1,286	1,351	1,370	139.4%
Liberia	1,765	484	350	358	360	−79.6%
Mauritius	3,729	6,115	10,987	11,472	11,659	312.7%
Nigeria	1,668	1,420	1,872	1,939	1,950	116.9%
South Africa	8,763	7,975	9,367	9,604	9,332	106.5%
Zimbabwe	247	265	–	–	–	–
Eastern Europe and Central Asia (developing)	–	1,393	4,800	5,167	5,507	395.3% (1990)
Czech Republic	–	16,320	22,863	23,223	22,098	135.4% (1990)
Lithuania	–	12,499	17,010	17,571	15,013	120.1% (1990)
Poland	–	8,171	15,655	16,436	16,705	204.4% (1990)
Russia	–	12,630	13,912	14,706	13,554	107.3% (1990)
Ukraine	–	8,063	6,547	6,721	5,737	−28.8% (1990)

Source: World Bank, *World Development Indicators*, http://databank.worldbank.org/ (accessed October 2010).

ent states took its place. A united Germany took in 3.6 million immigrants during the 1990s, up sharply from 1.85 million in the prior decade. A surge in asylum seekers and refugees resulted from regional conflicts in the Balkans and elsewhere. From 1980 to the present the foreign-born Chinese population quadrupled in the US from 363,277 to 1,570,999. Large numbers of Chinese students entered the US to complete college degrees. Many of these married and brought over family members. A number claimed political asylum.

Globalization impacted migration patterns in a big way during recent decades. Improved communications and cheap transportation, new patterns of trade and manufacturing, and the deregulation of business gave impetus to people movements for economic improvement. With better information about living conditions in other regions of the world, the gap in income levels between rich and poor countries prompted residents of developing countries to look beyond their own borders for economic opportunities. Most of these migrants were unskilled workers, but many had advanced education and professional skills.[8]

Europe and North America experienced the greatest immigration growth in the 20 years since 1990. The US gained nearly 20 million immigrants, and their share of the population rose from 9.1% in 1990 to 13.5% in 2010. Five countries in Latin America and Asia supplied 44% of the total immigrant population. The largest share came from adjoining Mexico, about one in every three. The others included the Philippines, India, China, and Vietnam – all in Asia. Germany received nearly 5 million immigrants, and their share of the population rose from 7.5% to 13.1%. Many came from Poland and Turkey, as well as other areas of Eastern and Central Europe. In the United Kingdom, there were nearly 4 million more immigrants, with the share rising from 6.5 to 10.4% of total population. The largest numbers came from former colonies India and Pakistan, South Africa, and Nigeria in the developing world. While these trends show the increasing mobility of the world's workforce, it is worth emphasizing that the migration of people accelerated somewhat faster (1.6% compounded annually from 1990 to 2010) than the world's population growth (1.3%).[9]

Much of this migration followed well-established corridors, reflecting the influence of networks. Ten point three million Mexicans moved across America's southern border, 3.5 million residents of Bangladesh entered India, 2.7 million Turks migrated to Germany, and 2.2 million Indians left for the United Arab Emirates. Large numbers of workers seeking temporary labor moved from South and Southeast Asia to countries in the Middle East. Thousands of Indonesians crossed into Malaysia in search of jobs, as did thousands of Burmese to Thailand, and large numbers of Filipinos to Singapore, Hong Kong, and Japan.[10]

Since 1980 waves of human migration have increased the racial diversity of many countries, including some historically white. According to the Migration Policy Institute, Britain was 94 percent white in 1991. In 2008 it was 81 percent white, with Asians and blacks having more than doubled their share of the population. Of the foreign-born population, the Irish (424,000) were outnumbered by Indians (639,000), Poles (526,000), and Pakistanis (436,000).[11]

Remittances to home countries

These migrants, whether temporary or permanent, continue to make substantial contributions to their countries of birth. Many remit a significant portion of their earnings to relatives and residents of their home countries, as migrants have done for centuries. In 2008, worldwide remittances were estimated at $444 billion. Of this amount $338 billion went to developing countries to support families. The largest of these recipients were India ($51.6 billion) and China ($48.5 billion), Mexico ($26.3 billion), and the Philippines ($18.6 billion). As a percentage of GDP, Tajikistan, Moldova, and Tonga each received remittances amounting to over 30 percent of GDP. With over 20 percent of GDP coming from remittances were the Kyrgyz Republic, Honduras, Lesotho, Guyana, Lebanon, Haiti, and Jordan. Remittances of this magnitude far exceeded development assistance from governments and international institutions.[12]

Continuing rural to urban migration

Another important trend involved the continuing migration from rural to urban areas within nations. In 1960, less than one-third of the world's population lived in urban areas. By 1980, 39% did, and by 2009, over half did. In high-income countries 77% of the population resided in urban areas in 2009 (90% in the United Kingdom; 82% in the US; 73% in the euro region). But large numbers of the world's population continued to live in abject, rural poverty in sections of Africa, Asia, and Latin America. In the world's least developed countries, a group of 49 countries with a population of 818 million, 71% lived in rural areas in 2009, compared to 83% in 1980. In the world's two most populous nations, China and India, residents of rural areas accounted for over half of the population. In China it was 56%, down from 80% in 1980, and in India, 70%, down from 77%

in 1980. The historical experience of high-income countries suggests that migration from rural to urban areas will remain an important trend in emerging markets – especially in India and neighboring South Asian countries – for years to come.[13]

Slower population growth

Why had per capita incomes risen so sharply? The dynamism of the global economy was obviously an important factor, but so was slower population growth. While world population rose over 50 percent from 4.4 billion in 1980 to 6.1 billion in 2000 and 6.7 billion in 2008, the rate of growth slowed. It was 2.5 percent worldwide in 1960, but fell to 1.7 percent in 1980, and 1.2 by 2008. In effect the world's population, which had been doubling every 29 years in 1960, doubled every 60 years in the early twenty-first century.

Yet population growth patterns were uneven. The population of low-income countries rose 93 percent over the period after 1980, far faster than for middle-income countries (51%) and high-income countries (22%). In some countries population growth actually turned negative. This occurred in the Ukraine, Russia, Poland, Japan, Hungary, Georgia, and other countries of Central Europe and Western Asia. There lifestyle issues, such as higher rates of smoking, alcohol consumption, and suicides, as well as the easier emigration of people had a negative impact. So did a declining birth rate among non-Muslim populations. In sub-Saharan Africa, the AIDS epidemic slowed population growth.[14]

Population control measures also had some impact. China took drastic steps in 1978, limiting couples to one child. As a result, the growth rate fell sharply from 2.8 percent in 1970 to 0.7 percent by 2000. In Mexico, government programs to encourage family planning, as well as a large outflow of migrants to the United States, helped to explain a drop from 3.2 percent population growth in 1970 to 1 percent by 2008. In Japan and some high-income areas of Western Europe, the population grew older, as couples chose not to have children.

Aging populations

Of course, greater longevity also meant older populations. In high-income countries, the percentage of people over age 64 to the working age population (dependency ratio) rose from 18% in 1980 to 23% in 2008. It soared in Germany (30%), Italy (31%), and Japan (33%). The rising numbers of senior citizens signaled problems for public officials responsible for providing social services, medical care, and other government assistance. The private sector and the working population would likely face higher tax burdens to pay for these inter-generational transfers. Emerging market countries faced no such burden. In China only 11% of the population was over 64; in India 8%. In much of Africa, the Middle East, and South Asia the ratio was even lower – 6 to 7%. In the developing world, a younger population wanted cars and consumer goods. Goldman Sachs economists have predicted that an expanding middle class in developing countries will continue to drive world growth and market opportunities in the decades ahead. Two billion people may join the middle class by 2030.[15]

Enhanced mobility

Another distinctive feature of the post-1980 global economy involved the enhanced mobility of goods, services, money, and information. As noted elsewhere, technological improvements in transportation, communications and information technologies gave a giant boost to market-opening and integration of national markets. Where border barriers and controls once impeded trade, their removal boosted imports. Corporations once rooted in the nation-state could move factories overseas to low labor-cost countries, and operate complex global supply chains. Jack Welch, the CEO of General Electric, vividly described this trend in 1998 when he told TV interviewer Lou Dobbs: "Ideally you'd have every plant you own on a barge to move with currencies and changes in the economy." He implied that plants could be moved wherever wages were lowest and regulations least intrusive.[16]

Big business's enthusiasm for offshoring and global sourcing diverged from the sentiments voiced by earlier generations of business leaders. In the early twentieth century business leaders thought in national terms, and with few exceptions relied on exports to serve foreign customers. By the late twentieth century Jack Welch's enthusiasm for global market opportunities better expressed the *zeitgeist*, or spirit of the times. The world of multinational enterprise now strongly backed economic and financial integration, and trade expansion.

Greater economic integration

World Bank data show the rising significance of these transactions. In the post-World War II period, trade grew far more rapidly than production for national consumption. The ratio of merchandise trade to GDP, a standard measure of a country's dependence on other nations, climbed steadily. World trade rose from 21 percent of GDP in 1970 to 35 percent in 1980 and to 53 percent in 2008, before the global recession disrupted trade flows. Trade exceeded 300 percent of GDP in 2008 for two small trading units, Hong Kong and Singapore. For euro-area countries, merchandise trade integration rose over 26 percentage points between 1980 and 2008. The US also became more reliant on the global economy. For the US, the ratio of trade to GDP climbed nearly 7 percentage points between 1980 and 2008. Incidentally, these figures do not take into account trade in services (such as banking, transportation, tourism, consulting, and the like), because services are more difficult to measure. Also, there are gaps in available service data, and delays in tabulating it.

Some of the most rapid integration with world markets involved former Communist countries. In 1970, merchandise trade represented only 5 percent of China's GDP, a decade later 20.1%, and then it surged to 56.7% in 2008. In 1990, Vietnam's trade to GDP ratio was 79.7%; in 2008, 176.4%. With the collapse of the Soviet Empire in Eastern Europe, countries of Central and Eastern Europe joined the global economy. In 1994 Russia's trade with the world amounted to 29.9% of GDP, but, 14 years later, it was 45.8%, comparable to many high-income countries.[17] The Czech Republic, Poland, and the Ukraine conform to this pattern.

Among developing countries the same pattern of growing engagement with the international economy applied generally. Low- and middle-income countries increased their trade dependence from 34.2 percent in 1980 to 55.6 percent in 2008. Some of the most rapid improvement occurred in East Asia and the Pacific where the merchandise trade ratio rose from 35.4 to 65.9 percent. Of course, a few troubled countries in the Caribbean and Africa slid backwards, but these situations appeared to reflect special and temporary circumstances, such as commodity-price fluctuations and internal unrest.[18]

Over the 30-year period, export-led growth – particularly exports of manufactures – enabled emerging nations, such as China and four smaller Asian "tigers" (Hong Kong, Singapore, South Korea, and Taiwan) to thrive in the global economy. These countries lured foreign investors to build factories, transfer technology, use inexpensive local labor, and produce goods for export. The developing countries of Asia saw exports of manufactures rise as a share of their total exports from 60 to 80 percent between 1990 and 2009. Annual GDP growth rates in some areas of Asia exceeded 8 percent, and the region offered an alternative model for developing countries around the world to imitate, one that hinged on active government leadership.[19]

The Asian export-led development strategy succeeded because it targeted the United States and other high-income markets in Western Europe, particularly the United Kingdom. From the mid-1980s both the US and the UK experienced widening, and chronic, deficits, as their consumers absorbed large quantities of goods from Asian countries. British imports of goods from developing countries of East Asia and the Pacific rose from 1% of total imports in 1980 to 10% in 2008. US imports of goods from those countries climbed from 5% of total imports in 1980 to 21% in 2008. For both countries the current account balance (the broadest measure of a country's relationship with the world) turned negative in the mid-1980s and remained negative for more than 20 years.† Between 1980 and 2009, the US experienced a cumulative current account deficit of $7,745 billion, and the UK had a cumulative deficit of $711 billion. Together the two English-speaking nations pumped $8.5 trillion dollars into the global economy. Both borrowed money from abroad to sustain consumption of foreign goods far in excess of their own capacity to produce and sell in the global market. In late 2009, overseas buyers held 28% of British government debt, up from 17% a decade earlier. In the US, foreign holdings of government debt rose from 18.8% of debt holdings in 2000 to 30.4% in 2010, indicating a growing dependence on foreign investors to sustain a high-consumption lifestyle.[20]

Poor, deeply-indebted countries also bought far more from the world than they sold during the 1980–2010 period. According to the World Bank, as a group poor, debt-ridden countries ran a deficit amounting to 11 percent of GDP in 2008. Unlike the two English-speaking nations (the US and the UK), which together account for about 19 percent of world imports, the poor debtors account for a very small share of world trade. Thirty-two of 38 are African. It is an uncomfortable fact that sub-Saharan Africa, with a population of 818 million, is less significant in international trade than Singapore, a city state with a population of only 5 million people.[21]

Large trade surpluses helped a number of other countries to build up currency reserves. Manufacturing powerhouses, like China, Japan, and South Korea, exported far more than they imported, and amassed

---

† The current account weighs trade in goods and services, plus income from investments and transfer payments (such as worker remittances and pensions). A surplus indicates a country is a creditor to the world, a deficit that it is a debtor.

Table 1.3 Ratio of merchandise trade to gross domestic product (percent)

Country or region	1970	1980	1990	2000	2008	2009
World	20.5	35.1	31.3	40.8	53.1	41.8
High income countries	21.0	35.4	31.3	39.8	52.2	40.5
Australia	23.6	29.4	26.0	32.5	37.3	34.6
Canada	36.0	48.4	43.1	71.9	58.4	48.4
Euro area	31.3	41.9	41.3	61.0	68.2	57.1
France	25.3	36.3	36.2	50.2	46.6	39.4
Germany	30.7	41.4	45.3	55.2	72.4	62.0
Japan	18.5	25.4	17.1	18.4	31.6	22.3
New Zealand	38.3	47.6	42.5	52.8	55.1	39.8
United Kingdom	33.1	41.6	40.3	42.9	41.0	38.4
United States	8.4	17.4	15.8	20.6	24.1	18.8
Low and middle income countries	18.2	34.2	31.7	45.2	55.6	45.0
Least developed countries	–	35.0	29.0	43.9	62.3	52.8
East Asia and the Pacific (developing)	12.2	35.4	47.0	59.5	65.9	51.5
China	5.0	20.1	32.3	39.6	56.7	44.3
Hong Kong	142.7	150.3	217.4	246.4	354.4	–
Indonesia	21.8	42.0	41.5	66.1	52.2	39.1
Malaysia	72.2	95.4	133.4	192.1	160.7	145.7
Philippines	34.1	43.3	47.8	101.2	65.7	52.3
Singapore	211.7	369.8	308.1	293.7	340.3	282.9
South Korea	31.7	62.4	51.1	62.4	92.0	82.5
Thailand	28.3	48.6	65.7	106.7	130.9	108.5
Vietnam	–	–	79.7	96.6	176.4	141.0
Latin America and the Caribbean	19.2	27.3	23.3	35.7	41.1	33.8
Argentina	11.0	24.1	11.6	18.1	39.0	30.7
Brazil	13.2	19.2	11.7	17.7	23.2	18.2
Chile	25.7	38.1	51.1	50.1	75.1	58.8
Mexico	10.9	20.7	32.1	59.5	55.9	53.9
Middle East and North Africa	33.5	48.0	42.4	47.9	65.9	53.5
Egypt	20.2	34.5	36.8	19.9	45.8	36.1
Israel	53.2	70.3	55.0	55.4	63.8	49.8
Saudi Arabia	61.1	84.7	58.6	57.2	90.2	78.0
Turkey	9.0	15.7	23.4	30.9	45.7	39.5
South Asia	8.4	16.9	16.4	24.0	42.7	32.3

(*Continued*)

Table 1.3 (*Continued*)

Country or region	1970	1980	1990	2000	2008	2009
Bangladesh	–	18.5	17.6	32.4	49.3	41.3
India	6.8	12.8	13.1	20.4	42.5	31.5
Pakistan	12.2	33.6	32.6	26.9	38.2	30.5
Sub-Saharan Africa	36.1	57.2	41.9	51.7	64.5	52.3
Ghana	39.2	53.7	35.7	93.3	54.5	52.1
Liberia	104.4	117.9	374.1	177.8	125.3	80.1
Mauritius	–	91.5	106.0	79.6	75.6	66.0
Nigeria	18.3	66.4	67.5	64.6	63.6	52.9
South Africa	40.3	55.9	37.4	44.9	65.6	47.6
Zimbabwe	39.7	42.9	40.7	51.2	–	–
Eastern and Central Europe						
Czech Republic	–	–	83.6*	107.7	133.7	114.9
Poland	–	–	43.9	47.2	71.8	65.4
Russia			29.9**	57.8	45.8	40.2
Ukraine			40.1**	91.3	84.5	75.0

Notes:
* = 1992, ** = 1994
Source: World Bank, *World Development Indicators*, http://databank.worldbank.org/ (accessed January 2011).

large current-account surpluses. They piled up huge holdings of foreign-exchange and reserve assets. By 2010, China had reserves of $2.5 trillion, Japan $1 trillion, and Russia $439 billion. Taiwan ($353 billion) and South Korea ($270 billion) also had large stockpiles of currency reserves.[22]

Transition from manufacturing to services

Another distinctive feature of the 1980–2010 period was the gradual transition of high-income economies away from manufacturing toward services – especially financial and information services. As explained in Chapter 5, futurist Alvin Toffler depicted this shift as a historic move away from smokestack industry to a post-industrial, knowledge-based economy. In a number of high-income countries emerging service sectors generated large numbers of jobs. This was especially so in the United Kingdom where the value of services rose from 56% to 76% of GDP between 1980 and 2007, reflecting the expansion of London as a world financial center. Employment in industry dropped from 37% to 22%, while employment in services rose from 59 to 76% of total employment. In the United States the value of services rose from 64 to 77% of GDP. The percent of employment in industry fell from 31% in 1980 to 21% in 2007, while service employment rose from 66 to 78%. Other major industrial countries mirrored this pattern to a lesser extent. In Germany services rose from 57 to 69% of GDP, and in Japan from 55 to 68%.[23]

Resurgence of financial markets

The resurgence of international financial movements and markets also distinguished the post-1980 period. One way to view this trend is to look at foreign direct investment (FDI), where a company in one country buys or builds a factory or facility in another. Data from the United Nations Conference on Trade and Development, an international institution with 193 members, show that the accumulated inward stock of world FDI soared from 9.8% in 1990 to 32.5% in 2007 before the economic collapse. For developing countries as a group it climbed from 13.6% in 1990 to 30% in 2007, and for developed countries from 9% to 33.3%. While Western Europe and the United States remained attractive to investors, large emerging markets such as China, India, and Brazil captured the lion's share of investment in developing countries. By 2007, investment flows to China increasingly targeted services, high-tech industries, and value-added activities, as multinationals shifted their strategies. Many no longer viewed China as principally a low-cost manufacturing base. Instead, they wanted access to a large, competitive market, and they sought to establish research and development centers.[24]

The growth of global stock exchanges provides another window to financial globalization. In 1990, the value of stocks traded on world stock exchanges equaled 28% of world GDP. Over that decade equity markets internationalized and soared. The value of stocks traded rose to 152% of GDP in 2000 and 184% in 2007 before falling back. In high-income OECD countries, the value of stocks traded as a share of GDP rose from 27% in 1990 to 216% in 2007. Markets in London and New York saw some of the greatest growth. In Britain the value of shares traded rose from 28% of GDP in 1990 to 368% in 2007. In the United States the pattern was similar. From 30% of GDP in 1990, it jumped to 259% in 2007. In Japan, where an economic slowdown cooled speculative trading in 1998, stock trading rose from 53% of GDP in 1990 to 148% in 2007.

Some of the most surprising developments were in former Communist countries, where capitalism revived with a flourish. Stock trading even boomed in Russia. Trading climbed from 8% of Russian GDP in 2000 to 58% in 2007. In China, a country with a mixed economy and Communist political leadership, stock trading leaped from 60% of GDP in 2000 to 230% in 2007. The stock-trading frenzy spread to developing markets around the world, such as Brazil, India, and South Africa. In Brazil stock trading rose from 1% of GDP in 1990 to 16% in 2000 and 46% in 2008. India saw stock trading jump from 7% of GDP in 1990 to 111% in 2000 and 91% in 2008. In South Africa stock trading amounted to 7% of GDP in 1990, 58% in 2000, and 150% by 2007.[25]

Deregulating markets and privatizing government

In the years after 1980, the decisions of governments to deregulate markets, privatize government-owned firms, and cut government spending also buoyed the private sector in many countries. In the US, where President Reagan and other presidents pushed deregulation and privatization, government spending declined from 16.8% of GDP in 1980 to 14.4% in 2000 before rising after the terrorist attacks of 2001 to 16.1% by 2007. In the United Kingdom, government spending dropped from 21.7% of GDP in 1980 to 18.6% in 2000.[26]

Countries in the developing world and East Asia have typically relied on extended family networks for old-age support. Government spending in the poorest countries is typically about 10 percent of GDP. Even in prosperous city states like Hong Kong (8%) and Singapore (11%), the percentage remains low. In emerging giants India (12%) and China (14%), government spending for consumption is a little higher.

Rise of Asia

During the contemporary period millions of new workers entered the global workforce and purchased goods in the marketplace. What is especially distinctive about this period is the acceleration of growth in East Asia, South Asia, and several other emerging countries, such as Brazil, as well as increased international competition in the high-income countries of Western Europe and North America. As world trade expanded rapidly, consumers in high-income countries experienced more choices and greater price competition. Big business in North America and Western Europe awakened to the potential of emerging markets, both for the growth of sales and for cutting costs of production. What management strategist Peter Drucker labeled production-sharing became widespread, as transnational corporations shifted production and later research and development to offshore facilities.

For residents of East Asian developing countries the progress was notable. Led by India, areas of South Asia also began to grow rapidly and embrace the global economy. As a result, the number of people in developing regions living in extreme poverty (defined as less than $1.25 per day in 2005) dropped to 1.4 billion in 2005 as compared with 1.8 billion in 1990. Most of that improvement occurred in China, where improved economic opportunities raised 475 million people from extreme poverty. A large concentration of poor remained in South Asia, where an estimated 600 million live on the equivalent of $1.25 per day. However, in sub-Saharan Africa conditions worsened with 100 million more people added to the ranks of the extremely poor than in 1990.[27]

Increasing volatility and dislocations

Clearly the open global economy did not benefit everyone. It had a down side for many in rich and poor countries. Change brought volatility, uncertainty, and dislocations. Workers who had once produced automobiles, steel, clothing, and shoes in markets insulated from world competition found themselves competing with young, highly-motivated, and relatively low-paid workers from developing countries. Many of the well-paid workers in high-income countries with retirement benefits and health care discovered themselves in a race to the bottom with the world's cheapest labor. Workers in some developing countries had parallel concerns. Family farmers in Korea, Japan, France, and India, among many locations, feared competition from commercial agriculture and the loss of their livelihoods. Inefficient businesses in developing countries opposed concessions on manufacturing tariffs, concerned about the consequences of vigorous competition. They lobbied national governments to resist concessions in multilateral trade negotiations. In Korea militant farmers fought with police and hurled epithets at legislators supportive of free-trade agreements. In France Jose Bove and a crowd of peasant farmers attacked and trashed a McDonald's outlet in 1999 to protest against industrial agriculture and the global trading system. One of the most successful protests occurred in Seattle, Washington, in December 1999 when a broad coalition of activists – consumer advocates, family farmers, trade unionists, environmentalists – disrupted a ministerial of the World Trade Organization. That, and other demonstrations at the annual meetings of the elite World Economic Forum in Davos, Switzerland, appeared to signal a backlash to corporate-led globalization. Polls showed that while ordinary people considered globalization a routine fact of everyday living, there was profound disquiet about the growing gap between rich and poor, the lack of good-paying jobs, and deteriorating working conditions.[28]

Technological revolutions

Another dimension of the global economic transformation involved key technological innovations in transportation and communications. These involved wide-bodied cargo aircraft (the Boeing 747), containers and container ships, satellite communications, fiber-optic lines, cell phones, the internet and personal computers, each of which helped dissolve the barriers of time, distance, and lack of information.

During the twentieth century people, goods, information, and money moved more rapidly across vast distances, as a result of innovations. The arrival of the wide-bodied Boeing 747 in 1969 brought markedly lower operating costs and facilitated the arrival of low-cost mass travel. In 2008, the US ATA reported that the world's airlines carried around 2.3 billion passengers annually, up 207% from 748 million passengers in 1980. More business people and tourists began to travel longer distances, and to visit developing countries. In 1980, 64% of tourists went to Europe, 22% to the Americas, 8% to Asia and the Pacific, 3% to the Middle East, and 3% to Africa. By 2009, Europe (52%) and the Americas (21%) had both lost share, but Asia and the Pacific (21%), the Middle East (6%), and Africa (5%) had gained. The World Tourism Organization reported that the number of tourist arrivals worldwide had climbed from 278.1 million in 1980 to 919 million in 2008, an increase of 230%. China had overtaken Italy as the fourth leading destination for tourists, after France, the US, and Spain. Apparently, tourists had become more interested in the Great Wall than in Roman walls.[29]

Lower jet-travel costs also facilitated air freight and enabled global production chains. A variation of the Boeing 747 produced for cargo service could carry 14 173-cubic-foot containers. In 2008, world airlines transported 40.5 million tons of freight up 265 percent from 11.1 million in 1980.[30]

Other improvements – particularly the development of wide-bodied cargo vessels and containerships – transformed ocean transportation and supported global business activity. Shipping companies, such as Maersk, the world's largest, put in service containerships, like the *Emma Maersk*, nearly 400 meters in length that could carry over 15,000 20-foot equivalent containers (TEU) and speed it along at over 25 knots. The large aluminum and steel containers could be easily loaded and unloaded with automated equipment in eight hours. Until containers arrived the 1960s, the loading process often took a week. It was an expensive and time-consuming process. Containerships could make the trip from China or Malaysia to Los Angeles or other West Coast ports in about two weeks. This fast service enabled merchants to keep smaller inventories, and to replenish them quickly, even using the 24-hour turnaround of jet freighters to restock high-value shipments.[31]

Innovations in communications during this period also expanded connections among people and nations, enhancing the flow of information. The International Telecommunications Union (ITU) estimated that by the end of 2009 there were 4.6 billion mobile phone subscribers around the world covering 90 percent of the world's population, up from 55.5 million in 1995. Cell phone usage increased 37 percent per year compounded.[32]

Similarly, internet usage grew rapidly. The ITU estimated that by the end of 2009 1.8 billion people used the internet, up from 279 million in 1999, a compound increase of over 20 percent annually.[33]

The easy flow of information facilitated business communications and enhanced flows of information among families and friends. It allowed social networking such as Facebook and Skype to connect individuals around the world. The rapid flow of information among individuals had enormous implications. It helped to homogenize tastes, harmonize cultures, and integrate markets in unprecedented ways. It also facilitated cultural diversity, as Chinese expatriates in the Americas retained regular contact with relatives and watched Chinese television. The communications revolution presented a challenge to autocratic regimes that sought to control content and suppress dissent.

One leader had foreseen the power of communications to transform the world. He was former President Ronald Reagan, himself once a radio broadcaster, who understood how information changed lives and expectations. Recognizing the vulnerability of the Soviet Union on this count in the 1980s, he expanded the operations of the Voice of America and Radio Liberty. Reagan knew the power of pictures, and he wanted to show residents of the Soviet Empire that ordinary Americans had cars, good homes, and even swimming pools. In so doing, he fueled discontent in Eastern Europe, hastened the demise of the Soviet Empire, and spurred the revival of market-led globalization.[34]

Conclusion

The period from 1980 to 2010 was an important era of economic transformations and turbulence. As the Cold War faded, and government regulations disappeared, a new market-driven global economy emerged. It was driven by new issues, new technologies, and the emergence of new economic power centers. Around the world living standards improved, life expectancy expanded, and flows of goods, money, people, and information rose sharply. But, as later events would show, late-twentieth century globalization enhanced both gains and vulnerabilities. The rising tide of globalization lifted many boats, and capsized others.

Chapter 2

The Global Economy before 1980

The contemporary global economy has roots in the globalization process and the dynamic international economy that emerged in the late nineteenth century. This chapter will summarize some of the key background developments, and show how that economy unraveled in a cycle of wars and economic dislocations, and then revived after World War II.

Globalization is an important unifying theme, essential to an understanding of the contemporary global economy. It is a process through which advances in technology and market-opening gradually erased barriers of time and distance and brought peoples and nations closer together. Globalization has remote origins, extending back to the irregular contacts of early merchants, adventurers, warriors, and crusaders with distant civilizations. For the early history of globalization, readers may wish to consult the "Suggested Readings."[1]

First Global Economy 1870–1913

During the late nineteenth century the globalization process accelerated. In an era of European industrialization, nation-building, imperialism, and rapid technological progress, Great Britain provided the leadership for constructing an international economy based on free trade and the gold standard. At the behest of classical free traders and export-oriented merchants, Great Britain repealed in 1846 its Corn Laws (import duties on corn imports) and adopted free-trade policies. Opening its home market to the

The Contemporary Global Economy: A History Since 1980, First Edition. Alfred E. Eckes, Jr.
© 2011 Alfred E. Eckes, Jr. Published 2011 by Blackwell Publishing Ltd.

world's trade and capital, Britain forged an open global economy that lasted until World War I. The international gold standard was a key element in the system. Britain defined its currency, the pound sterling, in terms of gold at a fixed rate and permitted free movements of gold. With the pound anchored to gold, international transactions became less risky. Investors and traders could have confidence in the payments system, knowing that national currencies would remain stable and that they could easily convert currencies from one to another at their convenience.

Britain's home market was open to the world – and its free-trade policies invited imports. The UK typically ran a trade deficit with the world (a trade surplus with its colonial empire) and financed its position with substantial surpluses on services – such as shipping and insurance – and earnings on its overseas investments. British cargo ships, accounting for one-third of the world's tonnage, carried the largest share of world trade. British investors exported a substantial amount of their own wealth to far corners of the world – developing railroads, ports, sewers, mines, and ranches. And the long arm of the British navy offered protection to shippers and investors against multiple risks – including piracy and expropriations.[2]

At the hub of the pre-World War I global economy was the City of London, a one-square mile area where the financial services industry was located. It employed 364,000 people in 1911. Within the city were located the privately-owned Bank of England, known as the Old Lady of Threadneedle Street, the London Stock Exchange, the gold and metal exchanges, and Lloyd's of London, insurance market to the world.[3]

In the period from 1870 to 1913 flows of goods, capital, and people all expanded rapidly. A global division of labor emerged along the lines of absolute advantage (see Chapter 5). European countries exported manufactured products to colonies and former colonies in exchange for imported agricultural products and raw materials. Among the benefits of this pattern was the availability of new products – especially meat – to improve the quality of European diets.

Large numbers of Europeans invested their savings overseas – in mines, ranches, plantations, railroads, and canals. Before World War I foreign assets climbed to 20 percent of world GDP, a figure not equaled again until the 1980s. Britain invested half of its wealth overseas during this period. France and the Netherlands also had large overseas investments.[4]

The arrival of steam-powered shipping and trans-oceanic submarine telegraph cables during this period lowered transportation costs, and improved communications. As a result, flows of people and goods expanded rapidly. Some 60 million people emigrated from Europe to the New World between 1820 and 1914. Before World War I information traveled by submarine telegraph between major financial centers in less than a minute.[5]

The period before World War I is often seen as a golden era of informal integration, progress, and private enterprise. There was greater mobility of information (via the telegraph), people (free immigration), goods (Britain's commitment to free trade), and capital among nations. The world's population grew rapidly but so did per capita incomes. World population rose from an estimated 1.27 billion in 1870 to 1.79 billion (an increase of about 41%), according to data compiled by the late economic historian Angus Maddison. To evaluate comparative economic performance, he focused on per capita gross domestic product (GDP), as the best available indicator of changes in well-being and production potential. Maddison's estimates show world per capita GDP climbing 75% from $870 to $1,524 in constant dollars over the period from 1870 to 1913. Incomes in Western Europe and the US increasingly diverged from those in China, India, and Africa where economic modernization was slow to arrive. Over the period per capita GDP rose 114% in the US and 73% in 12 West European nations, including Britain, France, and Germany. But growth lagged in the developing world. Africa's gains averaged 27%, and 16 East Asian countries averaged 24%. China tarried with only 4% growth over the period.[6]

Maddison's data offer evidence of enhanced income inequality. Incomes in Western European and the US far surpassed incomes in Asia and Africa – leading to criticisms that the world of *laissez-faire* capitalism enriched the rich and powerful, and pulled down the poor. Some economic historians respond that the divergence reflects the strong growth of industrial countries, not impoverishment of the poor. They say some peripheral countries benefitted strongly from increased exports of primary products – notably Brazil (rubber), Chile (copper), Central America (bananas), Argentina (beef and wheat), and Australia (wool and minerals).[7]

Longer life spans offer other evidence of improved conditions before World War I. Health care improved, infant mortality declined, and infectious diseases disappeared. Human diets benefitted from international trade in beef, fruits, and grains. In 1900, a person born in Western Europe had a life expectancy of 46 years and one born in the US 47 years. In Asia and Africa, it was perhaps 24 years. By 1950, Maddison estimates that life expectancy had reached 67 in Europe and 68 in the US, and 38 to 40 years in Asia and Africa.[8]

Given the extensive network of financial and commercial connections among nations, it is not surprising that some influential pundits and bankers thought the global economy robust enough to restrain warlike impulses. British peace activist, Norman Angell (Ralph Norman Angell Lane), claimed that economic interdependence promoted peace, and that military and political power gave no nation a commercial advantage. In *The Great Illusion* (1910), he wrote: "International finance has become so interdependent and so interwoven with trade and industry that ... political and military power can in reality do nothing. ..."[9] Others in the elite held similar views. Winston Churchill linked free trade to peace and interdependence. Free trade, he said, made towards the banding together of "the peoples of Europe and Christendom and ultimately of the whole world, so that forces and interests should becoming inextricably interwoven with each other." But renowned American geo-strategist Admiral A. T. Mahan dismissed Angell's thesis as itself a "great illusion," one that ignored how economic advantage had frequently resulted from use of military force and misread human action. "To regard the world as governed by self-interest only is to live in a non-existent world, an ideal world. ..."[10]

The views of Norman Angell, and Winston Churchill, reflected the Utopian faith of Victorian-Age liberals that free trade in goods and finance could produce peace. As it turned out, their expectations were misplaced, and the skepticism of Admiral Mahan confirmed.

De-Globalization 1914–50

The period from the outbreak of World War I to 1950 was one of de-globalization. Two world wars, a worldwide depression, and Cold War conflict disrupted the international economy. Economic progress was slower than before 1914. World population expanded 41 percent from 1.793 billion to 2.528 billion. GDP per capita climbed 38.5 percent from $1,524 to $2,111, a much slower than in the golden era from 1870 to 1913 (75%).[11]

World War I and aftermath

Historians sometimes claim the Great War that began in August 1914 brought to an end the first age of globalization.[12] Certainly, the blockade and widespread use of the submarine against neutral and belligerent shipping disrupted market-based patterns of exchange. Governments intervened to control trade and shipping, and the volume of trade fell sharply as a consequence. Governments also closed and regulated financial markets, and the belligerents liquidated overseas assets to finance the war. From 1914 to 1919, foreign investments in the US declined from $7.2 billion to $3.3

billion as Britain and other belligerents sold off assets. The US, which entered the war as the world's largest debtor, emerged from World War I as the largest creditor. The war also turned the US and Japan into maritime powers, as Britain lost substantial tonnage.[13]

Afterwards countries attempted to return to the gold standard and to revive international capital flows and trade. Bankers in New York and London took an active role in private efforts to promote stability and recovery. But dislocations and distortions remained. Europeans complained about high American tariffs complicating repayment of war debts. Protectionism was also a factor in Latin America where the war had dislocated traditional trading patterns, forcing countries to promote domestic industry. Agriculture, which over-expanded during the war, experienced oversupply and low prices during the decade. And Germany's hyper-inflation after World War I wiped out the savings of the middle class, and resulting political discontent facilitated the rise of the Nazis to power a decade later.[14]

Great Depression (1929–39)

The Great Depression was the second calamity to disrupt the international economy in the twentieth century, and its impact was worldwide. The beginnings of the collapse are associated with the New York Stock Market Crash of 1929, the failure of banks in Austria and continental Europe, and the collapse of the gold standard. Some scholars also blame the US Congress for enacting higher tariffs in 1930. Between 1929 and 1932, world trade dropped 25 percent in volume and 48 percent in value, as industrial output fell 36 percent. By 1931, most overseas borrowers were in default, and private capital flows had collapsed. Governments resorted to exchange controls and other regulatory measures to insulate economies from the global storm, and to promote national recovery.[15]

The US stock market collapse of 1929 offers intriguing parallels to the correction of 2008–9. The Dow Jones industrial average fell 89 percent from a peak of 381 on September 3, to a low of 41 in July 1932 before the presidential election. The market would not return to 1929 levels until 1954, some 25 years later. However, in the period 1929–32 the New York crash did not circle the globe. In most other countries, Italy excepted, the stock market declines were mild.[16]

While the exact causes of the US stock market crash continue to stimulate debate, the financial collapse followed a postwar decade of exuberant growth – a "new era" according to President Calvin Coolidge. Many thought that new techniques of scientific management and radical new innovations in communications – radio – and in transportation – automobiles and airplanes – would eliminate the boom-and-bust cycle of past decades. Enthusiasm for growth gave rise to excessive stock market speculation. During the war the government had aggressively promoted sales of Liberty Bonds with patriotic appeals, raising $21.5 billion to help finance the war. Afterward, with the reduction of government debt, investors turned to the stock market seeking high returns. Banks, which had made money selling war bonds, engaged in stock trading and lending to investors during the 1920s. This encouraged a speculative boom. Portfolios became over-leveraged and vulnerable to a correction in stock prices. Economist Milton Friedman later blamed the Federal Reserve for mistaken monetary policies. The Federal Reserve kept interest rates low from 1924 to 1927 to help strengthen the pound, support Great Britain's return to the gold standard, and promote currency stability in Europe. When the Federal Reserve tightened in early 1928 to curb speculators, it set in motion a monetary contraction that resulted in an economic collapse. As Federal Reserve governor Ben Bernanke said at Milton Friedman's 90th birthday party: "Regarding the Great Depression. You're right, we did it. We're very sorry. But thanks to you, we won't do it again."[17]

The economic collapse of the 1930s had many adverse consequences. The resulting joblessness and political discontent brought the National Socialists and Adolf Hitler to power in Germany determined to overthrow the World War I peace settlement. In Japan the depression emboldened the military and those favoring imperial expansion rather than international cooperation.

Everywhere the wartime emergency and later economic calamity strengthened the hand of the state and weakened the private sector and *laissez faire*. British politics during the interwar period was characterized by an expansion of the state and the mixed economy. At the end of the World War II the victorious Labor Party would extend government's reach nationalizing coal, steel, railroads, utilities, communications, and the Bank of England. A similar pattern unfolded in France with the nationalization of key industries at the end of World War II. In post-World War II West Germany, the mixed economy gained ground with the government holding substantial shares of most major corporations – and a corporatist philosophy taking hold through tripartite management of business, government, and labor.[18]

In the US President Franklin D. Roosevelt's New Deal increased the size of government as well. Federal officials undertook unprecedented public works programs, public spending, and efforts to set prices and wages. The regulatory state expanded most in the financial sector, where the banking and securities industries were considered responsible for the collapse. As will be discussed in Chapter 8, Congress enacted legislation barring commercial banks from engaging in investment banking and securities trading. It also established a Securities and Exchange Commission to regulate stock exchange trading and mandate disclosure of financial information to the investing public.

During the Great Depression commitment to an open global economy faded, as elected officials attempted to reduce unemployment. Joblessness soared in the US (reaching 25% in 1933), Germany (30% in 1932), and the United Kingdom (20% of insured work force, as high as 70% in some cities), arousing protests and demonstrations, and fears of political coups, or revolutions. Cambridge University economist John Maynard Keynes provided the intellectual rationale for the resort to deficit spending and government public works programs. He argued that government spending to stimulate aggregate demand would have a multiplier effect many times the original spending, thus stimulating production and generating jobs. In retrospect, it is clear that Keynesian spending during the New Deal did not end the depression; World War II deficits did. In 1943 US federal deficit amounted to nearly 28 percent of GDP, far above the 5–6 percent deficits of the New Deal years.[19]

Keynes had emphasized national recovery as the key to international recovery. During the depression, he came to question the priority assigned free trade and open capital markets during the *laissez-faire* world. He sympathized with those who wanted to minimize, rather than maximize, economic entanglement between nations. Ideas, knowledge, art, hospitality, travel, he said, should be international. "But let goods be homespun whenever it is reasonably and conveniently possible; and, above all, let finance be primarily national."[20]

Keynes, the era's most influential economist, was not the only one to question the benefits of economic interdependence in times of widespread unemployment and reduced demand. The depression hammered many countries dependent on raw-material exports, as had World War I. Among them were Argentina, Australia, Canada, Chile, New Zealand, and South Africa. The fall in world exports depressed demand for their agricultural and mineral exports, but the volume of trade in primary products fell only 13 percent compared to 42 percent for manufactures. This may help to explain why several of the peripheral countries – such as New Zealand and Australia – made rapid recoveries. Both devalued their currencies to boost exports and encouraged import-competing industries.[21]

Japan also recovered quickly, using Keynesian-style policies. It boosted spending on armaments and depreciated the yen. The latter boosted exports of Japanese textiles, and protected domestic industry from foreign competition. As a consequence, Japan largely escaped the depression. Its industrial production doubled, and Japan became increasingly self-sufficient. In Turkey a modernizing elite seized the opportunity to devalue the Turkish lira and promote industrialization. It experimented with central planning, and import-substitution industrialization. However, in adopting clearing arrangements with major trading partners, Turkey experimented with bilateral trading and became more reliant on Nazi Germany to which it sent coffee and raw materials in exchange for machinery.[22]

The Soviet Union, which had withdrawn from the capitalist system, also appeared to dodge the depression. It claimed to have no unemployment. Its propagandists delighted in contrasting the capitalist crisis and Bolshevik prosperity. A series of five-year economic plans boosted industrial production rapidly. In the Soviet Union per capita GDP reportedly rose 55 percent (from $1,386 in 1929 to $2,150 in 1938), reflecting Stalin's success with state planning. But, industrialization came at the expense of the farm sector, where the introduction of collectives and state farms depressed production and brought famine. Millions of workers were conscripted and forced to perform unpaid labor. Nonetheless, the economic expansion under a series of national plans appeared to confirm Marxist theories, led to romantic accounts in the Western press, and encouraged the Bolsheviks to promote a world revolution by imitation of their example. Some of the most slavish pro-Soviet reporting appeared in the *New York Times*, written by Walter Duranty. In 1931 Duranty claimed that "Soviet industry and agriculture are progressing at a fabulous rate while those pursuits in the rest of the world are lagging. ..." He reported that Soviet officials would welcome skilled workers from other countries. Thousands of foreigners responded to the dream of the "workers' paradise" with high pay, paid vacations, and free medical care, and accepted free passage to the Soviet Union.[23]

Along with the disintegration of the trading system and commodity markets, the calamity strengthened protectionist forces everywhere. US President Franklin Roosevelt, concerned about extensive unemployment in the US, chose to torpedo the London Economic Conference, called under League of Nations auspices, and to devalue the US dollar in terms of gold. Devaluation gave American exports a competitive advantage.

Other countries responded with exchange controls and trade barriers, and increasingly trade resumed on a bilateral basis. Nazi Germany and some other countries introduced bilateral balancing to manage trade flows and conserve foreign exchange. Great Britain and its Commonwealth enacted a preferential system, which discriminated against foreign trading partners outside the preferential arrangement – particularly the United States and Japan.[24]

The Great Depression had a devastating impact on international financial markets, as many debtor countries defaulted on obligations. Although these events have not been fully documented, studies show widespread defaults and suspensions of external debt payments throughout Europe and Latin America during the Great Depression.[25]

World War II and aftermath

The third catastrophic setback to the international economy was World War II. Like World War I, it exposed the vulnerabilities of dependence on foreign supplies, especially for Britain and Japan, which relied on imported raw materials and foodstuffs. Germany, although moving toward self-sufficiency in the 1930s, also depended heavily on imported basic raw materials, especially ferro-alloys needed to harden steel. Everywhere – but especially in Latin America and India – the dislocations to international trade reinforced pressures for industry protection. There were also resource shortages, especially of rubber and oil, which were required in large quantities for mechanized warfare. At the end of the war, there was considerable concern about resource vulnerabilities in the event of another global war. The US Secretary of the Interior warned that "We're running out of oil," giving emphasis to a postwar scramble to access oil reserves in the Middle East, Venezuela, and other locations. He claimed the war had bankrupted some of America's vital mineral resources. "We no longer deserve to be listed with Russia and the British Empire as one of the 'Have' nations of the world. We should be listed with the 'Have Nots,' such as Germany and Japan."[26]

World War II had several other profound consequences for the international economy. For one thing, it disrupted European empires, and ignited independence movements throughout the colonial world. Many of the new leaders in emerging areas were educated in Western Europe, and drew important lessons from interwar economic experiences. Because many newly-independent countries were excessively dependent on commodity exports (such as cocoa, copper, sugar, and rubber), diversification and industrialization seemed appropriate strategies. Drawing on the successful industrialization of the US in the nineteenth century, some of the new leaders opted for import substitution policies, in which the government regulated trade to promote key domestic industries. In other cases, the experience of the Soviet Union in achieving high levels of growth with state-led industrialization led to state planning and autarkic controls.[27]

Another significant result in the aftermath of World War II was the continued expansion of government ownership and regulation, and extension of the welfare state in Western Europe and North America. The successes of the public sector in mobilizing resources for war and the promises of democratically-elected leaders to extend the welfare state with cradle-to-grave benefits combined to strengthen the appeal of government planning and the mixed economy after World War II. In Britain victorious Labour party leaders spoke of a "New Jerusalem," while in the US some US-elected officials called for a global New Deal, or a "Century for the Common Man." In Australia and Canada leaders promised expansion of the welfare state in order to maintain support for the war effort. On the European continent expanded government planning and control of the economy underpinned efforts to reconstruct and integrate the economies of Europe, through the European Coal and Steel Community and later the European Economic Community.[28]

On the international level, there were similar government-led efforts to restructure and restore the global economic system. Unlike the aftermath of World War I when the US turned its back on the Versailles peace structure, this time the US government proved resolute. With the support of Great Britain, the US led efforts to rebuild the world financial system at Bretton Woods, New Hampshire, in July 1944. There representatives of 44 nations, including the Soviet Union, discussed, and established, twin financial institutions – the International Monetary Fund and the International Bank for Reconstruction and Development. The first was to restore and manage a system of fixed but adjustable rates of exchange. This was a gold-exchange monetary system, in which countries defined their currencies in terms of dollars, and the dollar was convertible to gold. However, only governments could exchange accumulated dollars for gold. To sustain the fixed parity system, the Fund stood ready to provide assistance to countries with temporary balance-of-payments problems. For the longer-term significance of Bretton Woods, see Chapter 8.

Another prong of postwar planning involved a multilateral International Trade Organization (ITO). It was largely the brainchild of the US State Department, and Secretary of State Cordell Hull, which waged a long battle during the 1930s to negotiate bilateral, reciprocal trade agreements and reduce barriers to trade. The ITO was to be a forum for multilateral trade negotiations, and it would administer a set of rules based on nondiscrimination and the most-favored-nation policy. Under the terms of the arrangement nations treated goods from other members of the organization no differently than products of the most-favored nation. As negotiated at the Havana Conference, the ITO's responsibilities went far beyond trade policy and engaged issues of foreign investments, commodities, and full-employment. The ITO charter was never ratified, because of opposition in the US Senate, but a temporary contractual arrangement intended to serve only until the ITO was approved by member governments, the General Agreement on Tariffs and Trade (GATT), lasted nearly fifty years. In 1995 the World Trade Organization, negotiated during the Uruguay Round of multilateral GATT negotiations, superseded GATT.

The end of the war against the Axis coalition led to the disintegration of cooperation among the US, the UK, and the Soviet Union. Stalin's government opted for an autarkic course rather than engaging the international economy and joining international economic institutions. The Soviet Union preferred to maintain its freedom of action without the legal obligations of membership in the Bretton Woods institutions or the GATT.[29]

The resulting Cold War, pitting the Western powers led by the US and the UK against the Eastern bloc led by the Soviet Union, was the fourth major factor disrupting efforts to restore an open international economy. East–West trade had accounted for 73.8% of the Eastern bloc's trade in 1938, but only 41.6% in 1948 and 14% in 1953. For Western nations trade with the East accounted for 9.5% of total trade in 1938, 4.1% in 1948, and 2.1% in 1950. For a period of nearly a half century after World War II, Cold War controls restricted commercial and financial activities. In effect, the Cold War imposed a form of regionalism upon the international economy.[30]

Renewed Globalization (1950–70)

Economic historians sometimes refer to the period from 1950 to about 1970 as another golden age of prosperity. During this 20-year period, world population grew fast from 2.5 billion in 1950 to 3.69 billion in 1970, but world GDP rose 5 percent annually. As a result, world per capita GDP climbed about 3 percent annually, meaning that incomes nearly doubled over the period. Also, international trade expanded about 8 percent annually, far faster than national GDP, signaling the growing interdependence of nations. There was other evidence of global economic integration. Private capital flows resumed, slowly at first and then more rapidly during the 1960s. And international migration resumed, with many of the migrants going to Western Europe from former colonies.[31]

There was a measure of income convergence as Western Europe and Japan grew more rapidly than the United States. In 1950 12 European countries had per capita incomes about half of the US level; in 1970 the Europeans had climbed to 73 percent. Over the same period, Japan soared from 20 percent of the US per capita income to 65 percent.[32]

Among the large developing countries growth was considerably slower during this period than among the industrial nations recovering from World War II. Brazil increased per capita GDP 83%, China 74%, and India only 40%. Latin American countries increased their GDP per capita 59%, while African countries elevated theirs 50%. In Asia some of the small economies (such as Hong Kong and Taiwan) began to grow rapidly, and their successes would soon energize the region. The period from 1950 to 1970 was generally a period of growing prosperity for workers and consumers in advanced countries.[33]

In the United States the generation that fought World War II and returned home, enjoyed government-educational benefits. Many completed college, and obtained good-paying employment. Despite wartime concerns about a possible renewal of the Depression after World War II, even low-skilled workers found abundant jobs in industry. They made automobiles, produced steel, or pursued other opportunities. In unionized industries, wages soared and healthcare and retirement benefits expanded. Weekly earnings in manufacturing rose 42 percent in constant dollars from $240.76 in 1950 to $342.34 in 1970, as manufacturing expanded from 15.2 million to 19.4 million. As a result, more and more Americans purchased automobiles, televisions, homes in the suburbs, and joined the rapidly expanding middle class.[34]

Globalization in a Turbulent Decade – the 1970s

As it turned out, for most advanced countries the good times came to an end in the 1970s. The turbulent period from 1970 to 1980 witnessed a series of dislocations – inflation, a steep recession, labor unrest, and surging energy prices. The Organization of Petroleum Exporting Countries (OPEC) succeeded in quadrupling the price of oil. Most nations experienced difficulty in maintaining previously high growth rates and boosting

GDP per capita significantly. World GDP per capita is estimated to have increased 21 percent, compared to 31.4 percent in the period 1950–60, and 34.5 percent between 1960 and 1970. Western Europe and North America struggled with stag-flation, a combination of slow growth and high inflation.[35]

By borrowing heavily from international banks, and inflating their economies, many Latin American countries delayed adjustment to the energy crisis. Eight of the largest Latin American economies grew GDP per capita 36.7 percent during the 1970s, compared to 27.2 percent in the preceding decade. But many African economies, less able to borrow from the banks recycling petro-dollars, experienced hard times. Maddison's data indicate that a significant number of African countries (20 of 52) experienced declining real per capita incomes. A small number of African countries benefited from the substantial increase in oil and commodity prices.

The real success stories were in East Asia, where the tiger economies, motivated by the example of Japanese recovery from World War II, and stimulated by Vietnam War spending, accelerated their growth. Per capita GDP grew 84.4% in Hong Kong (versus 81.7% in the prior decade), 104% in Singapore (versus 92.2%), 107.3% in Taiwan (compared to 87.5), and 90% in South Korea (versus 76.8%). China and India, however, continued to have undistinguished economic performances. During the 1970s China increased per capita income 36.3% (compared to 17.5% during the 1960s), while India grew per capita income an anemic 8.1%, less than 15.3% in the prior decade. Neither exhibited the dynamism of the 1980s when China displayed 76.3% growth and India 39.5% growth in GDP per capita.[36]

Meanwhile in high-income countries, the postwar boom was coming to a close. In the US manufacturing employment did rise from 19.4 million in 1970 to 20.3 million in 1980, but jobs in manufacturing dropped as a share of the non-farm labor force. For the baby-boom generation entering the work place, the job opportunities were in services, where employment expanded from 47.3 million to 64.7 million, this growth distributed among retail, government, and other services. In 1950, manufacturing had accounted for 33.7% of the non-farm labor force in 1950, but by 1970 it had fallen to 27.3%, and by 1980 to 22.4%. But from 1970 to 1980 manufacturing weekly wages in constant dollars rose slightly from $342.34 to $351.14, an increase of 2.6%. In the 1990s, manufacturing wages would actually fall to $338.57, a decline of 3.6%. While services offered more job opportunities, many of these jobs were in retail and areas with weekly wages two-thirds of those in manufacturing. It meant that dislocated manufacturing workers often experienced unemployment, retraining, and then reduced earnings in the expanding service sectors.[37]

Conclusion

During the first eight decades of the twentieth century, global economic integration reached a peak before World War I. Two world wars, the Great Depression, the breakdown of colonial empires, and the emergence of a socialist alternative in Eastern Europe frustrated repeated efforts to restore the global economy. Nonetheless, an integrated global economy continued to appeal to economists, business leaders, and some public officials.

Chapter 3

The Rich Nations

The dramatic changes associated with globalization and open markets have impacted and challenged all nations since 1980. Certain regions and nations have adapted more easily than others. In this chapter we consider how the rich countries in Western Europe, North America, Asia, and Oceania have adjusted in the period 1980 to 2010. Necessarily, our narrative is selective. An encyclopedic approach would exceed space available.

Since World War II high-income countries designed and sustained the open global economy. The rich countries shared certain characteristics. They were multi-party democracies with advanced legal systems providing substantial protection to individual and property rights. In all the press enjoyed freedom to criticize. Their economies permitted and rewarded private enterprise. In some countries the state took an active role in managing the economy, owning key enterprises and regulating markets. High-income countries had state-sponsored social safety nets – some more generous than others – for the elderly and the unemployed.

These rich countries dominated the world economy in 1980. With 21% of the world's population, they generated 79.1% of world merchandise exports, and 78.7% of world GDP. Nearly 30 years later – in 2009 – the rich countries, which now included South Korea, were less dominant. With 17% of the world's population, they accounted for 69.7% of world exports and 71.6% of GDP.

Most of the high-income countries participated actively in the Atlantic economy in the post-World War II period. But, globalization, the end of

The Contemporary Global Economy: A History Since 1980, First Edition. Alfred E. Eckes, Jr.
© 2011 Alfred E. Eckes, Jr. Published 2011 by Blackwell Publishing Ltd.

the Cold War, and emergence of new markets in Asia, Eastern Europe, and other developing areas broadened regional horizons. Big corporations based in Europe, North America, and Japan chose to compete in all major markets. Another important theme during the period involved the widening and deepening of regional economic integration. Nations in all areas of the world sought the advantages of membership in larger trading blocs, such as the EU and NAFTA, or in bilateral arrangements.[1]

Western Europe

European Union (EU)

During the early 1980s euro-pessimism was rampant. Western European economies stagnated, with declining smokestack industries losing millions of jobs. Meanwhile the US and Japanese economies surged forward. Some blamed militant labor unions, lavish welfare-state benefits, and lagging productivity for the job losses. Others emphasized a widening technology gap between Europe and its principal competitors. Italian author Luigi Barzini complained that Europeans had been reduced to the role of Greeks in the Roman Empire. He said that the most useful function an Italian or a Frenchman could perform was to teach Americans or Japanese the proper temperature at which to drink red wine. One former US Secretary of State even speculated that Europe could become a third-world country within a generation.[2]

Twenty-five years later – before the financial crisis of 2007 – Europe seemed more confident. Pundits celebrated a "golden age of integration," in which a long period of peace and prosperity enabled European countries to make giant strides. They created a single market for goods and services, a single currency, embraced the free movement of people, and expanded the bloc from the Atlantic Ocean to the borders of Russia. Brussels, the city some call the "New Rome," had become the center of the Europeanization process. Members of the EU had apparently succeeded in expanding welfare-state benefits, such as health care, pensions, and income transfers. Public social spending thus rose sharply as a share of GDP, from 20.8% in France and 22.7% in Germany in 1980 to 29.2 and 26.7% respectively in 2005. In the United Kingdom the increase was from 16.7 to 21.% . Mediterranean countries had some of the largest increases: 5.7 percentage points in Spain, 7 in Italy, 10.3 in Greece, and 12.9 in Portugal. The end of the Cold War, and a reduction of military expenditures, helped make this reallocation of resources possible. For Germany the huge increase reflected the need to spend 1.3 trillion euros over 20 years to stabilize social security systems in the East and facilitate reunification.[3]

On the cusp of achieving their ambitious goals of integrating Europe and extending social-protection programs, the experiment began to stall and then splinter. The Mediterranean financial crisis of 2010 exposed Europe's vulnerabilities, and the danger of monetary integration without fiscal union in which a central government controlled taxing and spending. In a revival of Euro-pessimism one historian concluded that the euro zone was in "mortal danger."[4]

In revisiting the period from 1980 to 2010 one important theme is how the European Economic Community (EEC) gradually expanded its membership from ten to 27 members, becoming the EU in 1993. While increasing its numbers, the EEC took important steps to deepen and harmonize economies within the bloc as it continued to integrate with the world. As is generally known this economic bloc, also known as the Common Market, originated in efforts after World War II to join the economies of longtime political enemies Germany and France in an coal-and-steel community. The architects of the new Europe were Robert Schuman, a French foreign minister, and Jean Monnet, a French cognac merchant and former official of the League of Nations who enjoyed a distinguished career in public service. They believed passionately that a disunited Europe inevitably resulted in war among competing nation-states. These two statesmen laid the foundation for the EEC.[5]

In 1957, Germany and France, the Benelux countries, and Italy signed the Treaty of Rome, creating the Common Market. The members agreed to remove internal tariffs and erect a common external tariff as well as a common agricultural policy. Over time the Common Market gradually expanded, adding three northern countries – Britain, Ireland, and Denmark – in 1973, and three Mediterranean countries – Greece, Spain, and Portugal – in the 1980s. After the Cold War ended former neutrals Austria, Finland, and Sweden joined the EU in 1995, making 15 members.[6]

With the dissolution of the Soviet Union in December 1991 a number of countries in Eastern and Central Europe sought to join the EEC. It established a series of conditions for membership. Applicants must be European states and have functioning market economies. They must also respect democracy, rule of law, human rights, and fundamental freedoms. In 2004, ten more countries met the criteria and joined – Cyprus, the Czech Republic, Estonia, Hungary, Latvia, Lithuania, Malta, Poland, Slovakia, and Slovenia. Two others, Romania and Bulgaria, acceded in 2007. Turkey,

Iceland, and a number of nations once part of the Soviet Empire aspire to membership, presenting difficult issues for EU officials.

Institutionally, the EU has evolved slowly from a common market into a type of federal system in which member states and the central authority share responsibilities. Concerned in the early 1980s about "euro sclerosis," or Europe's lack of competitiveness with Japan and the US, business leaders from Volvo, Philips, and Fiat, organized the 45-member European Round Table of Industrialists in 1983. They promoted the vision of a single market in which European firms could gain the economies of scale necessary to compete with non-European competitors. The round table urged deregulation of markets, harmonization of national regulations on product safety, and removal of border controls on flows of people, goods, information, and ideas. While public officials, like Schuman and Monnet, pushed European integration in the 1950s, business leaders pressed for the single market in the 1980s.[7]

When Euro-pessimism was at a peak in the mid-1980s, French Socialist Jacques Delors, an economist, became president of the European Commission. This tireless and determined political crusader focused on reviving the post-World War II vision of joining former enemies into an economic union. He zealously pushed the goal advanced by European business to achieve a single market by 1992. Delors championed abolishing frontier controls, leveling rates of taxation, institutionalizing workers' rights, and creating a European central bank.

His principal antagonist was Britain's Margaret Thatcher, an enthusiastic proponent of free-markets and the nation-state. She rejected the idea of a European super-state with a strong bureaucracy in Brussels. Instead of more regulation from the center, Thatcher called for deregulation, removal of exchange controls, and rejection of trade protectionism. She also fiercely opposed the single currency, and proposed an alternative, market-based approach of competing currencies and monetary policies. "I do not share the dream of a United States of Europe with a single currency," Thatcher said.[8]

Despite British skepticism and opposition to the euro, the initiative to achieve deeper integration succeeded. As a result of the Maastricht Treaty in 1992, Western Europe moved to complete a single market with 320 million consumers and 12 nations. European integration acquired new momentum. Maastricht deepened bonds of cooperation in defense and foreign policy, legal and judicial matters, and creation of an economic and monetary union – removing final border barriers. Also, the single-market initiative encouraged collaborative research between European business and universities, a form of industrial policy to make Europe more competitive in global markets.[9]

One of the most important developments came in January 1999 with the common currency (the euro), administered by the European Central Bank (ECB). Members of the so-called euro zone accepted monetary union and the euro as their common currency. Seventeen countries, but not Britain and Denmark, joined the euro zone. Sweden and other new EU members (Bulgaria, the Czech Republic, Estonia, Hungary, Latvia, Lithuania, Poland, and Romania) agreed to adopt the euro when they satisfied entry requirements. Among the other new EU members, Slovenia (2007) and Slovakia (2009) became the first former satellites of the Soviet Union to join the euro zone. Estonia adopted the euro in January 2011.

In less than a decade, the ECB, headquartered in Frankfurt, Germany, has emerged as one of the world's most important financial institutions. Not only does it define and implement monetary policy for the euro zone, it manages the euro and conducts foreign exchange operations. Modeled after the independent Bundesbank of Germany, the ECB has one monetary objective – promoting price stability – unlike the US Federal Reserve System which is also empowered to promote maximum employment and moderate long-term interest rates.[10]

European leaders took other important steps to tighten their bonds in the first decade of the new century. In 2004 governments of 25 EU member states signed a treaty establishing a Constitution for Europe. A complex agreement, it would have replaced existing treaties and expanded use of qualified majority voting to issues previously requiring unanimity. After British Prime Minister Tony Blair promised a public referendum, other member states did so. Voters in France and the Netherlands rejected the treaty in 2005, effectively killing it.

After a period of reflection European leaders opted for another approach. They would amend existing treaties rather than write a new one, and minimize the need for public votes of approval. Painstaking negotiations led to the Lisbon Treaty giving constitutional form to the supranational European state. Intended to consolidate the EU's power and streamline its bureaucracy, the union subordinated national parliaments and made citizens of EU members citizens of the European Union. It transformed EU governance, creating a union parliament, a Cabinet-style government, a permanent president with a five-year term, and upgraded the EU's role in foreign affairs. Qualified majority voting replaced unanimity in the Council of Ministers. But, given the opportunity to vote, the Irish public rejected the treaty, fearful Ireland would lose its sovereignty to a powerful EU. After further negotiations, Irish voters were persuaded to approve the treaty 16 months later. To avoid similar problems with democratic electorates, other European leaders opted to ratify the treaty by parliamentary vote. It entered into force in December 2009.

Because the 1957 Treaty of Rome established a common external tariff, the European Commission in Brussels has controlled external trade negotiations. Until the 1990s the EU's trade policy exhibited an Atlantic and Mediterranean focus. As principal partners in the GATT, Europe and the US worked together to promote multilateral trade liberalization and a stronger rules-based international trading system. Former colonial relationships presented some problems. Europe sought to maintain preferential arrangements with former colonies in the Mediterranean region and the Caribbean. For the United Kingdom, however, the price of becoming a European state was to re-orient its trade from the commonwealth to new partners on the continent.

By 2008 the EU apparently had succeeded in integrating the region. About two-thirds of members' trade (exports and imports) was with other members of the EU. As a result, the EU was the most integrated major regional trading bloc in the world. Even for the United Kingdom, with remnants of a vast formal and informal empire spanning the globe, the European relationship was primary. In 2008, 56.3% of its exports flowed to the 15 pre-1990 members of the EU; in return they supplied 45.3% of Britain's imports. In 1970, prior to joining the EU, those members took 40.3% of Britain's exports and supplied 36.8% of imports.[11]

Within the 27-member EU, lower-income nations along the periphery experienced faster growth in GDP and personal incomes. Spain, Portugal, and Ireland, which entered the regional market in the 1970s, grew rapidly as incomes converged with older members of the EU. Per capita GDP from 1980 to 2009 rose 188.2% in Ireland, 76.7% in Portugal, and 76% in Spain. However, Greece grew more slowly (up 53.9.%), about the same as the original members of the European Common Market. In recent years, the same rapid growth pattern appeared in Eastern Europe, where newer EU members, Poland, Hungary, and the Czech Republic, experienced rapid improvements in productivity.[12]

Over the course of its history, the EU has emerged as a major force in the global economy. In 2009 it had a population of 498.6 million (compared to 307 million for the US) and a GDP of $15.2 trillion (compared to $14.3 trillion for the US). The world's leading exporter and its larger importer, the EU accounted for 16.2 percent of world exports in 2009 and 17.4 percent of world imports (excluding internal EU trade). If trade among its members is included, the EU accounts for nearly 40 percent of world exports and imports. The EU is also the leading exporter and importer of trade in services – a diverse category that includes everything from tourism and transportation to finance and business consulting.

From a business perspective, the EU can claim 161 of the world's 500 largest corporations, compared to 139 for the US, 71 for Japan, and 46 for China. The EU's largest corporations by revenue include such prominent global brands as Shell, BP, Total, Volkswagen, Carrefour, Daimler (Mercedes), Siemens, and BMW.[13]

Within the EU, Germany is the leading merchandise exporter. Indeed, in 2009 after being overtaken by China, it was the world's second leading exporter accounting for 9% of world exports (including intra-EU trade), followed by the Netherlands 4% , France, 3.9%, Italy, 3.2%, Belgium, 3%, and the United Kingdom, 2.8%. In commercial services, however, the UK is the world's second leading exporter (behind the US, but ahead of Germany), a point that emphasizes London's historic role as a global financial and insurance center.[14]

Since World War II the EU nations and the US have competed and shared responsibility for leading the international economy. Along with commercial and financial ties, they have close political, military, and intelligence relationships. Influential ties also exist among businesses in the North Atlantic area through such associations as the International Chamber of Commerce, the World Economic Forum, and the European–American Business Council (EABC), which hold informal conversations between leaders in the public and private sectors. Founded in 1990, the 70-member body promotes unrestricted trade and investment between the US and the EU.

The geography of EU trade emphasizes trans-Atlantic interdependence. The European region's leading export market is the US (taking 18% of exports), and its second largest supplier (13.1%), behind China at 17.6 percent. Not surprisingly, for half a century the two Atlantic-area economic giants have worked closely together in multilateral trade negotiations under the auspices of the GATT and the WTO to open markets and promote nondiscrimination in international trade. Nonetheless, despite the close economic ties, China and Eastern Europe have emerged as major markets for European goods, services, and capital in recent years.[15]

Since the collapse of the Soviet Union, Eastern Europe has become an increasingly important business partner for the EU. The EU's economic power, manifest in trade and financial assets, has helped shape the economic transition of new market economies in Eastern Europe and Central

Asia. Belarus, Georgia, and the Ukraine, once part of the Soviet Union, look more to the EU for export markets than to neighboring Russia. Banks in Western Europe have supplied substantial amounts of credit to Eastern and Central Europe. By 2008, countries once part of the Soviet Union had a collective foreign debt of more than $1 trillion, much of that owed Austrian, German, Italian, and Swiss banks. On the trade front the EU's fourth largest export market (5.8%) is Russia, and that country supplies much of Europe's oil and gas. In 2007, Russian oil and gas provided more than 25 percent of EU energy consumption, accounting for 32.6 percent of oil imports and 38.7 percent of natural gas imports.[16]

Like the United States, the European Union has an unbalanced trading relationship with China. The EU's chronic trade deficit with China reflects the Asian country's cheap production costs, strength of the euro, and problems of access to the Chinese market. In 2009 China (excluding Hong Kong) took 7.2% of Europe's exports (up from 3% in 2000), but supplied 17.6% of imports, making China the EU's leading external supplier (up from 7.5% in 2000).[17]

One indicator of a country or economic bloc's integration with the world is its tariff schedule, the rates applied to imports. The EU applies relatively low duties to merchandise imports (4%), but relatively high duties on agricultural products (13.5%). Like the US, the EU has a relatively low ratio of trade to gross domestic product, 28.6%, when internal trade among members of the bloc is excluded.

In global finance, the EU has also established a leading role, reclaiming the position Western Europe countries held before World War I. The EU is the leading source of direct investment flows, accounting for 47.4% of the accumulated stock of outbound FDI in 2009, compared to 22.7% for the US and 3.9% for Japan. Among EU countries, France (9.1%), the United Kingdom (8.7%), and Germany (7.3%) are the leading investors.[18]

Not surprisingly, EU investors have a large stake in the US, accounting on a historical cost basis for 71.2 percent of US FDI in 2008. Firms like BP, Shell, Siemens, BMW, Mercedes, Michelin, Philips, and Volvo operate in the giant American market as easily as they do in Western Europe. Among EU nations the United Kingdom is the largest single foreign investor in the US, followed by the Netherlands and Germany. Similarly, 57 percent of US foreign direct investments go to Western Europe, with these concentrated in the Netherlands and the United Kingdom.[19]

By 2009 the euro was becoming widely accepted as a substitute in reserves for the dollar. The world's nations kept about 27% of their foreign exchange reserves in Euros, and 61% in US dollars. A decade earlier, the US dollar accounted for 71% of reserves and the euro less than 18%.[20]

But, then the Mediterranean debt crisis hit in early 2010. The EU and the ECB faced a critical challenge that threatened European unity and the euro zone. Unlike the federal system in the United States, member governments in Europe control their own fiscal (tax and spending) policies. Thus member governments can spend freely to address domestic concerns – particularly unemployment – and fund entitlement programs, such as health-care and pension benefits. A number of the Mediterranean members indulged in heavy deficit-spending, despite obligations under the Treaty of Maastricht. The treaty obliged member states to keep government deficits to 3% of GDP or less, and to keep debt-to-GDP ratios to 60% or less. But in 2010, every euro area government breached the 3% GDP deficit ratio, and the euro area debt ratio rose from 66% in 2007 to over 84% in 2010.[21]

Having borrowed heavily from foreign banks, some of the Mediterranean governments faced a debt refinancing crisis of staggering proportions. In particular, Greece's external liabilities were 87 percent of GDP, some 300 billion Euros owed primarily to German and French banks. Spain, Portugal, Italy, and Ireland also had high ratios of debt to GDP. As investors demanded higher yields to refinance Greek debt, the ECB and the EU faced a dilemma. If they did not bail out Greece and address the sovereign debt crisis, the euro might collapse and contagion could spread widely through the euro zone. Ireland, Italy, Spain, and Portugal all faced similar circumstances. But if Europe did bail out the free-spending Greeks, the example might invite further misgovernance. Moreover, the costs of a bailout would fall on unwilling taxpayers in Germany and France. Either way, the result might be disintegration of the EU and its banking system, and the collapse of the euro.

As it turned out, leaders of the euro zone chose to aid Greece and established a $950 billion program to assist other members. The ECB, which as an independent central bank saw its mandate as simply to fight inflation, agreed to buy the bonds of government members in order to lower their lending costs. In effect, this complex approach was designed to bail out the big international banks (French and German) that loaned large sums of money to Greece, and calm bond markets so that more potentially vulnerable governments did not face spiraling lending costs.

Greece did not escape the consequences of its spendthrift ways. Working hand-in-glove with the IMF, the rescue plan also involved stringent conditions for borrowing countries. Greece must cut its government spending, and slash costly pensions and welfare benefits, much as Thailand and Indonesia had done during the 1997 East Asian crisis. When word of the conditions circulated in Greece, protests and riots resulted, underscoring the difficulty of reconciling international monetary stability with democratic governance. Had Greece not adopted the euro, it might have followed the traditional approach of debtor countries – currency devaluation and inflation at home – shifting some of the adjustment burden to foreign lenders.

During the 1980s business and political leaders had fretted over the European region's declining competitiveness. Euro-pessimism was a major theme of the period. Thirty years later Europeans had a more sanguine perspective. The Cold War was over, Germany was reunited, and Western Europe was more integrated than ever before. The EU, which in 1980 was a loosely structured community of nine members with a population of 278 million, had become by 2010 a 27-member federal union with over 500 million people. Among the members 15 European nations had established themselves as world-class competitors. Ten of the 20 most competitive national economies in the world, according to the World Economic Forum's competitiveness report, were EU members – Sweden, Germany, Finland, the Netherlands, Denmark, the United Kingdom, France, Austria, Belgium, and Luxembourg. These members surround the world's most competitive nation – Switzerland – which is not an EU member. Only Greece among longtime members of the EU ranked low (83rd).[22]

North America

As in Western Europe, flows of trade and finance continued to integrate the North America region from 1980 to the present. The North American Free Trade Agreement (1994) was a major milestone along that path but it differed from the European approach. North American countries did not surrender control of agricultural and trade policies, and the money supply to supranational authorities. However, North America did achieve significant market integration. Whereas approximately two-thirds of the European Union's exports traveled to other members of the EU, about half of NAFTA member's exports went to other NAFTA members in 2008. However, only one-third of NAFTA imports came from other NAFTA members, and the vast majority of NAFTA trade involved the US. There was much less trade between Canada and Mexico.[23]

United States

Over the last generation the US witnessed a steady erosion of its relative position in the global economy. A half century ago in 1960, the US accounted for 35% of the world's production and the countries of the present euro area another 22%. By 2008, the US share had fallen to 28.8%, and the euro bloc to 17.7%, together accounting for less than half of global production. With a population of over 307 million in 2009, and a gross domestic product of $14.3 trillion, the US remained one of the world's largest, and most competitive, economic powers. The World Economic Forum's 2010–11 global competitiveness index ranked the US fourth, ahead of Germany and Japan, and far ahead of China (27th), India (51st), and Brazil (58th), the three big emerging markets some analysts expected to reshape the world of the twenty-first century. However, America's relative industrial position had declined, as the emergence of countries like Brazil, China, and India brought a new distribution of global production. The world's low and middle income countries, which accounted for about 15 percent of world GDP in 1960, had a much-expanded share in 2009 – nearly 25 percent.[24]

The decline of a leading power always invites commentary. Despite its relative decline, the US economy performed reasonably well since 1980. Per capita GDP in constant dollars rose some 62.4 percent, a solid performance comparable to Japan where GDP per capita climbed 59.2 percent but somewhat better than in the euro area (56.1%). US performance looks even better when its 33.6 percent population growth from 227.7 million in 1980 to 304.3 million in 2008 is considered. It is noteworthy that during this period population growth in Western Europe and Japan stagnated, rising ten percent or less. While the US population aged somewhat, it did not face the acute adjustments of Europe and Japan in funding social security and healthcare for aging populations. In 2008 the percent of the US population ages 65 and over was up two percentage points (from 11 to 13%), significantly less than the four percentage point (from 14 to 18%) rise in the euro area and 12 percentage point gain in Japan (from 9 to 21%).[25]

To many non-Americans the financial collapse of 2007–10, which began in the US, appeared to discredit the Washington consensus in behalf of free trade, deregulation, and neo-liberal economic policies. In particular, it raised questions about the appropriateness of monetary policies pursued while Alan Greenspan served as chairman of the Federal Reserve System (1987–2006). A libertarian who believed in free markets and the power of the individual, Greenspan disliked excessive government regulation and he pursued easy money policies after the Asian Crisis of 1997 and the 2001 terrorist attacks to stimulate the global economy. Critics say that Greenspan's easy credit policies, which brought the key Federal Funds rate to 1 percent in 2004, fueled the housing bubble and stock-market speculation. At the time, however, the press celebrated the introverted Greenspan as a concert maestro conducting the global economy. In February, 1999, *Time* magazine even heralded Greenspan as chairman of the "committee to save the world."[26]

The economic crisis elevated other criticisms of US economic performance. During the 1980s and 1990s observers sometimes marveled at America's economic dynamism and job creation compared to Western Europe and Japan. From 1980 to 2008 the US economy created millions of new jobs (nearly 47 million jobs net), the vast majority of these in services. With more flexible labor markets, the US typically had unemployment rates several percentage points below rates in Western Europe. But critics noted that this statistic ignored the unpleasant fact that the US was generating large numbers of low-level service jobs paying one-third less than factory jobs lost. Manufacturing's share of US nonfarm employment fell from 22.4 to 9.8 percent.

Economists affiliated with organized labor observed several other disturbing trends, including a rising maldistribution of income. For a 30-year period after World War II, the top tenth of wage earners made about 20 times the bottom 90% of wage earners. But, in the most recent 30-year period that ratio soared to 77 times. The top 1% of wage earners experienced earnings growth of 144.4% from 1979 to 2006, while the bottom 90% gained only 15.6%. Researchers also found higher poverty levels in the US than in similar high-income countries. Child poverty was more than double rates in other high-income countries.[27]

Despite soaring wealth, there was also evidence of stagnating personal incomes. Faced with the situation ordinary American rolled up their sleeves and worked longer hours than peers in other high-income countries. According to the Economic Policy Institute, the average annual hours worked in other high-income countries fell 10 percent from 1979 to 2006, but in the US they fell less than 2 percent.[28]

Americans also borrowed more to sustain their lifestyles and aspirations. The household savings rate fell sharply in the US from about 10 percent in the period 1973–84 to less than 1 percent in the first decade of the twenty-first century. Some thought this trend indicated the US was becoming a spendthrift nation dependent on foreign savings to sustain continued consumer spending, and less able to fund the retirement costs of an aging population. But the US was not the only major country with declining household savings. In the UK, Japan, and Canada there were parallel, and unexplained, declines. In the euro area, by contrast, the saving rate in Germany averaged nearly 8 percent, and in France well over 10 percent. Greece, the spendthrift among euro-zone countries, had a negative savings rate.[29]

Since 1980 US consumerism has had a major impact. The insatiable appetite of American consumers for imported jeans, electronics, shoes, automobiles, and other items has acted like a giant locomotive pulling the world economy, and generating millions of assembly-line jobs in Asia. During much of the late twentieth century the US economy thus served as the importer of last resort – the market on which other countries depended for the health of their export sectors. While the US supplied 11.2 percent of world exports in 2009, it bought 16.7 percent of world imports, a statistic that underscored the American economy as the locomotive for the world economy, and indicated a large trade deficit.[30]

America's trade relationship with the world has become quite asymmetrical over the last 30 years. The cumulative current account deficit from 1980 to 2009 was $7,745 billion. In 2009, the US ran a $501 billion merchandise trade deficit, which included deficits of $226.8 billion with China, a $47.5 billion with Mexico, $44.8 billion with Japan, and $20.2 with Canada. The deficit with NAFTA members was $67.8 billion, with Europe $72 billion, and $278.4 billion with Pacific Rim countries. On a commodity basis there was a $170 billion deficit on oil and gas.[31]

As the data indicate, the US economy has become far more dependent on, and integrated with, the global economy. America's merchandise trade to GDP ratio expanded from 17.4 percent in 1980 to 24.1 percent in 2008. With intra-European trade excluded from rankings, the US is the world's third largest exporter of merchandise (behind the European Union and China) and its second largest importer. In commercial services it is the second largest exporter and importer, behind the European Union. Part of the explanation for growing trade dependence could be found in the tariff structure. As a result of multilateral and bilateral reductions, America's duties on imports were relatively low – with applied duties averaging 3.3 percent on manufacturers and 4.7 percent on agricultural products.[32]

With relatively unobstructed access to the US market from foreign production bases, big business chose, as will be explained in Chapter 7, to develop global supply chains. Rather than producing in the large American market, firms could take advantage of the open door at the customs house to produce and assemble goods where it was most advantageous. While the global supply chain was obviously advantageous for corporate profits, there was a debate about whether the hollowing out process was advantageous for the nation. Certainly consumers benefitted from lower prices, but in the process they became more dependent on distant producers operating in a different regulatory environment where health, environmental, labor, and safety standards might differ widely from those in the market of last resort. Ignored in the discussion was any consideration of the day of reckoning. Neither individuals nor nations could live beyond their means for extended periods of time without selling off assets.

Canada

Between 1980 and 2010, Canada made a historic decision to integrate with emerging regional and global markets. During the 1980s Canada's leaders faced a critical decision. Long an important trading nation and active participant in world trade negotiations, it enjoyed a respectable 3.3 percent of world trade. But Canada's productivity growth lagged and its manufacturing costs exceeded the neighboring US by some 40 percent. Internal trade barriers among Canada's provinces contributed to these higher costs. Also, French Canadian separatist sentiment in economically depressed Quebec presented a continuing political threat to the survival of the Canadian federation.[33]

With 30 percent of its jobs dependent on trade, Canada's business and government leaders worried that a "fortress Europe," might restrict access after completion of the internal market in 1992. There was similar concern that US protectionism might jeopardize access to the American market, and threaten access of Canadian firms to an increasingly competitive world marketplace.[34]

As in Western Europe and the US during the same time period, big business pushed public officials to open markets and negotiate free trade agreements. Bell Canada, Stelco, B.C. Resources Investment Corporation, and others urged the new Conservative government of Brian Mulroney to reverse the former Trudeau government's nationalism, attract foreign investment, and pursue free-trade negotiations with the US along the lines recommended by a royal commission report on the future of the Canadian economy.[35]

Mulroney, a Quebec businessman, concurred with the recommendation, and turned his party's back on decades of outspoken nationalism. His government chose to integrate with the US and to deregulate the economy. The results were a bilateral free-trade agreement with the US in 1989, which was extended to include Mexico in 1993. Mulroney pushed the agreement through Parliament despite hostility from organized labor.

While columnists and interest groups continue to debate the wisdom of NAFTA, the basic data show that the Canadian economy performed reasonably well over the period. Per capita GDP rose 53.2% in constant dollars to $34,567 in 2009. This occurred despite a 37% increase in population from 24.6 million to 33.7 million people. One important factor in explaining the growth was access to the North American market. As a result of the US–Canada free-trade agreement, and then the three-way North American Free Trade Agreement (NAFTA), the share of Canada's exports directed to the NAFTA market rose from 61% in 1980 to 76.3% in 2009. Its exports to the EU dropped from 13% in 1980 to 8.3% in 2009. Like the US and Western Europe, Canada, which is the seventh largest exporter in the world, gradually became more dependent on Asian markets. Nonetheless, the US remained Canada's largest supplier, followed by the EU.[36]

A decade after NAFTA Canadian public opinion polls found support for the trade agreements high. Canadians apparently had become more comfortable with global integration. Nonetheless, a majority of Canadians thought the US had benefitted most from NAFTA, and 45 percent wanted to do whatever was necessary to renegotiate the terms. Dissatisfaction with NAFTA apparently did not diminish enthusiasm for other bilateral agreements. A majority of Canadians favored a free trade deal with India.[37]

In international trade negotiations, the Canadian government has long supported the multilateral trade liberalization process to advance its economic interests. Its trade specialists take active part in the WTO and help administer the global trading system. It has used the WTO dispute settlement mechanism to attack US corn subsidies. With vast deposits of oil sands in Alberta, Canada also has become a major player in international oil markets. On some lists Canada's proven oil reserves place it second only to Saudi Arabia.

Because assured access to the US market is vital to Canada's economic health, it has not hesitated in recent years to pursue bilateral and regional agreements. While seeking improved access to foreign markets, Canada seeks to preserve its distinctive culture with restrictions on foreign magazines and films. Foreign firms entering Canada quickly find that provincial barriers restrict internal trade. Inter-provincial barriers also handicap internal trade. Three western provinces – British Columbia, Alberta, and Saskatchewan – signed an agreement to remove trade barriers and allow unfettered interprovincial investment and labor mobility. Ontario and Quebec have also discussed an inter-provincial free-trade agreement.

Oceania

Australia

Australia is a good example of a successful agriculture and raw-materials-oriented economy dependent on open trade. Australia had a population of about 21.9 million (2009), up 50 percent from 14.6 million in 1980, but during these years it succeeded in boosting per capita GDP 71 percent. The World Economic Forum competitiveness index places Australia in sixteenth position overall and commends its ability to balance the government budget and reduce its public debt to one of the lowest among high-income countries.

An important part of the explanation for Australia's general prosperity is its growing integration with the global economy, and proximity to booming Asian markets. The emergence of China as an industrial power has benefitted Australia as a nearby supplier of minerals and raw materials, such as iron ore and natural gas. Exports of minerals and metals constitute over 60 percent of Australia's exports, with farm products another 13 percent.

As a trading nation, Australia ranks seventeenth in the world as an exporter, and thirteenth as an importer of merchandise with per capita trade of $18,699. Australia's principal export markets are China, Japan, the EU, Korea, and India. For Australia the rise of China has been an important stimulus. China imports more than 300 million tons of Australian iron ore annually and large quantities of liquid natural gas. Chinese investments, tourists (a half million annually), and exchange students promise to reshape Australia and its world outlook.[38]

Long a protectionist nation, Australia began to deregulate its economy, privatize state industries, and reduce its tariffs in the 1980s under Prime Minister Bob Hawke, a former labor leader. Eager to gain assured access to its major overseas markets, Australia has negotiated bilateral FTAs with a number of countries in the Asia–Pacific region, including the US.

New Zealand

Once-remote New Zealand became integrated into the global economy during the last 30 years as a result of developments in transportation and communications.[39] With a population of only 4.3 million, up 34% from 3.2 million in 1980, New Zealand increased GDP 46.7% over the period.

Unlike neighboring Australia, which relies heavily on its exports of indus-trial raw materials, New Zealand remains dependent on food exports. They accounted for a rising share of New Zealand's merchandise exports, up from 48% in 1980 to 62% in 2009.[40]

An agricultural country with more sheep than people, New Zealand has historically relied on exports of lamb meat and butter to support its import needs. Because it is reliant on imported manufactures, New Zealand has virtually no duties on imports. Its principal export markets are Australia, the European Union, the US, Japan, and China.[41]

Japan

With guidance from a strong civil service, oriented to promoting growth and recovery from the devastation of World War II, Japan exhibited mete-oric double-digit growth into the 1980s. Conscious of how the US indus-trialized in the nineteenth century, Japan deliberately restricted imports and foreign investments, while encouraging technology transfer. It suc-ceeded in boosting per capita GDP 59.2 percent between 1980 and 2009. In 2010 it had foreign exchange reserves ($1 trillion) second only to China.

During the 1980s the world media regularly carried stories about Japan as number one, and touted the successes of Japanese industrial policy. Before the bubble burst in 1990, real estate valuations soared, so much so that the area of the Imperial Palace in Tokyo at one point had a valuation in excess of the entire state of California. Japanese investors roamed the world, purchasing real high-profile estate such as New York's Rockefeller Center and California's Pebble Beach Golf Club, building green-field man-ufacturing facilities to gain a presence in major markets, and buying US Treasury securities.

With a population of about 127.6 million, Japan has an economy of about $4.1 trillion, roughly one-third the size of the US economy in pro-duction. Among major trading nations Japan enjoys some of the least expensive security, a result of its defense alliance with the US. After World War I Japan pledged not to rebuild its military. It spends less than 1% of GDP on its military, far less in 2008 than the US (4.3%), Korea (2.6%), or China (2%). Japan is the fourth leading exporter of both merchandise and commercial services. Its principal merchandise export markets in 2009 were China (18.9%), the US (16.4%), the EU (12.5%), and Korea (8.1%). On the import side, Japan is the fourth leading importer of merchandise, much of it from China. Japanese multinationals have followed their European and American rivals in shifting assembly to China. Like the EU,

Japan has relatively low average tariff levels (2.5%), but keeps tariffs on agricultural products much higher (21%). As a matter of national policy Japan seeks to produce half of its food.[42]

Among high-income countries, Japan is one of the least globalized. It has relatively low levels of trade and inbound foreign investment as a share of GDP. And it has the lowest number of foreign workers among OECD members. Nor is Japan open to migration. Migrants compose about 2 percent of Japan's population compared to 13 percent in the US. Part of this reflects regulatory policies adopted after World War II to speed the recovery of domestic industries, but it also reflects Japan's traditional cultural and racial homogeneity intended to promote harmony.[43]

Conclusion

During the 30-year focus of this book, the high-income countries became more tightly integrated into the global economy. In Western Europe and North America, they also pursued regional integration through the European Union and NAFTA. Merchandise trade as a share of GDP continued to grow, but the greatest expansion occurred in financial and service markets, where globalization and trade negotiations had substantial impact during this period. But, as we shall discover in a later chapter, these efficiencies came at a steep future price. When financial markets collapsed in 2008, integration facilitated the spread of disruption far and wide. The high-income countries that overreached in efforts to open and integrate markets faced particularly difficult adjustments and a slow recovery.

Chapter 4

The Developing World

Six weeks after the events of September 11, 2001 unsettled markets and appeared to signal a decade of strife and terrorism, Goldman Sachs economist Jim O'Neill introduced a catchy new acronym – "BRIC". With it he directed the attention of investors and public officials to four large emerging markets – Brazil, Russia, India, and China – each with enormous growth potential. O'Neill predicted that the quartet would produce more than 10 percent of global output by the end of the decade. As it turned out, the BRICs surpassed that level in 2008.[1]

In this chapter, we examine briefly the BRICs and other countries with the potential to move rapidly up the economic development ladder. Goldman Sachs says another group including Turkey, Mexico, Nigeria, and Indonesia could grow rapidly. Over time some of these emerging economic powers may join Taiwan, Hong Kong, Korea, and Singapore, among the middle-income countries successfully moving up to developed-country status during the 1980–2010 period. The chapter also looks at another monumental achievement during the period – the restructuring of state-planned economies in Eastern Europe and Asia. Along with these emerging and transitioning economies, we spotlight some of the countries slogging behind. These have enormous problems and face a difficult future.[2]

As used among economic development specialists, the term "developing world" covers a broad array of nations – some 150 altogether. The World Bank classifies developing countries as those with per capita incomes below $12,196. The IMF also includes as developing countries oil-exporting nations with high per capita incomes but heavy export dependence on a

The Contemporary Global Economy: A History Since 1980, First Edition. Alfred E. Eckes, Jr.
© 2011 Alfred E. Eckes, Jr. Published 2011 by Blackwell Publishing Ltd.

single commodity. For the purposes of this narrative, we have elected to place these oil-exporting nations among the ranks of developing countries. One other point deserves emphasis. Not all developing countries are developing at the same pace. Some of the countries are emerging rapidly and have the potential to achieve high-income status in the next generation. Others wallow in corruption and conflict, and must overcome great obstacles. Our broad category of "developing countries" thus includes the world's two most populous nations (India and China), leading oil exporters (Saudi Arabia and others), a fallen superpower (the Russian Federation, successor to the Soviet Union), and several regional giants thought to have enormous potential – Brazil, China, and India.[3]

Asia

A World Bank study of the *East Asian Miracle* (1993) attributed the economic resurgence of Asia to strong state guidance (industrial policy), market-directed incentives, and prudent macroeconomic policies. While stimulating growth and exports, governments successfully kept inflation in check. As noted in Table 1.2, countries in East Asia and the Pacific increased their per capita GDP 594 percent from 1980 to 2009, far faster than the 60 percent rise for the world. The Asians achieved these gains despite their population growth (66%) exceeding world growth (51%).

Export-led development and integration with the global economy were critical to Asia's winning strategy. By the end of the first decade of the twenty-first century, 11 of the 21 largest exporting nations were located in the Pacific region – China, Japan, Korea, Hong Kong, Singapore, Taiwan, Malaysia, Australia, Thailand, India, and Indonesia. These 11 trading powers accounted for over 37 percent of world exports and their share continues to grow, reflecting the dynamism of the region. In services the same nations exported nearly 38 percent of the world total, and imported about 25 percent.[4]

China

Until the first decades of the nineteenth century China had a higher GDP than Western Europe or its offshoots in North America and along the Tasman Sea. But China, a seafaring country with trading and exploration interests, turned inward in the fifteenth century, rejecting foreign science and technology. Chinese leaders were convinced that their Celestial Empire was the center of the universe. Until the late twentieth century China largely ignored the world economy, and pursued isolationism under the Manchu dynasty and the Communists until pragmatists, such as Deng Xiaoping (1904–97), chose to modernize and open up the country through trade, tourism, and educational exchanges. From Mao's China with its Cultural Revolution, re-education, and peasant labor camps emerged a new China under Deng's leadership after 1978. It attempted to synthesize Marxism and capitalism, and establish a socialist market economy, one that looked outward to the world for investments, machinery, technology, and markets.

The results were impressive. During a period when China's population climbed from 981 million to 1.3 billion, an increase of 35 percent, the Chinese economy increased per capita GDP a phenomenal 1,083 percent (from $524 in 1980 to $6,200 in 2009). Behind the statistical measures of progress is a story of human sacrifices described in detail in Chapter 10. Millions of Chinese peasants, many of them young women, migrated to urban areas to work in low-wage factories assembling apparel, electronics, toys, and other products for export markets. Many worked 70 hours or more per week for less than $200 per month. At Longhua where Foxconn, a Taiwanese assembler for major international brand products, employed 300,000 to 400,000 workers, the pace was so intense and the discipline so tight that dozens of workers attempted suicide.[5]

Although China's overall GDP is about half the size of the American economy, this fast-growing country has emerged as one of the most important trading countries. Its growing appetite for aluminum, coal, copper, petroleum, food, and other raw materials contributed to a spectacular surge in commodity prices in 2007–8. After the European Union China is the world's largest exporter, accounting for about 12.7% of exports. China is the third largest importer, taking 10.5% of imports. China's leading export markets are the EU and the US. Its imports come from Japan, the EU, Korea, and Taiwan. While the US is one of China's leading export markets, it does not rank among China's five leading suppliers of imports.[6]

One of the keys to China's expanding trade, and indeed to its large currency reserves, has been foreign investment. Over the last ten years China has attracted about 20 percent of all foreign direct investment (FDI) to developing countries. The Chinese government says that foreign enterprises account for over half of exports and imports, and provide 30 percent of industrial output. Initially China's inbound FDI was concentrated in export-oriented manufacturing. Since 2000, as China has opened its service sectors to competition, hotels, retailers, and financial firms, among others, have entered. FDI in services has expanded much more rapidly than investment in industry.[7]

By the turn of the twenty-first century China had established itself as the world's discount factory. It imported raw materials from Australia, Brazil, and many other countries, then added cheap labor, and exported the results. But China aspired to become more than a supplier of cheap goods to the world market. It aspired to move up the value chain and produce high-technology products, and to this end China demanded that foreign investors bring technology as well as capital. In opening its doors, the Chinese government adopted a "pay-to-play" policy, mandating joint ventures in key industries, imposing local manufacturing rules, and mandating technology transfers as the price of admission. China also wanted foreign business to support its efforts to join the WTO and gain assured access to world export markets at the most favorable tariff rates.

Eamonn Fingleton, an international trade analyst based in Tokyo, was one of the first to observe that China's approach to world trade diverged sharply from the private enterprise model espoused in North America and Europe. He noted that multinational businesses operating in China had become instruments of Chinese government mercantilism. Mercantilists seek to export more than they import, and to accumulate monetary reserves for national advantages. Fingleton criticized big business for transferring advanced technology to China to gain market access, and then lobbying for Chinese interests in foreign capitals.[8]

In 2010 multinationals voiced concerns about the environment for foreign business in China. Western business lobbyists complained that China was advancing a different economic model, one that involved state domination of key sectors like automobiles, electronic information, iron and steel, science and technology, and others. They cited instances of Chinese protectionism – including subsidies and preferences – used to support national champions. Also, they complained that Chinese enterprises, supported by the Communist party and state, had expanded beyond China, using profits from a protected home market to compete for global resources and markets with Western private enterprises.[9]

With over $2.5 trillion in foreign currency reserve, China began to play a more active role in trade and finance. Its state enterprises expanded rapidly. In 2010 three – Sinopec, State Grid, and China National Petroleum – ranked among the top ten on *Fortune* magazine's "Global 500" list of the world's largest corporations. Altogether 46 Chinese corporations made the list. Many of them foraged for natural resources in far corners of the world – from iron in Brazil and Australia to oil in Africa, Canada, and the Middle East – paying premium prices for assets.[10]

Whether state-directed capitalism – and the Beijing consensus – would succeed over the long-term in supplanting the Western market-driven model was an open question. But China's export-led development model, similar in some respects to methods employed successfully in Japan, South Korea, and Taiwan, appeared to challenge the neo-liberal Washington consensus that shaped US thinking before the economic crisis of 2007–10.[11]

Asia's Tigers

The four so-called tigers of Asia – Hong Kong, Singapore, South Korea, and Taiwan – have demonstrated over the last 40 years that nations with strong and farsighted leadership can overcome poverty and colonialism, and develop rapidly. Following the example of postwar Japan, these four led the way. Each of them, incidentally, had experienced a brutal Japanese occupation during World War II. In the 1960s, South Korea and Taiwan had incomes not materially different from some newly independent African countries, such as Ghana. By 2009, two Asian tigers had a per capita GDP more than 15 times Ghana's $1,370. The Asian approach to development – relying on export-led growth, industrial policies to promote domestic enterprises, and some import restrictions – achieved wonders for the four tiger economies. By the early twenty-first century they had joined the developed world and other countries in the region, inspired by their example, sought to do the same.[12]

Hong Kong

Once a British colony on the Asian Mainland, Hong Kong reverted to Chinese control in 1997. However, it continues to operate somewhat autonomously ("one country, two systems"), as an international commercial and financial center. Hong Kong is even a member of the World Trade Organization. A trading city, like Singapore, Hong Kong had 7 million people in 2008, up from 5.1 million in 1980. Over that period Hong Kong increased its per capita GDP 191 percent. It enjoys one of the highest standards of living in the region. It exports 3.5 percent of world exports. Whereas Hong Kong once traded extensively with Europe, it has grown closer to the mainland economically since the turnover. About half of its trade is with China.[13]

Singapore

The trading state of Singapore has only 5 million people, but as a trading center it dwarfs much larger areas. In 2008 Singapore ranked as the ninth leading exporter and importer in the world, accounting for 2.9 percent of world exports. It exports more merchandise than the South Asian sub-continent, home to about a quarter of the world's population. From 1980 to 2009, Singapore raised its per capita GDP in constant dollars 218 percent from $14,454 to $45,974 to lead the Asian region.[14]

Singapore preaches and practices free trade, but it relies on government intervention. Under the pragmatic leadership of Prime Minister Lee Kuan Yew (1959 to 1990), it emphasized "Confucian values," a philosophy that places the good of society over welfare of individuals. Lee's authoritarian approach stressed order and discouraged democratic criticism as dysfunctional to the quest for economic growth. After Malaysia voted to expel predominantly Chinese Singapore in 1965, the island state declared independence. With virtually no resources except the intelligence of its people, Singapore opened to trade and foreign investment. The government intervened to create competitive advantages. Singapore's industrial policy succeeded in transforming a regional hub into a world-class competitor in manufactures, services, and knowledge.

Contemporary Singapore has one of the most business-friendly and competitive environments in the world. It imposes no duties on imports. With one of the world's largest container ports, Singapore trades with all regions. World competitiveness surveys usually list Singapore among the top countries.[15]

South Korea

During the last decades of the twentieth century South Korea recovered from the devastating Korean War and emerged as a major exporter of manufactures, including automobiles, electronics, ships, and machinery. In 1980 South Korea was a developing country with a per capita GDP lower than Ecuador, Peru, or South Africa. By the mid-1990s South Korea had joined the ranks of the advanced countries and become a member of the prestigious Organization for Economic Cooperation and Development (OECD), a group of 30 wealthy nations. From 1980 to 2009, Korea's GDP per capita (in constant dollars) climbed an impressive 360 percent from $5,544 to $25,493, a performance surpassed only by China among emerging economic powers.

Korea's business conglomerates (chaebols), such as Hyundai, LG (Lucky GoldStar), and Samsung, have worldwide activities and brand recognition. Korea is also a major exporter of services, particularly engineering and construction. Samsung engineers built one of the Petronas connecting-towers in Kuala Lumpur, Taipei 101, and Burj Dubai, a skyscraper with 160 habitable floors and a spire reaching 2,717 feet. Korean engineering and construction firms have participated in projects in 118 countries, with about two-thirds of their foreign contracts in the Middle East, especially Saudi Arabia, the United Arab Emirates, and Libya.[16]

With a population of 48.7 million and a GDP of $1.3 trillion (2008), South Korea is the fifth leading exporter and the seventh leading importer. It was the first of the OECD group to emerge from the global recession. A double-digit expansion in exports, combined with a Keynesian-type deficit spending to stimulate domestic demand, facilitated the rebound.[17] Korea is realigning its economic relationships, and growing closer to China. In the aftermath of the Korean War, it depended on the American market for export opportunities, but in recent years China has become its leading customer, followed by the EU, and the US. As for South Korea's imports, China leads, followed by Japan, the US, the EU, and Saudi Arabia.

Despite Korea's role as a major exporter of goods and services, its home market remains highly protected for agricultural products. Korean subsidizes its agricultural sector at a higher rate than any OECD member. About 2.4% of GDP goes for farm support in Korea, compared to 1.1% in Japan, 0.9% in the EU and 0.7% in the US.[18] Korea applies 48.6% *ad valorem* duties on agricultural products to please its militant farm sector, but the rate on nonagricultural products is 6.6%. Korea has long sought to limit the influence of Japanese automobile and electronics manufacturers, and so it maintains restrictions on these imports.[19]

As discussed in Chapter 6, President Lee Myung-bak, a former Hyundai executive, has attempted to integrate Korea into the world economy through bilateral and regional free-trade agreements. He envisages South Korea offering a leadership model for developing nations.

Taiwan (Taipei, Chinese)

Taiwan's status as an independent economy is complicated by its delicate relationship with nearby China. With only 23 million people, it has become the eleventh most important trading power in the world, accounting for 2.2 percent of world exports. Its trade per capita ($22,049) surpasses all non-oil producing nations, except Singapore. But mainland China on the other side of the Taiwan Straits regards tiny Taiwan as a break-away prov-ince, and its military has prepared to reunify China by force, if necessary. At the time China was admitted to the World Trade Organization, Taiwan was admitted as Taipei, Chinese, a diplomatic phrase that fudges claims of sovereignty.

Taiwan has flowered as a trading country, raising its living standards by its own bootstraps from the early 1960s when Taiwan first invited foreign electronics firms to assemble in its foreign-trade-zones, making use of low-cost labor. Because of its tense relationship with China, Taiwan protects its domestic agriculture (agricultural tariffs average 16.9%), while nonagricul-tural tariffs average 4.5%. Its principal export trading partners, paradoxi-cally are China and Hong Kong, followed by the US, the EU, and Japan.[20]

Despite the risk of conflict, business ties between Taiwan and the main-land have flourished. During the mid-1980s Taiwan gradually removed restrictions on exports to mainland China via Hong Kong and Macao, and in 1991 it eased a ban on Taiwanese investments. Taiwanese businesses saw very early the opportunity to shift labor-intensive manufacturing of shoes and apparel to the low-cost mainland, and they recognized the profit-making opportunities presented by the huge China market. Despite the absence of direct air service until 2008, Taiwanese investors began to flock to China in the 1990s. Reportedly, one-half of Taiwan's direct investment stock (perhaps $175 billion in 2008) is in China.[21] There are 750,000, or more, Taiwanese residents living in China, and Taiwanese firms remit profits to Taiwan.

Under President Ma Ying-jeou, a Harvard University-educated lawyer, Taiwan has pursued a policy intended to achieve closer economic integra-tion with the mainland through free trade and technical business accords. Critics feared Ma would promote unification with the mainland, while compromising its independence and opening Taiwan to the disruption of cheap Chinese goods.[22]

Association of Southeast Asian Nations

Regional integration is another strategy that the nations of South East Asia have adopted in order to achieve and sustain high growth. In August 1967 Indonesia, Malaysia, the Philippines, and Thailand joined Singapore in organizing the Association of Southeast Asian Nations (ASEAN). Subsequently, Brunei, Cambodia, Laos, Myanmar (Burma), and Vietnam became members. ASEAN is a regional association with the goals of promoting economic and social progress and cultural development. In 2009, ASEAN had a population of 584 million and average per capita GDP of $2,577. But ASEAN members had achieved different levels of development. Per capita wealth ranged widely from Singapore at the upper end to economically backward Burma. In 2009 ASEAN accounted for $814 billion in exports, approximately 6.5 percent of the world total. Decisions about goals, plans of action, and the like are the subject of negotiations among governments, and do not depend on the approval of voters.

In 1992 ASEAN members agreed to move to an ASEAN Economic Community (AEC) by 2015. One of the foundations of AEC is the ASEAN Free Trade Area (AFTA), while another is the ASEAN Comprehensive Investment Area (ACIA). In essence the goal is to create a single market and production base without permitting free movement of unskilled labor or other standardization and harmonization. ASEAN aspires to complete a single market, a customs union after 2015.

In January 2010 the six original members removed import tariffs on most commodities. The other four must implement this provision by 2015. At present only about 25 percent of ASEAN trade is intra-regional, while one fifth is with the United States and Europe, and some 29 percent with Japan.[23] To achieve greater integration through a customs union will require considerable institutional support, but in 2010 ASEAN had a tiny bureaucracy of only 70 professionals, many of them focused on conducting conferences. The European Commission by contrast had over 25,000 civil servants to administer the EU.

Indonesia

Singapore's successful development has inspired its larger neighbors, Indonesia and Malaysia. Indonesia, a former Dutch colony, has rich natural resources – including oil, rubber, and timber. Its leaders face a harsh environment with periodic monsoons and earthquakes, and a rapidly growing population. Over the period from 1980 to 2008, Indonesia's population increased 56 percent from 147.5 million to 230 million. Indonesia succeeded in boosting per capita GDP from $1,361 to $3,813, an increase of 180.2 percent in constant dollars. Compared to its dynamic Asian neighbors this was unimpressive, but it surpassed economic performance in high-income countries and signaled Indonesia's long-term potential.[24]

More than 200 million Moslems live in Indonesia, giving it the largest Moslem population in the world. Nonetheless, Indonesia is a secular country. Christians compose about 9 percent of the population. An ethnic

Chinese minority (about 1%) has prospered in industry, retailing, and finance, despite discrimination and violent hostility. Ethnic Chinese control the vast majority of the nation's private wealth.

Government corruption, an inefficient bureaucracy, and military dominance have long handicapped Indonesia's development. After gaining independence from the Netherlands in 1945, two nationalists – Sukarno (1945–67) and Suharto (1967–2008) – ruled. Both collaborated with the Japanese occupation. Under Sukarno Indonesia nationalized Dutch businesses and took steps to reduce the economic influence of ethnic Chinese over rural and retail trade. He discouraged foreign investment. In 1967 Suharto inherited a bankrupt economy and reversed socialist policies in order to promote development. His regime provided protection to ethnic Chinese business conglomerates. But widespread corruption and fluctuating attitudes toward foreign investment remained obstacles to growth.[25]

Despite its potential as a big emerging market, Indonesia is not a major trading power. Its share of world exports is a little over 1 percent. However, the meteoric growth of China has presented new markets for Indonesia's raw-material exports, and the general prosperity of the region bodes well for Indonesia's economy.[26]

Malaysia

Malaysia, once British Malaya, is a relatively prosperous Moslem country with 27.5 million people. It has abundant natural resources for export, including oil and gas, timber, and palm oil. Adjoining Singapore, it has benefitted from the phenomenal growth of that city state. Malaysia's tolerant, pro-business approach lured Western electronics firms and other investors in the 1970s to make use of its inexpensive labor.

Growing rapidly, Malaysia has enjoyed a long period of economic growth, which in turn has helped overcome racial tensions between the Malay majority and its Chinese and Indian minorities. Like leaders of adjoining countries, Malaysia's leaders saw the opportunity to promote export-led development. They actively encouraged Western firms to assemble goods in Malaysia. During the period from 1980 to 2009, Malaysia increased GDP per capita 159.2 percent from $4,891 to $12,678.[27]

During the Asian economic crisis of 1997, the Malaysian government of Prime Minister Mohamad Mahathir took a different approach than Thailand or Indonesia. Those countries had opened their financial markets to global capital flows (capital account convertibility) at the request of the IMF. But during the crisis they had to accept stringent IMF stabilization plans involving budget cuts and structural reforms. Mahathir imposed capital controls, in effect regulating markets and currency speculation, and the Malaysian economy weathered the storm without an onerous IMF adjustment plan. In effect, Mahathir thumbed his nose at the IMF and won.

The Philippines

The Philippines is a low, middle-income democracy struggling to find a competitive niche in a world where China and Vietnam offer the cheapest manufacturing labor. With a well-educated labor force of college graduates who know English, the Philippines has succeeded in exporting services (including legal services) and attracting call centers. It also exports workers. Large numbers of Filipinos work abroad – in healthcare, construction, and home services – and remit large sums ($18.6 billion in 2008) helping relatives who remain at home. Since 1980 the composition of Philippine exports has changed dramatically with manufactures rising sharply. Foreign investment, particularly in computer equipment, is largely responsible for this shift.

The Philippine economy has underperformed neighboring countries, in particular Taiwan and Malaysia. During the period 1980 to 2009, the Philippines increased GDP per capita only 22.8 percent, while population climbed 80.7 percent from 50.9 million to 92 million. Rapid population growth reflects a high birth rate, for the Philippines is a predominantly Roman Catholic country. Political corruption, a fact of life in many developing countries, is endemic in the Philippines. According to international corruption ratings, it ranks among the bottom 25 percent of nations.[28]

Thailand

In Southeast Asia one of the most dynamic manufacturing economies in the region is Thailand. Benefitting from Vietnam War orders and spending, and subsequent foreign investment, Thailand transformed itself from a country of smiling Buddhas, elephants, and rice farmers into a significant exporter of manufactures. Manufactures rose from 25 percent of merchandise exports in 1980 to 74 percent in 2008.[29]

The Asian economic crash of 1997 began in Thailand with the bursting of a real estate bubble, and a run on the Thai currency, the baht. Nonetheless, over the longer period the Thai economy has performed relatively well. While its population grew 44 percent (from 47 million to 67.8 million) between 1980 and 2008, per capita GDP climbed an impressive 225 percent from $2,231 to $7,258. However, political instability with occasional riots, ballot-box corruption, and military rule has raised concerns about Thailand's ability to sustain an ambitious economic development program.

Vietnam

Vietnam is another Communist country that reformed, embraced capitalism, joined the WTO in 2009, and enjoyed rapid, export-led growth. Vietnam's transition to a socialist market economy began in the mid-1980s when leaders chose to follow the Chinese example and liberalize the economy. With labor costs lower than China, they attracted garment and footwear makers, and targeted consumers in the US and Europe. From 1980 to 2009, Vietnam's population grew 63 percent from 53.7 to 87.3 million people, but with a surge of foreign investment Vietnam succeeded in increasing per capita GDP 197.2 percent in constant dollars. Vietnam's success has made it a poster child for Asian-style economic development.[30]

South Asia

In South Asia there have been halting steps toward economic integration but poverty and political rivalries, especially between India and Pakistan, have impeded efforts to open markets and reduce trade barriers. This densely populated region has the world's largest concentration of poor people with one billion living on less than $2 per day. Half of the region's population is illiterate. Nonetheless, the region weathered the recent global recession better than high-income countries and returned to growth. The dynamic services sector leads the recovery. But World Bank economists say growth is inadequate to create 150 million jobs for new workers over the next decade.[31]

India

India, with 1.1 billion people, is an emerging giant with a growing middle class of some 300 million. Since 1980 India's population rose 70 percent from 679 million to 1,155 million, but it succeeded in increasing per capita GDP an impressive 230.4 percent from $899 in 1980 to $2,970 in 2009.[32]

For much of its history since gaining independence in 1947, India rejected free-market economics and relied on central planning, industrial policy to promote manufacturing, and government control over foreign trade and foreign investment. India's protectionist trade policy sought to substitute domestic production for imports. The average tariff surpassed 200 percent, and quotas also restricted trade. India's growth from 1950 to 1980 averaged about 3.5 percent.[33]

With the collapse in 1991 of its major trading partner, the Soviet Union, India began to liberalize its economy and open up to trade and investment. But inadequate ports, roads, power, and other infrastructure complicate efforts to expand exports of manufactures. However, India has large numbers of well-educated people eager to take service-related jobs. Annually India's colleges and universities turn out 2.5 million graduates, including 350,000 engineers. Call centers and back-office operations flourish in India, as North American and European firms have moved jobs to India to take advantage of well-educated but relatively inexpensive labor. Also, large numbers of transnational firms, such as General Electric, have established operations and research centers in India. In addition, Indian entrepreneurs have developed a number of world-class competitors such as Reliance Industries, a conglomerate; Tata in engineering and manufacturing; and Infosys and Wipro in software and information technology. The 2010 *Fortune Global 500* lists eight Indian corporations.[34]

As a trading country, India ranks relatively low – fifteenth in merchandise exports. It is more competitive in services, and is the sixth leading exporter. As a founding member of GATT in 1947, India takes an active role in global trade negotiations. It has rallied developing countries in the WTO as a counterweight to the influence of the EU and the US, but, while seeking market access for manufactures and agricultural exports in the rich industrial countries, instances of Indian protectionism abound. In WTO negotiations, India declined to open its agricultural market to world competition and to lower tariffs on imported manufactures. In deference to its generic drug manufacturers, who reproduce overseas patented drugs by a different process, and to consumers who benefit from low-prices, India has been slow to comply with the WTO's code protecting intellectual property rights. And, to protect small retailers and 42 million jobs from Wal-Mart, Tesco, and Carrefour, India bans foreign investment in multi-line stores.

Bangladesh

Bangladesh separated from Pakistan in 1971. A Moslem country, it is poor and overpopulated. Between 1980 and 2009, GDP per capita rose from $604 to $1,288, an increase of 113 percent at a time when population surged from 88 million to 162 million, an increase of 84 percent. To create jobs, Bangladesh focused its low-cost labor force on producing textiles and apparel for the global market. In the apparel plants large numbers of women labor for low wages ($24 per month minimum wage in 2010) in difficult working conditions, including poor ventilation and inadequate fire safety. With the end of international textile quotas in 2005, Bangladesh found the apparel trade more competitive than ever. Its exports go to distant markets, such as the European Union and the US, while China and India are the leading suppliers of imports.[35]

Pakistan

Created from Moslem-majority areas of British India, Pakistan gained independence in 1947. Over time its leaders industrialized this poor, agricultural nation. The growth of the textile and apparel industries produced jobs and exports (nearly 60 percent of total exports). Nonetheless, for a country of 166 million people, Pakistan's share of world exports is far below 1 percent. Over the period since 1980, Pakistan has increased its GDP per capita by 100 percent (from $1,191 to $2,381 in constant dollars), while population rose 99 percent from 85.2 million to 169.7 million.

Because of political hostilities, there is little official trade between Pakistan and neighboring India, less than 1 percent of total exports. However, smuggling is widespread. Like Bangladesh, Pakistan looks to the European Union and the US for export sales. A petroleum importer, it depends heavily on Saudi Arabia for imports. Other leading suppliers include the European Union and China. With widespread corruption and terrorism, Pakistan has difficulty attracting outside investment.[36]

Latin America

For much of the post-World War II period, Latin America pursued import-substitution policies intended to promote domestic industries. But as a result of a debt crisis in the early 1980s, Latin American leaders shifted course, restructured their economies, and opened their markets to international trade and finance.

Mexico

Difficult economic circumstances forced the ruling party in Mexico to rethink its international relationships during the 1980s and to engage the global economy. Ruled by one political party since the Mexican Revolution, Mexico had pursued isolationist economic policies, and attempted to keep its distance from the US, its large North American neighbor, despite a 1,969 mile common border. During the late 1970s Mexico, flush with oil-export earnings, sought to grow rapidly, and to borrow on the strength of prospective earnings. But, in 1982 with rising interest rates and falling oil prices, this approach proved unsustainable. Mexico announced that it could no longer meet payments on some $80 billion in debts owed to foreign banks. The Mexican stock market collapsed, as did the currency.

The situation was dire. Population was rising rapidly, up 57.2 percent from 68.3 million in 1980 to 107.4 million in 2009. With more mouths to feed, large numbers of *campesinos* (farmers) left the land and migrated to urban areas to find jobs. But unemployment remained high. Mexico's per capita GDP fell 4 percent in the 1980s, a recipe for social and political unrest. In this situation, Mexico's leadership made a crucial decision to look outward for foreign investment to create jobs. It agreed to deregulate the economy, join GATT in 1986, and negotiate market-opening trade agreements that would attract foreign investors. With Europe engaged in market integration and expansion, the US was the only prospective partner available. To officials in Washington the Mexican overture seemed an historic opportunity to promote growth, prosperity, and stability in an important neighbor. Against that were the enormous challenges, particularly the problems of integrating a low–middle-income country (Mexico) with two high-income economies.

As it turned out, NAFTA did bind Mexico to North America and integrate it into the international trading system. One result was a modest improvement in living standards for its people. Over the period from 1980 to 2009 Mexico succeeded in raising per capita GDP 19.3%. Its trade as a share of GDP climbed from 21% in 1980 to 58.1% in 2009. NAFTA attracted foreign investors, and they built manufacturing facilities to serve the North American market. Manufactures as a share of Mexican exports rose from 12 to 65%.[37]

In a short time, Mexico became a major trading country – ranking tenth among the world's exporters (excluding intra-EU trade) and tenth among importers. Of its exports over 80 percent goes to the US, 5 percent to the EU, and slightly over 3.6 percent to Canada. Nearly half of Mexico's imports arrive from the US. Much of Mexico's trade consists of cross-border trade in intermediate products, as multinational corporations move parts and components to locations for less-expensive assembly, and then ship finished products such as automobiles back across the border to high-income consumers. In 2009 more finished motor vehicles entered the US from Mexico than from either Canada or Japan.[38]

NAFTA increased cross-border illicit trade. With more containers moving northward, drug smugglers found Mexico an attractive staging ground for serving US customers. Drug wars among rival smuggling gangs soon turned border cities into terror zones, threatening the stability of Mexican political institutions. Violence and organized crime impair Mexico's efforts to attract foreign investors and tourists.[39]

South and Central America

In South and Central America regional economic integration has not advanced as far as in Western Europe and North America. Mercosur, the most successful grouping, brought together Argentina and Brazil, and two smaller countries, Uruguay and Paraguay, in 1991. Integration was slow. In 2009, 15 percent of Mercosur exports went to other Mercosur countries, but only 17 percent of imports came from Mercosur partners. Another smaller regional grouping, the Andean Community, seeks to promote trade among Andean countries – Bolivia, Colombia, Ecuador, and Peru – but its members have achieved even less integration.[40]

The stimulus of NAFTA to the Mexican economy encouraged smaller countries in the region to pursue economic integration. One such undertaking was the Central American Free Trade Agreement (CAFTA), negotiated in 2003 and including the Dominican Republic. After a referendum in Costa Rica the agreement took effect in early 2009. Some saw it as an extension of NAFTA southward and an important step toward building a Free Trade Area of the Americas (FTAA).

Free-trade negotiations also proceeded bilaterally. Colombia, the Dominican Republic (a party to CAFTA), and Panama negotiated free-trade agreements (FTA) with the United States. While these countries already generally enjoyed unimpeded access to the large North American markets as a result of low US tariffs and the generalized system of preferences, the FTAs offered a broader framework for settling disputes and providing access to the services sector, intended to promote greater flows of private investment.

Since the nineteenth century Latin America has looked to the US and Western Europe for markets, but China emerged in the early twenty-first century as a major market for the region's raw materials and as a significant supplier of low-cost manufactured goods. For Argentina (2008), Chile

(2008), and Brazil, sales to China have became more important than exports to the United States.

Brazil

One of the big emerging markets, Portuguese-speaking Brazil is the leading industrial power of South America, and increasingly a global leader. Between 1980 and 2009 Brazil's population rose 57 percent from 123 million to 193.7 million. It succeeded in raising GDP per capita only 26 percent, but in the first decade of the twenty-first century Brazil enjoyed much more rapid growth. It suffered only a brief setback in the 2007–10 recession. The largest country in Latin America by area and population, Brazil (with a GDP of about $2 trillion) has industrialized and become a diversified exporter of manufactures (including airplanes and armaments), as well as agricultural products such as coffee and cotton. Agricultural products and manufacturers each account for about 40 percent of exports. China is Brazil's second leading export market behind the EU. Some of Brazil's largest corporations, such as Embraer, the maker of commuter airplanes, energy giant Petrobras, and Vale, a mining company, have world-class reputations.

With a large domestic market, a diversified economy with strengths in agriculture, raw materials, manufacturing, and technology, Brazil historically has sought to limit access to its market. It pursued an import substitution policy, and continues to use subsidies and government procurement policies to stimulate national production. In services it has been slow to open up the domestic market to foreign financial, telecommunications, cable, and media companies. But Brazil wants foreign investment, and because of its market size and growth potential has enjoyed considerable success in attracting outside capital.[41]

Eager to improve market access for its products abroad, Brazil has taken an increasingly active interest in the WTO. It has encouraged trade among countries in the southern hemisphere, and has used the WTO dispute settlement mechanism (discussed in Chapter 6) to challenge successfully US subsidies for cotton and EU subsidies for sugar.

Argentina

Once a leader in Latin America, Argentina fell on hard times in the twentieth century, when nationalistic policies, social conflict, shortsighted fiscal policies, and excessive borrowing weakened the national economy. So did the misguided attempt to invade the Falkland Islands, precipitating war with Britain in 1982. A financial crisis, resulting from large foreign debts, domestic overspending, and declining competitiveness, pushed Argentina into chaos in 2001–2. The collapse brought bank runs, deadly protests, defaults on debts to foreign banks, and a plunge in direct investment to South America.

Over the 30-year period Argentina's relative economic position has declined. In 1980 Argentina had a per capita income ($10,067) higher than any South American country, except oil-rich Venezuela. Chile, which adopted market-oriented reforms, surpassed it in the mid-1990s. With a population of 40.3 million in 2009, Argentina remains a major exporter of agricultural products, such as wheat and beef from the rich Pampas, to world markets. But its share of world exports is 0.6 percent. Brazil and the European Union are its largest markets with China close behind.[42]

Chile

Under military dictator Augusto Pinochet (1974–90), Chile opened its economy to global trade. Lowering tariffs, deregulating industries, and adopting a floating exchange rate, Chile experienced the highest rate of economic growth in Latin America. During a time when its population grew 53 percent from 11.1 million in 1980 to 17 million in 2009, the dynamic Chilean economy grew per capita GDP 143 percent from $5,366 to $13,057. As a result, Chile one of the highest standards of living in South America. On the WEF competitiveness index, Chile ranks thirtieth of 139 nations, ahead of all other Latin American nations.[43]

The Middle East and North Africa

This region is an area of contrasts between modernizing democratic regimes in Turkey and Israel, and autocratic regimes in oil-rich lands such as Iran and Saudi Arabia. Unlike most other areas, the winds of change have also aroused the passions and fears of clerics who envisage a future shaped by religious fundamentalism.

Turkey

With 74.8 million people and a relatively large domestic market Turkey is one of the more moderate and advanced countries in the Middle East. It is also one of the largest, most secular and democratic states in the Muslim world. Over the period 1980 to 2008, Turkey succeeded in more than doubling GDP per capita while population climbed 66 percent.[44]

Turkey has a relatively small share of world exports (less than 1%), but it is much more integrated into the global economy than in 1980. In 1980 merchandise trade amounted to 15.7 percent of GDP, in 2008 it was 45.7 percent. Turkey aspires to join the European Union, and has taken steps to integrate with that bloc. Over two million of its natives have taken up residence in Germany, and about half of Turkey's trade is with the EU.[45] Because of extensive trade and financial linkages to the EU, the global financial crisis of 2007–10 hit Turkey hard, despite good economic management and low public debt.

Israel

One of the most dynamic economies in the Middle East with a thriving high-tech industry is Israel, a country with 7.4 million people. Over the period 1980 to 2008, Israel acquired developed-country standing. It succeeded in boosting GDP per capita 70 percent, even as its population nearly doubled. A pariah to the Arab world, Israel has cultivated its overseas network, negotiating a free-trade agreement with the United States in 1984 and similar arrangements with the EU. Its leading export markets are the US and the EU. The EU supplies over one-third of imports, followed by the US and China. Israel maintains high tariffs on imported agricultural products (averaging 16.5%) to encourage local production.[46]

Gulf Cooperation Council

An agreement among Bahrain, Kuwait, Oman, Qatar, Saudi Arabia, and United Arab Emirates, the Gulf Cooperation Council (GCC), negotiated in 1981, has political, defense, and economic dimensions. Economically, the members launched a common market and aspire to a common currency. They have attempted to use oil riches to modernize and to integrate with world financial centers. The GCC countries enjoyed enormous success when oil prices soared, but were hard hit during 2007–10 when oil prices dropped, banks froze credit, and the real-estate bubble burst.[47]

Saudi Arabia

As a leader of OPEC and the world's leading oil exporter, Saudi Arabia exercises an influence in international relations disproportionate to its 25.4 million population. The ruling Al Saud family has held a monopoly of power since founding of the Saudi Arabian state in 1932. With about one-fifth of the world's proven oil reserves, the petroleum sector continues to drive the economy, and accounts for 90 percent of export earnings. Among its leading export markets are Japan, Taiwan, the US, the EU, and the United Arab Emirates. About one-third of imports come from the EU, with the US, China, Japan, and Korea supplying smaller portions. Saudi Arabia depends on 5.5 million foreign workers to keep the energy sector running. Saudi Arabia has $410 billion of gold and foreign currency reserves.[48]

Egypt

One of the most populous countries in the region, Egypt sits astride one of the world's great shipping routes – the Suez Canal. Nonetheless, Egypt accounts for considerably less than 1 percent of world exports, and its ratio of trade to GDP (65.2%) has not changed significantly over the last generation. Egypt's principal trading partner is the European Union, which takes about one-third of its exports, and provides about the same share of import. Between 1980 and 2008 Egypt's population spiraled from 42.6 million to 83 million, an increase of 95 percent; per capita GDP rose 106 percent over the period. While it has a reasonably large domestic market, Egypt is not a magnet for foreign investments. Its handicaps include rapid population growth, inflation, budget deficits, political instability and corruption, a weak educational system, inefficient labor markets, and few natural resources.[49]

Sub-Saharan Africa

No region experienced greater difficulty adapting to the challenges of globalization than sub-Saharan Africa, a vast region of independent nations. Many have rich natural resources but lack roads, railroads, and modern port facilities to support the expansion of commerce. Until the arrival of cell phones, few residents of this region could use telephones. Many live without electricity or refrigeration. Only one in four Africans has electricity. In the sub-Saharan region generally, life spans were short and per capita incomes negligible. Tribalism, disease, political corruption, and the absence of an educated work force discouraged foreign investment. Except for South Africa and Nigeria, sub-Saharan countries have small markets and thus do not benefit from the economies of scale that large domestic and foreign markets offer.

Africa's growth – almost 5 percent annually from 1997 to 2007 – softened during the global financial crisis. The crisis reduced remittances, private capital flows, foreign aid, and commodity prices. In addition to cyclical problems Africa has profound structural problems handicapping efforts to integrate with the global economy. When compared to other regions, a study for the World Economic Forum concluded that Africa was one of the most expensive places in the world to produce. Poor infrastructure, inadequate credit, crime and corruption, and an unpredictable regulatory environment more than offset any advantage from low-cost labor. High transportation costs are a barrier to expanding trade within the region.[50]

One of the most egregious examples of misgovernment involves Zimbabwe, the former Southern Rhodesia. Once a prosperous farming area, and producer of tobacco, and a country with unmatched tourist attractions, Zimbabwe fell under the one-party misrule of President Robert Mugabe and faced economic collapse. With a population of 12.5 million people, Zimbabwe experienced a sharp decline in per capita GDP between 1980 and 2009. A bungled land reform program damaged commercial farming and turned the country into a net importer of food. The Global Competitiveness Index ranks Zimbabwe among the world's least competitive economies – 136 of 139 countries, and Transparency International lists it among the most corrupt countries. It has spiraling inflation, a huge government debt, and one of the world's highest birth rates. However, Zimbabwe's government has massive reserves of diamonds (estimated at $2 billion) available for sale.[51]

Another resource-rich Africa country with similar problems is the Democratic Republic of the Congo, formerly the Belgian Congo and Zaire (1971–97). A vast under-populated country, the Congo has large mineral resources, but it is misgoverned and debt-ridden. Per capita GDP fell from $774 in 1980 to $290 in 2008, a decline of 63 percent. Meanwhile, several other sub-Saharan African countries benefitted from oil production – particularly populous Nigeria and Angola. Angola saw GDP per capita rise 65 percent. Nigeria, with rapid population growth, did less well. Its GDP per capita climbed only 17 percent, as population jumped from 74.8 million to 154.7 million, 107 percent, but with increasing oil exports it became more engaged in the global economy. Like South Africa, Nigeria is a large emerging market (over 143 million people) and might succeed over the long term in achieving high levels of growth.[52]

One of the bright spots among nations associated with Africa is Mauritius, a small island country located 500 miles east of Madagascar in the Indian Ocean. As a former colony of Britain, it enjoys duty-free access to the

European Union. A majority of its 1.3 million people are of Indian descent, and Hinduism is the majority religion. Once reliant on sugar exports, Mauritius has successfully diversified into manufacturing and services, including tourism. It has specialized in textiles, attracting Chinese and Indian investors to produce goods destined for the European and North American markets. These exports also qualify for special preferences under the US African Growth and Opportunity Act (AGOA). Mauritius has done relatively well since 1980, increasing GDP per capita from $3,729 to $11,659, an increase of 213 percent. Life expectancy at birth has climbed from 66 to 73 years, far above the average for sub-Saharan Africa, which rose from 48 to 52 years during the same period.[53]

South Africa

As an African country with enormous mineral wealth (including platinum and diamonds), and one of the highest standards of living, South Africa attempted the difficult transition from white Afrikaner rule to a multiracial democracy in the early 1990s. Under the newly elected African National Congress government, officials integrated the disadvantaged black majority into the economy and sought to revive an economy weakened by external sanctions. South Africa dismantled its previous system of high tariffs and government intervention in favor of an open, market-driven system compatible with its obligations under the World Trade Organization. After the end of apartheid and foreign economic sanctions, trade as a share of GDP rose from 37 percent to 66 percent during the period 1990 to 2009 as South Africa became reintegrated into the global economy. During the political transition per capita GDP in constant dollars fell about 20 percent, but ended the period at $9,332 (6.5% above the 1980 level).[54]

A number of factors complicated the political transition from Afrikaner rule. During the political changeover crime soared and more than a million white South Africans emigrated. Many of these were highly-skilled medical professionals. Their migration complicated efforts to fight HIV/AIDS in a country with AIDs infecting nearly 20 percent of adults. In this dire situation it is not surprising that South Africa's average life expectancy at birth fell from 57 to 51 years from 1980 to 2008.

Having hosted the 2010 World Cup finals in association football, South Africa aspires to an expanded leadership role on the continent. Its trade officials see South Africa pulling smaller markets into a more cohesive regional trade zone stretching from the Cape to Cairo.[55]

Central and Eastern Europe

From the end of World War II until the break-up of the Soviet Union in 1991, Central and Eastern Europe pursued its own version of regional integration. Under Soviet direction the region acquiesced to socialism and central planning rather than engagement with the economies of Western Europe and North America. Under the Soviet system, government owned the means of production, and government planners, not market mechanisms, allocated resources in order to achieve growth and economic development.

During the 1960s the Eastern bloc claimed high rates of growth and succeeded in challenging the West militarily and politically. But economic growth slowed in the 1970s. Without incentives, worker productivity remained low, and economies stagnated, unable to produce adequate consumer goods. Alcoholism and corruption also hampered economic performance. Gradually the population became restive, as improved communications – such television and fax machines – heightened awareness of the enormous gap between economic conditions in Eastern bloc and the prosperous West. Shortages also helped sow the seeds of revolution. Although the Eastern bloc was relatively self-sufficient in energy, Soviet efforts to reorganize agriculture with collective and state farms to improve efficiency proved disastrous in practice. Without private property and incentives for growers, the farm sector did not produce enough food, particularly grain and meat. As a result the region became increasingly dependent on imports of grain, and credits from overseas suppliers.[56]

After the breakup of the Soviet Union, 12 of the former Soviet republics joined a loose association – the Commonwealth of Independent States (CIS) – and promoted their own version of a common market, labeled a common economic space. As noted earlier, eight others joined the EU, but it rebuffed overtures from Armenia, Azerbaijan, Belarus, Georgia, Moldova, and the Ukraine for membership, apparently not wanting to provoke Russia. Instead, the EU offered association agreements, including free trade, economic aid, technical expertise, and visa-free trade if these neighbors commit to democracy, the rule of law, and sound human rights and economic policies.[57]

Because the new transitional states generally had well-educated labor forces and relatively low-wages, multinational corporations expanded operations rapidly in this region, often at the expense of previous low-cost producers like Spain. Fiat, Ford, Renault, General Motors, Volkswagen, and other carmakers opened auto assembly plants in Eastern Europe. So did

Asian car makers like Toyota, Nissan, Hyundai, and Kia. Slovakia, with 5.4 million people, soon became known as the "Detroit of the east," as three automobile manufacturers opened plants. To automakers the attractions included skilled labor, wages about one-fifth of those in high-income members of the EU, a low 19 percent flat-tax rate, and proximity to European markets. Volkswagen was the first international carmaker to open a plant in Slovakia; Peugeot Citroen of France and Kia of Korea followed.[58]

Western companies also turned to Russia for talented workers, making use of offshoring and outsourcing opportunities as they sought to cut labor costs. With computer programmers available for as little as little as $1,000 a month, Western enterprise recruited East European workers. As noted in Chapter 7, Boeing made use of Russian engineers to help build its 787 "dreamliner."

With more open economies and enhanced flows of trade, capital, and information these countries sought to join the global economy, build relationships with the West, and secure middle-class lifestyles. By 2009, some of them had made significant progress – incomes were up, and life expectancy much improved. In Poland, per capita GDP had risen 104 percent from 1994 to 2009, and life expectancy expanded four years. There were significant improvements in the Czech Republic, Hungary, Slovakia, and Romania, where per capita GDP rose from 35 to 54 percent. Some of the most impressive growth occurred in the tiny Baltic states of Estonia, Latvia, and Lithuania. Between 1994 and 2008, GDP per capita rose 158 percent in Estonia and 143 percent in both Latvia and Lithuania. The Baltic countries benefitted from privatization, thriving export markets in nearby Finland and Sweden, and an influx of foreign investment, but they also borrowed heavily in foreign currencies. This dependence left them particularly vulnerable to the financial collapse of 2008–9.[59]

The global crisis hit this region especially hard as credit markets tightened and currencies fell. In some countries one of the first steps in adapting to the open global economy involved heavy foreign borrowing. Eager home buyers took out mortgages in foreign currencies (borrowing from Swiss or Austrian banks), where interest rates were lower. When the collapse came, many borrowers found themselves unable to make payments. As a result, the International Monetary Fund provided bailouts to Hungary, Latvia, Serbia, the Ukraine, Belarus, and Romania, among others, requiring that recipients bring down government debt and reduce current-account deficits. But, unlike the stringent IMF approach to the 1997 Asian debt crisis, recipients received time to make adjustments. The IMF's new rules of engagement even involved supporting expanded social safety nets so as to cushion the most vulnerable in society.[60]

Russian Federation

The old Soviet Union (USSR) practiced self-sufficiency and carefully controlled economic contacts with the West. Stretching over one-sixth of the earth's surface in 1990, the USSR had a population of 291 million. This population included more than 100 ethnic groups – Russians, Ukrainians, Uzbeks, Belarusians, Kazakhs, Azeris, Armenians, Georgians, and others. Trade amounted to perhaps 4 percent of GDP, the vast majority with other communist countries in Eastern Europe. While the USSR wanted Western technology with military applications it had little to sell, except gold, caviar, vodka, and raw materials. It relied heavily on espionage to obtain Western industrial and military secrets.

After the USSR collapsed in December 1991, a trimmed-down Russian Federation with 142 million people, but one-eighth of the earth's land area, threw off the communist system based on state planning and collective farms. It attempted the transition to a market-driven economy. At first adopting the advice of outside economists, such as Harvard economist Jeffrey Sachs, and the IMF, President Boris Yeltsin's government introduced market-oriented reforms. However, "shock therapy" – the removal of price controls and subsidies – contributed to hyper-inflation of 2,500 percent and plunged millions of pensioners into misery. Efforts to privatize and restructure state-controlled enterprises in a country with a system of vouchers led to the sale of government assets at fire-sale prices. Reportedly, there was widespread corruption and the privatization program enriched organized crime. It also accelerated the emergence of a group of oligarchs who obtained key companies and exerted substantial political influence. Without firm foundations of law and order, the new market economy in Yeltsin's Russia empowered criminal gangs, and corruption flourished.[61]

Eager to support democracy in the Soviet Union, the Clinton administration in the US and the IMF encouraged Yeltsin to remove capital controls and borrow heavily from abroad, as they did emerging economies in Latin America and East Asia. But after the 1997 Asian crisis interest rates soared internationally, oil prices dropped 40 percent, and the Russian stock market collapsed. Fearful of ruble devaluation the Russian oligarchs began moving money out of the country, forcing the government to negotiate a $22.6 billion rescue package from the international institutions.

Three weeks later the ruble collapsed and Russia declared a moratorium on private debt payments to foreign creditors. What happened was that the oligarchs and their banks continued to remove money from Russia; and the Western banks received repayment. The IMF and its supporters, including the US, were left holding the bag. But, the resulting devaluation apparently benefitted import-competing industries, and spurred Russia's economic growth.

The Russian crisis, coming as it did immediately after the East Asian financial crisis, exposed the shortcomings of IMF advice to developing nations. Those that followed IMF recommendations and opened their economies to global financial markets suffered most, while China and India, two economies that ignored the IMF and retained controls, avoided the turmoil.[62]

A decade later, the Russian economic situation was much improved. A humbled Russia gradually integrated into the global economy, and used energy exports to promote recovery and replenish currency reserves. During the Putin administration the economy enjoyed rapid growth averaging 7 percent. Nine years of growth produced budget surpluses. High oil prices, a major source of government revenue, aided the recovery. As the world's largest exporter of natural gas and the second largest exporter of oil, Russia quickly became a major player in world commodity trade. By the end of 2009 it had accumulated $439 billion in foreign exchange reserves, third only to China and Japan.[63]

Russia's principal export market is the EU (46% of total exports in 2009), and it relies on Western Europe for large quantities of imported manufactures (45% of total imports). Trade with Asia has expanded rapidly with China accounting for 14 percent of imports and Japan another 4.5 percent. Reflecting its growing dependence on international markets, Russia has assigned high priority to joining the World Trade Organization.[64]

But, fearful of Russia's geopolitical ambitions, Western Europe remains uneasy about growing dependence on Russian energy. During the winter of 2009 a financial dispute with the Ukraine led to the disruption of Russian gas shipments, leaving large areas of Eastern Europe freezing. Similarly, Russia appears unwilling to become overly dependent on foreign food supplies. In early 2010 President Dmitry Medvedev approved a Russian Food Security Doctrine intended to cut imports of major agricultural commodities to below 20 percent of consumption.[65]

Nonetheless, contemporary Russia is far more dependent on global markets than the Soviet Union was. Because of lack of credit and an underdeveloped financial market, Russian business oligarchs have borrowed heavily from international capital markets in dollars and euros. In 2007, before the financial crisis, financing from capital markets amounted to 12 percent of Russia's GDP compared to South Africa (10%), India (5%), Brazil (5%), and China (3%). When foreign credit dried up, the oligarchs discovered hard times. In 2008, Russia's 25 richest oligarchs lost more than $220 billion, and reportedly had to beg for bail-out loans from the Kremlin.[66]

Conclusion

As this chapter indicates, in the generation after 1980 most of the world's nations chose to open up and participate actively in the global economy. One of the best measures of this integration is the share of merchandise trade (exports and imports) to GDP. For rich nations, the increase was from 35.4% in 1980 to 52.2% in 2008, before the recession severely impacted trade flows. But for middle- and lower-income developing countries, the increase was even greater, from 34.2 to 55.6%. Not surprisingly, China and India set the pace. China's merchandise trade to GDP ratio nearly tripled from 20.1 to 56.7%, while India's multiplied from 12.8 to 42.5%.[67] While there were some exceptions in sub-Saharan Africa and Latin America, and among war-torn nations, the data demonstrate the impact of the globalization process. But, as later chapters in this book explain, open economies – especially countries with open financial markets – are especially vulnerable to external economic shocks. While increasing openness is associated with greater prosperity, it can produce great instability, and even contagion, when bubbles burst. This lesson is likely to shape future policy responses as nations reflect on recent experiences.

Chapter 5

Thinking about the Global Economy

The most influential economist of the mid-twentieth century was John Maynard Keynes, a brilliant and self-assured Cambridge University scholar. His thinking shaped government efforts to cope with widespread unemployment during the Great Depression and later, as head of the British delegation to the Bretton Woods Conference, Keynes helped design the International Monetary Fund and the World Bank, twin pillars of the post-World War II international economy. Keynes is also remembered for his clever remarks. He observed that "… the ideas of economists and political philosophers, both when they are right and when they are wrong, are more powerful than is commonly understood. Indeed the world is ruled by little else. Practical men, who believe themselves to be quite exempt from any intellectual influences, are usually the slaves of some defunct economist."[1] Stated differently, economic ideas do have consequences in the hands of public officials.

To understand developments over the last 30 years, it is important to introduce some of the economists and business strategists whose ideas shaped the emergence of the global economy, influencing the actions of corporate and government officials. For many of these thinkers their ideas continued to resonate long after they passed from the scene. In this chapter we meet the leading proponents of free-market economics, free trade, and deregulation. The chapter also looks at others who favored a variety of state-owned and regulated approaches to managing and developing the economic order. Finally, the chapter focuses on some of the pundits and strategists who shaped business thought on globalization and competitiveness. Many of them earned advanced academic degrees in economics.

The Contemporary Global Economy: A History Since 1980, First Edition. Alfred E. Eckes, Jr.
© 2011 Alfred E. Eckes, Jr. Published 2011 by Blackwell Publishing Ltd.

One of the important themes is how the pendulum swings from one current of thought to another and back again. Periods of state intervention and control gave way to periods of deregulation and market self-regulation, until new global financial crises in 1929–30 and 2007 prompted governments to intervene and expand their regulatory efforts. Another important theme is how the global economy that emerged during the last decades of the twentieth century had intellectual roots in the thinking of influential British economists some two centuries earlier.

Early Free Traders

Adam Smith

The foundation pilings for the contemporary international trading system can be found in the writings of two British economists – Adam Smith (1723–90) and David Ricardo (1772–1823). Smith, a Scottish professor of moral philosophy, authored *The Wealth of Nations* in 1776, one of the most famous economics books of all time. It originated as an attack on the prevailing economic philosophy of mercantilism. In eighteenth-century Britain, and on the continent, leaders sought to use the power of the state to enhance national power. To this goal, they employed government subsidies, monopolies, and regulations over trade. Governments sought to protect emerging industries, such as textiles, and to accumulate gold and bullion in treasuries. Smith challenged the tenets of mercantilism, and offered a *laissez-faire* (a French phrase meaning "let do") alternative. He said that if individuals pursued their own self interest and profit, within a framework restricted by law, custom, and religion, they would contribute more to the wealth and satisfaction of the nation. His formulation, as Margaret Thatcher noted, was based on a keen psychological insight – the propensity of humans to "truck, barter, and exchange one thing for another."[2]

In making his point, Smith introduced the metaphor of the "invisible hand" in which individuals pursued their own self-interest as producers and consumers and in the process promoted an end not part of their intention. If individuals sold dear and bought cheaply, he reasoned that the "invisible hand" of market forces would coordinate their activities and improve welfare. In a comment that has echoed over centuries Smith asserted: "It is not from the benevolence of the butcher, the brewer, or the baker that we expect our dinner but from their regard to their own interest." Yes, individuals prospered but so did the entire community.[3]

Smith also laid the intellectual foundation for the contemporary global economy. He reasoned that if individuals specialized in their work, this division of labor would stimulate economic growth and enhance the wealth of nations. In a famous example, he noted that a worker not familiar with pin-making might make one per day. But in a manufacturing operation involving a division of labor among a number of workers specializing in distinct aspects of the process, each worker would become more skillful, perhaps producing the equivalent of 4,800 pins per day. Smith's case for expanded international trade rested on the same division, and specialization, of labor. Nations, like individuals, could specialize in producing different products, improve their productivity through larger-scale operations, and exchange their surpluses for mutual advantage.[4] Under Smith's formulation nations should import goods that were produced more cheaply abroad. Trade economists often describe Smith's rationale for trade as the theory of absolute advantage.

In the late twentieth century public officials and pundits often recalled enthusiastically Adam Smith's support for free trade. In the *Wealth of Nations* and other writings, the great Scotsman did argue for liberalizing commerce and removing barriers to trade. For example, in criticizing mercantilism, he said "in every country it always is and must be the interest of the great body of the people to buy whatever they want of those who sell it cheapest." He asserted that Britain "should by all means be made a free port, that there should be no interruptions of any kind made to foreign trade. ..." Smith said that "if it were possible to defray the expenses of government by any other method, all duties, customs, and excise should be abolished, and that free commerce and liberty of exchange should be allowed with all nations and for all things."[5]

Adam Smith was not as dogmatic as some of his modern-day interpreters. As the title of his book suggests, he was primarily concerned with the "wealth of nations," not the fortunes of individuals. Thus, he recognized the national-defense exception – "... defense ... is of much more importance than opulence. ..." He also thought tariff retaliation might sometimes be needed on to open export markets. And he understood that freedom of trade "should be restored only by slow gradations and with a good deal of reserve and circumspection" in instances where it has been interrupted for some time.[6]

Smith's career shows that he was no academic out of touch with practical problems of governance. Late in life he spent 13 years as a Scottish customs collector. Essentially, in this phase of his career he was a bureaucrat collecting taxes for the mercantile state. It is especially ironic that the economist who wrote such a devastating critique of British mercantilism spent his own final years helping to administer and sustain that system. During his stint as a customs collector Smith's enthusiasm for reform appears to have taken a back seat to his administrative duties defending the mercantile state.[7]

Indeed, a close reading of the *Wealth of Nations,* published two years before he became a trade administrator, shows Smith to be both a critic and defender of the mercantile system. Along with recognizing the defense exception to the theory of free trade, he vigorously defended the navigation acts intended to support the Royal Navy and to give British shipping a monopoly of the carrying trade. These, he said, were "perhaps, the wisest of all the commercial regulations of England. ..." While appreciating the connection between the mercantile system, and Britain's capacity to win wars, Smith sought to discourage the American colonists from building their own manufacturing facilities. This would "obstruct ... the progress of their country towards real wealth and greatness." No wonder that some of Adam Smith's critics (such as Friedrich List, discussed below) considered the eminent Scotsman an apologist for the status quo and British free-trade imperialism. It is worth remembering that Adam Smith and the classical economists were first and foremost patriots and citizens of the nation-state, not libertarians intent on promoting individual rights. Smith said, for example, "The great object of the political economy of every country is to increase the riches and power of that country."[8]

In contemporary times Adam Smith is sometimes remembered as the "father of capitalism," but he did not originate capitalism, or even use the term. What he did was to offer a persuasive rationale for giving market-forces free reign. Interestingly, he gave little attention to the role of entrepreneurs, instead seeing the economy as a big machine. Nor was he especially fond of merchants and manufacturers. "People of the same trade seldom meet together, even for merriment and diversion, but the conversation ends in a conspiracy against the public, or in some contrivance to raise prices." Despite these sentiments, the international business community subsequently embraced Smith and celebrated him as the world's most prominent exponent of private enterprise. So have prime ministers and presidents. Margaret Thatcher of the United Kingdom lauded Smith; some of her supporters credited Smith with inspiring Thatcherism. Even East European leaders, like Vaclav Klaus, the president of the Czech Republic, praised Smith for providing a "clear compass" for looking at the world.

Probably Adam Smith would have been surprised at how recent genera-tions interpreted his message and made him the "godfather" of modern capitalism.[9]

As efforts to deregulate private enterprise gained momentum during the 1980s, some enthusiasts attempted to identify the famous Scotsman with the deregulation movement. During the Reagan administration some in the White House began wearing Adam Smith ties to signal their enthusiasm for getting government off the backs of business people. In fact, Smith's views were more nuanced. While he did rail against the excesses of government regulation in the era of mercantilism, he thought govern-ment had multiple responsibilities. It should maintain national defense, support a stable monetary system, undertake public works, and support public institutions for education. Like other classical economists, he believed government should establish a legal system supportive of free markets.[10]

David Ricardo

In 1817 David Ricardo, an English stockbroker who never attended college, expanded on Smith's theory to show how a country could benefit from imports. In his theory of comparative costs Ricardo explained why nations should specialize in items in which they have cost advantages, thus enhanc-ing global wealth and consumer gains. Ricardo presented his important insights with a simple static model – one with only two countries, two products, and labor being the only factor of production. Using arithmetic he easily demonstrated how if Britain specialized in the production of cloth and Portugal in wine, the two countries could engage in mutually beneficial exchange. This was true, Ricardo argued, even if one of the two countries was more efficient in the production of both products. He established that total production would be greater if each country specialized, and did not attempt to produce both products. Over the next two centuries economics evolved but Ricardo's basic theory of comparative advantage has endured.

Subsequently, economists expanded upon the insights of Smith and Ricardo. They demonstrated that the case for free trade holds when more countries and products are added to the model, and when more factors of production are included. The famous Heckscher–Ohlin model, named after Eli Heckscher and Bertil Ohlin, two Swedish economists, is based on different resource endowments (such as fertile land). It offers another explanation for comparative advantage. Free traders, from Ricardo to the present, have insisted that free trade is advantageous even if practiced unilaterally.[11]

Free-Trade Skeptics

Friedrich List

If contemporary support for free trade and open markets has its roots in the theories of the classical economists, modern-day trade critics of the global economy look back to those who criticized Smith and Ricardo for inspiration. Perhaps the most important was Friedrich List (1789–1846), a native of Wurttemberg in Germany, who criticized Smith's "cosmopolitical" thinking. While Smith and the English classical economists rebelled against the mercantile state, List, an economic nationalist, saw tariffs, subsidies, and industrial policy as essential to national economic development. List was not opposed to free-trade for developed countries, but he saw Britain's enthusiasm for knocking down trade barriers as driven by self-interest. London wanted to kick away the ladder so that late-developing countries would not achieve Britain's success at economic development and challenge its industries. The problem with Ricardo's theory of comparative advantage, as List and other critics recognized, was that it forced countries to accept their current level of technology. In effect, it doomed agricultural countries to specialize in farm products, and resource-rich countries to export raw materials. But countries that wanted to achieve higher income levels might need to protect infant industries and gain some breathing space from international competition.[12]

The American experience shaped List's emphasis on protectionism for national development. A political refugee, List lived during the 1820s in the United States, and saw first-hand efforts to promote domestic industry behind high tariff walls. He exchanged ideas with those who considered protection the key to national economic development. Like Alexander Hamilton, List is associated with the "infant-industry" argument for protecting start-up industries with subsidies and tariff until they can survive in open competition. But List also saw protectionism as intermediate step on the path to free trade, and favored free trade among the German states before the idea became popular.

In the twentieth century List's thinking resonated with nationalist elites in many countries. In India, for example, economic nationalists had long urged industrialization and infant-industry protection. List's thinking, and

America's experiences, would influence Japan's late-comer efforts to industrialize in the early twentieth century and recover from the devastation of World War II.[13]

Gunnar Myrdal and Raul Prebisch

After World War II some heterodox economists rediscovered aspects of List's development strategy. In *Rich Lands and Poor* (1957) Swedish economist and sociologist Gunnar Myrdal (1898–1987), who shared the 1974 Nobel Prize with Austrian Friedrich Hayek, criticized orthodox trade theory for failing to explain growing inequalities between developed and underdeveloped countries.[14]

Another free-trade skeptic was Raul Prebisch (1901–86), the Argentine accountant and self-trained economist who became head of the United Nations Commission for Latin America and the first director-general of the United Nations Conference on Trade and Development (UNCTAD). He shared Myrdal's view of a world in which the rich countries got richer and the poor, poorer. Prebisch was one of the first economists to offer a structuralist critique of the world trading system. His answer was to encourage import substitution, and he urged developing countries to use active government policies to facilitate development, among them the use of tariffs and exchange controls. In advocating state intervention, Prebisch was rejecting the advice of free-trade orthodoxy associated with the United Kingdom, the US, and the Bretton Woods institutions.[15]

List's perspective would also guide economic development in many other newly independent nations. His thinking influenced the nation-building process in a variety of late-developing countries, including Brazil, India, Indonesia, Ireland, Ghana, Japan, South Korea, Turkey, and others. Political scientists and developmental economists have commented on how support for import-substitution industrialization, whatever its origin, spread around the world. Journalist James Fallows has noted that copies of List's books were available in Asian book stores. List's ideas may have influenced the export-oriented, import-restricting industrial policies of mainland China under Deng Xiaoping's developmental dictatorship.[16]

Karl Marx and the communist revolution

A second prominent critic of Adam Smith's capitalist world was a contemporary of Friedrich List's. He was Karl Marx (1818–83), co-author of the *Communist Manifesto* (1848) with Friedrich Engels. In it and *Das Kapital*

(1867) he offered a different view of the global economy – one divided not by nationality but by class. While Smith had argued that the division of labor, and specialization, facilitated economic and social progress, Marx claimed that the owners of the means of production – the capitalists – exploited the workers (the proletariat). Increasing alienation would lead to a revolution of the proletariat, and the state would seize the factories preparatory to the communist revolution. Workers of the world would throw off their chains and unite against their exploiters, the capitalists, he believed. In his view, the adoption of free-trade policies would accelerate the international revolution. "It breaks up old nationalities and pushes the antagonism of the proletariat and the bourgeoisie to the extreme point. In a word, the free trade system hastens the social revolution. It is in this revolutionary sense alone, gentlemen, that I vote in favor of free trade." In the *Communist Manifesto* Marx and his collaborator Friedrich Engels foresaw the globalization of capitalism. They asserted that "the need of a constantly expanding market for its products chases the bourgeoisie over the entire surface of the globe." They noted also how the bourgeoisie, using vastly improved means of communications (probably the steam engine and the telegraph), drew even "the most barbarian nations into civilization." In short, the bourgeoisie "creates a world after its own image."[17]

Marx and Engels are relevant to contemporary circumstances for several reasons. For one, as their modern supporters stress, they predicted that capitalist-style globalization would make the world more unstable and vulnerable to political revolutions. In their words, the bourgeoisie paved "the way for more extensive and more destructive crises." Another reason is that they inspired the Soviet alternative to market-based capitalism. Vladimir Lenin (1870–1924), a lawyer who brought a socialist revolution to Russia at the end of World War I, rejected the market economy. But, in his New Economic Policy of 1922, Lenin relented somewhat, permitting some market activity in agriculture. However he promised the state would control the "commanding heights" – the railroads, power plants, steel mills, other major industries, and coal mines – on which the economy depended. Like British writer J. A. Hobson, Lenin was especially critical of finance or monopoly capitalism. He deemed it the final stage of capitalism with wealth concentrated in the hands of financial and corporate oligarchs.[18]

Third-world nationalists

Marxian thought, and the Soviet example, reverberated around the world after World War II as European colonial powers lost their empires. Many developing-world nationalists saw Marxism and its reliance on the state to promote economic development as the approach to emulate in the early stages of nation building. Some were infatuated with the Soviet Union. There reliance on central planning appeared to produce high economic growth. The emergence of a non-capitalist superpower capable of launching space satellites and intercontinental ballistic missiles offered an appealing alternative model.[19]

India was one of many developing countries where Marxist thinking influenced public policies. Jawaharlal Nehru, the son of a prosperous barrister and a Brahmin aristocrat, encountered socialist thought while studying in Great Britain and adapted socialist rhetoric to the cause of Indian nationalism. Despite his left-wing support in the Congress Party, Nehru was viewed as a modernizer, one who would bring planning to India's circumstances, and strengthen Indian businesses. In power as India's first post-independence prime minister (1947–64), Nehru pursued national economic development with technocratic planning. Protectionism (with high tariffs and restrictions on foreign investments) and industrial development with five-year plans and extensive state intervention characterized his reign. Unlike developing countries that continued to rely on exports of raw materials or agricultural products, India turned inward. It produced its own steel, railroad cars, automobiles, and machinery, and achieved high economic growth by focusing on the domestic economy. Perceiving that India, like the United States in the nineteenth century, was a vast continental market, its leaders ignored export promotion, and focused on autarky. In part, this was a rejection of India's colonial past, when Britain's East India Company had managed India's trade to the advantage of the home country.[20]

Other developing-world nationalists, including Gamal Abdel Nasser in Egypt (1918–70), Sukarno (1901–70) in Indonesia, Ho Chi Minh in Vietnam (1890–1969), Fidel Castro in Cuba (1926–), and Kwame Nkrumah (1909–72) in Ghana all emphasized socialist-style national development. Upon taking power they generally nationalized industry, finance, and commerce, and pursued land reform. They expanded state bureaucracies and experimented with planning in order to spur development.[21]

In East Asia, except for China, Marx's influence was less important than nationalism and other factors – including Japan's recovery from World War II. Scholars have observed that Japan devised the developmental state relying on government guidance, bureaucratic intervention, technology transfer, and a variety of protectionist trade policies to facilitate rapid economic growth with private ownership. Later Singapore, South Korea, and

Taiwan, among others, used variants of the Japanese approach to modernize.[22]

Great Depression and Managed Economies

The Great Depression also had an enormous impact on post-World War II approaches to managing economies. It raised doubts about the long-run viability of capitalism and shattered the faith of economists, and policy-makers, for a time in the self-regulating marketplace. Before the depression, economists in Britain and the United States relied on neo-classical economic models consistent with the teachings of Adam Smith and David Ricardo. These had been modified and updated by a series of eminent economists, notably Alfred Marshall (1842–1924), the high-priest of Victorian economic thought. His text, *Principles of Economics*, which went through eight editions from 1890 to 1920, was widely used by young economists. Marshall, who was trained as a mathematician, effectively translated the theories of Ricardo into geometry and algebra. He is remembered for developing demand and supply analysis. John Maynard Keynes, one of Marshall's students, said that the training of a good economist required only knowledge of Marshall's text and reading of the daily newspaper. Generally, Marshall and the neo-classicals discouraged meddling with the marketplace, taking the view that the invisible hand of market forces would bring necessary adjustments.[23]

James Landis and the regulatory state

The Great Depression shattered public faith in the free-market, trickle-down economics, and limited government policies. Indeed, they were widely blamed for the excesses of Wall Street during the Great Depression. Public sentiment became supportive of efforts to regulate and reform the free-enterprise model, including legislation to separate commercial banking from more risky investment banking. The resulting regulatory state had its intellectual origins in the writings of a brilliant lawyer, James Landis, and a similarly talented economist, John Maynard Keynes. Landis, a professor at Harvard Law School, came to Washington to design and help administer the Securities and Exchange Commission, and to clean up the mess on Wall Street. In his book, *The Administrative Process*, Landis made the argument for expert commissions to oversee specialized areas of the economy. In particular, Landis favored the use of informal advisory opinions before formal regulatory action. He supported the growth of the administrative process against court review that involved judges in technical issues for which they had little preparation. This approach shaped the growth of government intervention and regulation of stock markets, finance, transportation, utilities, and other sectors of the economy.[24]

John Maynard Keynes (1883–1946)

During the Great Depression, Cambridge University economist John Maynard Keynes inspired new thinking about how government intervention could promote recovery. Emphasizing fiscal policy (taxing and spending), Keynes offered a theoretical explanation for how government policy impacted the economy. Adam Smith and the classical economists thought the most important duty of government was to enforce laws so that invisible hand – individuals pursuing self-interest – would promote wealth and happiness. While Smith and Ricardo engaged in debate and even held government positions (Smith a customs collector, and Ricardo a member of parliament), many of their successors took the view by the mid-nineteenth century that economists should not meddle with market forces.[25]

The Great Depression encouraged academic economists, like Keynes, to take a more active role in making and administering economic policy. In Britain and the United States, a number of economists became heavily involved. Some, such as the neo-classicists, insisted that no action should be taken because market forces would heal the system. Others, such as the Marxists, insisted that capitalism was inherently flawed and required radical structural reforms. But John Maynard Keynes' theoretical contributions convinced many economists that specialists in macroeconomics could control aggregate demand, and thus boost employment in periods of recession and restrain inflation in wartime. In the *General Theory of Employment, Interest, and Money* (1936), Keynes argued that the private economy might not achieve full employment, because the return on capital was too low to stimulate business investment. This was the so-called liquidity trap. In short, the private economy seemed to have a deflationary bias. During a recession when government tax revenues fell, many orthodox economists wanted to cut spending or to increase taxes. Keynes showed that either of these options squeezed the economy and made the situation worse. He believed that government spending (deficit spending) could close the gap and stimulate aggregate demand. He recommended deficit spending in times of unemployment, and accumulating budget surpluses in times of surplus. Despite some initial resistance, the proof was in the pudding.

Keynesian deficit spending promoted recovery during World War II and helped avoid a postwar slump. By 1971, even conservative Republican president Richard Nixon announced he was a Keynesian.[26]

As it turned out, the Keynesian model had some flaws – visible by the mid-1970s. It was easier for politicians to increase spending and borrowing, or to cut taxes, than it was to do the reverse. The Keynesian program had an inflationary bias. Also, Keynesian-style deficits did not succeed in maintaining full employment.

With their activism and commitment to public service, Landis and Keynes inspired a generation of young lawyers and economists. Many of them entered the government sector to advise officials and administer programs. During the 1930s and World War II economists became involved in everything from setting agricultural prices to choosing bombing targets. Young lawyers drafted sweeping federal rules and regulations for the private sector. Not only did government employment soar, but government's share of the gross domestic product rose substantially. In the US the central government's share of GNP more than tripled from 1928 to 1934 (rising from 3 to 10.1%).[27] Businessmen, unaccustomed to regulatory oversight, soon found themselves filling out forms and implementing government regulations. Congressional committees and government administrators held them accountable. Not surprisingly, affluent business-people soon founded think-tanks critical of big government and supportive of deregulation. These included the Adam Smith Institute (founded 1977), and Institute of Economic Affairs (1955), both in London, and the American Enterprise Institute (1954), Heritage Foundation (1973), and Cato Institute (1977), all three in Washington, DC.

The Free-Market Counter-Revolution

In the 1970s the Keynesian pro-regulatory consensus endured on domestic issues, while governments in Western Europe and North America (the OECD countries) continued to push forward on trade liberalization in manufactured goods. But, increasingly, efforts to open commerce touched on issues of domestic regulation, involving services, standards, procurement, intellectual property, and soon environmental and health/safety issues. In this climate, it is not surprising that critics mounted a serious challenge to the Keynesian consensus. Among the leading protagonists were Austrian economist and philosopher Friedrich Hayek (1899–1992) and monetarist/libertarian Milton Friedman (1912–2006).

Friedrich Hayek

Hayek, who shared the 1974 Nobel Prize in Economics with Gunnar Myrdal, believed that a good economist must be more than an economist. Rather than dealing exclusively with technical issues, he thought about issues of social and political philosophy. Hayek held that law was essential to operations of the market, because it created a stable structure of expectation for economic activity. Like other Austrian economists of his generation, Hayek was concerned about the spread of state socialism. In his widely read 1944 book *The Road to Serfdom* he attacked centrally planned economies. In his view the shortcomings of central planning led inexorably to tyranny and totalitarian government. The process would lead to the dismantling of the free-market system and destroy personal freedoms. Hayek branded the idea that individuals can shape the world about them according to their wishes a "fatal conceit" in socialism. This philosophy resonated with Prime Minister Margaret Thatcher (1925–), who made Hayek's critique of socialism a centerpiece of her national election in 1979. She was one of the public figures most influenced by the ideas of economists.[28]

Milton Friedman

In the United States the political current was moving in the same direction after World War II. Hayek took up residence at the University of Chicago in 1950, where its economics department had long-disputed Keynesian-style deficit spending. Milton Friedman, a brilliant University of Chicago economist, would lead the counter-attack on Keynesian thought and acquire the reputation as the most influential economist in the last quarter of the twentieth century. Because Friedman's free-market ideas attracted interest in China and flowered in Britain and America under Margaret Thatcher and Ronald Reagan, some have referred to the last quarter century as "the Age of Milton Friedman."[29]

A masterful debater, Friedman began as a Keynesian but launched a counterrevolution with an alternative method of managing the macro economy. For Friedman the remedy was to control the money supply. "Money matters," said Friedman and his followers as they focused on the quantity of money in circulation. His personal license tag even emphasized the quantity theory of money: $MV = PY$.* These monetarists thought the independent Federal Reserve could achieve optimal economic performance

---

* Money Supply Times Velocity of Money Equals Price Level Times Output.

by tweaking the money supply. Keynesians, however, put their emphasis on managing government fiscal policy – essentially spending and taxes.

In his academic writings and commentary for *Newsweek* Friedman discussed a variety of policy issues and proposed flexible exchange rates, the draft, and privatization of the postal service. In his 1962 bestseller *Capitalism and Freedom* he argued for deregulating industry, including transportation and banking, and privatizing welfare programs. Friedman was also critical of Keynes' use of the government as a balance wheel in the macro economy. He claimed that not only had Keynesianism failed to offset recessions but also it fostered an expansion in the government sector and prevented a reduction in tax burdens. Ironically, during World War II, a much younger Milton Friedman had worked in the US Treasury and devised the program of payroll tax withholding.

Friedman and his colleagues at the University of Chicago were the intellectual fathers of the contemporary deregulation movement. While Keynesians thought the economy could be actively managed, the Chicago economists dissented. They held that scientific regulation was a myth and that government should let market mechanisms and prices allocate resources. They believed that markets were more rational than government actions. Their theories appealed to the business community and some public officials during the 1970s as economic stagnation and inflation exposed the shortcomings of Keynesian analysis. Friedman and his colleagues offered an alternative approach – one in which the hands of government regulators became less active.

Friedman advised Republican candidate Barry Goldwater in 1964, and then wrote a *Newsweek* column for a popular audience from 1966 to 1984. In 1975 he flew to Chile and encouraged dictator Augusto Pinochet to adopt a "shock program," including control of the money supply to cool inflation, cuts in government spending, and free trade. Friedman's students, the so-called "Chicago Boys," succeeded in taming inflation and reviving growth. They also played a major role in bringing free-market economics to Eastern Europe after the collapse of the Soviet Union. Friedman himself traveled widely, advising even leaders of the People's Republic of China on monetary matters.

Ronald Reagan (1911–2004), who had majored in economics at Eureka College in Illinois before the Keynesian Revolution, became president of the US in 1981. He had an instinctive enthusiasm for tax-cuts and deregulation. Among Reagan's economic advisers were Milton Friedman and Alan Greenspan (1926–). Reagan would confer the Presidential Medal of Freedom on Friedman in 1988 for restoring "common sense to the world of economics. ..." He named Greenspan chairman of the Federal Reserve Board in 1987. In his advice to Reagan, Friedman emphasized the central role of money in controlling the economy. It was less important, he thought, to balance the budget than to get spending priorities right.[30]

Alan Greenspan

Greenspan, a private consulting economist, was a disciple of Soviet-émigré philosopher Ayn Rand, a radical exponent of *laissez-faire* as the ideal form of social organization. He described himself as a "libertarian Republican." In government during the Nixon, Ford, Reagan, Bush, Clinton, and Bush presidencies he pushed the philosophy of free-market capitalism. He believed in efficient self-correcting markets, and abhorred government oversight that might curtail risk taking, or "inhibit the pollinating of bees on Wall Street." As chairman of the Federal Reserve Greenspan would back the so-called Washington consensus, pushing the free-trade, deregulatory agenda, and encouraging foreign governments to open their capital markets to Western banks. As a zealous critic of government regulations, Greenspan had long considered the Glass-Steagall Act of 1933, which separated commercial banking from investment banking, a mistake. And, he enthusiastically supported changes to make institutions more adaptable to the circumstances of globalization.[31]

After the stock-market collapse of 2008, Greenspan acknowledged to a congressional committee that he had some responsibility for the collapse. "Those of us who have looked to the self-interest of lending institutions to protect shareholder's equity – myself especially – are in a state of shocked disbelief. ..." In response to a question asking if Greenspan found his view of the world, his ideology, was not working, the former central banker said: "Absolutely, precisely. You know, that's precisely the reason I was shocked, because I have been going for 40 years or more with very considerable evidence that it was working exceptionally well." In effect, he was acknowledging that the classical faith in efficiently operating markets had flaws. "I made a mistake in presuming that the self-interests of organizations, specifically banks and others, were such that they were best capable of protecting their own shareholders and their equity in the firms."[32]

Rational-market theorists

Greenspan's faith in rational and efficient markets appeared to have academic blessing. While Milton Friedman had taken the position that market-based decision-making was superior to government decisions, some of his Chicago colleagues carried faith in the rationality of markets to a higher level during the 1970s. In 1978, Michael Jensen, a Chicago economics Ph.D., asserted that there was no other proposition in economics which has more solid empirical evidence supporting it than the efficient-markets hypothesis. The theory held that markets rationally priced assets. Markets collected and distributed information, more efficiently than government regulation could do. Confident of theoretical underpinnings, financial economists devised mathematical investment models that sought to value risk by diversification. Their work spawned the growth of derivatives (complex credit swaps) and other new financial instruments, such as securitized sub-prime mortgages. In the process, thousands of young financial economists found high-paying employment on Wall Street.[33]

Irving Fisher

But as later events showed, the confident financial economists had miscalculated. And a $683 trillion market in derivatives would soon collapse. Their colossal mistake was not unprecedented. In 1929 another mathematical economist Irving Fisher of Yale University asserted two weeks before the stock market collapse that stock prices had reached a "permanently high plateau." Fisher's work offered a foundation for later efforts to diversify and reduce risk, including securitization. "The more unsafe the investments are, taken individually, the safer they are collectively … ," he said in 1929. Fisher lost a fortune and his home in the Great Depression, as well as much of his reputation.[34]

Conflicting Currents

In 2008 Wall Street, as well as elected officials, was again shown to be vulnerable to the siren call of defunct economic theories. At the time Wall Street was going overboard on derivatives, some economists were challenging the theoretical foundation for efficient markets. One was Joseph Stiglitz, an MIT-trained economist, and modern-day Keynesian, who would later become chief economist for the World Bank and would share the Nobel Prize for economics in 2001, for his analysis of markets with asymmetric information. In essence Stiglitz and several colleagues had warned that information imperfections and institutional frictions, such as the banking system, limited the ability to arbitrage risk and contributed to investment bubbles. Another critic was Robert Shiller, another MIT-trained economist, who demonstrated that markets were volatile, and who stated in 1984 that the rational markets theory was "one of the most remarkable errors in the history of economic thought." Stiglitz pointedly blamed Chicago economists for providing an apparent intellectual foundation for the belief that markets self adjusted and that government should do nothing.[35]

Phil Gramm, architect of banking deregulation

Another economist who abandoned the classroom to shape public policy and promote deregulation was Phil Gramm (1942–), a Republican senator from Texas. He taught at Texas A&M University before entering politics. Gramm held a Ph.D. in economics from the University of Georgia, where he had written a short 79-page dissertation containing little mathematics. Gramm was an enthusiastic and doctrinaire exponent of *laissez-faire* economics in the tradition of British economist Alfred Marshall. He attributed the inflation of the 1970s to excessive government spending to finance the Vietnam War. Blaming the bankruptcy of government, Gramm argued that market forces should drive the economy with minimal government regulation.

As chairman of the Senate Banking Committee in 1999, Gramm spearheaded efforts to repeal Glass-Steagall and deregulate banking, saying "We have learned government is not the answer." He blocked measures to curtail predatory or deceptive lending, and pushed through legislation that effectively blocked regulation of derivatives and other complex financial instruments. Gramm referred to Wall Street as a "holy place," and sought to strengthen its competitive position internationally by reducing regulatory oversight.[36]

Jeffrey Sachs and "shock therapy"

The collapse of the Soviet Union, and its empire in Central Europe, offered many opportunities for free-market experimentation. US economists, supported by substantial sums in Western aid money, attempted to privatize state industries and deregulate command economies. The principal architect of "shock therapy," the draconian deregulation and privatization measures used to integrate Eastern and Central Europe into the global marketplace, was the flamboyant economist Jeffrey Sachs of Harvard University. Sachs, a mid-30s wunderkind, has been described in the press as the Indiana Jones of economics, a reference to a fictional movie adventurer who skipped his teaching job and trotted around the globe. Sachs and his graduate students offered standard neo-classical advice to governments – slash government subsidies, sell-off state industries, control inflation, and lift price controls to allow the market pricing system to operate. This no-nonsense approach soon made Sachs and his Harvard colleagues much reviled in Poland and Russia. And their privatization efforts facilitated the transfer of property to a new class of Russian oligarchs.[37]

Sachs' reputation for administering successful "shock therapy" stemmed from his activities in Bolivia during the mid-1980s. Called to a country with 24,000 percent annual inflation, Sachs designed an austerity program that reduced inflation to 15 percent within months. But the iconoclastic Sachs was too radical for the banking establishment. He encouraged third-world countries to default on debt payments to avoid hyperinflation.[38]

Washington consensus

The Latin-American debt crisis of the 1980s, which followed the second surge in oil prices in 1979, had produced a consensus about the best policies to promote economic growth and stimulate development in developing economies. John Williamson, an economist with the Peterson Institute for International Economics, a Washington think-tank, introduced the term "Washington consensus" to summarize the conventional wisdom about policies thought to be wise. His listing included fiscal discipline, financial liberalization, trade openness, inward foreign direct investment, privatization, and deregulation. While there were differences over exchange rate policies and capital-account liberalization, the formula was market-oriented. In the US Treasury, on Wall Street, and at the Bretton Woods institutions (the International Monetary Fund and the World Bank), there was broad support for this approach.[39]

In both London and Washington the Washington consensus was associated with market economics and good governance as the best way to stimulate economic growth. It represented a coupling of mainstream and development economics. Import substitution and state intervention, once popular among developing countries, had fallen out of favor. Anne O. Krueger, an international economist and former first deputy managing director of the IMF, argued that the rapid growth of the so-called Asian tigers by opening up their economies to trade between 1960 and 1990 contributed to the change in thought. So did, she said, the third-world debt crisis of the early 1980s. Krueger, sometimes seen as the high priestess of market fundamentalism, advanced the case for the Washington consensus forcefully first within the World Bank during the 1980s, and then in the IMF, beginning in 2001.[40]

Critics construed the Washington consensus, pushed by the IMF and the US Treasury, as a neo-liberal manifesto. It defined the economic policies of Margaret Thatcher and Ronald Reagan, and was inspired by Milton Friedman and Friedrich Hayek. At its core were privatization, liberalization and integration of trade and capital markets through free trade, and stringent efforts to control inflation with sound money and balanced budgets.[41]

As the economic crisis of 2007–10 unfolded critics of the Washington consensus would later comment on its alleged failures. Countries that pursued neo-liberal policies, Stiglitz claimed, lost the growth sweepstakes and witnessed a disproportionate shift of benefits to individuals at the top of the economic ladder. James K. Galbraith noted that Argentina, once a poster boy for the conservative model, found recovery only after repudiating foreign debts. Stiglitz also argued that market fundamentalism, such as reflected in the so-called Washington consensus, produced a colossal misallocation of resources to housing and the financial sector.[42] The most horrifying examples of how market fundamentalism worked, Stiglitz claimed, could be found in post-Communist Russia. Life expectancy was lower. Private monopolies replaced state monopolies. The result was a system of crony and Mafia capitalism.[43]

In developing countries – including Brazil, India, and China – the Washington consensus was considered the high-water mark of American market fundamentalism. By 2009, after Wall Street's crash had spread globally, that model had been discredited. Nowhere was the resentment greater than in Asia where, following the financial crisis in 1997, Washington and the IMF lectured and imposed stringent adjustment terms. Twelve years later, as markets in North America and Western Europe crashed, Asians began talking openly about a new Himalayan or Beijing consensus. The former reportedly rejected economic theories and models based on ideology, and relied more on Asian values and experiences. The Beijing consensus appeared to rest on three pillars – market-oriented reforms with a big role for state enterprise, authoritarian rule, and independence and self-reliance to avoid the influence of powerful external institutions and forces. Unlike the Washington consensus it emphasized political stability and non-interference.[44]

In mid-2009, the leading emerging countries – Brazil, Russia, India, and China (the so-called BRIC countries), met to share their perspectives on a multipolar world, to complain about Washington's domination, and to explore ideas for terminating the dollar's special status. They noted that while the US is the world's largest debtor, it had avoided the painful structural adjustments it prescribed for others. They saw a bankrupt financial system supporting an interventionist government with aircraft carriers and military bases encircling the world. The four desired to replace the dollar as the world's principal reserve currency, so that the US could not live off the savings of others and print money for unlimited military interventions.

The pendulum of economic thought and policy thus continued to swing. The financial mess of 2007–10 had revived the Keynesian-regulatory approach, and discredited free-market fundamentalism, much as the collapse of 1929 and the Great Depression had done for earlier generations. Stiglitz and other Keynesians, whose advice had been rejected during the heady days of market fundamentalism and global Friedmanism, gloated. Economist James Galbraith, son of Keynesian John Kenneth Galbraith, dismissed the "straight jacket dictated by the 'magic of the markets.'"[45]

Father of the euro

Several other prominent academic economists made major contributions to the evolution of the global economy. One was Robert Mundell, a Canadian-born monetary economist who teaches at Columbia University. A supply-side economist, who worked at the University of Chicago in the 1960s and later at the International Monetary Fund, Mundell analyzed monetary and fiscal policy under different exchange-rate regimes. He also worked on optimum currency areas. This body of research won him a Nobel Prize in Economics in 1999, and influenced the introduction of the euro. As the Nobel committee stated, he demonstrated that under a system of fixed exchange rates monetary policy had limited impact. But, under a floating exchange-rate system, monetary policy became powerful and fiscal policy powerless, an insight that shaped Europe's approach to the euro. The world's press would label Mundell the intellectual father of the euro.

Paul Krugman and new trade theories

Princeton University economist Paul Krugman, who is also a *New York Times* columnist, won the 2008 Nobel Prize for his new trade theories linking international trade and economic geography. David Ricardo thought that countries differed – particularly in their endowments of land, labor, and capital – and this explained why Portugal exported wine and Britain textiles in his simple two-country model explaining comparative advantage. Krugman offered a different explanation for why the bulk of world trade involved similar countries exporting similar products. His theory focused on the benefits of specialization and large-scale production, and reduced transportation costs. These lowered prices and created greater diversity for consumers.

After winning his Nobel Prize for elaborating traditional free-trade theories, Krugman began to offer more heretical thoughts. In his opinion columns for the *New York Times* Krugman argued that misaligned exchange rates undercut the benefits of free trade. He urged the US to pressure China to realign its currency rate and end its currency manipulation. He also asserted that trade between countries at different levels of economic development created a large class of losers in countries with higher wage rates. With the US importing a substantial portion of its manufactured goods from third world-economies, he complained that the ranks of highly educated workers who clearly benefit from this trade were "greatly outnumbered by those who probably lose."[46]

Business strategists

Numerous futurists and pundits sought to educate business, and the general public, on the profound changes reshaping the world economy late in the twentieth century. Generally they emphasized buzz phrases, such as globalization, the transition to a post-industrial society based on services and knowledge, and the transfer of manufacturing to low labor-cost countries. Sometimes they appeared to be synthesizing familiar trends.

In 1980 futurist Alvin Toffler stirred discussion with his book *The Third Wave*. A former *Fortune* magazine business writer and editor who focused on the impact of technological change, Toffler has been described as the "world's most famous futurologist." According to Toffler, social and economic change came in waves. In the first wave agriculture replaced hunters and gatherers. Then, beginning in the late seventeenth century, the industrial revolution based on the nuclear family, the corporation with its approaches to mass production and distribution dominated. After World War II, Toffler argued that most countries began to move away from a second-wave society built on industry to a "third wave" constructed on post-industrial lines. A decade later he would argue that a power shift in which wealth became dependent on instant communication and the dissemination of data, ideas, symbols, and symbolism was transforming the old smokestack society. Some interpreted *Future Shock* to predict that "we would all be living a life of leisure by the year 2000."[47]

Another influential professional prophet was John Naisbitt, once President Lyndon Johnson's pollster. In his 1984 bestselling book *Megatrends*, Naisbitt explained that America was restructuring from an industrial society to an information society, as it moved from a national to a global economy. Naisbitt claimed that all of the developed countries were de-industrializing with Japan, for example, moving out of cars and steel, because nearby Korea was underselling Japan. Naisbitt predicted that smokestack industry would soon be relegated to third-world nations, as the Information Age transformed US manufacturing. He confidently asserted that America's economic strength depended more on information services than on goods.[48]

One prominent businessman who engaged in public debate and trumpeted the arrival of the information society was Walter Wriston, the CEO of Citicorp. Improvements in communications, he said, had enabled data to flow across borders unimpeded. "The ability to move capital to where it is needed and wanted is fundamental to the continual effort of mankind to live a better world." Later Wriston would describe the "marriage of computers and telecommunications" as ushering in a revolutionary change. The Information Age, he said, was as different from the Industrial Age as that period was from the Agricultural Age. "For the first time in history, rich and poor, north and south, east and west, city and countryside are linked in a global electronic network of shared images in real time. Ideas move across borders as if they did not exist."[49]

Peter Drucker

The pundit with the greatest credibility in the business community was an Austrian émigré, Peter Drucker (1909–2005), who devoted his career to studying and writing about management trends. Educated in law, Drucker left Nazi Germany and migrated to Britain and later America. Noting that economists were interested in commodities while he was focused on people, Drucker became a management consultant and author, writing 35 books with millions of sales.

An incrementalist, not a Utopian, Drucker had by the early 1980s identified three fundamental changes transforming the global economy, particularly world demographics. With slow population growth in high-income countries, he foresaw shortages of semi-skilled labor. Similarly, with high-surging population growth in developing countries, he anticipated a growing need for jobs outside the agricultural sector. He also asserted that the market for primary products had become "uncoupled" from the industrial economy, as material intensity declined. For developing countries the great opportunity was to employ cheap labor in "production-sharing" activities with multinational corporations. Drucker coined the term "production sharing" in 1977, and said that it was the "newest world economic trend." In production-sharing industrialized countries manufactured components of goods and shipped them to developing countries. The finished goods then came back to industrialized countries for marketing. He recommended that developing countries emulate the examples of Singapore, Hong Kong, and Taiwan in using their labor advantage to become subcontractors for developed-country manufacturers. Drucker was not the first scholar to identify this phenomenon, but his ideas reached the largest audience through the media and his bestselling books.[50]

Drucker foresaw a second decoupling, this one of production from employment in industrial economies. With automation, manufacturing employment was declining steadily (down 5 million in the US between 1973 and 1985), while output rose. He predicted the transition of workers from labor-intensive industries to knowledge-intensive industries.

Last, Drucker trumpeted the emergence of the "symbol economy" – involving capital flows, credit flows, and exchange rates – as the "flywheel" of the future world economy. By the mid-1980s he noted that the London Eurodollar market turned over $75 trillion a year, 25 times world trade. He attributed the rise of the symbol economy to the change from fixed to floating exchange rates, and the deregulation of capital flows, and also to two oil shocks which forced oil producers and banks to recycle earnings.

Drucker also observed that the US had used the international economy to avoid tackling disagreeable domestic problems, such as balancing government tax revenues and expenditures. Japan – he did not foresee China – had encouraged this as it used exports to maintain employment in a sluggish domestic economy, but recycled trade surpluses to purchases of American government bonds. The two countries – America and Japan – lived in an Alice-in-Wonderland environment where the Japanese preferred to absorb heavy losses on their dollar holdings to confronting domestic unemployment.[51]

In promoting "production sharing" arrangements, Drucker's advice resonated with the needs and aspirations of big business. It appealed to Ruben F. Mettler, the CEO of TRW, a manufacturing firm once involved in producing aerospace and automotive equipment, as well as credit reporting. He called Drucker's term a "magic phrase" and envisaged hundreds of complex production-sharing relationships uniting nations throughout the world. He said: "... it's easy to imagine a 21st-century world economy whose guiding principle would be: 'Make Trade, Not War!'" [52]

Business leaders praised Mexico's *maquiladora* (twin-plant) program, the North American Free Trade Agreement (NAFTA), and the Caribbean Basin Initiative (CBI) as government-initiated programs that encouraged production-sharing. Firms shifting assembly abroad found they could save thousands of dollars per worker. Commenting on his firm's plants in Haiti and the Dominican Republic, Alfred J. Roach, chairman of TII Industries, a maker of overvoltage protection devices for the telecommunications industry, described the Caribbean as a golden opportunity. Twin plants in the Caribbean allowed his firm to lower production costs. He found supportive local governments and motivated labor. "The visionary cry of the pioneer 49ers that 'thar's gold in them thar hills' befits the situation," he said. [53]

Kenichi Ohmae

Also influencing business strategies in the rapidly-changing world of the 1980s and 1990s was a prominent Asian management consultant, Kenichi Ohmae (1943–), a Japanese executive with McKinsey & Company. One of his great contributions was interpreting Japanese business thinking to the Western business community. Ohmae exhorted his Japanese countrymen to become more outward looking in their approaches. An unapologetic globalist, Ohmae celebrated global business in a series of books. He advocated a form of cosmopolitanism in which managers transcend the limitations of national and local origins. [54] In his mind the corporation had become a transnational source of identity, replacing the local community or the nation-state.

Ohmae also heralded the decline of the nation-state and the rise of region-states in a borderless world. He said that while boundaries between countries existed on maps, they had largely disappeared on a competitive map. "What has eaten them away is the persistent, ever speedier flow of information." But, while emphasizing a global outlook, Ohmae was one of the first to emphasize that most international business was conducted in the triad, high-income countries including Japan, Western Europe, and the United States. [55]

Michael Porter

Another academic leader of management thinking during the period – and especially after Drucker's death – was Michael Porter (1947–) of the Harvard Business School. Porter entered the management area after completing a Ph.D. in business economics, and attempted to apply economic thinking to the study of business. The *Times* of London labeled him "the most influential management guru."[56]

Author of a series of texts on corporate strategy, Porter wrote the widely-discussed *Competitive Advantage of Nations* (1990). Using economic principles to address management issues, Porter attempted to answer the question – how do firms compete? He attributed much of the success of individual firms to national business environments, and concluded that location was important – particularly at regional and local levels. Whereas traditional international trade theory focused on the factor endowments of land, labor, and capital, Porter concluded that other factors shaped the patterns of trade among nations – especially technology and the efficient utilization of inputs. These governments and nations could influence.

While Ohmae and some other strategists claimed corporations were becoming stateless and their managers cosmopolitan citizens detached from their nationalities of origin, Porter, who later served on the President Reagan's Commission on Industrial Competitiveness, took a different view. Based on research in ten countries, he concluded that the nation remained important in shaping the competitiveness of firms. He assigned special significance to educational systems, the dynamism of government regulatory and trade policies, macroeconomic policies, and cultural factors in explaining why industries excel in some areas but not in others. These impacted innovation and helped develop clusters of competitive companies in various industries.[57]

Industrial policy advocates

Porter saw the free market as a key to national competitiveness, and relegated government to a supportive role in providing infrastructure, education, a legal system to settle property disputes, and the like. Others – especially liberal Democrats – took another approach, and urged national industrial policies. Among the most influential proponents of government intervention to pick winners-and-losers were two Rhodes scholars, Ira Magaziner and Robert Reich, both friends of Bill Clinton, another Rhodes scholar. The two co-authored a book, *Minding America's Business*, in which they advanced a proposal for US industrial policy intended to stimulate industries in which the US had a cost advantage. They argued for public policies to ease the movement of capital and labor out of declining industries and into industries that can be highly competitive in the world economy.[58]

In a 1983 book *The Next American Frontier*, Reich, who served his friend President Bill Clinton as Secretary of Labor, concluded the American economy was slowly unraveling. Claiming that American industries remained tied to the mass production of standardized products when these goods could be produced more cheaply elsewhere, while industrial competitors in Japan and Europe unified and coordinated policymaking across industries, he called for imitating MITI's success.

Another articulate proponent of industrial policy was economist Lester Thurow, dean of the Sloan School of Management at Massachusetts Institute of Technology. In *The Zero-Sum Solution* Thurow worried about Americans becoming "low-wage haulers of water and hewers of wood," and recommended government involvement in investment banking and a domestic industrial R&D foundation. His book, implicitly a response to Reagan-administration policies of deregulation and limited state intervention, rested on the belief that government financial support and intervention was necessary to expedite technical progress. While claiming to reject protectionist approaches to industrial competitiveness, Thurow favored other forms of government intervention including administrative guidance as in Japan. His industrial policy thus involved tripartite consultation and bargaining among industry, labor, and government. His proposal assumed that government officials, who operated in a political environment, could agree on what rising industries should be assisted and which declining industries should be buried.[59]

Subsequently, many other scholars echoed their concerns about decline. They included the president of the American assembly who asserted that "America can't compete," and Yale historian Paul Kennedy, who thought American leaders had to manage a relative erosion of its world position. By the early 1990s many ordinary Americans were convinced that America was on the decline. A poll by the Council on Competitiveness found that, by a margin of seven to one, Americans thought Japan had become the number one economy.[60]

As it turned out, the Japanese challenge proved short-lived. By the early twenty-first century attention had turned to China, where an authoritarian regime embraced aspects of the free market and successfully adopted the export-led growth strategy that had served Japan and the smaller Asian tiger economies well in the 1980s.

Conclusion

From this review of thought it is evident that the insights of Adam Smith, David Ricardo, Friedrich List, and other critics of free trade remain relevant to policy discussions on trade and development in the contemporary world. So do the perspectives of John Maynard Keynes and Milton Friedman on managing economies in cyclical downturns, and those of Peter Drucker and other management strategists on adapting to the new era of integrated national markets. On many occasions during the contemporary period, leaders and policymakers have invoked the names of Smith, Keynes, Hayek, Friedman, and other prominent economists to rationalize policy responses to the forces transforming and disrupting the global economy.

It is apparent from the sometimes contradictory views presented in this chapter that economists may disagree fundamentally on policy issues. One senior economist, Barbara R. Bergmann, has observed that economic recommendations frequently lack an empirical foundation, unlike the physical sciences where factual observations lead inductively to theories. Economists, she says, are prone to theorizing without observing. As a result, political ideology and value judgments may shape policy recommendations. Her insight could help us understand how the contemporary global economy became unstable and vulnerable to contagion in recent years despite so much high-powered economic advice.[61]

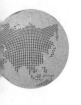

Chapter 6

International Trade

As nations opened their borders and engaged the evolving global economy, international trade expanded rapidly in the late twentieth century. The phenomenal growth of China, and of six smaller Asian economies, spurred commerce in the Pacific region, and transformed traditional trading patterns. As emerging Asian nations focused on exporting manufactures, several mature economies in Europe and North America turned to services. The United Kingdom and the United States became net importers of goods. Meanwhile, trading countries sought to promote trade liberalization through multilateral negotiations and to establish a broader set of rules to guide world trade in the next century.

Trade Trends and Transitions

For centuries trade between higher income countries in the northern hemisphere and poorer countries in tropical regions adhered to a simple complementary pattern. Countries in the north produced and exported manufactures (textiles, steel, and machinery). They imported raw materials (bananas, coffee, cotton, spices, minerals, and precious metals) from the south. Trade between north and south tended to mirror the crude specialization of production described in the writings of Adam Smith. It reflected the principle of absolute advantage based on differences in factor endowments (the natural distribution of resources) and labor costs.[1] Trade among high-income countries, however, often involved two-way, intra-industry trade in differentiated manufactures. This competition corresponded more

The Contemporary Global Economy: A History Since 1980, First Edition. Alfred E. Eckes, Jr.
© 2011 Alfred E. Eckes, Jr. Published 2011 by Blackwell Publishing Ltd.

to Ricardo's theory of comparative advantage, or comparative costs, based on differences in technology and productivity.[2]

For some two centuries – from the late eighteenth to the late twentieth century – the northern hemisphere dominated production of manufactures. During the final decades of the twentieth century they lost that advantage. In 1980 the European Union, Japan, and the US produced 72% of world manufacturing exports. In 2008 this elite group produced only 60% of world manufacturing exports. An emergent China and six smaller emerging "tigers" of East Asia (Hong Kong, Korea, Malaysia, Singapore, Taiwan, and Thailand) generated another 21.6%, up from 6.6% in 1980. China, on the verge of becoming the world's largest exporter of manufactures, accounted for 12.7% of exports, up from 0.8% as late as 1980.[3]

The rise of China and its smaller Asian neighbors as exporters of manufactures signaled a new era in global economic relations, as the world moved beyond the traditional north–south model described earlier. Indeed, south–south trade among developing countries grew twice as fast as world trade after 1990. Among developing countries the shift to manufacturing was evident in the rising share of manufactures as a percent of total exports. In Latin America and South Asia the share of manufacturing in total exports rose from 17 and 54 percent respectively in 1980 to 51 percent and 65 percent in 2008.[4] This pattern did not extend to the Middle East and the Commonwealth of Independent States (CIS), a successor to the Soviet Union. Most of these countries remained highly dependent on exports of fuels and mining products, which accounted for more than two-thirds of export revenues. In Africa and Latin America a number of countries – such as Argentina – continued to earn a majority of merchandise export revenue from the sale of food products.[5]

Among some older industrial countries evolving trade patterns highlighted another significant transition: the shift from manufacturing to services. Commercial services accounted for 29.3 percent of the United Kingdom's total exports in 2000, and 39.8 percent in 2009. For the US the comparable figures were 26.2 percent in 2000 and 31 percent in 2009.[6]

The growth of interregional trade in manufactures underscored a third theme: the emergence of "production sharing" and offshoring. About 1980 significant numbers of multinational corporations began moving raw materials and parts around the world to the most advantageous point of assembly. Business strategist Peter Drucker had been the first to popularize this trend, which he termed "production sharing." Recognizing that developing countries had surplus workers eager for labor-intensive work, and that developed countries faced higher labor costs, he predicted a rapid growth in production-sharing activities. Products designed and marketed in high-income countries would be assembled in low-income nations to the mutual advantage of both developed and developing countries.[7]

In order to spread costs and risks, multinationals soon began to outsource tasks to offshore suppliers rather than to operate their own foreign assembly plants. Much offshore work was done in tax-exempt foreign trade zones, such as the ones established in Taiwan during the 1960s. Usually these facilities assembled low-tech items like apparel, shoes, and electronics. Over time the pattern changed. Workers in developing countries, such as Singapore, Taiwan, and Korea, became highly educated and technically sophisticated. The diffusion of technology meant that tasks once done only in high-income industrial countries could be done anywhere. As a result, upscale jobs in back-office operations, research, and engineering also began to move offshore. While US-based firms led in offshoring to East and South Asia, European firms were not far behind. Many of them found it advantageous to move work to Eastern Europe, where German was widely spoken.[8]

By the first decade of the twenty-first century the sharing of work in corporate strategies had evolved so far that on major projects corporations often employed teams in countries far distant from one another and workers with different skill levels. One example was Boeing's approach to designing and producing the Boeing 787 "dreamliner." Boeing opted to operate as the final assembler and integrator of parts and components. It outsourced 70 percent of design and production, contracting with some 50 suppliers, more than half outside the US. In turn, the external suppliers turned to more than 900 small subcontractors.

Utilizing lightweight composites (plastics and carbon fiber), development and production of this plane became a global project involving a vast network of suppliers. Japanese and Italians designed and built composite fuselage sections and wings. Some 200 Russian engineers designed titanium aircraft parts. Giant Boeing 747s – so-called "Dreamlifters" – transported the parts and subassemblies to Everett, Washington, where unionized workers snapped them together. In this instance production-sharing worked imperfectly. The Boeing 787 project fell more than two years behind schedule. Supplier problems included language difficulties and other snafus. To keep the outsourcing model intact, Boeing discovered that it even had to buy out some suppliers and to lend money to others.[9]

Despite the growth of global sourcing, and inter-regional trade, trade within individual regions (intra-regional trade) continued to account for the majority of world merchandise trade. Much of that intra-regional trade occurred among members of the European Union. However, within South and Central America, the Middle East, and Africa, intra-regional trade amounted to only 2.5 percent of total exports.[10]

Trade specialists frequently emphasize that over the entire period since the end of World War II international trade has increased faster than the gross domestic products of individual nations. According to WTO data, world exports expanded 26-fold in volume terms from 1950 to 2009, while world GDP climbed only eight-fold. Trade in manufactures grew far more rapidly than did energy/mining products and agriculture.[11] The fastest growth took place between 1950 and the 1973 oil shock. Then higher fuel prices and inflation slowed real growth, but rapid growth resumed in the 1990s. Among the key factors were lower fuel prices and the collapse of the Soviet Union. Subsequent decisions of more developing countries to open their economies to trade and investments added four to five billion persons to the world marketplace.

It is worth noting while trade soared during the first three decades after World War II, much of it reflected the recovery of Europe and Japan. During this period, much of the world did not participate actively in the global economy. Governments regulated much trade with exchange controls, permits, and other administrative devices. The Soviet Union, China, and their allies pursued autarkic, regional policies. They desired to advance an alternative form of economic organization, one that involved state ownership of the means of production (socialism) and central planning. A third group of countries, some of them newly independent in Asia, Africa, and the Americas, adopted import-substitution policies. They sought to stimulate domestic manufactures and to break the colonial pattern of dependence on advanced economies in Europe and North America in which they exported minerals and agricultural commodities.

For smaller developing countries in Asia, the rapid recovery of Japan, using an export-oriented growth model, proved a stimulating example. Beginning in the mid-1960s, Taiwan, Hong Kong, Singapore, Malaysia, Korea, and Thailand all adopted similar outward-oriented trade models. Taiwan began the trend with its export-processing zones for textiles, apparel, and electronics. Over the course of the following generation Taiwan succeeded in expanding its share of world exports tenfold from 0.2 percent in 1963 to over 2 percent in the late 1980s.[12]

Middle East oil producers engaged the global economy differently. Between 1973 and 1983, oil-exporting countries in the Middle East enhanced their share of world trade, but these gains, derived from higher oil prices, dropped when prices fell during the 1980s. Oil prices soared again in the first decade of the twenty-first century, as more and more residents of China and India acquired automobiles and global demand for oil soared.

Another major change in international trade patterns occurred in the early 1990s. With the collapse of the Soviet Union, the global economy entered another market-opening phase. Many former Soviet states sought to join the Europe Union. China, once an Asian model for socialism, also changed course, adopting an outward-oriented model and inviting foreign investment and technology transfers. These events inspired neo-liberal hubris in such tomes as Francis Fukuyama's *End of History* and journalist Thomas L. Friedman's *Lexus and the Olive Tree*. Both celebrated the return of free markets and free trade.[13]

As the repercussions of these dramatic events ricocheted around the developing world, other developing countries adopted open trading policies. Prompted by the successes of the Asian tigers and the collapse of command economies in Eastern Europe, many industrializing countries chose to liberalize their own economies and attract foreign investors. They lowered tariffs, deregulated industries, and scaled back subsidies. Many of them abolished state-trading monopolies and adopted convertible currencies. After the conclusion of the Uruguay Round of multilateral trade negotiations in 1994, more of them took seriously their rights and obligations in the open-trading system.[14]

Some of the more important transitions occurred in the western hemisphere. Argentina, Brazil, Chile, and Mexico adopted more open and pro-business policies, deregulating their economies and engaging the global marketplace. One of the most remarkable changes in trade policy occurred in Mexico during the late 1980s, as noted in Chapter 4. Recognizing that Mexico needed to generate more jobs for its burgeoning population, President Miguel de la Madrid listened to the advice of a group of US-educated economists. They included the man he would select as his successor, Carlos Salinas de Gotari. The economists advised abandoning import-substitution industrialization and integrating Mexico into the global economy. Soon Mexico began luring foreign investors, and privatizing some state industries. It joined the General Agreement on Tariffs and Trade (GATT), and encouraged the expansion of in-bond *maquiladoras*, essentially facilities to assemble apparel, auto parts, and electronics for the US market from duty-free imports.

Meanwhile, other developments transformed the post-Cold War international economy, and buoyed certain emerging powers. China and Russia re-entered the international economy – the former as an exporter of manufactures, the latter as an exporter of oil and gas. A boom in commodity prices benefitted developing countries in Africa, the Middle East, and the Americas. One result of these profound changes was that the share of global exports held by North America, the expanded European Union, and Japan began to decline. Expansion of regional trade in North America through NAFTA and the growth of the European Union were not enough to alter this pattern. The mirror image of the industrial countries' relative decline was the emergence of a diverse group of developing nations manufacturing labor-intensive products. They accounted for two-thirds of world apparel exports and more than half of exports of cell phones and office equipment.[15]

By the end of the first decade of the twenty-first century, China had become the world's largest exporter – and nine Asian countries ranked among the world's top 20 exporters. After China, the list included Japan, Korea, Hong Kong, Singapore, Taiwan, Malaysia, Thailand, and India. Five other major trading nations abutting the Pacific Ocean were the United States, Russia, Canada, Mexico, and Australia. Altogether the top 20 accounted for over 65 percent of world trade.

The rise of developing countries as exporters of manufactures and the transition of older industrial countries to substantial importers of manufactures had widespread political and economic ramifications. Anxious and dislocated workers in advanced countries, led by unions, backed protectionist trade policies, hoping to save their jobs. Also, the surge in imports produced huge trade imbalances, and chronic current account deficits, in Britain and the US.

Another fundamental factor supporting the trade expansion involved lower transportation and communications costs. High freight rates and storage costs act like a protective tariff in discouraging international trade. But the shift to air travel and enhanced use of containerization helped reduce overall costs. In 1965, air shipments accounted for about 6 percent of US imports. By 1998, they accounted for nearly 25 percent. Air transportation accounted for 8 percent of exports in 1965, and over 29 percent in 1994. In particular, improved long-range air shipping enabled global supply networks to flourish, especially for higher-valued items. Faster container ships and wide-bodied tankers also accelerated trends, reflecting the increased speed of ships and the reduced time required for loading and unloading. Costs of making international calls and transmitting information fell dramatically, while the internet markedly improved communications and information flows.[16]

Multilateral Trade Negotiations

Along with economic factors and technological developments, many trade specialists cite another reason for the expansion of international trade,

Table 6.1 Top twenty merchandise exporters (2009)

Country or unit	Population (millions)	Total trade/ GDP (%)	Merchandise exports* (%)	Commercial services* (%)
1. European Union*	498.6	28.6	16.2	26.3
2. China	1,331.5	58.6	12.7	5.2
3. United States	307.0	27.3	11.2	19.2
4. Japan	127.6	32.2	6.2	5.1
5. Korea, South	48.7	96.9	3.9	2.3
6. Hong Kong	7.0	406.6	3.5	3.5
7. Canada	33.7	64.3	3.4	2.3
8. Russia	141.9	51.4	3.2	1.7
9. Singapore	5.0	406.0	2.9	3.5
10. Mexico	107.4	58.1	2.4	0.6
11. Taiwan	23.1	129.7	2.2	1.2
12. Saudi Arabia	25.4	96.5	2.0	0.4
13. United Arab Emirates	4.6	171.3	1.9	0.4
14. Switzerland	7.7	111.2	1.8	2.8
15. India	1,155.0	46.2	1.7	3.5
16. Malaysia	27.5	185.8	1.7	1.1
17. Australia	21.9	44.5	1.6	1.7
18. Brazil	193.7	24.8	1.6	1.1
19. Thailand	67.8	139.4	1.6	1.2
20. Norway	4.8	74.3	1.3	1.5

*Share of world trade not including trade among EU members.
Source: World Trade Organization, *ITS 2010*, 14, 16.

namely policy changes resulting from international negotiations. For over 60 years multilateral negotiations under the auspices of the General Agreement on Tariffs and Trade (GATT) and the World Trade Organization (WTO) have removed barriers to trade in goods and services. They have established a rules-based dispute settlement mechanism conducive to business expansion. By lowering tariffs among its members, the GATT/WTO system contributed to the surge in trade. The WTO estimates that the average tariff rate for industrial countries fell from the 20 to 30 percent range in 1947 to less than 4 percent by 1995 as a result of multilateral negotiations.[17]

The GATT, a contractual arrangement among governments, began in 1948 with 23 members. The leaders of this trade club were the US and the United Kingdom, as well as other leaders of the British Commonwealth

– Australia, Canada, and New Zealand. Half of the founding members were developing countries, including Brazil, Chile, India, Pakistan, and South Africa. In its earliest days GATT was a forum for trade liberalizing negotiations and trade policy discussions. Until the 1970s it was a small, low-profile organization, and countries of the North Atlantic, the nations most involved in international trade, provided leadership. Whenever the US and the Europeans agreed, the developing countries generally followed suit. GATT's leaders initially insisted on the universal application of the organization's key principles of non-discrimination and reciprocity and developing countries, lacking the capacity to engage the system, often ignored their rights and obligations.

Over time developing countries would become more assertive, especially after the formation of the United Nations Conference on Trade and Development (UNCTAD) in 1964. They would insist on special treatment and a special dispensation from the rules for their import-substitution industrialization polices. During the late 1960s and 1970s UNCTAD members would demand one-way trade preferences, permitting them easy access to the markets of the advanced countries without providing reciprocal access to their own. The Tokyo Round, concluded in 1979, confirmed special and differential treatment for developing countries.

During the Uruguay Round (1986–94), developing countries became more engaged in the multilateral process. When the GATT metamorphosed into the World Trade Organization (WTO), the new organization soon had 111 members, the majority of them developing nations. By 2010 the WTO had 153 members, 111 of them developing countries. It was apparent the balance of power was shifting from the nations with the greatest stake in international trade to a broader coalition of emerging countries determined to enhance their own growth by participation in the world economy. Moreover, they were eager to protect their rights against discrimination that might jeopardize the principle of non-discrimination.

To understand developments in the multilateral trading system during the 30-year period under review, it is helpful to review the GATT process and the principal negotiating rounds.

GATT Negotiations

Under the GATT a series of multilateral trade negotiating rounds occurred. The negotiations took place at Geneva (1947) before the formal establishment of GATT; Annecy, France (1949); Torquay, England (1950–1); Geneva

(1956); and Geneva (1960–2). These negotiations focused on lowering tariffs and involved product-by-product bilateral negotiations among principal suppliers. The resulting concessions were then generalized on a most-favored-nation basis to all members of GATT. This approach, while it facilitated negotiations among the countries most concerned about a single product, enabled emerging and recovering industrial powers, such as Japan, to gain access to markets without making reciprocal concessions of their own. During the Kennedy Round (1962–7), negotiators adopted a linear formula for across-the-board tariffs, an approach that avoided the cumbersome and time-consuming product-by-product negotiations with leading suppliers.

The most successful rounds under GATT are generally thought to have been the first Geneva Round and the Kennedy Round. In these two the US Congress authorized major duty reductions (up to 50% of existing rates) and reductions averaged about 35 percent. Some scholars have observed that the stated concessions impacted nations taking part in the negotiations differently. While the US rolled back its tariff from high 1930 levels, many war-damaged European countries used exchange controls and quantitative restrictions to delay access to their markets. Much of this was justified by the need to rebuild war-damaged economies, but the effect was to benefit protectionist forces and enable certain European governments to pursue industrial policies benefiting domestic producers.[18]

The Kennedy Round produced other asymmetrical results. While the US and the Common Market negotiated down duties on industrial products, producing cuts of between 36 and 39 percent, the Common Market, having recently fashioned its common agricultural policy, declined to make significant concessions on agriculture. Developing countries did not actively participate in the round. Forty-one GATT members, including emerging trading powers Singapore and Malaysia, refused to join the negotiations. Another 17 negotiated under special arrangements that did not mandate reciprocity. Thus, big emerging markets like Argentina, Brazil, India, Indonesia, Korea, and Pakistan gained the benefit of concessions made by industrial powers, but refrained from lowering or binding their own tariffs. Japan also declined to make substantially equivalent concessions, recognizing that the US was determined to push through an agreement to satisfy a congressional timetable for concluding negotiations.[19]

While the Kennedy Round began with high expectations, the principal achievements were in removing tariffs on industrial products traded by the principal trading countries of Europe and North America. The average *ad valorem* equivalent on dutiable US imports fell from 12.2 percent in 1967 to 8.6 percent in 1972, when Kennedy Round concessions were fully implemented, effectively opening the huge American market to international competition.

Until the 1970s multilateral trade negotiations under GATT auspices focused on tariff reduction. The Tokyo Round (1973–9) also included border barriers – such as tariffs and quotas – but in addition it sought to address a variety of non-tariff barriers and to extend the GATT system to other areas of concern to multilateral business, such as government procurement. But overall the results proved disappointing. The Tokyo Round achieved far less than the prior Kennedy Round, which had concluded in 1967. While advanced countries agreed to reduce tariffs on industrial goods about one-third, there was little progress on agriculture. The European Community refused to roll back its variable levy system for protecting agriculture.

Perhaps the round's greatest achievement was in extending GATT rules to non-tariff matters. Governments approved several non-tariff "codes" relating to countervailing duties and subsidies, antidumping duties, product standards and technical barriers, import licensing, government procurement, and customs valuation.

As in prior GATT negotiations, developing nations did not participate actively. Although they asserted rights to all of the tariff concessions granted by rich countries to one another, they had a different set of priorities and few resources to engage in negotiations. In the 1970s they looked the United Nations Conference on Trade and Development (UNCTAD) and its director Raul Prebisch for leadership. Prebisch, the Argentine economist who once urged tariffs and import substitution as the path to development, now exhorted the industrial nations to provide one-way tariff preferences to exports of the poor. And in the Tokyo Round GATT members chose to make permanent the Generalized System of Preferences (GSP). In doing so, GATT members essentially waived the core principle of nondiscrimination for developing countries.

The US and the European Community administered similar preferential programs. The US program allowed developing countries duty-free access to the US market subject to certain limitations. The executive branch annually reviewed each country's eligibility to determine if its exports exceeded certain levels, and on occasion graduated countries or removed products eligible for preferences. One of the results of these unilateral preference programs was that developing countries continued to assume little responsibility for the multilateral system, and instead looked to bilateral negotiations with the EU and the US for trade benefits. They also made little effort to liberalize and bind their tariffs against future changes.

While many were disappointed with the outcome, it is arguable that the Tokyo Round did more than sustain the multilateral process. It took important steps to accommodate the world trading system to changing circumstances, as it extended international trade rules to non-tariff issues. Europe and the United States chose not to address the problem of free riders on tariff issues – that is, countries such as Japan that sought to benefit from other country's tariff cuts without giving much in return. They did apply the concept of reciprocity to various non-tariff codes, however. To benefit from the codes a nation had to assume obligations. Not surprisingly most of the developing nations opted out of these arrangements. A decade later only 25 countries had adhered to the codes on dumping and subsidies, and only 12 had agreed to open up government procurement to foreign competition.

During the early 1980s there was little enthusiasm for another multilateral round, as high unemployment and economic stagnation prompted nations to look inward. But fears of resurgent protectionism and bilateral free-trade agreements prompted the European Community, Japan, and the US to launch the so-called Uruguay Round, the eighth and last GATT round. They did so in September 1986, when GATT held a ministerial at Punta del Este, Uruguay. As it turned out, the Uruguay Round proved to be a marathon round, taking seven-and-a-half years to conclude in 1994, but involving a record 123 countries.

Among the goals of the Uruguay Round was improving the workings of the international trade system, particularly in agriculture, subsidies, safeguards, dispute settlement, and non-tariff measures. For the US a principal goal was to revise the ineffective GATT dispute-settlement process, which allowed members to block an adverse finding. The US also wanted to promote more open and fair conditions of trade in agricultural commodities and improvements in GATT provisions to address certain unfair trading practices. Frustrated with free-riding countries and the lack of reciprocity, Congress had directed negotiators to obtain improved market access for US exports to developing countries. The European Union differed on agriculture but had a similar set of interests – improving dispute settlement, establishing rules for services, and gaining greater access to developing-country markets.

With so many goals and so many participants, it is not surprising that the Uruguay Round proved a frustrating exercise. Whereas during previous rounds the United States and the European Community were the major players, this time developing countries took a more active role. Of the 123 participants, two-thirds were developing countries.

A deal involving developing and developed nations was the key to the final agreement. The rich countries agreed to phase out restraints on textiles and apparel imports and to improve market access for developing-world agricultural products, in exchange for extending the multilateral system to intellectual property, services, and trade-related investments. Behind the compromise was a business reality. Large transnational corporations wanted improved access to emerging markets. Many of them were frustrated with local-content restrictions in host countries, which regulated their economic activities. The MNCs sought greater freedom to run their operations in the most efficient way possible. Also Wall Street, the insurance industry, and telecommunications giants sought opportunities to sell products and services in developing markets on the same terms as host-country competitors. Entertainment and pharmaceuticals industries insisted on stronger protections for patents and copyrights.

The most significant result was an institutional one. The final agreement established a permanent organization – the World Trade Organization (WTO) – replacing a temporary contractual arrangement – the GATT – which had endured for nearly 50 years. The WTO would serve as a forum and a vehicle for implementing trade agreements. The Uruguay Round agreement contained 13 different accords covering trade in goods and agriculture; sanitary and phytosanitary measures; textiles and clothing; technical barriers to trade (standards); trade-related investment measures (TRIMS); antidumping, customs valuation, preshipment inspection, rules of origin, import licensing procedures, subsidies, and countervailing measures; and safeguards. In addition, the negotiators approved a General Agreement on Trade in Services (GATS); an Agreement on Trade-Related Aspects of Intellectual Property Rights (TRIPS); a dispute settlement understanding; trade policy review mechanism; and four plurilateral trade agreements covering government procurement, civil aircraft, dairy, and bovine meat. These plurilaterals, however, did not include all members. The final act also set out an additional negotiating agenda, one including financial services, basic telecommunications services, and civil aircraft. These matters were left largely unresolved until later negotiations.

From the standpoint of developing countries, agreements on textiles and clothing and on agriculture were most important. The textile pact promised to end country-by-country quotas on imports of textiles and apparel by January 1, 2005. This was implemented, benefitting low-cost textile exporters – China, Bangladesh, and Vietnam. But, many inefficient African producers experienced heavy losses, as did medium-income countries with higher cost structures, such as the Philippines, Taiwan, Turkey, and South

Korea. In agriculture member countries agreed to establish a fair and market-oriented system. They pledged to improve access to their markets, cut support to agriculture, and reduce export subsidies. But the Uruguay Round left for future negotiations agreement on how these goals were to be achieved, and the poor countries would argue with some justification that the US and EU did not keep their side of the bargain.

As it turned out the most controversial aspects of the trade package was the WTO and its dispute-settlement mechanism. The GATT had operated by consensus, so that one country could block action. In the new international organization there was a determination to continue the GATT practice of decision-making, but in the event of a formal vote each nation would have one vote, no matter the size of its stake in the global economy. Thus it appeared that India (then with 936 million people) had voting power equal to Grenada with 108,000, while an anomaly enhanced Europe's influence. Although on trade matters the European Union in Brussels negotiated and administered trade policy, its constituent members each could cast votes equivalent to the EU's total member states (15 in 1995, 27 in 2007).

As created in the Uruguay Round the new WTO was quite different from its predecessor, sometimes described as a "rich man's club." Developing nations now held more than two-thirds of the votes, although they accounted for only a small share of world trade. As a result, development issues and the concerns of the poorest countries shaped the WTO negotiating agenda far more than they did under the GATT during its first 20 years. Indeed, the Doha Round launched in November 2001 had as its explicit goal making international trade rules fairer for developing countries. "The majority of WTO members are developing countries. We seek to place their needs and interests at the heart of the Work Programme adopted in this Declaration."[20]

WTO in Transition

Under the auspices of GATT, the US and the European Union, the two largest trading areas, dominated the organization. Smaller trading countries, such as Australia and Canada, took an active leadership role and made important contributions. But when Europe and the US agreed the others generally acquiesced. Even though GATT functioned by consensus (giving each member a veto), dissent was rare.

In the WTO, an organization in which two-thirds of the members were low-income countries, India, Brazil, and South Africa, all longtime members of GATT, proposed to lead the developing world. Their first triumph came in 2002 when the developing countries challenged the US and Europeans on the selection of a new director-general, the top official. Under GATT, tradition dictated that the head official be a European. In 1999, when WTO members sought to choose a new leader, a deadlock emerged. The unusual compromise involved sharing the six-year term between Mike Moore, a former prime minister of New Zealand, and Supachai Panitchpakdi of Thailand. For the first time, the director-general of the international trade organization was a resident of a Pacific country, a choice that signaled the rising importance of Asia in trade matters.

Moore had the misfortune to preside over the turbulent WTO ministerial in Seattle in December 1999. He had wanted to launch a new multilateral round of negotiations – a development round – to address some of the complaints about the uneven distribution of gains from the Uruguay Round. Poor countries complained that rich countries had agreed to cut farm subsidies, but had not. Frustrated at not having improved access for their agricultural exports, developing countries refused to lower tariffs and open markets to high-income-country manufactures and service providers.

The unrest in Seattle was a blow to international business determined to strengthen and extend the rules-based multilateral system. However, the terrorist attacks of September 2001 afforded another opportunity for nations to unite behind the launching of another trade round – the so-called Doha Development Round (DDR), named for Doha, Qatar, where the WTO met in November 2001. In this round, participants proposed to use trade liberalization to integrate poor countries into the international system. They sought to reduce poverty and promote economic development, thus promoting greater prosperity, social stability, and world peace. Some members, notably the Europeans, hoped to address a variety of new issues in the context of the multilateral round. These involved investment, competition, transparency in government procurement, and trade facilitation. The same issues, the so-called Singapore issues, had been raised initially at a 1996 WTO ministerial in Singapore. Critics – particularly India – claimed that the first three of the items were strictly speaking non-trade issues and impinged on domestic sovereignty.

Big business initially applauded the Doha Round. The International Chamber of Commerce (ICC) said that early agreement would send a confidence-boosting signal to investors, traders, and consumers. According to the ICC, the message was that governments would continue to open markets and "develop multilateral rules in line with new business realties and requirements."[21] Other big-business groups repeatedly urged world leaders to keep the Doha Round on track and to reassure global companies considering new investments. Among the most vocal were the Business Roundtable, European Round Table of Industrialists, the Nippon Keidanren in Japan, the Canadian Council of Chief Executives, the International Chamber of Commerce, and Union of Industrial and Employers Confederations of Europe.

As the concerns of big business suggest, the Doha Round had a turbulent history. Initial enthusiasm gave way to frustrations, deadlock, and fiascos, such as the turbulent ministerial in Cancun, Mexico, in 2003. There rich and poor countries disagreed about the scope of the round. African countries declined to extend the negotiations into new areas, and blamed the rich countries for refusing to dismantle farm subsidies.

Gradually the deadlock led to the postponement and eventual suspension of the negotiations in July 2006. Indian Trade Minister Kamal Nath asserted the round was not dead but was somewhere between intensive care and the crematorium. While the US and Europe pointed fingers at each other for the deadlock, the confrontational approach of developing countries was another important factor.

Dispute Settlement

Under GATT dispute settlement emphasized diplomatic solutions, and as a result obligations were often not enforced to the letter.[22] The WTO agreement introduced a highly legalistic dispute-settlement process in which member nations can file complaints alleging violation of WTO rules. Private parties – such as transnational corporations – do not have the requisite standing to bring cases directly. At the core of the new-dispute settlement process is implementation, compensation, or retaliation. If the losing party to a complaint does not implement the decision and make compensation, the party bringing the complaint may retaliate by suspending equivalent concessions. In effect, the dispute-settlement process makes the WTO an international regulatory authority. Many of its decisions impinge on national economic governance.

Since 1995, members have filed 418 complaints (through December 2010). The US and the European Union brought 178 complaints (43%), and had to respond to 180 (43%) complaints. The US was a party – either a complainant or a respondent – in nearly half of all cases (206). Two other developed economies, Canada and Korea, have filed 47 cases. Twenty cases named China as a respondent, but China has filed only seven cases. In recent years the US and the EU have brought fewer cases, but developing countries have filed increasing numbers of dispute settlement cases. The most active have been Argentina, Brazil, India, Mexico, and Thailand. The five filed 93 cases (22% of all complaints). Brazil, Mexico, and Thailand have brought nearly twice as many cases as have been filed against them. Least developed countries, including Bangladesh, most of Africa, and other countries so classified by the UN, seldom have been involved in dispute settlement cases. They tend to account for a small share of world trade, and lack the resources and experience to utilize dispute settlement successfully.[23]

Emerging countries have adapted to the requirements of the rules-based system, and increasingly retained foreign law firms to assist with their legal challenges. Brazil, Canada, China, the European Union, Mexico, South Korea, and Vietnam are among the countries that have hired US lawyers to represent their interests in WTO proceedings.[24]

While the dispute-settlement system is relatively new, scholarly analysis suggests that it has been relatively successful. The implementation rate of WTO panel decisions is about 75 percent. But there appear to be compliance problems, in which remedies have been delayed or their implementation disputed. The US, the country that promoted the rules-based approach to trade governance, is alleged to be the "biggest troublemaker" because of its refusal to implement major rulings. The reason given for non-compliance has been congressional reluctance to enact implementing legislation. The troublesome US cases involve steel products, copyright law, trademarks, tax law involving foreign sales corporations, cotton subsidies, and export credit guarantees. Also difficult was the so-called Byrd amendment named for the late Senator Robert Byrd (D-WV). It authorized distribution of anti-dumping and countervailing duties collected from trade cases to petitioning companies. In effect, it invited them to continue retaining lawyers and filing trade cases. The European Union also refused to implement WTO decisions in high-profile cases involving bananas and meat hormones. It resolved the banana dispute after some 16 years in December 2009, when the EU agreed to a process for lowering its customs duties on bananas each year until 2017.[25]

In the Brazilian case brought against US cotton subsidies, Brazil requested $2.5 billion in retaliatory trade sanctions, but the WTO authorized $294.7 million. In mid-2010 the US government began monthly payments of $12.3 million to Brazil to avoid dismantling the support program.

Bilateral and Regional Trade Negotiations

When WTO ministerials at Cancun, Mexico, (September 2003) and Hong Kong (December 2005) failed to break political deadlocks and make progress toward concluding the Doha Round of multilateral negotiations, major trading powers began to pursue alternative approaches. Under pressure from big business to break down trade barriers and improve terms of access to emerging markets, they shifted negotiating strategies away from the multilateral approach favored since the end of World War II. Each of the major trading nations began to pursue bilateral and regional agreements. By July 2010 the WTO reported that it had received notification of 474 regional trade agreements (RTAs), and 283 were in force.[26]

At first impression the various regional, bilateral, and multilateral approaches appeared contradictory. Bilateral and regional agreements seemed to violate the principle of nondiscrimination that underpinned multilateralism, the foundation for GATT/WTO. But the founders of the GATT system envisaged a place for bilateral and regional agreements for trade in goods, as a first step toward extending gains from trade to all countries. The GATS agreement negotiated during the Uruguay Round for services also contemplated bilateral and regional agreements. Basically, the WTO wants regional and bilateral agreements to promote trade openness, and not lead to greater discrimination against outside parties. The spirit of GATT/WTO is inclusiveness, that bilateral agreements be expanded to include more parties.

Many of the recently negotiated bilateral and regional agreements seek deeper levels of integration than under the WTO. Some include measures to liberalize and harmonize trade-impeding regulatory policies. Others strive to enlarge and integrate regional blocs in Europe, North America, South America, and Asia. Others link countries in different regions and at different levels of development, such as US FTAs with Jordan and Chile. In light of these trends it is necessary to examine briefly the trade policy strategies of leading powers.

The United States

For 35 years – until the early 1980s – the US gave top priority in trade negotiations to advancing the GATT-based multilateral system. During the Reagan administration US officials grew frustrated with the reluctance of allies in Western Europe and Japan to sponsor another multilateral round to address unresolved issues of non-tariff barriers, services, intellectual property, trade-related investments, and strengthened dispute settlement. To encourage multilateral negotiations, and to contain domestic protectionist impulses, the US opted in 1983 to pursue a two-track path to trade liberalization. On the one hand, the US would pursue bilateral free-trade agreements, and on the other it would exhort other GATT members to authorize multilateral negotiations.

For domestic political reasons, the Reagan administration chose to negotiate the first bilateral FTA with Israel. The agreement proposed to eliminate tariffs and non-tariff barriers on virtually all trade between the two countries over a ten-year period ending in 1995. This pact included provisions not covered in GATT, such as intellectual property, services, and performance requirements. Both countries insisted on exceptions. The US retained quotas and restraints on textiles and apparel, and Israel maintained non-tariff barriers and levies on agricultural items. The message to the international community was clear – if others would not discuss these issues in a multilateral context, the US would do so on a bilateral level with selected trading partners. Bilateralism had thus become a second-best alternative to multilateralism.

The second such agreement, signed in January 1988, was with neighboring Canada. For Ottawa the deviation from multilateralism represented an opportunity to secure preferred access to its most important foreign market (the US market took almost 80% of Canada's exports) at a time when anti-dumping and other non-tariff barriers threatened access. For the US it was both fulfillment of a long-time aspiration to integrate the North American market as well as an opportunity to strike down non-tariff and investment restrictions, establish rules for services, direct investments, and intellectual property that might influence the Uruguay Round negotiations.

The North American Free Trade Agreement (NAFTA), completed in 1992, represented an extension of the US–Canadian agreement to another North American nation. It opened many sectors of the Mexican market to foreign investments (but not petroleum), and importantly included a mandatory dispute-settlement process ensuring that foreign investors would receive national treatment and prompt compensation for any expropriation at market prices. The dispute settlement procedures in this agreement, and in the US–Canadian pact, involved new and questionable precedents. NAFTA Chapter 11, for example, allowed private parties to bring disputes against governments before private tribunals. According to Citizen Trade Watch, an activist organization, corporate investors used

NAFTA's investor-statement enforcement system to dispute domestic court rulings, federal and state anti-gambling policies, water rights, and even public postal services.[27]

Under presidents Bill Clinton and George W. Bush the American quest for regional and bilateral agreements continued, as the US sought to energize and nurture the multilateral process. Clinton pushed a Free Trade Agreement for the Americas, and bilateral agreements with Chile, Jordan, and Singapore. After the terrorist attacks of September 11, 2001, Bush gained renewed trade-negotiating authority from Congress, and put his free-trade initiative in overdrive. At one point his administration was negotiating 19 agreements with 47 countries, all except for Brazil and Australia having relatively small markets. When Bush left office in January 2009, his administration could point to seven bilaterals completed and approved by Congress (Australia, Bahrain, Chile, Morocco, Oman, Peru, and Singapore) as well as a regional agreement, the so-called Central American/Dominican Republic Free Trade Agreement (CAFTA/DR). Three more agreements had been completed (Colombia, Panama, and South Korea), but not approved by Congress.

Economists sometimes say that a free-trade agreement can be written on a postcard. President Bush's agreements were long, lawyer-drafted tomes that contained hundreds of pages of legal text detailing tariffs, quotas, services, finance, and other information. They contained dispute-resolution procedures, intellectual property protections, investment guarantees, government procurement, and various provisions to establish rules for global business. As a way of comparison, NAFTA had 824 pages, the US–Singapore bilateral 1,586 pages, and CAFTA/DR 3,725 pages. Proponents of free-trade agreements said that they benefited producers, and consumers, and enhanced world welfare. Judging from the length of free-trade treaties, one unmistakable winner was the paper industry.

Public dissatisfaction with free trade mounted in the US as the economy weakened. In October 2010 a *Wall Street Journal/NBC News* poll showed more than half of those surveyed, 53 percent, said free-trade agreements have hurt the US. In 1999, only 32 percent held that view. Many Americans associated lost jobs with trade liberalization. Recognizing that he lacked support among congressional Democrats for enacting trade agreements, President Barack Obama delayed submitting to Congress bilaterals completed with Panama, Colombia, and South Korea.[28]

Instead the new US administration proposed to engage new trade negotiations with the Trans-Pacific Partnership (TPP), a regional free-trade agreement that took effect in 2006. A comprehensive agreement, it covers trade in goods and services, intellectual property, government procurement, and a variety of non-tariff barriers, such as rules of origin, sanitary and phytosanitary measures, and other technical barriers. Its founding members are Singapore, New Zealand, Brunei, and Chile, two of which have bilateral FTAs with the US. The US, Australia, Peru, and Vietnam want to join, and others may be interested. Aside from the administration's desire to signal its support for free-trade negotiations, America's interest is to help shape a platform for economic integration across the Asia Pacific region, and to avoid the discriminatory effect of an East Asian regional agreement excluding the US.

European Union

From its inception as the European Common Market in 1957, the European Union has been conflicted between regionalism and multilateralism. In establishing a common external tariff and a common agricultural policy to bolster regional economic integration, the six-member Common Market discriminated between members and non-members and indulged in policies in conflict with the spirit of GATT. For political reasons – the need to anchor Germany firmly to Western Europe – the US and other GATT members tolerated this exception, while encouraging the European Community to negotiate in GATT rounds for member countries. The Kennedy and Tokyo Rounds tied Europe firmly to the multilateral process, and made it a pillar along with the US in promoting a rules-based economic system open to trade and investments.

Frustrated with the GATT/WTO process and needing to address issues of economic instability on its eastern and southern borders, the European Union has chosen, like the US, to pursue regional and bilateral liberalization. These initiatives are considered the best options for advancing the international business interests of European manufacturers, service providers, and investors. In this regard, the European Commission in Brussels has directed its trade negotiators to fashion bilateral and regional economic arrangements with neighboring countries, former colonies, and major trading partners in distant corners of the world. Thus it is apparent that both Europe and the US are pursuing similar bilateral-regional strategies. Some of the EU initiatives were defensive moves intended to preserve access to distant markets, such as FTAs with Mexico and Korea, where Europe apparently feared further loss in market share to the US.

Others involved integrating nearby countries more tightly into the European orbit. In 1995 the European Union and ten Mediterranean governments – Algeria, Egypt, Israel, Jordan, Lebanon, Morocco, Syria, Tunisia, Turkey, and the Palestinian Authority – issued a declaration in Barcelona, Spain, calling for a Euro-Mediterranean Free Trade Area (EMFTA) by 2010. It involved negotiating bilateral association agreements with each country and gradually implementing free trade. EMFTA envisaged free trade in manufactures and the gradual opening of trade in agricultural products. The bilateral agreements have all been concluded with the European Union, except for Syria, and the parties are committed to implementing free trade among themselves. The Euro-Mediterranean Association Agreements differ but have certain common aspects – including respect for human rights and democracy, establishment of WTO-compatible free trade over a 12-year transition period, and provisions relating to intellectual property, services, public procurement, competition, subsidies, and monopolies. The EMFTA initiative reflected Europe's appreciation that its own economic prosperity and political stability depended on improving economic conditions in North Africa. The ambitious objective remains creation of a Euro-Mediterranean free-trade zone, open to 600 million inhabitants.

In 2000 the EU proposed economic partnership agreements with a number of developing nations, the so-called Asia-Caribbean-Pacific (ACP) group, essentially 77 former colonies with about 700 million people (12% of the world's population), but generating only 2.8% of world trade. For decades these countries enjoyed preferential access to Europe's market, but the preferences violated WTO rules which required reciprocity, not dependency. The EU proposed regional partnership arrangements, in which the countries would open their markets to EU businesses, enjoy generous access to the EU market, and trade more freely among themselves. Under the threat of losing preferences on their exports to the EU, some 35 countries made initial interim agreements with the EU by a December 31, 2007 deadline. But the agreements are controversial both in the developing countries and with other members of the WTO. Critics have accused the countries signing initial economic partnership agreements with the EU of acting imprudently because of political and economic pressures.[29]

After North American countries completed NAFTA in 1992 the European Union, not wishing to be excluded from a fortress America, negotiated its own free-trade agreement with Mexico, which took effect in 2000. The EU feared losing market share to the United States, and Mexico sought to diversify its exports and attract European investment capital so as to create jobs. In 2008 the EU took 5.9% of Mexico's exports, and supplied 12.7% of Mexico's imports, making it Mexico's second largest trading partner after the US. The EU also negotiated one with Chile, which went into effect in

February 2003, a year before a similar FTA agreement with the United States. In 2008, the EU took 24.6% of Chile's exports, and supplied 12.4% of Chile's imports. The EU surpassed the US as Chile's leading trading partner.

With Canada the EU opened negotiations in May 2009. Canada accounts for 1.7% of the EU's external trade, and the EU is Canada's second most important trading partner behind the US. The negotiations continued into 2011 with difficult discussions on intellectual property, investments, technical barriers, sanitary and phytosanitary measures, and some aspects of trade in goods. The EU is also negotiating a FTA with the Central American countries.

The EU has also turned its attentions to FTA negotiations with other major trading partners in the Asia. It is negotiating bilateral free-trade agreements with the Association of South East Asian Nations (ASEAN) and the Gulf Cooperation Council, two regional blocs, and also with India and Korea. In December 2009, the EU opted to pursue the ASEAN negotiations in a bilateral format with individual countries. Vietnam has signaled that it wishes to negotiate a bilateral FTA with the EU. Subsequently, it suspended negotiations with the Gulf Cooperation Council.

The EU initialed a bilateral with Korea in October 2009, and negotiated with India and Singapore. The EU agreement with Korea has encountered some of the same resistance that the US–Korean agreement faced in the US. Europe's small car manufacturers feared greater competition from Korean carmakers. As a result of the Lisbon Treaty enhancing the role of the European Parliament, this bilateral was the first trade agreement subject to parliamentary debate. Italian automaker Fiat fanned parliamentary resistance, and won a six-month delay in implementation.

The EU also encountered difficulties in its negotiation of a bilateral free-trade agreement with Mercosur. This agreement was scheduled to be completed in 2004 but differences over Brazilian access to the European agricultural market and EU access to the Brazilian telecommunications sector stalled negotiations. The outcome may depend on the outcome of the multilateral Doha Round, and any agricultural concessions. In May 2010, ten European nations, led by France, objected to resumption of talks with Mercosur, warning that the strategic agricultural interests of the European Union were at stake.

Japan

For Japan the turbulent WTO conference in Seattle was a turning point. It began to pursue regional trading options, as Europe and the US had done.

To lessen dependence on the American market, Japan looked to Asia, where it hoped to balance off China's attempts to expand its regional influence. With ASEAN, Japan signed a general framework for bilateral free trade in October 2000. Negotiations began in April 2005 and concluded with an agreement in 2007. The Comprehensive Economic Partnership agreement covered trade in goods, services, investments, dispute settlement, sanitary and phytosanitary regulations, intellectual property, rules of origin, and technical barriers to trade. Japan thus sought to achieve a stronger trade position in Asia relative to China, Korea, and the United States. When Korea and the European Union signed a free-trade agreement, Japan, fearing it could lose a competitive edge in European markets, proposed a free-trade pact with the EU.[30]

Previously Japan signed a bilateral free-trade agreement with Singapore in 2001. This one did not include agriculture. It focused on liberalizing trade in services, especially finance and telecommunications, investments, the movement of people, and dispute settlement. Japan subsequently signed agreements with Malaysia (2005), Indonesia (2006), Philippines (2006), Brunei (2007), Thailand (2007), and Vietnam (2009). In these Japan made concessions on admitting some agricultural products, but not rice. The agreement with the Philippines opened Japan's nursing-care market to Japanese-speaking Filipinos. Japan also completed negotiations with Switzerland for a free-trade agreement in 2009, the first agreement with a European nation.

Japan also made defensive trade moves in the western hemisphere. It signed its second bilateral free-trade agreement with Mexico in September 2004, so as to ensure its corporations use of NAFTA. Japan did address sensitive agricultural issues. It set import quotas for Mexican beef, chicken, and oranges. Mexico agreed to liberalize imports of Japanese automobiles and steel. The agreement also covered dispute settlement, safeguards, competition policy, and investment protections. Another with Chile in March 2007 followed similar actions by the US and the EU.

Canada

Canada, a longtime supporter of multilateral trade liberalization, was one of the first to play the bilateral card. Fearful of losing access to a fortress Europe and to the US, it proposed free-trade negotiations with the US in 1985 that led to the Canadian–US Free Trade Agreement (CUSFTA) bilateral and eventually to NAFTA (including Mexico) in 1994. Subsequently, it negotiated bilateral free-trade agreements with Israel (1997), Chile (1997),

Costa Rica (2002), the European Free Trade Association (EFTA) (2002), Jordan (2008), Peru (2008), and Colombia (2008). EFTA includes Iceland, Liechtenstein, Norway, and Switzerland.

Canada was slower than the US to pursue bilateral and regional FTAs aggressively – preferring to think that the multilateral WTO negotiating process held the greatest potential for the largest gains. However, Canadian agriculture fears falling behind the US in negotiating FTAs with countries that are important markets.

In May 2009, Canada opened negotiations with the European Union for a Comprehensive Economic and Trade Agreement (CETA), a pact that would be broader than NAFTA. The negotiations go beyond tariff issues and attempt to address technical and administrative barriers, reciprocity, labor flexibility, government purchasing, capital flows, and environmental issues. Controversial issues involve agriculture, where the EU wants greater access for dairy products, and Canada seeks lower EU duties on beef, cereals, and pork. Also troublesome is government procurement. Ontario, a manufacturing province, fears major losses if Canadian provincial and local government procurement is opened to the EU. Some citizen activists fear the agreement will lead to the privatization of public services in Canada, and include an investment provision permitting private companies to challenge in private tribunals the laws and regulations of a government party to the agreement.[31]

China

China is another late-comer to regionalization. Determined to win membership in the WTO and thus eligibility for nondiscriminatory tariff treatment of its exports, China kept a low profile in multilateral negotiations. When it became clear that gains from the Doha multilateral round would be insignificant, China also began to pursue regional and bilateral approaches. Aware of the danger of relying on the US and Western Europe for export markets, China recognized the opportunity to find both export markets and resources in the Asian region. China's immediate goals are to promote East Asian economic integration, tying smaller countries of the region with abundant resources – like Indonesia – more closely to China. It also desires to promote a Northeast Asian FTA with Japan and Korea. Free-trade agreements are thus a way to enhance competitiveness, not to achieve the political benefits of integration, as in Western Europe. China also seeks to secure access to critical energy and industrial raw materials.[32]

It opened negotiations first with countries having close regional ties, such as Australia, Hong Kong and Macao, and New Zealand. China also began negotiations in November 2001 with the ten-member ASEAN bloc, and concluded a framework agreement in 2002. This FTA took effect in January 2010 for 1.7 billion people. The provisions apply to newer members of ASEAN in 2015. The parties had an early harvest of agreements on goods, dispute settlement, and trade in services. China and Thailand concluded a limited FTA in October 2003 removing tariffs for 188 types of fruits and vegetables. The two parties hoped to conclude a comprehensive agreement by 2010.

To obtain access to foreign natural resources China has also employed FTAs. Among them are pacts with the Gulf Cooperation Council, Chile (2006), and Peru (2008). In April 2010, it signed an FTA with Costa Rica, enabling Costa to export agricultural products like coffee, meat, and juice, as well as high-tech products like Intel's computer microprocessors, to China in exchange for a wide variety of Chinese consumer goods.

Unlike lengthy US FTAs, Chinese agreements are usually brief and focused on trade in goods. Chinese agreements typically do not address intellectual property, investment, service issues, and dispute settlement. Nor do they consider non-WTO matters such as labor and the environment.

India

A founding member of GATT, India, like other major trading powers, has pursued regional and bilateral trade agreements with Sri Lanka, Bangladesh, Bhutan, Sri Lanka, Maldives, Nepal, China, ASEAN, and South Korea. There is also an economic cooperation agreement with Singapore and framework agreements with ASEAN and Chile. India's policy initially emphasized its smaller neighbors in the South Asian region, and its agreements are riddled with exceptions and cover a small share of two-way trade.[33]

The ASEAN–India Free Trade Agreement (AIFTA), concluded in 2009, covered goods and will eliminate tariffs gradually on 80 percent of all trade. The parties are continuing to negotiate liberalization of trade in services and investments, both deeper forms of economic integration.

The comprehensive partnership agreement with South Korea also phases out tariffs slowly over a ten-year period. It excludes fisheries and some agricultural products, but covers services and investments. A provision pertaining to skilled professionals opens the way for computer programmers and engineers to work temporarily in each country.[34]

India opened negotiations with the European Union in June 2007 on a bilateral free-trade and investment agreement, but a series of controversies have delayed the discussions. The European Parliament wants the sensitive topics of child labor and environmental carbon emissions included. Another controversy involves stricter standards for India's generic drug makers that might limit the sale of drugs to developing countries. The EU also has sought to gain access to India's services sector and government procurement, and obtain liberalized rules for foreign investment, which India resists. And the EU has been reluctant to ease stringent food safety standards and rules governing Indian professionals working in the EU.[35]

India and China are negotiating a bilateral trade agreement, described as similar to a free-trade agreement. Trade between the two countries has been growing rapidly – more than 30 percent annually – but much of it involves exports of India's raw materials which return as China's higher value finished goods. India's small- and medium-sized businesses complain about cheap Chinese imports undercutting their markets. Meanwhile, India's service exporters say that China's non-tariff barriers and restrictions on procurement handicap Indian exporters.[36]

South Korea

As the new millennium opened South Korea, long renowned for its protectionist trade policies, initiated bilateral and regional free-trade negotiations to improve its access to key markets. As an economy highly dependent on imports of Middle East oil, Korea relied on export earnings to support its appetite for petroleum. Government officials feared Korea could not survive without joining the quest for free-trade agreements. Many of its leading trading partners – the US, the EU, and Japan – were negotiating bilateral deals. Korean industry worried about exclusion from key markets. Export industries faced competition from China in lower price brackets, and from Japan in the higher end.

Recognizing that free-trade deals faced vehement opposition from farmers and workers in import-sensitive industries, Korea turned first to a distant non-Asian country, Chile, and then to smaller Singapore. It excluded politically sensitive rice from the negotiations. Even so the Chilean agreement faced massive resistance from farmers and anti-globalization activists.

Korea then focused on the US. In 2006–7 the two countries negotiated a bilateral FTA that apparently opened Korea's protected home market to US beef imports and improved access for American movies. The agreement aroused militant opposition from Korean farmers and workers, who marched and demonstrated. President Lee Myung-bak did not back down, saying that Korea is "sandwiched between China and Japan. ..." Parliamentary ratification of the pact would "help Korea overcome its economic sandwich position."[37]

Elected in 2007, President Lee, a former chief executive of Hyundai, was a free-marketer determined to revive Korea's economy and achieve 7 percent growth. Known as the bulldozer because of his forceful style, Lee was a pragmatic businessman and globalization enthusiast, determined to advance his country's competitiveness. To revive the Korean economy after a decade of leftist rule and social spending, he set out to revive 7 percent growth, attract foreign investment, and generate export-related jobs. To do so, Lee looked to free-trade agreements with the US, the European Union, Peru, Colombia, Canada, and Australia. He also wanted such agreements with neighboring China and Japan.[38]

By early 2010 Korea had secured and implemented FTAs with Chile, Singapore, the European Free Trade Association, ASEAN, and India. It had negotiated agreements with the US and the EU, and was holding negotiations with Peru, Australia, New Zealand, Canada, Mexico, Colombia, and the Gulf Cooperation Council.

Brazil

As the economic leader of the Mercosur bloc, which includes Argentina, Paraguay, and Uruguay, Brazil is eager to negotiate with the European Union and the US as an equal. The Mercosur group has concluded FTAs with Colombia, Ecuador, Venezuela, and Peru to establish the base for a proposed South American Community of Nations. Negotiations with the EU have foundered over issues of European agricultural subsidies, services, and removal of duties on auto products, but Mercosur concluded an agreement with Israel in 2007.[39]

President Lula Da Silva, a former left-wing union leader, came to power in 2000 criticizing the proposed Free Trade Agreement for the Americas (FTAA). He later advocated free-trade agreements that take into account the interests of developing countries. Eager to advance Brazil's role as a leader of an emerging nations bloc, he proposed a free-trade pact between Mercosur and India and South Africa, on the grounds that this grouping would create the world's largest free-trade area. In 2010 he pushed an agreement between Mercosur and Caricom, the 14-member Caribbean Community, as well as one between Mercosur and Palestine. Brazil also agreed to move forward on a bilateral trade agreement with Mexico. It had long viewed an agreement with Mexico as a Trojan horse for US investors. But by 2010 a different perspective prevailed. An emerging Brazil saw the opportunity to lure Mexico into a relationship with fellow Latin American countries and to expand Brazil's interests in Mexico.

Conclusion

During the period beginning in 1980 trade revived but trading patterns changed markedly. Led by China and Japan, East Asia emerged as an export powerhouse, accumulating large monetary reserves from export sales and inbound investments. The US and the UK evolved into major importers of developing-world manufactures and leading suppliers of financial and business services. The temporary GATT multilateral system metamorphosed into the permanent WTO. It had a stronger dispute-resolution system and a broader mandate to address non-tariff issues. Differences between emerging and developed countries over key issues stymied multilateral negotiations. Instead trading powers turned to narrower regional and bilateral agreements to gain improved market access, while not abandoning the WTO process.

Chapter 7

Global Business

During the last decades of the twentieth century the integration and internationalization of markets transformed the world of business. Corporations based in Western Europe, North America, and Japan gradually expanded beyond national boundaries. They established positions in other high-income markets, and by the 1990s moved into key emerging markets, such as Brazil, China, and India. Many of these multinational corporations fashioned global supply networks, enabling them to produce, distribute, and market goods and services wherever they chose at the most advantageous price. Border barriers they deemed an unwarranted relic of the Cold War nationalism, a burden to mutually beneficial commerce, and an interference with free-market forces transforming the world. While much of the new international business involved regional activity, pundits and business leaders increasingly spoke about the global economy as if it were a single market, rather than the sum of differentiated regional and national markets. In the words of Japanese management consultant Kenichi Ohmae, "Being a global player means viewing the world global market as your proper soil, your place to plant trees and nourish them."[1]

Over the last generation globalization has had far-reaching effects. None was more significant than the integration of markets. Prior to the late twentieth century, independent nations used tariffs, immigration barriers, and currency controls to preserve their own markets, traditions, cultures, and forms of government. Behind these border barriers the pace of life often seemed slower and less risky. Sometimes there was little change from generation to generation.

With the emergence of integrated regional and global markets, workers in once remote locations specialized and competed for work in the sometimes chaotic world market. These new workers, and consumers,

The Contemporary Global Economy: A History Since 1980, First Edition. Alfred E. Eckes, Jr.
© 2011 Alfred E. Eckes, Jr. Published 2011 by Blackwell Publishing Ltd.

benefitting from higher incomes, began to buy internationally traded apparel, electronics, and even motor vehicles, such as scooters and entry-level cars and trucks. Using the internet and cell phones, they could easily contact relatives and friends in distant locations. With the freer flow of information and economic opportunities, individuals became more engaged in discussing issues of concern, such as global warming, pollution, sweatshops, and even political issues involving the Kurds, Tibetans, and other minorities. As a consequence of globalization, and the opportunities presented by wider markets, access to capital, and technology, a number of newly industrializing countries – Brazil, China, India, South Korea, and a number of smaller countries in East and Southeast Asia – became low-cost suppliers to world markets and advanced rapidly up the ladder of economic growth. Some even launched their own multinational firms.[2]

The emergence of these new competitors – and their corporate champions – brought a radical transformation to the world's industrial map, as major centers of production shifted to the Pacific and East Asia. The last similar realignment in the world's industrial production had occurred before and during World War I when Germany, the United States, and Japan challenged Britain's leadership in manufacturing.

As noted earlier, the phenomenal expansion of international business in the last generation of the twentieth century reflected a variety of factors – political, technological, economic, and demographic. The end of the Cold War, improvements in communications, transportation, and information processing all were important, as was renewed growth and price stability. Several long-term demographic and economic trends also shaped the new environment. As noted in Chapter 1, they included rapid population growth and urbanization in developing countries, as well as rapid economic growth. The latter empowered millions of new consumers with middle-class incomes and aspirations, and attracted multinational business. To business strategists the message was clear: to prosper in the twenty-first century corporations needed a strong commitment to the world's emerging and rapidly growing markets.[3]

Increasing International Business Activity

Multinationals and transnationals

Given long-run trends, it is not surprising that more and more companies awakened to opportunities outside their home markets. Corporations with operations in more than one country are usually called multinational corporations (MNCs) or transnational corporations (TNCs).* Some are resource-oriented firms, like ExxonMobil, Shell, or BP (formerly British Petroleum). Others are manufacturing firms supplying intermediate goods, or selling consumer products. Among them are General Electric (US), Toyota Motor Corporation (Japan), and Ford Motor Company (US). Still others are insurance, banking, or shipping companies, which trade in services. Among the largest service providers are Vodaphone (UK), and a variety of telecommunications and utility companies in Western Europe. Deutsche Post AG, for example, has 283,699 foreign employees, many working for DHL, its parcel service provider and logistics firm which competes with UPS and FedEx.

According to UNCTAD, in 2008 there were an estimated 82,000 transnational corporations with 810,000 foreign affiliates. The total stock of foreign direct investment stood at some $16.2 trillion, with annual outflows of nearly $2 trillion. In 1990, when the UN agency began to report on transnationals, there were 35,000 with 150,000 foreign affiliates. At that time the total stock of FDI stood at some $1.7 trillion with annual flows of $225 billion. Affiliates of transnationals are thought to account for one-third of world exports of goods and services and to employ about 80 million people worldwide, 16 million of them in China. In the mid-1980s these affiliates accounted for a similar share of world exports and employed 22 million outside their home countries. Among the largest and most prominent MNCs as measured by employment are retailers Wal-Mart (US) with over 648,905 foreign workers out of 2.1 million, and Carrefour (France) with 363,311 foreign workers among 495,287.[4]

A list of the 100 largest non-financial TNCs shows that the majority are in manufacturing, but that an increasing number are in services. Also, most TNCs count North America, Western Europe, or Japan as their home economy. Among the top 100 transnationals, 92 listed one of the above as home. A small but rising number are based in developing countries. Among the top 100 nonfinancial firms in 2008, Korea and China both had two, while Hong Kong, Malaysia, and Mexico each had one. However, UNCTAD estimates that TNCs from developing and transition economies account for more than a quarter of 82,000 transnationals.[5]

It is worth emphasizing that international business is the domain of large corporations. Inexperience and the complexity of operating in different regulatory and cultural environments discourage many medium-size and

---

* We use the terms multinational and transnational corporations interchangeably to avoid confusion.

small businesses. In the European Union and the United States few small and medium-sized firms export, despite official efforts to promote trade. In the US the top 10 percent of exporting firms account for well over 90 percent of exports by value. UNCTAD has reported that the 100 largest corporations combine to produce value-added approximately equal to 4 percent of world GDP.[6]

State-owned enterprises

Many multinationals are state-owned enterprises. In various sectors private multinationals compete head-to-head with state-owned enterprises supported politically and financially by governments with substantial holdings of foreign reserves. Brazil, China, India, and Russia are among the most active. Between 2005 and 2010, 40 companies from those four countries moved onto the *Forbes* Global 500 list of the world's largest companies. Altogether developing and former Eastern bloc countries accounted for 95 of the 500 firms. Their activities ranged from finance and services to manufacturing and resources. Governments owned and operated the world's largest energy companies. These included Saudi Aramco, Gazprom (Russia), China National Petroleum Corp., Petrobras (Brazil), and others. Political scientist Ian Bremmer says that state-owned oil companies control more than 75 percent of all crude oil production. In 2005, China's state-owned companies accounted for 16 percent of that country's total trade.[7]

The global expansion of state-owned enterprises has aroused concerns in some countries. In April 2010 when Sinopec, one of China's national energy companies, announced it was buying a share of Canadian oil sands producer Syncrude, there were fears that China might use its stake as a vehicle to pressure Canada on public policy, or for espionage. In Australia, Chinese state-owned enterprises have purchased stakes in Australian natural resource companies, and have encountered government restrictions. Australia's Foreign Investment Review Board indicated that state-owned enterprises should not seek more than 15 percent of major producers and less than 50 percent of green-fields projects. Of China's $51.1 billion in outbound investment for mergers and acquisitions in 2008, more than 60 percent targeted natural resource firms.[8]

Prelude to Corporate Globalism

To understand recent controversies, an historical perspective is needed. After the Great Depression and World War II, international business revived slowly. Europe and Japan suffered heavy war damage, and their governments restricted trade and payments for balance-of-payments reasons. In the developing world, nationalism and political instability discouraged risk-taking. US firms, which had been active in Europe during the interwar period, soon returned and sought to establish a strong presence in the European Common Market and the European Free Trade Association (EFTA). The latter, a less-binding association of seven European countries, offered an alternative form of economic integration. Its members – the so-called "Outer Seven" – included Austria, Denmark, Norway, Portugal, Sweden, Switzerland, and the United Kingdom. From 1966 to 1970, the value of US foreign direct investment in Europe (historical cost basis) rose from $16.4 billion to $25.3 billion. It climbed to $96.3 billion in 1980. US multinationals like IBM, Ford, and General Motors expanded rapidly in Western Europe to serve consumer markets.[9]

As trans-oceanic jet travel and a reliable international telephone service became available in the late 1950s, many large corporations moved to fashion globally integrated production and marketing systems. Initially there was an absence of central control. That would come in the 1970s with improved communications technology (satellites), container ships, and wide-bodied passenger jets. What distinguished the new multinationals from earlier forms was equity control of globally, or regionally, integrated production and marketing systems. Controlled by a headquarters corporation, the new MNCs were essentially owned and managed by residents of the home country.

Corporate leaders like Irving Shapiro, chairman of DuPont, began to tout one-world economics. According to Shapiro, developments in technology, including communications and transportation, made it possible for corporations to look beyond national boundaries to the challenges of serving worldwide markets. Henry Schacht, the CEO of Cummins Engine, put it more bluntly: "Business cannot continue to think in terms of national boundaries; they are no longer relevant. Aggressive business institutions, in the last ten years, have rapidly adopted the global point of view." The multinational corporation, he said, wanted "the opportunity to compete" without hiding behind national boundaries. There should be no restrictions on where a multinational corporation obtains its material, money, and labor.[10]

American challenge

The European Economic Community with its common external tariff attracted a surge of US investments to continental Europe in the 1960s. This flow, along with concerns about home-country dominated corporate structures, aroused host-country political sensitivities to foreign takeovers. French journalist Jean-Jacques Servan-Schreiber's 1967 book, *The American Challenge,* played to those concerns. Better-organized American companies, he asserted, were rolling from Naples to Amsterdam with the ease of Israeli tanks in Sinai during the 1967 war. He warned that Europe might lose its economic identity and become a US subsidiary, overrun by US technology and corporate influence.[11]

Servan-Schreiber's book helped fan discontent in Europe, and over the next decade several host governments moved to regulate international business. Some European leaders interpreted the "American challenge" as a call to arms and responded with a series of new industrial policies, national enterprise boards, and joint projects in technology, from Eureka to Esprit and Airbus Industrie. They sought to establish regional champions and to restrict US investments. Airbus, the European collaborative project to build a world-class aircraft industry, had origins in European aspirations to compete with US manufacturers. Cooperation in aviation was viewed as a means to promote long-term economic and technological progress in Europe. As noted in Chapter 8, President Charles de Gaulle of France sought to slow the American corporate advance by converting France's dollar reserves into gold. Because the US Treasury had inadequate gold to honor its pledge to convert upon demand, the Johnson administration had to impose controls on US capital exports to avoid a dollar crisis. By August, 1971, US authorities could postpone dollar devaluation no longer, and over time the world moved to a system of floating currency rates.[12]

Turbulent times and economic malaise

The long and costly war in Vietnam, ending in America's defeat, also contributed to business pessimism during the 1970s. So did quadrupling of oil prices, resulting from the OPEC oil embargo of 1973, which ignited price inflation around the world. The saturation of consumer markets in the high-income countries, proliferation of government regulatory activity to achieve health, safety, and environmental concerns, and deficient tax and monetary policies led to slower business growth, rising unemployment, and resource shortages. Declining productivity gains and stagnant gains in real income contributed to the economic malaise.

In Europe, the first signs of "Euro sclerosis," or economic stagnation, appeared with sluggish growth and high unemployment in welfare states. Unemployment, which had been 2 percent in the 1960s, reached 11 percent in 1984. Economists attributed the sluggish situation to higher energy costs, slower population growth, high marginal tax rates, and technological advances. One of the chief causes was thought to be rigid labor markets with centralized wage bargaining. Whereas US firms were able to shed their least productive workers in hard times, and hire new workers at lower wages, the labor market rigidities discouraged European firms from hiring new workers. As a result, while the US economy generated 20 million new jobs in the decade after the oil shock, Europe produced an army of unemployed – some 19 million by the mid-1980s.[13]

On top of these problems, other Cassandras voiced prophecies of environmental disasters and famine during the 1970s. Scientists and technocrats associated with the Club of Rome, an international group funded by Italian industrialist Aurelio Peccei, issued an urgent warning that uncontrolled growth of population and technology must be regulated or human society faced total collapse. They predicted food and resource shortages as economic and population growth pressed on finite resources. The doomsayers, whose dire predictions hearkened back to the pessimistic forecasts of the Reverend Robert Malthus (1766–1834), called for reduced consumption and greater sensitivity to environmental consequences.

These were not the only gloomy forecasts to dash business optimism in the 1970s. To make matters worse, meteorologists warned of global cooling, another Ice Age, and reduced food production. Some predicted catastrophic famines. In a book titled *Famine 1975!* William and Paul Paddock asserted in 1967 that the world's population growth would soon overtake the capacity of developing countries to feed their populations.

Multinationals and third-world nationalism

Meanwhile the political environment for business deteriorated internationally. In the developing world, a Group of 77 nations organized at the end of the first session of the United Nations Conference on Trade and Development in 1965. The leaders railed about exploitation, and called for a new economic order with automatic transfers of resources from developed to developing countries. In May 1974 the UN General Assembly joined the fray, approving a declaration on the establishment of a new international economic order. It complained about the remaining vestiges of foreign occupation, alien and colonial domination, and neo-colonialism in all forms, and observed that developing countries constituting 70 percent of the world's population accounted for only 30 percent of the world's income. The declaration encouraged as a sovereign right the nationalization of natural resources and "all economic activities." It asserted the right of sovereign countries to regulate and supervise the activities of transnational corporations. It demanded preferential and non-reciprocal treatment for developing countries in all fields of international economic cooperation. It also demanded technology transfers, financial aid, and restitution and full compensation for past exploitation.[14]

In effect, the new militance among developing countries mirrored the success of OPEC in quadrupling oil prices in 1973. OPEC's initiative had awakened the Group of 77 to their power, and given them a sense of purpose and direction. Developing nations thus sought to employ their voting majority in the UN system to reorganize the rules of the international economy. The appearance of north–south conflict between "haves" and "have-nots," and involvement of the UN thus represented a distinct challenge to multinational enterprise and foreign investment.

Protests about the dark activities of multinationals were not confined to poor countries and their governments. The United Nations organized a study group on multinationals to investigate the impact of MNCs on development and international relations. Witnesses railed about the insensitive behavior of MNCs in failing to make decisions locally and in bribing host governments. From the hostile tone of the UN hearing, the international business community concluded that it should expect the hostility of host countries toward MNCs to increase. Multinational business was told to expect greater national planning in developing countries and more regulations and restrictions.

Grim expectations for the 1980s

As the 1970s ended, major economies faced double-digit inflation, labor unrest, and a second oil price hike, this one stemming from the overthrow of the Shah's regime in Iran. Once again consumers in high-income nations found their prosperity jeopardized by events in the oil-rich, but turbulent, Middle East. Business pundits in Europe and North America expected the 1980s to see more of the same. So did economists at respected international agencies. They released bleak forecasts predicting more unemployment, inflation, and stagnant business conditions in the new decade. The IMF in Washington observed that "the current environment of great uncertainty clearly foreshadows a period of severe strains in the world economy. ..." The Bank for International Settlements in Basel warned about the acceleration of inflation in all industrial countries. The Paris-based Organization for Economic Cooperation and Development predicted a 21 percent hike in oil prices, and double-digit inflation. It forecast a recession in the US (as it turned out, the sharpest since the Great Depression) and sub-par growth in Western Europe.[15]

Declining competitiveness and the Japanese challenge

Against these short-term and cyclical conditions big business saw limited investment opportunities and much-increased foreign competition in home markets. In Europe and North America there was growing apprehension about the competitiveness of industries and their abilities to survive the Japanese business challenge. While the Japanese did not hesitate to cut prices to gain market share, they also produced quality products that appealed to consumers. In both Western Europe and North America Japanese products steadily picked up market share as consumers bought Canon cameras, Sony electronics, and Toyota cars, among the better Japanese exports. This gain in market share came at the expense of traditional suppliers like Kodak, Grundig, Philips, and General Motors. From 1960 to 1980, Japan had more than doubled its share of world exports from 3.1 to 6.4 percent, whereas Britain's share had fallen from 8.2 to 5.4 percent and America's from 15.1 to 11.1 percent. France and West Germany had improved their own shares of world exports by less than a percentage point, as they gradually abandoned product markets.[16]

The Japanese business incursion set off alarm bells in North America and Europe. In 1979 Harvard professor Ezra Vogel captured public attention with the publication of his best-selling book, *Japan as Number One: Lessons for America*. Concluding that America was in trouble, Vogel warned that Japan was on the verge of surpassing the United States to become the dominant economic power. He attributed Japan's successful challenge to superior industrial competitiveness, partly a result of innovative management practices and successful business–government cooperation. Vogel urged America to respond not simply with adjustments to fiscal and monetary policies but also with industrial policy in which government could target selected industries. He recommended establishing a cadre of senior bureaucrats to implement a strategy that nurtured export-competitive industries and phased-out declining ones – essentially picking winners and losers.[17]

Industrial policy debate: US

Vogel's proposals stimulated heated debate, and the idea of a national competitiveness policy appealed to some Democrats in the US, including

Senator Walter Mondale, the 1984 presidential nominee. It also enjoyed support from organized labor, economists like Lester Thurow of MIT, and investment banker Felix Rohatyn who wanted Congress to establish a new version of the Reconstruction Finance Corporation to aid distressed industries. Robert Reich and Ira Magaziner also pushed industrial-policy during this period, and later influenced the Clinton administration's approach.[18]

Among big businesses and their Republican allies there was little support for interventionist industrial policy, that is, managed by government officials. President Ronald Reagan, and his successor George H. W. Bush, preferred market-based solutions involving deregulation and tax incentives. Martin Feldstein, the Reagan administration's chief economist, questioned whether industrial policy was responsible for Japan's economic success and whether it could be successfully transplanted abroad. He dismissed any policy that increased government planning as a "burden on our economic life and a threat to our long-term economic prosperity."[19]

Public interest in the competitiveness issue prompted the Reagan administration to establish a presidential commission on industrial competitiveness. Chaired by Hewlett-Packard CEO John Young, it was directed to examine the issues and make recommendations after the 1984 presidential election. The commission's report, reflecting the high-tech perspectives of some members, emphasized that while the United States was still the world's strongest economy, it was "losing its ability to compete in the world's markets." The report proposed four specific measures to improve competitiveness: (a) creating an economic climate that encourages public and private investment; (b) emphasizing education, training, and regular retraining; (c) supplementing the existing commitment to basic science with an active technology policy; and (d) promoting US exports and adopting a foreign economic policy to open markets around the world. Nonetheless, Young's report disturbed the free-enterprise Reagan administration with its insistence that government was responsible for creating an environment within which American business could effectively compete. He also claimed that "government has not yet effectively performed the legitimate roles it already has."[20]

Not surprisingly, given its activist conclusions, the presidential commission had little impact on policy during the Reagan administration. During a Cabinet briefing the president reportedly asked in a note "If the US is in such trouble, why are the Europeans so jealous?" After the 1984 elections, the domestic economy seemed stronger, and the administration celebrated, "It's morning in America again!"[21]

As it turned out, the first Bush administration was more supportive of action on the competitiveness front with its efforts to reduce government deficits and promote educational reform. But it was the Clinton adminis- tration that articulated a competitiveness strategy and took a series of interventionist actions. It increased funding for the internet and for pro- grams to speed the transfer of technologies from universities and national laboratories to the commercial market. Clinton also emphasized training and lifelong learning to prepare ordinary Americans for an era of global competition and rapid change. And the strategy rested on a mixture of fiscal and monetary policies that produced low interest rates and nurtured business innovation.[22]

Industrial policy: Europe

In Europe, where there was a long tradition of government intervention and industrial policy, the Japanese challenge produced different policy reactions. After World War II socialist governments in that region saw nationalization as a way for governments to control the "commanding heights" of national economies. During the 1970s, in response to growing international competition, industrial policy gained new life. In France the socialists and communists worked together during the 1970s to expand the role of the state, nationalizing industries and encouraging state enterprises to expand their scope. One state enterprise, Renault, purchased major stakes in Mack Trucks and American Motors, and diversified into agricul- tural machinery, machine tools, and robotics. French industrial policy focused on automobiles, electronics, and steel, as well as emerging infor- mation and biotech industries. In Italy industrial policy focused on devel- oping state champions in electronics, aerospace, and nuclear energy. In the late 1970s state-owned banks rescued failing state firms and industrial groups.

In Britain and Germany, industrial policies were less ambitious. During the 1970s the British government acted defensively to prevent widespread unemployment when it took over automakers Rolls Royce and Leyland, and then British Steel. Conservative Prime Minister Margaret Thatcher talked the language of privatization and free enterprise, but her govern- ment encouraged public investment in computers, microtechnology, and other exotic areas where the private sector might not invest. German politi- cians also spoke the language of the free market, but they too encouraged state investment in public corporations. The public corporations were advised to enter new areas and expand overseas.[23]

The Challenge of Open Markets

Rising import competition

Until the late 1970s few industries in high-income countries had experienced serious competition in their home market. Imports from cheap-labor countries first hammered labor-intensive industries such as textiles, apparel, footwear, and consumer electronics. By the early 1980s imports impacted most major industries, particularly steel, automobiles, and machine tools, where unions had used their negotiating power in the post-World War II period to exact high wages and benefits. The large American market, with 227 million high-income consumers and a per capita GDP of $22,568 (constant 2000 US$), was an inviting target – and a market relatively open to foreign exporters. As a result of multilateral negotiations begun in 1947 under the auspices of GATT, tariff barriers were no longer a significant barrier to trade in industrial products. Completion of the GATT Kennedy Round of tariff reductions in 1967 (implemented over a five-year period) and the Tokyo Round in 1979 effectively opened the US market. The US average *ad valorem* tariff on dutiable products fell from 12.2 percent in 1967 to 8.6 percent in 1972, and to an inconsequential 5.7 percent by 1980 at the close of the Tokyo Round of GATT negotiations. American leaders embraced and encouraged these changes, partly for national security reasons. They perceived that a prosperous Japan and Europe would be stronger allies in the Cold War competition with the Soviet Union and China. At the end of the Kennedy Round, the US Secretary of Commerce saw the writing on the wall and alerted the business community that tariff reductions represented a large step toward a "truly one-world market." The large and lucrative American market, he added, was "no longer the private preserve of the American businessman."[24]

In Japan and the European Community governments yielded more slowly to the global-market imperative. While GATT negotiations also lowered their duties on imported manufactures, some governments – especially France and Japan – employed a variety of ingenious non-tariff barriers (voluntary restraint agreements, product standards, and customs procedures) to manage import competition and reduce pressure on domestic manufacturers. France, eager to develop its own video recorder industry, required all importers of Japanese video recorders in 1982 to bring their shipments through customs at the remote, understaffed customs post of Poitiers, 210 miles south of Paris. The regulation virtually ended the flow of foreign VCR imports.

The Japanese were even more imaginative, using quotas and safety standards to keep out foreign competition. To reduce competition from European and American ski manufacturers, the Japanese imposed new safety standards claiming that Japanese snow conditions were different. Japan required that imported cars be tested in Japan rather than in foreign plants where they were assembled. They required that cosmetics companies test production in Japan because Japanese skin was different. Similar arguments were employed to restrict US beef, citrus, rice, leather, and tobacco, as well as semiconductors, supercomputers, and telecommunications.

Other factors, in addition to trade liberalization, boosted global competition during the 1980s. The widespread use of containers, jet freighters, and wide-bodied ships reduced freight rates and facilitated the expansion of trade. So did the widespread use of subsidies to stimulate exports and sustain domestic employment. State-owned European steel producers entered the American market and, benefitting from government subsidies, seized market share from US producers. Rather than cut jobs, they chose to export steel with steep discounts on hot- and cold-rolled steel products, forcing foreign competitors to cut back. In effect, it was a beggar-thy-neighbor strategy.

Surging foreign investments

Devaluation of the dollar during the 1970s made it more attractive for European and Japanese businesses to invest in the US market, take over existing plants, or build new facilities, and compete with American multinationals on their home turf. Over a 20-year period, the dollar-purchasing power of the German mark, the Dutch guilder, Japanese yen, and Swiss franc doubled, enabling the surge in overseas investments. The influx of foreign investment was so large that the net book-value of foreign investment in the US, which doubled after 1974, expanded at nearly twice the rate of US outward investment during the 1970s. British Petroleum completed its purchase of Sohio, and foreign companies became big investors in autos, electronics, chemicals, machinery, real estate, and retail. European banks took advantage of a favorable regulatory climate to expand their presence.

Thus by the 1980s the shoe was on the other foot. European and Japanese industrialists had turned the tables on American multinationals, and targeted the lucrative American market. French tire-maker Michelin and German carmaker Volkswagen set up North American plants. Electrolux of Sweden, Philips of the Netherlands, and Thomson of France all purchased US competitors. Because Europe had rigid work rules and high labor costs, the European business giants frequently chose to serve the affluent North American market through local production rather than exports from Europe.

Japanese competition intensified – particularly for US makers of steel, automobiles, machine tools, and televisions and electronics. The bilateral US trade balance with Japan became increasingly unbalanced, with merchandise deficits rising from $1.7 billion in 1975, to $10.4 billion in 1980, $46.2 billion in 1985, and remaining at $41.1 billion in 1990.[25]

Beginning in 1972 Japanese investors snapped up prestigious hotels in Hawaii, bought the famed Pebble Beach golf course in California, the Rockefeller Center in New York, and Columbia Pictures. But their investments in manufacturing often took a different form. Rather than buying older unionized facilities, they invested in green-field manufacturing facilities, such as auto plants in Kentucky, Ohio, and Tennessee. The Japanese located the plants in rural areas near interstate highways where they could hire good quality labor with a strong work ethic, and avoid conflicts with unions and minorities. The politically sophisticated Japanese spread their investments across America, gaining political leverage in Washington from grateful officials at the state and local levels.

The US response

Like Europeans 20 years earlier, Americans became uneasy in the early 1980s about the rising tide of foreign imports and investments. During the severe recession of 1981–3, protectionist solutions gained appeal. In Washington, DC, there was growing support in Congress for buy-America proposals, voluntary restraint measures, and other political solutions to protect US industry from Japanese competition. The legal approach also attracted interest as trade lawyers filed hundreds of cases under US import remedy laws seeking relief from import surges or unfair trading practices, such as dumping, harmful subsidies, and infringement of intellectual property rights. Under the anti-dumping and countervailing duty laws, industries could file cases with the US Department of Commerce and the independent US International Trade Commission, setting in motion an investigative process that often ended with the imposition of duties. Agency decisions were reviewable in courts of law, and could not be set aside for policy reasons by the Executive Branch. In 1982 and 1983 US steel producers filed hundreds of cases aimed at reducing import competition from Europe and Japan, as well as some emerging producers in countries like

Brazil and Korea. In 1982 Harley-Davidson, the iconic motorcycle producer, faced a surge of imports from Japanese competitors, and filed for temporary protection under the so-called escape clause. An investigative process led the US International Trade Commission to recommend, and the Reagan administration to impose a high tariff on heavy motorcycle imports. The resulting relief sheltered Harley from import competition, and enabled it to restructure and become export competitive. Later President Reagan traveled to Harley's manufacturing facility and effused: "Like America, Harley is back and standing tall." He asserted that "where US firms have suffered from temporary surges in foreign competition, we haven't been shy about using our import laws to produce temporary relief. ..."[26]

As other industries sought to use similar import remedy laws to gain similar relief, many media pundits worried about increasing protectionism and trade wars. The Reagan administration signaled its opposition to long-term protection, and encouraged Japanese producers to invest in US manufacturing facilities. During the 1980s Japanese investment grew from $4.2 billion in 1980 to $70 billion in 1990, reflecting the influx of Japanese auto producers and their suppliers.[27]

Practical experience competing with imports during the 1980s was a major factor influencing more corporations to embrace globalization and accept inevitable adjustments. During that decade the auto industry lost a third of the domestic market, and steel producers a quarter of their market. The pressure from imports forced American firms to abandon product lines that they had pioneered. Famous electronics brands such as Magnavox, Sylvania, and Philco were sold to Philips of the Netherlands. Zenith, the last American television maker, sold out later to Lucky Goldstar of Korea. At the end of the 1980s *Forbes* magazine interviewed 24 chief executives about what they had learned from the new competition. The principal lesson was "go global or die." According to David Roderick, the chairman of USX, who fought a long and costly battle to protect the American market from dumped and subsidized steel, "we learned we were in an irreversible, growing globalization of the marketplace," and that survival required painful steps to improve productivity and improve product quality. Said Ford Chairman Donald Petersen, "We learned that there's no market for lousy cars; we tested it. ..."[28]

As a result, corporations adopted a number of survival strategies – including sharp cost-cutting, efforts to reduce personnel costs with fewer white- and blue-collar workers, investing in new technologies, and joint ventures to improve opportunities for competing in foreign markets. CEOs operated with guns at their heads.

Europe's response

As in the US, the Japanese competitive challenge aroused concern among European businesses and governments. Before trade policy was transferred to the European Commission, member states imposed quotas on sensitive products. In 1970, for example, Italy had quotas on more than 50 Japanese products, France 30, and West Germany more than 10. European officials complained that Japan was not sufficiently integrated with the international economy. In employing anti-dumping and voluntary export restraints to restrain the Asian advance, officials in Brussels took a defensive approach. The European Commission also negotiated voluntary restraint agreements on Japanese automobiles, and similar agreements covering trade in textile and steel products. Enthusiasm for unilateral measures and Japanese bashing would decline in the late 1980s, as Japanese investments soared. There was growing concern in some European capitals – notably London – that pursuing the hard line would jeopardize inflows of investments that generated high-skilled jobs and manufactured exports from Japanese-owned factories in Europe. During the decade Japanese investment in Europe rose from $4.7 billion to $45 billion, a 25 to 1 ratio over European investments in Japan.[29]

While Japanese industrial policy and aggressive export practices contributed to the decline of some industries in North America and Japan, the competitiveness problem had many dimensions. One aspect related to the character of the Japanese worker – prepared to work long hours producing quality products. One EC report, drafted by Sir Roy Denman, described the Japanese as "workaholics living in what Westerners would regard as little more than rabbit hutches, who have only recently emerged from a feudal society."[30] In Europe competitiveness problems involved to a significant degree the absence of a large market. With small, segmented economies European business simply could not achieve cost reductions from large scale production.

Over the longer term European business leaders saw further integration of the European market as an antidote to foreign competition and "Euro-pessimism." Rather than 12 compartmentalized national markets, they wanted to remove customs barriers and harmonize product standards. The European Round Table of Industrialists, an association of founded in 1983, sought to educate European governments about the precarious state of the regional economy. In particular, they argued that red tape, customs barriers, national currencies, and fragmented markets stultified growth. The round table's core strategy was to secure and implement a European Single

Market program, which later involved a single currency, to restore growth, employment, and prosperity. The big industrialists, led by Swedish motor vehicle maker Volvo, saw the single market bringing greater efficiencies and an opportunity for European business to counter-attack against powerful foreign competitors.[31]

Many North Americans worried that Europe's relentless pursuit of a single market might enhance a "fortress Europe mentality." But European business leaders who understood the potential of new communications and information technologies also began to preach global expansion and cosmopolitanism. Saying that European companies remained too provincial, Claude-Noel Martin of France's Generale Biscuit exhorted them to cooperate and compete internationally against similar large North American and Japanese corporations. A European flag, he asserted, should fly over company headquarters. Wisse Dekker, the chairman of Dutch electronics giant Philips, warned that multinationals might leave Europe if it failed to complete the single market process. "If Europe does not unite, industrial innovation will pass Europe by. Multinational companies will then be forced to adjust their geographic priorities." The new technologies, Dekker and other industrialists recognized, made global competition a fact of life. High costs of product development required corporations to amortize costs over a larger base of consumers, and to compete globally.[32]

Along with expanding in the evolving European regional market, the big European firms focused on obtaining plants and distribution networks in North America. This was part of their strategy of achieving competitive positions in the high-income triad countries (North America, Japan, and the European Union). European inflows to the US soared in the 1980s, totaling $216 billion for the decade versus cumulative inflows of merely $28 billion in the 1970s. At the beginning of the decade Europe's investment position in the US on a historical-cost basis approximately equaled America's investment stake in Europe. But by the end of the 1980s Europe's investment position in America was considerably larger than comparable US investments in Europe.[33]

One World?

Corporate free traders

By 1990 two opposing, and competing, perspectives had emerged in the international business community. One was optimistic and internationalist. It represented the views of big business as reflected by the International Chamber of Commerce, its American affiliate the US Council for International Business, the Business Roundtable, the Canadian Council of Chief Executives, the European Round Table of Industrialists, the World Economic Forum, and Japan's Keidanren and other similar associations. These groups embraced international business, and sought expanded opportunities in high-income and emerging markets. Fearful of nationalism and protectionism, they discouraged unilateral trade remedies. Such measures might invite retaliation against corporate efforts to expand market share abroad and to gain positions in China and Japan. Big business sought a set of multilateral rules for the international trading system and they promoted a world investment agreement as well. While applauding conclusion of the Uruguay Round, the ICC said it was no longer adequate to focus on trade barriers as the principal impediments to international business. They wanted a framework of rules for doing business on a global basis that adopted a broader conception of market access. The International Chamber of Commerce proposed to extend the rules-based system to international investments. It asserted that worldwide economic integration requires business to produce and market goods and services on a global scale, by integrating the skills of people and various assets – tangible (e.g., land and resources), intangible (e.g., intellectual property), and monetary (e.g., stocks). In this process, trade and investment have become indistinguishable parts of a single strategy. Companies trade to invest and they invest to trade.[34]

Business protectionists

Taking a defensive position on globalization were less internationally competitive firms determined to protect their domestic markets. Often these were smaller, family-owned firms in higher income countries, or they had a relatively high-cost structure resulting from labor agreements with unions. They had little interest in global expansion and primarily wanted to preserve and protect their presence in national and regional markets. To achieve these goals, they used political influence where possible, and retained lawyers to initiate trade-remedy proceedings. Their goal was to erect barriers to vigorous foreign competition. In the high-income countries these firms often included those producing textiles, apparel, and footwear. They achieved their greatest success with a series of international textile quota arrangements. The so-called Multifiber Arrangement, an agreement among 42 exporting and importing countries that took effect in 1974 and was extended until 2005, regulated trade in textiles and apparel. In essence, it enabled industrialized countries to manage imports from developing countries with country-by-country quotas. In the US these business groups, and a broader coalition of activists, sought unsuccessfully to bloc NAFTA (the North American Free Trade Agreement) in 1993, the admission of China to the World Trade Organization, and the passage of CAFTA (the Central American Free Trade Agreement). Gradually, the opponents lost ground, beaten by big business with its enthusiasm for global engagement. Although the multinationals had the money to influence public policy decisions, public opinion polls showed that at the grass roots ordinary citizens remained apprehensive of globalization and concerned about dislocations to employment and communities.[35]

Global Business Advocates and Activists

Management consultants and strategists, more visible in the last decades of the twentieth century than in earlier times, pushed the internationalist, cosmopolitan vision and urged business to seize the opportunities offered by global competition. With easier oil supplies, floating exchange rates, new information and communications technologies, and worldwide pools of cheap, low-skilled labor, they saw enormous incentives for corporations to integrate and compete globally. One management consultant warned that changes in technology were creating a world "in which anything can be made and sold anywhere else." Companies that didn't seize the opportunities presented by globalization would not survive.[36]

Restructuring

To that end, many big publicly held corporations began to restructure and cut costs. Companies obtained agreement from unions for more flexible work rules, reducing labor costs as much as 30 percent in one plant. Becoming leaner, industry increasingly put premiums on innovation, marketing, entrepreneurship, and growth-based investments in automation to enhance productivity. At General Electric, one of the largest and most successful transnational corporations, CEO Jack Welch emphasized that "American corporations have a great responsibility to be the lowest-cost, highest-quality producers of goods and services."[37] He spun off unproductive units and transferred labor-intensive operations overseas where returns would be greater.

One of the most infamous corporate turn-around specialists was Albert J. "Chainsaw" Dunlap, the so-called Rambo in Pinstripes. A West Point graduate, Dunlap developed a career parachuting in to troubled firms, firing employees, and closing unproductive units to cut costs and restore profitability. Dunlap's tough-guy approach pleased investors as their stock prices soared. Hired in 1996 as the CEO of Sunbeam Corporation, Dunlap fired 6,000 of 12,000 employees. He closed 16 of 26 factories and shipped labor-intensive operations, such as the hair-clipper unit in McMinnville, Tennessee with 650 jobs, to Mexico. Later the Sunbeam Board fired Dunlap who had used unorthodox accounting practices to conceal losses.[38]

Business Strategists and Globalization

Since 1977 pundits like Peter Drucker had urged big business to meet the challenges of global competition by moving low-cost assembly operations to developing countries with cheap labor and focusing on emerging markets. Others like Japanese strategist Kenichi Ohmae encouraged large multinationals to focus on the high-income, regional markets – the so-called triad – encompassing Western Europe, North America, and Japan. And Harvard University marketing professor Theodore Levitt, another leading scholar, focused attention on how globalization was fashioning a single world market. Everywhere children played with PacMan games and used Sony Walkmen. Shopping centers from Rio to Manila to Dusseldorf all sold Gucci shoes, Yves St Laurent suits, and Gloria Vanderbilt jeans. Around the world elites traveled in Mercedes Benz sedans, and the middle classes in Toyota Corollas. His widely read article on "The Globalization of Markets," published in the prestigious *Harvard Business Review* (1983), argued that technological changes were a powerful force promoting convergence in the world economy. "It has proletarianized communication, transport, and travel. It has made isolated places and impoverished peoples eager for modernity's allurements. Almost everyone everywhere wants all the things they have heard about, seen, or experienced via the new technologies. ... The result is a new commercial reality – the emergence of global markets ... the globalization of markets is at hand."[39]

Arguably, Levitt was ahead of his times in the 1980s. While global brands had arrived – notably, Marlboro, Mercedes Benz, Coca-Cola, IBM, Nestle, and Heinz – it was debatable whether the same standard product could be marketed everywhere. Culture and tastes still differed widely, but elite opinion was beginning to homogenize. Almost everywhere in the triad business and public leaders read the *Wall Street Journal* and the *Financial Times*, shared similar consumer tastes, and vacationed in high-end resorts.

Adapting to the Age of Globalization

Some industries responded to the attraction of international production, and cost savings, earlier than others. Labor-intensive electronics firms set up assembly facilities in Taiwan during the 1960s, and Hewlett-Packard soon had a manufacturing chain stretching halfway around the globe. It included skilled engineers in California and low-wage assembly workers in Malaysia. General Electric, faced with growing European and Japanese competition in its electronic products, centralized its world production of audio products in Singapore. During the 1980s *maquiladoras*, or border-assembly plants, in Mexico became a population option for firms eager to tap low-cost labor but serve the US market closer to home. Mexican wages, which had been higher than those in Singapore, Korea, and Hong Kong in the 1970s, dropped below Asian competitors during the 1980s as a result of Mexico's devaluation. Cheaper labor costs, and incentives to set-up assembly facilities, led to a boom in employment growth (rising from an average of 9,213 jobs in the 1970s to 40,407 in the late 1980s). After passage of NAFTA job growth rose to 46,448 in the early 1990s, before large numbers of assembly jobs began to migrate to China. From 2001 to 2004, after China entered the WTO and became the low-cost supplier of labor-intensive goods, Mexico lost 28 percent of its *maquiladora* plants.[40]

Among European multinationals there were similar adjustments to the new competitive environment. Plans to complete integration of the European market in 1992 prompted European firms to merge to achieve global economies of scale. At that time only a small number of European companies qualified as global competitors – Fiat, Pechiney, Siemens, Solvay, Unilever, and Volkswagen. Others would soon join their ranks. In 1987, for example, Swedish–Swiss ASEA and Brown-Boveri merged to restructure Europe's electric engineering and equipment industry. Some took advantage of strong European currencies and open markets to buy up foreign assets and reinvent themselves. Sweden's Volvo sold its automotive division to Ford in 1999, and purchased the truck divisions of Mack and Renault, transforming the company from a minor player in the world auto market into the third largest producer of trucks. Eleven years later Ford would sell the Swedish automaker to Geely of China.

Faced with high labor costs (labor in France and Germany cost $22 per hour, compared to about $20 in the US), lagging productivity, and cultural barriers to risk-taking and innovation, many big firms chose to invest abroad where costs were lower. Some pursued "green-field" investments in new markets, and built factories. To gain assured access to the growing American market for luxury vehicles, automakers BMW and Mercedes, as well as their suppliers, constructed assembly facilities in South Carolina (completed 1994) and Alabama (1997), where labor unions lacked influence and state governments offered generous incentives. Alabama offered $253 million in incentives to attract Mercedes, paying an estimated $169,000 per created job.[41]

Offshoring and outsourcing

During the 1990s the world's transnational corporations awoke to the benefits of outsourcing and offshoring, many shifting plants and jobs to China or India. For European manufacturers, there were major sources of cheap labor – many with German language and technical skills – closer to home. They constructed new plants in Eastern and Central Europe where wages were 15 percent of German levels, and encouraged suppliers to join them. For Volkswagen, which employed 37,000 workers and another 200,000 at supplier companies, Central Europe offered a low-cost supply base – one that made a huge contribution to profits. In such circumstances, it was not surprising to find trade union leaders in the older established countries of Europe complaining about a "race to the bottom."[42]

At the beginning of the twenty-first century, the environment for international business was much different than a generation earlier. In 1980 policy walls insulated national markets, and the requirements of Cold War competition required substantial government management of international trade. In Western Europe state-owned enterprises and government regulations hampered business enterprises. In both Europe and North America high inflation and high unemployment combined to produce economic stagnation and malaise. By 2000, the Cold War was over, and markets deregulated. Negotiating under the auspices of GATT, trading nations had approved a new set of rules and dispute-settlement procedures in the Uruguay Round (completed in 1994) to shape the environment for international business, and take further steps to reduce trade barriers covering goods and services. Along with policy changes came the information-technology revolution. Computer chips, satellites, and the internet had reduced telecommunications costs dramatically. As a result, highly mobile multinational enterprises had become increasingly liberated from national jurisdictions, and in a position to play one government off against another.

Stateless multinationals?

The globalization revolution also altered business thinking about the nation-state. In the 1970s and 1980s business had curried favor with public officials, but by the 1990s some pundits and executives had become so openly cosmopolitan in thinking that they celebrated the demise of the nation-state. Kenichi Ohmae pronounced the nation-state a dinosaur waiting to die. In his view companies were becoming stateless world citizens free from national identifications. Consumer sovereignty would trump appeals to nationality, he thought, as people around the globe strived to purchase the world's best goods. Some MNC executives adopted this cosmopolitan world view. Gilbert Williamson, president of NCR, intoned: "We at NCR think of ourselves as a globally competitive company that happens to be headquartered in the United States."[43]

Speaking in Beijing about Cisco's plans to expand its business and sourcing, CEO John Chambers raved: "If I wasn't American, I would be Chinese." *Time* magazine columnist Strobe Talbott effused about nationhood becoming obsolete and all states recognizing a single global authority. He predicted that the phrase "citizen of the world" would assume real meaning by the end of the twenty-first century.[44]

Flat or spiky world?

Pursuing the globalization theme, *New York Times* columnist Thomas Friedman argued in a 2005 bestseller that the world was flat.[45] But, many business professionals had a different view of the global economy. To them the global marketplace was not flat but uneven – perhaps even spiky. It was divided into three broad geographic regions – namely, North America, the European Union, and Japan. This core triad enjoyed high rates of innovation and sophisticated consumers with high purchasing power. The triad housed the largest multinational enterprises. Business researchers reported that only nine of 380 Fortune 500 companies, for which data was available, truly had a global market presence at the turn of the twenty-first century. They defined a global market presence as having less than 50 percent of sales in the home region, and at least 20 percent in each of the three regions. By this standard only nine firms qualified: IBM, Sony, Royal Dutch Philips, Nokia, Intel, Canon, Coca-Cola, Flextronic, and Moet Hennessy-Louis Vuitton.[46]

Nonetheless, there was ample evidence of increasingly sophisticated forms of integration. The classical, hierarchical model for a multinational enterprise involved high degrees of centralization as the parent company sought to coordinate differentiated activities. In the 1980s much was written about the post-industrial corporation, or virtual corporation, where outside designers and engineers conceived new products, and the corporation farmed out manufacturing to contractors in Asia, which in turn passed along the labor-intensive work to subcontractors in China. Oregon-based Nike was an example of the virtual corporation. It operated none of its factories, relying on sub-contractors in cheap labor countries. At first it offshored manufacturing to Japan, but when labor costs rose it shifted production to South Korea and Taiwan. Later, it moved to China, Indonesia, and Vietnam.

Globally integrated enterprise

Another form was the "globally integrated enterprise," a term associated with IBM CEO Sam Palmisano. He said that IBM no longer considered companies a series of units defined by geography. Rather the units were defined by purpose (sales, research and development, and production), and they were located anywhere on the globe where work could be done most efficiently. IBM, which metamorphosed from a multinational International Business Machines that sold office equipment and computers into a global services provider, detached from its home country, the United States. Its employees worked on a variety of projects bringing different skill sets.[47]

A utility project in Texas illustrated IBM's globally integrated formula. The work team involved research scientists in Yorktown Heights, NY, and Austin, TX, software developers in Pune and Bangalore, India, engineering equipment and quality-control specialists in Miami and New York, and utility experts and software designers that have come from Philadelphia, San Francisco, Los Angeles, Chicago, Raleigh, NC, and elsewhere.[48]

A huge improvement in information and communications technologies during the era had permitted such complex structure. It also promoted a measure of convergence in which more and more products were sold in the same, or similar, form in national markets. And more and more firms were outsourcing portions of their value-adding operations. By the mid-1990s more and more foreign direct investment flowed to developing countries. Indeed, FDI flowing to developing countries had been larger than official inflows in every year since 1993. Developing countries received 40 percent of all FDI flows by 1993. Much of that focused on China. In 1993, with $26 billion in FDI inflows, China had become the second largest host country, behind the US. China surpassed the US in 2003.

Offshoring controversies and opportunities

Firms choosing to access cheap offshore labor either directly or through sub-contractors sometimes found their activities subjected to a harsh media spotlight. During the 1990s Nike, the world's largest athletic shoe-maker, faced criticisms for the hazardous and exploitive working conditions imposed by suppliers in Indonesia, Vietnam, and China. Nike responded by installing a code of conduct for its suppliers and monitoring their activities. Other retailers and clothing manufacturers, such as Adidas, Benetton, Banana Republic, the Gap, and Old Navy have faced similar charges. More recently, software maker Microsoft experienced criticism for sweatshop conditions at a subcontractor's plant in China where teenage workers toiled 12 to 15 hours a day, earning 43 cents an hour.[49]

But, while some investment remained controversial, UNCTAD has reported that investment in China is no longer directed exclusively to labor-intensive industries with low labor costs. Capital-intensive and technology-intensive industries also attract FDI. By 2000 four out of five Fortune 500 firms had invested in China, and much of that was flowing into research and development. Microsoft, Motorola, GM, GE, JVC, Lucent-Bell, Samsung, Nortel, IBM, Intel, DuPont, P&G, Ericsson, Nokia, Panasonic, Mitsubishi, AT&T, and Siemens were among the ones having research and development facilities in China. As these examples suggest, another important trend at the beginning of the twenty-first century was the location of research and development facilities in developing countries. These facilities went beyond adapting products to local markets and involved core innovation strategies. GE's R&D facilities in India employed 2,400 people working on aircraft engines, medical equipment, and consumer durables for the global market. Major pharmaceutical companies, like Eli Lilly, GlaxoSmithKline, Novartis, Pfizer, and others, conducted clinical research activities in India.[50]

Why had multinationals shifted R&D to developing countries in Eastern Europe, South and East Asia? According to UNCTAD, intensifying pressures to increase research and development so as to bring products quickly to market forced multinationals to move research to countries with lower costs and well-educated scientific manpower. In China or India companies could hire ten or more engineers for the cost of one in Silicon Valley. And these engineers were well educated. In GE's laboratory in China more than

80 percent of engineers held doctoral degrees, while in Bangalore, India, 60 percent had post-graduate science credentials.[51]

A third important trend in the internationalization and integration of business was the rising importance of services in FDI. UNCTAD found that in the 1970s less than one quarter of world FDI stock involved services. In 1990 less than one half involved services, but by 2002 the share accounting for services had risen to about 60 percent, or $4 trillion. Meanwhile the share of manufacturing in the stock of world foreign direct investment fell to 34 percent. One reason for the rising share of services in foreign direct investment related to the fact that most services were not tradable. They needed to be produced where they were consumed. Thus, retailers like Carrefour and Wal-Mart had to invest in foreign retail and distribution outlets to serve customers outside the home market. Another reason for rising investment in services involved the pressure to cut costs. Businesses found they could serve customers in triad markets with customer call centers in India, the Philippines, or other locations, and achieve cost savings of 20 to 40 percent. They also found that back office operations, involving the processing of transactions, could be handled less expensively offshore.[52]

By the beginning of the twenty-first century, the global economy was more competitive than ever. For executives of multinational corporations, coping with globalization remained the top challenge. They saw the integration of markets – particularly of large emerging markets such as China, India, and Brazil – as an irreversible reality. High rates of growth in emerging markets they considered unstable and subject to sudden crises, but nonetheless richly rewarding. The successful multinationals, they said, were not those that exported business models and products designed for the US and Western Europe. Rather they adapted to unique local structures and geographic challenges, and produced products and services intended for local markets. Sensitivity to local conditions (localization) led Hindustan Unilever to develop a low-cost detergent, Wheel, to encourage people to move from soaps to detergents. Their product has 20 percent of the market, and impacts 600 million people.[53]

The rise of India and China, and other emerging markets, has also increased competition as these markets develop their own national champions who then enter the world stage. While foreign firms focused on entering the Chinese and Indian markets, a number of Chinese and Indian firms emerged as powerful international rivals. The Haier Group, a state-owned enterprise in China, captured almost half of the US market for small refrigerators in 2002. In 2005, Lenovo, a computer technology company partly owned by the Chinese government, acquired IBM's personal computer division. Many of the emerging market competitors were state-owned enterprises, which accounted for some 85 percent of China's FDI in 2004–5.[54]

But globalization also brought some unanticipated rewards. During the global financial crisis of 2007–10 some multinationals discovered the value of global business diversification strategies involving a commitment to both advanced and emerging markets. General Motors, which faced bankruptcy in the United States, flourished in China, where it successfully cashed in on the arrival of the auto age, while auto sales plummeted in mature markets.[55]

Conclusion

As this chapter shows, private business awoke to the opportunities and challenges of global competition in the 1980s. Rapid growth in developing areas, declining opportunities in advanced markets, new technologies of communications and transportation, and a changing international environment at the end of the Cold War combined to alter the environment for international business. In the face of more vigorous competition, some firms and governments did use the power of the state to protect markets and devise industrial policies benefiting national champions. But, over the last decades of the twentieth century, multinational corporations gradually concluded that the path to survival involved adapting to a world with deregulated markets, open borders, and global competition. The largest and most successful firms engaged globalization and devised strategies to expand market share and profits. Their approaches frequently involved shifting business activities offshore, outsourcing many activities to subcontractors, and developing sophisticated global supply chains and integrated enterprises. To cut costs and gain improved access to high-growth markets, such as China and India, the big firms soon transferred state-of-the art technology and established research facilities abroad. By the first decade of the twenty-first century there was some evidence that the pro-globalization strategy had hidden perils. State-owned enterprises in China and other emerging market countries, having benefited from technology transfer and cooperative arrangements with multinationals, were themselves entering the global competition in a quest for markets and critical resources.

Chapter 8

Internationalization of Finance

The world of finance is a complex one that ordinary people contact when they routinely cash a check or use a credit card, buy a stock or bond, obtain a home mortgage, or exchange currencies for their foreign travel. Few consumers seek to master the intricacies. The mysteries of finance are usually left to bankers, traders, investors, and other professionals whose occupations require a higher level of understanding. Many of the most successful financial professionals work in a few of the world's money centers – London, New York, Tokyo, Frankfurt, and Hong Kong among others. In this interconnected world, it is possible for sophisticated investors to play the global markets from almost any location where there are cell phones and computers with internet access.

Introduction to International Finance

So what is international finance, and why has it become so volatile and controversial in recent years? The Bank for International Settlements (BIS), which is a bank for central bankers, based in Basel, Switzerland, compares the financial system to the plumbing on a home. When it works, it is taken for granted, but when it doesn't the results can be highly disruptive. Just as a plumbing system depends on a steady flow of water, an economic system relies on available financing and dependable intermediaries like banks, credit unions, stock brokers, insurance firms, and the like. These institutions serve the important function of funneling money from persons who wish to save a portion of earnings to those who need to borrow to finance

The Contemporary Global Economy: A History Since 1980, First Edition. Alfred E. Eckes, Jr.
© 2011 Alfred E. Eckes, Jr. Published 2011 by Blackwell Publishing Ltd.

business activities or make large purchases. And these institutions, and their instruments, help shift the risk of failure to those better able to assume it.[1]

But when these intermediaries – banks, brokerages, and insurance companies – lose trust in one another, perhaps because they cannot assess risks and value assets properly, the financial system clogs up, like a home's plumbing. Without trade financing, exporters and importers cannot conduct business. Without credit, businesses cannot borrow to purchase needed materials and meet payrolls. And, in instances where banks cannot meet the demands for cash of their depositors and become insolvent, irrational behavior (panic) may ensue, paralyzing the whole economic system.

Over the centuries, there have been a large number of financial crises that had international repercussions. Many of them began as banking crises. Banks typically borrow money from depositors that can be redeemed on short notice. They lend over a longer term, and many of these loans cannot be repaid upon demand and converted easily into cash. Thus in a financial crisis banks can become illiquid – unable to meet current obligations – or even insolvent – when the value of the bank's assets is less than the value of its liabilities. Something similar can happen to governments, particularly those that borrow in foreign currencies. Sovereign defaults, as they are known, occur when a government does not make scheduled payments on its domestic or foreign debt.

Sometimes exchange rate crises trigger a financial collapse. If, for example, a government pursued high-growth policies at home, perhaps with heavy borrowing from abroad, it might be unable to maintain existing exchange rates. Sensing vulnerabilities, speculators might move out of the weak currency, forcing devaluation and igniting a panic as borrowers found themselves unable to pay off foreign loans. After reviewing eight centuries of financial crises, Carmen Reinhart and Kenneth Rogoff, two economists, have concluded that "financial crises are nothing new." They affect rich and poor countries alike. Thus the Great Recession of 2007–10 was the latest of a long series of disruptive economic events extending back to at least the 1340s. The first international debt crisis reportedly occurred when King Edward III of England, having squandered funds on the Hundred Years' War with France, defaulted on debts to Italian bankers.[2]

De-Globalization and National Regulation of Finance

The golden age of finance that preceded World War I disintegrated in that conflict, and was never fully restored during the difficult period of recovery.

As it turned out a series of calamities – two world wars, a great economic collapse, and the resurgence of interventionist thought – produced a highly regulated environment for all international and domestic financial transactions. As noted in earlier chapters, government leaders gradually adopted Keynesian-style spending to restore prosperity within the context of national economies. There was little coordinated action by finance ministries and central banks to promote global recovery. Instead, countries looked inward and took unilateral action. Not until the 1970s – a quarter century after World War II – did enthusiasm for self-regulating markets revive and bring about a significant relaxation of government controls over the financial system.

Glass-Steagall and other reforms

During this 40-year period governments generally employed exchange controls and other restrictions to control international transactions. Distrustful of the market mechanism that had produced serial bankruptcies and a crisis of confidence, governments intervened to impose new rules on the financial system. They regulated domestic stock exchanges and banking to protect investors and depositors and to prevent contagion. In the United States, for example, congressional hearings in 1933 after the stock-market crash revealed conflicts of interest between banking and securities firms. Counsel for the Senate Banking and Currency Committee Ferdinand Pecora exposed numerous examples of stock market manipulation and insider trading. Albert Wiggin, the president of Chase Bank, had shorted his own bank's shares. Charles E. Mitchell's National City Bank (forerunner of Citibank) passed off bad loans to Latin American countries by securitizing them and selling them to naive investors. The hearings disclosed that some commercial banks engaged in speculative trading of securities, unloading risky bonds on unsuspecting investors. Congressional investigators concluded that extravagant compensation incentives had encouraged bank officials to indulge in unsound practices. The resulting Glass-Steagall Act (the Banking Act of 1933) brought radical reforms. It imposed a wall between risky investment banking and commercial banking, and set up the Federal Deposit Insurance Corporation, an agency of the federal government, to insure customer deposits. Regulation Q set a maximum interest rate that banks could pay on deposits. Other legislation established the Securities and Exchange Commission, an independent regulatory agency, to oversee securities trading and stock exchanges. Senator Phil Gramm (R-TX), the chairman of the Senate banking committee which repealed the segmentation of banking provision in November 1999, observed that Glass-Steagall passed at a time when people believed that "government was the answer" and that stability and growth came from the government regulating free markets.[3]

Everywhere memories of turmoil during the Great Depression shaped government actions pertaining to banking and securities markets from the 1930s to the early 1970s. To maintain economic stability, national regulatory authorities guarded access to domestic markets. Regulators recognized their fiduciary responsibilities to maintain a safe and sound banking system. In the US these laws and regulations involved restrictions on interstate banking, ceilings on interest rates paid on bank deposits, and limitations on competition. Thus, legal barriers and regulatory oversight kept the financial services industry segmented among banks, investment banks, and insurance companies. A variety of regulatory authorities, including the Federal Reserve, the Comptroller of the Currency in the Treasury, the Federal Deposit Insurance Corporation, and the Securities and Exchange Commission, as well as state banking authorities, shared responsibilities for regulation. In the United Kingdom, because the Great Depression did not lead to widespread bank failures, bank regulation had remained informal. The regulatory supervisor, the Bank of England, used moral suasion as the basis for regulation to promote stability. It also exerted informal control over the London Stock Exchange. Interestingly, during this extended period of tight financial regulation and restricted capital flows, there were few banking crises, perhaps confirming the cautious approach of regulators in supervising domestic financial markets and maintaining "heavy-handed … capital controls."[4]

Bretton Woods and international finance

Distrust of private bankers and their reckless practices also influenced the determination of governments to control the reconstruction of international finance after World War II. Public agencies, not quasi-public central banks such as the New York Federal Reserve Bank and the Bank of England, which had facilitated reconstruction from World War I, would supervise the financial domain. The leaders of this undertaking were two academic economists – Britain's John Maynard Keynes and America's Harry Dexter White – who represented the finance ministries of the two governments leading the coalition against the Axis. The resulting Bretton Woods agreements constructed a wall between private international banking and the government sector. Given the enthusiasm that Roosevelt's New Dealers had for cleaning up Wall Street and restraining the power of private interests, it is not surprising that the US Treasury took the lead in establishing a postwar structure that gave public institutions and intergovernmental agencies principal responsibility for regulating international finance. The British government, represented by John Maynard Keynes, agreed with that approach. Central banks operating autonomously might implement policies, but finance ministries were more accountable to voters. At the July 1944 Bretton Woods Conference, setting up the International Monetary Fund and the International Bank for Reconstruction and Development (later the World Bank), Treasury Secretary Henry Morgenthau, Jr. lashed out at private finance. He asserted that the bank would "provide capital for those who need it at lower interest rates than in the past and ... drive only the usurious money lenders from the temple of international finance."[5]

Architects of the postwar international monetary system contemplated that currencies would be freely convertible only for trade in goods and services. In light of the disintegration of private capital markets during the Great Depression, they held little hope for the revival of private investment. During the interwar period short-term capital flows disrupted efforts to maintain stable exchange rates. And so, many economists believed that flows of private capital were incompatible with an open international trade system. As an alternative to private lending, Keynes and White agreed on an International Bank for Reconstruction and Development that would borrow private capital and lend it to deserving countries. Given the founders' enthusiasm for international institutions and government regulation of markets, it is not surprising that the postwar arrangements made no provision for capital-account convertibility. Keynes and White could not envisage the revival of private capital flows and global securities markets after World War II. Thus, the institutional arrangements made no provision for monitoring and regulating private investment.

The Bretton Woods arrangements established a gold-exchange standard, a modified version of the pre-World War I gold standard. To maintain confidence in the system, the US defined its currency in terms of gold and pledged to buy and sell gold from other governments at a fixed price ($35 per ounce of gold). With this commitment other governments pledged to peg their rates of exchange to the dollar. For countries experiencing temporary balance-of-payments difficulties, the IMF could provide assistance. Also, after consulting with the IMF, governments could adjust currency pegs to correct a "fundamental disequilibrium." Members of the IMF agreed to make currencies convertible for trade purposes, and to use exchange controls and restrictions only under tightly regulated circumstances. Under this so-called gold-exchange standard, other governments accumulated reserves of dollars, instead of gold, which they used in the market to maintain the fixed value of their currency.

Slow recovery of private investment

As Keynes and White had anticipated, long-term private capital flows were slow to revive after World War II. The New York financial market floated only $4.2 billion in foreign issues between 1955 and 1962, a modest amount compared to the $126.5 billion floated for national issues. Foreign governments learned to rely on official aid. The US government financed the European Recovery Program, or Marshall Plan (about $13 billion). Altogether the US provided $98 billion in economic and military aid to other countries during the years 1945 to 1952. Various bilateral and multilateral sources (such as the World Bank) provided limited amounts of capital for newly independent nations seeking outside assistance to spur economic development. From 1948 to 1961, the World Bank committed $2.9 billion to less developed countries, 41 percent of it to Latin America, and 24 percent to a single client, India.[6]

During the 1950s and 1960s, despite the continuance of exchange controls to protect balances of payments, private capital flows would gradually revive, initially among developed countries. Establishment of the Eurodollar market in London facilitated the trend. Eurodollars were dollars held outside the United States beyond the reach of the Federal Reserve. During the 1950s the Soviet Union preferred to hold its dollars in London, and during the 1960s this market grew as US multinationals found they could earn more on deposits in London than in the US where Regulation Q restricted interest rates. The Eurodollar market grew from $1.5 billion in 1958 to $25 billion in 1968 and $132 billion in 1973. Soon there were Eurobond and Eurocredit markets as well, and the presence of the Euromarkets helped revive the City of London as a financial center. The growth of the London market also attracted foreign banks, and by 1970 American competitors controlled 54 percent of the Eurocurrency market. The rebirth of London as an international financial center occurred despite the weakness of the British pound, which was devalued in 1967 and floated in 1972.[7]

In 1970, the world's outward flows of foreign direct investment (FDI) amounted to $13.4 billion. Over 60 percent went to eight high-income countries – Australia, Canada, France, Germany, Italy, the Netherlands, the United Kingdom, and the United States – with 13 percent of the world's population. Twenty-nine percent ($3.85 billion) flowed to some 150 developing countries with 71 percent of the world's population. Poor countries relied mostly on intergovernmental aid for outside assistance. In 1970 government aid to developing countries was $8.6 billion, while private direct investment to the same group was less than half ($3.9 billion).[8]

In the climate of the times private investors were reluctant to risk lending to politically unstable and impoverished countries. There was too much risk of default in the developing world, where many countries had only recently gained independence. And indeed across the developing world newly independent regimes demonstrated their nationalism by expropriating foreign-owned properties – copper mines, telephones, electrical utilities, and others.

The rise and demise of Bretton Woods

The gold-exchange standard system established at Bretton Woods in 1944 essentially was placed in mothballs for about 15 years after the war until countries recovered. Because of inadequate monetary reserves, most countries could not maintain their IMF parities and meet their IMF obligations. Instead they opted to retain exchange restrictions to protect their balances of payments. In September 1949 24 countries, including Britain, devalued their currencies, hoping to improve their competitive positions. Over the next decade their reserve positions gradually improved so that on December 31, 1958, Western European countries generally abandoned exchange controls and made their currencies convertible for trade purposes.[9]

With limited convertibility restored, the Bretton Woods system finally began to function in 1959 as the founders envisaged. Soon unexpected problems surfaced. One arose from a basic flaw in the Bretton Woods system – the special privilege afforded the key currency, the US dollar. The growth of world trade required reserves of dollars and liquidity (or the availability of a widely acceptable currency) to finance transactions. In the postwar period the reserve currency of choice was the US dollar. It provided approximately two-thirds of the world's expanding monetary reserves, and merchants and traders could easily convert it to finance business transactions. Commodities, like oil, traded in dollars. But the availability of the dollar hinged on the US running a persistent payments deficit. Belgian-born economist Robert Triffin, a former Federal Reserve economist who taught at Yale University, called attention to the dilemma: the world economy could grow and prosper only so long as other countries retained confidence in the dollar as convertible to gold. But, when foreign reserves of dollars exceeded the US gold supply, the world might lose confidence in the dollar. Without confidence in America's pledge to convert dollars for gold upon demand the international monetary system could become unstable. The international economy could also break down if there were inadequate supplies of dollars, or some widely acceptable currency, to support the growth of transactions outside the US.[10]

Meanwhile, America's appetite for foreign cars and other imported products grew. Its students, tourists, bankers, and multinational corporations roamed the world, buying goods and services with dollars that could not be converted into gold. This situation vexed President Charles de Gaulle of France, one European leader concerned about America's "exorbitant privilege." In his view the gold-exchange standard enabled the US as a reserve currency country to live beyond its means and pursue hegemony. De Gaulle perceived that the dollar's unique reserve status enabled the US government to prosecute an unpopular war in Vietnam without facing the financial consequences.[11]

For more than a decade, governments attempted to shore up Bretton Woods. During the 1960s the Kennedy and Johnson administrations struggled to preserve the dollar's unique role. They arranged swap agreements among central banks to provide credit to countries with inadequate reserves. They backed an IMF plan in 1967 to create a new international reserve unit, the SDR or Special Drawing Right, which was to supplement the dollar. And they pursued unilateral measures. Capital controls in the form of an interest-equalization tax were imposed to reduce outflows and reduce pressure on the dollar. Other efforts sought to discourage multinational corporations from investing, and banks from lending, abroad. These restraints energized the Eurodollar market in London. Wall Street complained that activity and jobs moved to London at the expense of New York, and that Britain had become the center of the large Eurodollar market. Led by New York's Citibank, a number of US banks opened or expanded their London operations to circumvent US regulations.[12]

Triffin had predicted that eventually a crisis would bring down the dollar and the monetary system. Such a crisis occurred in 1971, when the United States – unable to honor its gold-redemption pledge and effectively facing a run on the bank – chose to abandon its commitment at Bretton Woods. Soon the Nixon administration allowed the dollar to float against other leading currencies, and removed restrictions on capital flows, a move popular with the New York banking community and big business. Many smaller countries pegged their currency to the dollar. Some, like Japan and members of the European Community, and later China, intervened in exchange markets – buying and selling dollars – to influence their rate against the dollar. Thus, in the post-Bretton Woods era, although the dollar fluctuated in value, it remained the linchpin of the monetary system. It continued as the currency of preference for financing trade and for accumulating national reserves. In addition, sellers of commodities, such as oil, continued to price in dollars.[13]

The demise of the Bretton Woods exchange-rate system emphasized another key analytical point about international monetary relations. It was the idea of the incompatible trinity, namely that fixed exchange rates, independent monetary policies, and perfect capital mobility were mutually incompatible. Simply stated, during the heyday of the gold standard before World War I fixed exchange rates and capital mobility co-existed but internal monetary policies adjusted to preserve the other two external policies. From the Great Depression to 1970 the international economy had experienced fixed exchange rates and independent national monetary policies but not external capital mobility. After the breakdown of Bretton Woods, the trading community in effect chose monetary independence and capital mobility, but not exchange rate stability. Canadian-born economist Robert Mundell, who taught at the University of Chicago and worked for the IMF, developed this basic analysis, for which he was awarded the Nobel Prize in economics in 1999.

Second Era of Financial Deregulation

During the last quarter of the twentieth century two English-speaking countries – the United States and the United Kingdom – would lead the way to a new era of financial globalization. They both opened their domestic markets to trade and capital flows, and deregulated their financial sectors. Simply stated four factors drove the second era of financial globalization – ideas, leadership, innovations, and inflation.

Friedman and free-market ideas

Perhaps most important was a seismic shift in thought among intellectuals and public officials about the proper role of the state in regulating the economy. As a result of experiences in the Great Depression, the conventional wisdom favored government intervention to reduce uncertainty, maintain full employment, and thus to strengthen capitalism against radical forces seeking to overthrow it. By the late 1960s, however, opinion began to swing back toward free-market ideas. As economic growth slowed, and unemployment and inflation re-appeared, public officials became more receptive to the libertarian, *laissez-faire* thinking of Milton Friedman, Friedrich Hayek, and other academic economists who challenged the pre-vailing Keynesian consensus.

Friedman, an elf-like economist with big ears, and an enthusiasm for public debate, led the assault. Of course, we are familiar with his ideas from the discussion in Chapter 5. One of his first targets during the 1950s was the Bretton Woods fixed-exchange-rate system. Disputing depression-era claims, he argued that flexible rates left greater freedom to individuals. As recognition of these efforts, the Swedish Nobel Committee awarded Friedman the Nobel Prize in economics in 1976. In announcing the prize, the Nobel Committee observed that Friedman was a pioneer among those recommending free rates of exchange. He was among those who first realized – and could explain – why the Bretton Woods system, with relatively fixed rates of exchange, was bound to break down sooner or later.[14]

Among Friedman and his colleagues at the University of Chicago there was also a growing faith in rational, efficient markets, which their academic research appeared to confirm. In 1990 the Nobel Committee gave its stamp of approval. It awarded the prize in economics to three US economists (Harry Markowitz, Merton Miller, and William Sharpe) for their pioneer-ing work in the theory of financial economics. In 1997 the committee awarded the Nobel in economics to two other Americans, Robert Merton and Myron Scholes, for their method of determining the value of deriva-tives. According to the Nobel committee Merton and Scholes developed a pioneering formula for the efficient management of risk in derivatives and other financial products. The two laureates subsequently joined Long-Term Capital Management (LCTM), a US hedge fund that used their much-touted strategies in highly leveraged trading. It lost $4.6 billion in 1998 following the Russian financial crisis.[15]

Nonetheless, the work of these prominent economists would inspire a generation of young "quants." These were students interested in mathemat-ical and statistical models and their method of taming risk. And Wall Street seemed hungry for quantitative models. Thus, as memories of the Great Depression receded, support for economic deregulation and market com-petition surged among academics and policymakers. A "this-time-is-different" mentality had arrived. It was based on the conceit that although free markets had failed in the circumstances of the 1920s, self-regulation would work this time.

Not everyone shared the financial economists' enthusiasm for unregulated financial markets and innovative new products, such as the securitization of debt. In effect, securitization enabled original lenders to convert nonmarketable assets (such as traditional home loans) into marketable ones. They did so by packaging and pooling the debt, and then marketing it. As early as 1987, the BIS reported that securitization had become "particularly popular in the United States." It noted that new instruments such as collateralized mortgage obligations (CMOs) were growing rapidly. These were private-sector debt securities offering returns from a pool of mortgages. Also, institutional investors increasingly used portfolio insurance techniques relying on futures and options. The BIS noted that the principal benefit from such developments arose from more efficient operations of the market, with a lower cost of funds to borrowers and higher returns for savers. But the BIS stated that the new techniques had not been tested over business or interest-rate cycles and "potential costs are therefore difficult to assess." The new methods the bank associated with greater volatility in markets and it warned of greater systemic risk: "... The failure of a major market-maker could lead to severe consequences, not only for the market in which the failure occurs, but 'contagiously' for other markets in which the market-maker operates. ..." The bank indicated a need for tightening and expanding regulation, and greater international coordination and cooperation. It noted that the blurring of distinction between commercial and investment banking in the US, and Japan, "may lead to an aggravation of the problems of contagion, systemic risk and conflicts of interest."[16]

Subsequent events would show the shortcomings of the quantitative risk models. The general counsel of Long-Term Capital Management would later write that Wall Street and regulators used the wrong paradigm of risk assessment. The sophisticated models assumed that risk was "randomly distributed and that each event has no bearing on the next event in a sequence." Instead, he asserted that capital markets were complex dynamic systems in which risk was truly unpredictable and "cannot be modeled with even the most powerful computers." Other economists, noted Carmen M. Reinhart and Kenneth S. Rogoff, have observed that standard data sets, on which risks are calculated, rest on a narrow range of countries and time periods.[17]

Thatcher and Reagan press financial deregulation

Among the political leaders most receptive to free-market ideas and supportive of financial deregulation were Prime Minister Margaret Thatcher (elected in 1979) and President Ronald Reagan (elected in 1980). As a student at Oxford University Margaret Roberts, later Margaret Thatcher, had read Hayek's famous *Road to Serfdom*, and considered it a powerful critique of socialist planning. As prime minister, she publicly recognized Hayek's influence by nominating him for a royal honor, the Order of the Companions of Honour (CH).[18]

Determined to reverse Britain's decline, Thatcher resolved to achieve a fundamental change in direction. The restoration of free markets was an important component of her election platform. She and the Conservative government elected in May 1979 put their "faith in freedom and free markets, limited government, and a strong national defense." One of her targets was Britain's system of exchange controls. From 1938 to October 1979, British residents had faced government restrictions on buying and using foreign exchange for travel, foreign investments, or private property. A resident of Britain could take only 500 pounds in cash when traveling abroad in the late 1970s. Unable to participate in foreign investment opportunities, pension funds kept their funds invested close to home. In stock exchanges cumbersome traditional practices reigned. An individual wanting to purchase a stock contacted a broker, who in turn contacted a jobber who made markets. The whole transaction involved several telephone calls and was costly and time-consuming. That began to change after Thatcher's election in 1979. In its first budget the new Conservative government removed exchange controls. In the United States, Milton Friedman applauded: "Hooray for Margaret Thatcher." Her government "did precisely what she had promised to do."[19]

The United States had previously abolished capital controls in 1974 after the OPEC oil embargo, in part to help US banks recycle petro-dollars to developing countries. George Shultz, a neo-liberal economist from the University of Chicago, was President Nixon's Treasury Secretary, and he took the lead in removing controls, much to the delight of his friend Walter Wriston, head of Citibank.[20] With the US and Britain having abandoned attempts to control capital flows, other governments soon moved to do the same, Australia and New Zealand taking this action in 1984–5. Members of the European Community committed to capital account liberalization by 1990. The result was that by 1990 the major countries had abandoned, or relaxed, capital controls. Private capital could traverse the world economy with greater freedom than at any time since the 1920s. With less national regulation large British, German, Japanese, and US banks began to operate easily on a global scale.

One measure of the new-found strength of market forces involved foreign exchange trading. Until the 1970s trading in currencies was inconsequential. In 1973, the average daily turnover in foreign markets was about $15 billion. Twenty-five years later – in 1998 – $1.5 trillion changed hands every day. By comparison, total world exports of merchandise during the calendar year 1998 were $5.5 trillion, less than four days of exchange trading.[21]

Similar liberalization occurred in equity markets. The arrival of the microprocessor in the 1970s markedly reduced the price of computers and along with technological developments, such as fiber-optic lines, joined markets around the world. In a bid to dominate trade in equities, the New York Stock Exchange automated and deregulated in the 1970s. Fixed commissions were abolished, hours extended, and foreign brokers allowed to join the exchange. Fearful of growing competition from New York's more open trading practices, London began to liberalize trading practices in 1986. The so-called "Big Bang" abolished fixed commission trading and adopted new electronic, screen-based trading, and allowed foreign banks to buy British investment houses. British banks could set up integrated investment banking operations.

London's "Big Bang"

For the stodgy City of London, the "Big Bang" brought a cold shower of American-style competition. The result was an avalanche of new investors, many of them foreign banks, buying up old brokerages and merchant banks. Goldman Sachs joined the London Stock Exchange, and by 1986 had become one of the top ten banks handling mergers and acquisitions in the United Kingdom. Dresdner Bank purchased Kleinwort Benson in 1995, and Swiss banking giant UBS took over venerable S. G. Warburg the same year. Citigroup bought Schroders in 2000. Over the course of 20 years the value of traded shares rose 1,500 percent from 161 billion pounds in 1986 to 2,496 billion in 2006. For the British government deregulation produced a surge in tax receipts, with the financial services industry providing 26 percent of corporate tax receipts in 2006, up from 18 percent before the "Big Bang."[22]

Gradually the two major international financial centers came to resemble Siamese twins, conducting the same transactions with similar institutions and regulations. By 2009 London appeared to have established a lead as a global financial center, thanks to post-Enron scandal legislation in the US imposing complex financial reporting requirements for firms listed on US exchanges. In London 50% of all shares traded on the Stock Exchange were held by overseas shareholders, up from 7% in 1963, 12.8% in 1989 after the Big Bang, and 40% in 2008. Free-spending sovereign wealth funds from the Middle East bolstered the surge. It is estimated that 75% of Fortune 500 companies had London offices and foreign firms paid 40% of the City's work force. The London Stock Exchange listed some 630 foreign companies from 72 countries.[23]

In Canada, where Conservative Premier Brian Mulroney opted to abandon nationalistic trade policies and negotiate a free-trade agreement with the US, supporters of deregulation in the Ontario provincial government pushed through a "Little Bang" in 1987. It essentially removed separations between banks, securities firms, trust companies, and insurers. As in Britain the reforms opened the cozy world of Bay Street, Toronto's financial district, to foreign competition. But initially the competition was not as fierce as the locals feared. Canadian banks bought up brokerages and chose to focus on the Canadian market, not on expanding internationally.[24]

The reforms initiated in New York and London impacted other markets, as electronic communications enhanced competition. But until the 1990s the changes were largely confined to a portion of the English-speaking world. Australia, Canada, New Zealand, the United Kingdom, and the United States took the lead. Japan, India, and South Africa were largely unreformed, as was most of continental Europe. There security markets remained tightly regulated, as politicians and economists adhered to the belief that government intervention was necessary for successful economic management.[25]

Tokyo opens financial market

Tokyo was the most important Asian financial market. In the course of 20 years from the early 1970s to about 1990, it emerged as a major world financial market. Until the 1970s Japan concentrated on recovery from World War II, and the tightly regulated banking system focused on lending to industry to finance expansion. The Japanese government tightly controlled access to the financial market. It regulated capital flows into and out of Japan, the purchase of Japanese stocks by foreigners, and borrowing by Japanese firms. As a result, until the late 1970s Japan remained outside the evolving international financial system. But the breakdown of the Bretton Woods system, and the shift to floating rates, encouraged Japan to open its financial market. By 1979, authorities had removed many restrictions and integrated Japan into the financial system. By then the Tokyo stock market had capitalization second only to New York, and Japanese capital had begun to flow abroad seeking investment opportunities. By 1980 Japan's five top banks ranked among the top 20 in the world, and Tokyo had become one of the three leading international financial centers, along with London and New York.[26]

Technology and inflation spur change

During the early 1980s technological innovations and economic conditions also stimulated the move to deregulate and make financial services more competitive. In particular, a series of innovations transformed the operating environment in financial services. Faster computers, automated office equipment, and improved transportation enabled big banks to serve the global financial market and benefit from economies of large-scale operations. In the face of these innovations Walter Wriston, the articulate chairman of New York banking giant Citibank, decried the continuation of "fortress banking" in the United States. He grumbled that regulators kept bankers locked inside the fortress while "everyone else with imagination and drive harvest the cash crops growing beyond the stockade."[27]

The re-emergence of inflation as an international problem was another important underlying factor influencing developments. In 1980 consumer prices increased at double digit levels in France (14%), Japan (8%), the US (14%), and the United Kingdom (14%). In many developing countries, prices rose even faster: Chile (35% but down from 375% in 1975), Mexico (26%), Philippines (18%), South Korea (29%), and (20%). To cope with inflation, central banks, like the Federal Reserve in the US, adopted stringent monetary policies that saw interest rates reach unprecedented peaks in 1979 and 1980. In the US the Federal funds rate and prime lending rates peaked at over 20 percent, and then dropped 7 percentage points in early 1981. Rates in most other industrial countries moved up in line with US rates.[28]

Inflation impacted all segments of society, but especially competition in the financial services industry. Banks had traditionally earned profits by charging borrowers more than they paid depositors. This process of intermediation enabled borrowers to buy cars, purchase homes and real estate, and meet payrolls – in effect, lubricating the wheels of the economy. But the early 1980s inflation hindered bank competitiveness in the US. Federal regulations (so-called Regulation Q) placed an interest-rate ceiling on bank savings (about 5%), at a time when inflation had reached double-digit levels. Savings and loan associations, not under similar restrictions, paid 12 percent and thus attracted deposits away from banks.

Not surprisingly the resurgence of inflation gave ambitious institutions and entrepreneurs incentives to circumvent regulatory barriers. One chief executive with the entrepreneurial imagination to transform the brokerage business was Donald Regan. He was a tough-minded former Marine who served as chief executive of Merrill Lynch, a staid brokerage firm. Determined to expand business and increase profits, Regan pushed for new products that tied customers to the firm, not to individual brokers who sometimes took their customers as they switched employers. His subordinates developed the highly successful Cash Management Account (CMA), essentially combining a brokerage-margin account with cash sweeps into a money market mutual fund. It allowed customers to write checks and use a debit card on brokerage accounts. Unlike bank deposits, CMAs were not insured by the federal government through the Federal Deposit Insurance Corporation (FDIC). Customers assumed the risk.[29]

Banking deregulation

As commercial banks lost deposits to new competitors, like savings and loans and brokerage firms, they in turn placed pressure on regulators. In 39 states they sought to relax depression-era rules barring branch banking and to permit some consolidation. US banks also sought to expand operations overseas, as foreign banks sought a presence in the US. In 1978 Congress passed a landmark International Banking Act of 1978, which established a new framework for the regulation of foreign banks. Essentially, it provided national treatment to international banks. A number had already entered the US market but could not obtain FDIC insurance to compete for retail deposits. By 2007 foreign banks held 27.6 percent of US banking deposits and made nearly 15 percent of all loans.[30]

As other countries deregulated banking and adopted the principle of national treatment (literally the same as domestic banks) American banks raced overseas to find opportunities. In 1979 there were 144 US banks operating 777 branches overseas. More than 48 percent of the total loan portfolios of the ten largest US banks involved loans to foreign clients. Between 1972 and 1978 the assets in foreign branches of US banks had tripled.[31]

Wriston's Citibank adds risk

Citibank's Wriston was one of the most visible and persuasive proponents of change in the banking industry. A banking entrepreneur, the daring and confident chairman of Citibank appreciated the opportunities that globalization presented. An internationalist, Wriston saw the world as a global marketplace. His interest and experience in international banking stemmed from 1956 to 1966 when he headed the bank's European operations. By 1959 a total of 30 European and associated nations had made currencies freely convertible for non-residents, creating opportunities for investors and borrowers. One of the big opportunities involved lending in the so-called Eurodollar market. As dollars flowed out of the United States, they accumulated in European branches of US banks outside of the Federal Reserve's control. As the CEO of Citibank from 1967 to 1984 Wriston proved dynamic and visionary. The financial press labeled him one of the twentieth century's great banking innovators. One of his most significant innovations involved an esoteric product known as a negotiable certificate of deposit (CD) in the early 1960s. With CDs Wriston helped transform the banking industry as he pressed to expand Citibank's profits 15 percent annually. Previously, bank lending was limited by the deposits of customers, and the Federal Reserve had imposed limits on the interest rate banks could pay. With CDs banks could compete effectively for corporate and international deposits.

Citibank, formerly the National City Bank, had a long tradition of involvement in foreign banking. It had been active in Germany and Latin America during the 1920s and in China during the 1930s. One of Wriston's boldest and most controversial ventures was the central role Citibank assumed during the oil crisis of the 1970s after OPEC pushed up oil prices. In 1974–5, and again in 1979 after the Iran crisis, OPEC pushed up prices sharply. The first time it was a five-fold increase in the price of crude oil. During the second crisis crude prices doubled. Citibank, and other banks, seized the opportunity to recycle OPEC's dollars to hard-pressed developing countries. For a time the bankers made big profits on the spread (the difference between what a banker charges borrowers and what it pays depositors). Defaults of the depression era were a distant memory to Wriston's generation of international bankers. His aggressive lending rested on the assumption that sovereign countries don't go bankrupt, unlike private borrowers. "When problems arise, they are problems of liquidity, not insolvency," he said. If a county took steps to solve its balance-of-payments problems, he believed that it would find that financing for investment projects and for any temporary balance-of-payments gap. Wriston downplayed risk, anticipating that borrowing governments could meet payment obligations if banks and government extended more credit. Implicit in his thinking apparently was the belief that if debtor governments suspended payments the big bankers could turn to Washington and the IMF for aid.[32]

Not everyone in the financial community shared Wriston's enthusiasm for growth and risk. Henry Kaufman, the legendary "Dr. Doom," of Salomon Brothers, a Wall Street investment bank which developed the first mortgage-backed securities, faulted Wriston's emphasis on growing profits and expansion. Kaufman claimed this encouraged a risk-taking culture in banking that eventually had "disastrous consequences for third world economies, for global financial markets, and for Citibank itself." There were similar concerns at the IMF and the BIS, two staid institutions with oversight and reporting responsibilities. They worried about the quality of loans and the risks to financial stability. Noting a shift in bank lending patterns from private corporations to governments, the BIS raised the issue of "sovereign" risks. It expressed concerns that banks had too little experience evaluating the risks of government loans. The IMF feared it might foster a climate of all-too-easy borrowing by deficit countries, thus facilitating inflation and delaying necessary reforms. However, the IMF was out of political favor. Finance ministers of developing countries objected to its nagging and stringent conditions for loans.[33]

Latin American debt crisis

In the course of lending petrodollars to developing countries – such as Argentina, Brazil, and Mexico – the banks did increase their exposure to risk globally. According to the BIS, private banks lent $158.5 billion from 1974 to 1980, of which $92.5 went to non-oil developing countries. The banks raised $82 billion of this from OPEC countries. In lending amounts of this magnitude to developing countries, the banks took risks that would come back to haunt them, particularly in their dealings with Mexico and Brazil. During the early 1980s, as central banks in developed countries hiked interest rates to combat inflation, Latin American countries encountered difficulties servicing debts. Some had to cut imports as much as 50 percent.[34]

The crisis hit after the Falkland Islands War of May 1982, when the bankers awakened to the fact Latin American countries were overextended. Unable to pay its debts, Mexico negotiated a loan from the US and agreed to reschedule its debts with the bankers. The IMF took a prominent role in arranging credit and helping borrowers restructure. In return for its credits, the IMF demanded that borrowers accept conditions, such as cutting government spending, reducing imports, and devaluing currencies. The IMF action thus prevented a major default, which might have sparked a series of bank failures endangering the international banking system.

The rescheduling postponed a crisis, but ultimately the banks had to write off many of their Latin American loans. John Reed, Wriston's successor at Citibank, set aside $3 billion to cover losses on Wriston's loans to Latin America, which was the total amount of the bank's earnings for the last four years of Wriston's tenure as CEO. The developing-countries debt crisis thus underscored the fragility of the deregulated financial system. The banks lent money to foreign governments on the basis of little disclosure. As large institutions too big to fail, they relied on governments to bail them out of difficulties. The administrations of presidents Ronald Reagan and George H. W. Bush did so with the Baker and Brady plans to address the crisis and avert systemic failure. This was a classic example of moral hazard, where the risk takers were too large to fail. In this situation they could make risky loans that pay high returns without fear of the consequences if loans did not perform as expected. If all else failed, taxpayers could be counted on for bailing out the banking sector. As it turned out, the Latin American crisis was the prelude for worse to come.[35]

Financial Globalization in the 1990s

By the early 1990s, as the Cold War came to a close and the Berlin Wall collapsed, the globalization of finance was far advanced. Big banks and financial firms were scouring the world for business, facilitating the flow of private capital, financing the expansion of trade. The world's stock markets, once separated by time and distance, or at least the telegraph, were increasingly linked by fiber optics, satellites, and high speed computers. As a result of the "Big Boom" in Britain in 1986, and successful efforts by Western service providers to enter the Japanese market, London, Tokyo, and New York had the largest security markets. At the end of 1990, the New York market (NYSE and NASDAQ) was the largest with a domestic capitalization of $3 trillion, Tokyo was second with $2.9 trillion, and London $850 billion. It is estimated that the total market value of securities in circulation was $21.2 trillion, divided almost equally between stocks ($10.8 trillion) and bonds ($10.4 trillion). Ten years later (2000) New York was $15.1 trillion, Tokyo, $3.2 trillion, London, $2.6 trillion, and the New York Stock Exchange Europe $2.3 trillion.[36]

Japanese crisis

The relative decline of Japan in the 1990s merits comment. By the late 1980s Japan was on top of the world. Ezra Vogel's *Japan as Number One*, published in 1979, warned that America was being overtaken by Japan and that power was shifting to the Pacific. Vogel claimed that Japanese institutions coped more successfully than their American counterparts. Behind Japan's surge were a hard-working people determined to rebuild from the devastation of World War II. Its economy had grown at a 6 percent rate since the 1950s, far surpassing other developed countries. Japanese products – such as Toyota cars, Sony electronics, and Canon cameras – appealed to consumers everywhere for their quality and affordability. As noted in Chapter 3, Japanese investors flush with cash bought trophy properties around the world. As *The Economist* wrote: "… the Japanese are now stinking rich." In 1987, the market capitalization of the Tokyo Stock Exchange exceeded that of New York. Japan's banks dominated the world's top ten. Nomura Securities, an investment bank and brokerage company, had profits larger than Citibank and Merrill Lynch. The financial and business press carried reports about how Tokyo stood to replace New York and London as the capital of international finance.[37]

But, as it turned out, Japan's financial strength was a mirage, constructed on an undervalued exchange rate, over-leveraged banks, and a real-estate bubble. A square meter of prime Ginza (shopping district) real estate cost $300,000. The value of all land in Japan (about $20 trillion) was about 2.5 times that of the entire United States.[38]

When the bubble burst, the fall was fast and hard. The Nikkei index dropped two-thirds over two years. Commercial land values in big cities fell 80 percent between 1991 and 2000. The fall in land and stock values reportedly wiped out the equivalent of three years of Japan's gross domestic product.

Along with their heavily leveraged lending to industrial corporations and real estate, Japanese banks were the victims of new international rules, the Basel Accords of 1987. Negotiated under the BIS they sought to require that international banks hold equity capital equal to 8 percent of liabilities. At the time the equity in Japanese banks was closer to 2 percent, although their assets included shares in other companies valued at their purchase price. Japanese regulators had permitted these to count as equity capital. But the collapse of the Japanese market forced many Japanese banks to withdraw from international activities. In response to this situation Japanese regulators announced in 1997 their own "Big Bang," which was implemented between 1998 and 2001. To entice savers back into the market they abolished barriers separating banking, investment, and insurance, liberalized foreign exchange transactions, and brought accounting systems in line with international standards. These steps prepared the way for Tokyo to re-enter international markets.[39]

Offshore banking and sovereign wealth funds

Several new phenomena gathered speed during the 1990s – offshore banking and sovereign wealth funds (SWFs). Offshore banking became a significant factor in international finance. Both Switzerland and the Cayman Islands emerged as major players in this business, driven by the desire of some customers to achieve personal privacy and to avoid national tax and regulatory authorities. Before the tragic events of September 11, 2001, led to increased scrutiny over offshore banks, it was widely estimated that the world's wealthiest individuals held nearly $6 trillion offshore in tax havens. Some of that money was illicit money – the product of drug laundering and other criminal activity.[40]

SWFs are government owned and managed funds that invest oil revenues and trade surpluses in higher-risk, higher-return assets, including stocks, hedge funds, bonds, commodities, and real estate. Kuwait established the first SWF in 1953; Norway organized its government pension fund in 1990. In more recent years China, Iran, Russia, Qatar, and the United Arab Emirates have established SWFs. It is estimated that these government funds manage between $1.9 and $2.9 trillion, and some estimates have them managing $12 trillion by 2015. In 2007 the largest were the Abu Dhabi Investment Authority (United Arab Emirates), $500–875 billion; Norway's Government Pension Fund, $373 billion; Singapore's Government Investment Corporation, $330 billion; and Saudi Arabia's Monetary Authority, $327 billion. One of the ten largest was the California Public Employees' Retirement System, $237 billion.[41] There are concerns that these funds, which operate in a non-transparent way, may have geopolitical interests – including the acquisition of natural resources – as well as financial interests.

On one level financial internationalization appeared to be a great success. By 1989 it was estimated by the BIS that daily foreign exchange trading amounted to $650 billion per day, nearly 40 times the value of exports of goods and services. The US dollar was used in 90 percent of all deals. London retained a significant lead in foreign exchange trading in April 2009, IFSL reported. The UK accounted for 36 percent of global foreign exchange trading, well ahead of the US (14%), Japan (7%), and Singapore (6%). It was apparent that foreign trade accounted for only a fraction of foreign exchange transactions. International capital flows – particularly transactions among banks – accounted for the bulk. FDI had revived smartly. In the 1970s, UNCTAD figures show FDI flows averaging $24 billion per year; in the 1980s, $92.7 billion; and in the 1990s, $401 billion.

During 2000 to 2008, FDI flows averaged $1,138.1 billion. According to BIS staff, non-official inflows to emerging market economies averaged $15.6 billion during the 1980s, of these $12.2 billion was FDI. During the 1990s, inflows were $173.8 billion, of which $102.2 billion was FDI. And, from 2000 to 2007, FDI inflows to emerging markets were $542.6 billion, of which $267.3 was FDI. In 2007, gross non-official inflows to emerging market economies exceeded $1,440.2 billion – a phenomenal expansion of capital flows.[42]

It appeared too that the expansion of trade and financial flows was associated with high growth and with reduced inflation. Over the period 1992 to 2007 as inflation subsided, real growth expanded robustly in many countries. The emerging countries of East Asia enjoyed particularly high rates of growth, averaging 7.26% annually. China averaged nearly 10% growth, followed by Vietnam 7.4% and Korea 5%. Several other large emerging markets enjoyed strong growth: India (6.5%), Brazil (2.7%), and Russia (2.6%). However, among developed countries Germany (1.5%) and Japan (1.15%) offered disappointing examples. The United Kingdom (2.9%) and the US (3.15%) did better.[43]

Capital-account convertibility

In Western Europe and the US a consensus had emerged about the optimal path for development. This so-called Washington consensus, a phrase associated with economist John Williamson, rested on a neo-liberal foundation of assumptions – free trade, free flows of capital, balanced budgets, and the like. And in the international institutions there was a determination to advance the policies, especially capital-account convertibility, so that investors could easily move their money from one location to another. The Washington consensus viewed open-capital markets as a key fundamental for sustained growth, even though countries like China had regulated capital flows and yet experienced double-digit growth. Interestingly, the international campaign to open capital markets was not led by Wall Street and Washington, but by European leaders, several of them French socialists.

Many other world leaders cooperated in the campaign to deregulate markets and privatize government enterprises. Curiously, some of the most effective proponents for deregulating and opening capital markets were French socialists and European bureaucrats. As part of efforts to integrate the European Union, and achieve monetary union, the EU required in 1988 that member states remove barriers to capital flows among themselves, and with non-members. Jacques Delors, the French socialist who was president of the European Commission, and his chief of staff Pascal Lamy, now head of the World Trade Organization, pushed the neo-liberal set of rules for capital. In the International Monetary Fund another French socialist, Michel Camdessus, embraced capital-account liberalization and began to urge it on developing countries. They sought to use international codes and institutions to manage financial globalization for the benefit of the middle class, whereas the US and its powerful banks regarded the IMF and its bureaucrats with skepticism.[44]

During the 1990s the IMF encouraged developing countries to open their capital markets and liberalize trade, even though there was no professional consensus about the value of capital-account liberalization. Argentina, Mexico, Venezuela, and several other Latin American countries undertook rapid and radical deregulation in the late 1980s and early 1990s. The same liberalization trend occurred in Indonesia and Malaysia, although at a slower pace. The IMF argued that robust growth in many developing countries was "associated with increased openness and greater integration into the global economy." In February and April 1997, the Fund's Directors agreed "that an open and liberal system of capital movements fostered economic growth and prosperity by contributing to an efficient allocation of world saving and investment." In consultations with individual developing countries, such as India, Malaysia, and South Korea, they encouraged deregulation and removal of obstacles to foreign investment. The IMF officials pointed to the "considerable efficiency gains from freer capital flows." In effect, the international monetary institutions had become advocates for financial globalization, promoting a vast network of loosely regulated private capital markets and urging structural reforms in emerging markets to accommodate capital flows. As established at Bretton Woods, the IMF had a less ambitious mission – promoting financial stability.[45]

With the removal of controls on capital flows, there was a considerable increase in capital moving to developing countries. FDI flows rose from $13.4 billion in 1970 to $55.3 billion in 1980, $201.6 billion in 1990, and $1,411 billion in 2000, a 105-fold increase. FDI flows to developing countries soared from $3.9 billion in 1970 to $7.7 billion in 1980, $35.9 billion in 1990, and $133.3 billion in 2000. This was a 34-fold increase in 30 years. In 1970 developing countries obtained twice as much from official aid as from private investment; 30 years later, private investment was 2.7 times official flows. Among developing countries the largest share of private investment went to big emerging markets. In 2000 Brazil ($32.8 billion), China and Hong Kong ($102.6 billion), and Mexico ($17.8 billion) received $153.2 billion, or 60 percent of investment flows to developing countries.[46]

Asian economic crisis

The Asian economic crisis of 1997–8 was a warning signal of dangers to come as a deregulated global economy took shape. Until 1997 the emerging markets of Asia had been a model for the future. They had high rates of savings, high-rates of growth (exceeding 7%), and currencies pegged to the US dollar. Korea and Thailand had recently opened their financial markets to foreign investors. This encouraged foreign investors searching for high yields to invest in Asian securities. In 1996, the year before the roof caved in, FDI poured into the developing countries of Asia. They received $94 billion (64 percent) of the world total of $147 billion invested in developing countries. China and Hong Kong obtained $52.2 billion, Korea $2 billion. The countries of Southeast Asia (including Indonesia, Malaysia, Singapore, and Vietnam) gained $30.5 billion.[47]

Other forms of external financing soared, particularly volatile short-term bank lending. As a result, the economies became dependent on dollar-denominated debt and vulnerable to fluctuations in investor sentiment. According to the BIS, international bank lending and bond finance for five Asian countries (Indonesia, Korea, Malaysia, the Philippines, and Thailand) rose from a $19 billion annual average in the early 1990s to $75 billion in 1995–6. Short-term external debt as a percentage of foreign exchange reserves rose sharply for several countries. In the case of Korea it rose from 148% in 1993 to 214% in mid-2007; Malaysia from 28 to 62%; and Thailand from 89% to 153%.[48]

In Thailand borrowing in foreign currencies fueled an asset bubble in real-estate construction. In their enthusiasm for returns, foreign investors again underestimated risk in developing markets, and assumed that local governments would support financial institutions. Years of uninterrupted growth lulled investors to the dangers of rising external indebtedness in a deregulated environment. The BIS reported that by mid-1997 Thailand's short-term external debt was 153 percent of foreign exchange reserves. For Indonesia and Korea it was even higher – 182 percent and 214 percent respectively.[49]

When Thailand's exports started to slip in the spring of 1997, the baht came under speculative pressure forcing the kingdom to devalue. This triggered pressure on the Philippine peso, the Malaysian ringgit, and the Indonesian rupiah. After these currencies fell, contagion spread to the

Korean won. To obtain outside financial support ($117 billion was offered), Thailand, Indonesia, and Korea accepted IMF stabilization plans. They required harsh domestic austerity. The most humiliating image from the period, and the one that outraged many Asians, was that of IMF managing director Michel Camdessus towering over Indonesian President Suharto as he signed a stabilization agreement requiring harsh stabilization measures.

The Asian crisis of 1997 reinforced the dominant position of the dollar. As the experience of the Asian countries demonstrated, smaller countries needed large reserves of dollars to ward off speculative attacks in times of turmoil. In the aftermath they chose to keep their currencies cheap, promote exports, and build up large reserves of dollars to avoid a similar crisis in the future. Some began to talk of dollar hegemony as a consequence. The dollar seemed indispensable, for under the system of floating rates that succeeded Bretton Woods the dollar remained the linchpin of international finance. Major commodities, such as oil, continued to be priced in dollars. And the world needed dollar reserves to finance trade and to maintain the value of national currencies. Many governments intervened in exchange markets, using dollars, to influence the value of their currencies.

Conclusion

In this chapter we have examined how the winds of globalization transformed the tightly regulated financial world that grew out of the Great Depression. In that era bank failures, unsound investment practices, and disruptive capital movements had compelled governments to regulate banking, finance, and international capital flows. A half century later, as memories of prior events dimmed, pressure mounted for deregulating financial markets. Lobbyists and free-market enthusiasts succeeded in relaxing controls, and enabling a revolution in global finance. Private capital flows soared, assisted by new communications and information technologies. To facilitate the process, governments in high-income countries and the IMF aided and abetted efforts to open developing-world capital markets. While the reforms lowered capital costs, and produced many benefits, there were early indications that deregulated markets operated imperfectly, and sometimes broke down. During the last two decades of the twentieth century, a series of developing-market financial crises warned, like silent canaries in a coal mine, of imminent danger in a financial world with few controls.

Chapter 9

The Global Financial Crisis of 2007–10

The vibrant global economy quickly shrugged off the Asian crisis and resumed its growth. Like a powerful locomotive, growing consumer demand in the US pulled economic activity in other regions. As the world's largest and most open market, the US generated 30 percent of global GDP in 2000, and consumed 19 percent of world imports.

Around the world investor confidence rebounded swiftly. In 1999, two years after the regional financial crisis, Asian markets in Singapore, Sydney, and Hong Kong capped a remarkable recovery. Bullish sentiment at year's end marked a sharp turnaround. Among European markets Britain's FTSE touched a new all-time peak on the last trading day, up 17.8 percent for the year, with technology shares leading the way. Technology shares also pushed the Paris bourse to a new record level, and technology was behind the US boom that saw stocks soar to record levels in late 1999. US stocks had risen for 105 months, the longest period of expansion since the 1960s.

As rising flows of trade and finance continued to integrate nations, transactions in foreign exchange markets expanded rapidly. In 1998, $1.5 trillion changed hands every day. By 2007 the daily turnover in currencies was $3.5 trillion, up 133 percent. By comparison, total world exports of merchandise amounted to $14 trillion, the equivalent of four days of exchange trading.

Like many others, Alan Greenspan, chairman of the US Federal Reserve System, thought the world economy generally prosperous and stable. Along with strong growth inflation remained low. Since the early 1980s economic downturns in high-income countries had been shallow. Advanced

The Contemporary Global Economy: A History Since 1980, First Edition. Alfred E. Eckes, Jr.
© 2011 Alfred E. Eckes, Jr. Published 2011 by Blackwell Publishing Ltd.

economies proved resilient to shocks and collapses in Argentina, Mexico, East Asia, and Russia. To Greenspan the global capitalist economy seemed fast-changing and self-correcting. Open markets and free trade had lifted millions of the world's people from poverty.[1]

Developments in global securities markets during the first years of the new millennium appeared to support Greenspan's faith in free enterprise. Stock markets continued to expand, consolidate, and integrate. New York Stock Exchange's capitalization, which stood at $11.4 trillion at the end of 1999, rose to $15.7 trillion by the end of 2007. The New York Stock Exchange Europe climbed from $2.4 trillion to $4.2 trillion, and London from $2.9 to $3.9 trillion. A new market, Shanghai, emerged from nowhere and had a valuation of $3.7 trillion. It was in fifth place ahead of Hong Kong, which had a valuation $2.7 trillion. As markets grew and technology improved, consolidation continued. By 2007 the New York exchange had merged with Euronext, creating a global marketing group. Euronext, founded in 2000, united exchanges in Paris, Brussels, and Amsterdam.[2]

Bulls and Bears

Among a majority of forecasters and financial analysts, the mood at the beginning of the new century was upbeat. Some foresaw a robust, long-term expansion as technological innovations and the shift to a service-dominated, knowledge-based economy shaped a new economic paradigm. Rosy predictions flowed freely from the lips and pens of pundits. Journalist James K. Glassman and economist Kevin Hassett predicted the Dow Jones industrial average would rise to 36,000 in three to five years. That was an increase of 213 percent over the 11,497 average on December 31, 1999. The authors claimed that stocks were undervalued, because technological advances and improved sources of information had reduced risks. Not to be outdone, financial adviser Charles Kadlec forecast a rise in the Dow industrials to 100,000 in 2020.[3]

In this euphoric environment bulls remained on the rampage and pessimistic bears faced media scorn. In November 1999 Louis Rukeyser, the ebullient bullish host of "Wall Street Week," a popular television program for US investors, expelled the only Cassandra from his panel of market "elves." For 156 weeks Gail Dudack of Warburg Dillon had offered bearish forecasts and poured cold water on market optimism. Several months after her departure, the market shifted directions in dramatic fashion. The crash of technology stocks in the US signaled the end of the dot.com bubble. But it did not destabilize the global economy, nor did terrorist attacks in 2001 and the surprising collapse of energy giant Enron due to accounting fraud. These events had little impact on gold prices, traditionally a signal of bearish sentiments. Gold prices ended 2001 at $276.50, lower than any average price since 1978.[4]

Optimism at the beginning of the twenty-first century was reminiscent of the mood before World War I. In that golden era a similar open economy existed. Trade, investments, and migration soared. Many thoughtful people of that period anticipated continued growth and improvement, as nations prospered, matured, and integrated their economies. While there were doomsayers predicting a European war or the collapse of capitalism, the sudden collapse of globalization in 1914 seems to have surprised European investors.[5]

Contemporary circumstances differed significantly from the era that came to a close in the summer of 1914. Nonetheless, there were fascinating parallels. The buoyant internationalism of *New York Times* commentator Thomas Friedman resembled that of Norman Angell in 1911. Like the pre-World War I writer, Friedman saw a world too interconnected for war. In the *Lexus and the Olive Tree* (1999), and in other writings, Friedman offered his own upbeat theory of an interdependent world: the "Golden Arches" thesis. He stated that "no two countries that both have a McDonald's have ever fought a war against each other." As incomes rise and nations become middle class, supporting a McDonald's network, Friedman believed that economic and digital integration, and the spread of capitalist values, constrained foreign policy behavior. Or stated differently, "people in McDonald's countries don't like to fight wars anymore, they prefer to wait in line for burgers."[6]

Despite euphoric forecasts, some influential observers did have concerns about the health of the global economy at the beginning of the new millennium. *The Economist*, which offered an international perspective on trends, worried about the world's two largest economies, Japan and the United States. Excessive borrowing made these economies appear vulnerable. Japan, recovering from the collapse of its stock and real-estate markets in 1990, would soon have the "biggest debt (as a percentage of GDP) that has ever been owed by any developed economy during peacetime." Public-sector debt in Japan contrasted with America's "private profligacy," manifest in rising consumer debt, huge bonuses to corporate executives, and soaring equity prices. While acknowledging that new economic conditions were bringing genuine gains, it asserted "that markets are ... being driven by unrealistic expectations of future productivity and profits growth."[7]

To financial overseers one incident was especially disturbing. The crash of a hedge fund (Long Term Capital Management) rang an alarm. LTCM lost $4.6 billion in 1998 following the Russian financial crisis. It had been using complex mathematical trading techniques to take highly leveraged positions, using derivatives and other new financial instruments. The New York Federal Reserve Bank organized a private-sector bail-out from among LTCM's creditors in order to avoid wider systemic damage. Later overseers discussed the lessons and implications and whether the failure of new techniques at LTCM posed a broader threat to the financial system. Perhaps because the collapse had been contained without spreading to Main Street, the reviewers chose not to recommend government intervention to curb innovation in financial markets. But the episode highlighted the dangers of interdependent markets and permissive attitudes toward risk.[8]

Free-market economics and deregulation remained the watchwords of the day. Federal Reserve chairman Greenspan took the view that derivatives made markets more efficient, and President Clinton's treasury secretary Larry Summers agreed. When regulators at the Commodity Futures Trading Commission sought to exert authority over derivatives, industry lobbyists blocked efforts to strengthen regulation. They had help from Texas Senator Phil Gramm, the chairman of the Senate banking committee, who played a central role in writing the Commodity Futures Modernization Act in 2000, closing the door to regulation of swaps and derivatives.[9]

The Bank for International Settlements in Basel, which serves central banks, had reservations about the "virtual explosion in the issue of sub-investment-grade bonds in the United States" and about permissive and imprudent lending. It noted that a long period of financial deregulation and consolidation made the world financial system "more market driven, globalized, interconnected, and fast-moving than ever before." While appreciating new techniques for transferring credit risk, the BIS warned that "efficiency is not everything." Attention must be given to safety and stability. It manifest concern that the distribution of risk within the system had become less transparent.[10]

The International Monetary Fund had similar misgivings. In its *Global Stability Report* (March 2002), it warned about over-leveraging and credit quality deterioration growing out of the exposure to traded financial assets. The rapid growth of over-the-counter derivatives trade had doubled to nearly $100 trillion (notional size) between 1995 and 2001. The IMF said the complexity of derivatives trading could leave parties vulnerable to unrecognized risks and "expose the overall system if mistakes are large."[11]

Several prominent private investors expressed concerns about the new financial instruments. Henry Kaufman, a savvy Wall Street money manager whose gloomy views won him the nickname "Dr. Doom," criticized the flawed reasoning of "financial soothsayers" who "tout the New Paradigm." He also voiced doubts about rational market theories and the use of quantitative risk-management systems. These techniques reinforced "the illusion that risk can be dissected and predicted with a high degree of precision. ..." Paul Volcker, the former chairman of the US Federal Reserve System, agreed with Kaufman. He thought that modern risk-management and trading techniques were rooted more in mathematics than in clear understanding of financial markets and human nature.[12]

Another prominent investor, Nebraska billionaire Warren Buffett, called attention to the risks in derivatives. These were complex financial contracts used to speculate and mitigate risk. The value of the contract depended on future price movements of an underlying asset. Buffett noted that even financially sophisticated investors could not learn from disclosure documents what risks lurked in positions. He deemed the latent dangers "potentially lethal," and branded derivatives "financial weapons of mass destruction."[13]

Problems in the Making

Despite growing concerns, monetary authorities did not remove the punch bowl of cheap money from the party. After the Dow industrials broke 6,000 in October 1996, Federal Reserve Chairman Greenspan warned about the "irrational exuberance" of markets, but the bulls charged on. The Federal Reserve was not disposed to raise interest rates and provoke a political firestorm of criticism. After the Asian Crisis of 1997 and the collapse of the dot.com bubble in 2000–1, it eased interest rates to stimulate consumption. The Fed did so again after the terrorist attacks of September 11, 2001.[14]

Nor were US monetary authorities unduly alarmed about imbalances resulting from expanding consumer debt and excessive government spending and borrowing. The ratio of household debt to personal disposable income rose from 65 percent in the mid-1980s to an all-time high of 133 percent in 2007. Greenspan rationalized that rising debt went hand-in-hand with progress in a market economy. In his view a rising ratio of debt to household income did not indicate "stress." Nor was the "maestro" of the Federal Reserve troubled about America's persistent external imbalance (current account) and growing reliance on foreign capital to finance that deficit. As noted previously, the current account is the broadest measure of a country's economic relationships with the world. It takes into account trade in goods and services, transfers and remittances, and interest and investment earnings. Greenspan observed that there were many imbalances – including the federal deficit – and he placed the current account deficit (CAD) "far down the list." So did treasury secretary Paul O'Neill, who called the CAD a "meaningless concept." He echoed the Bush administration line that deficits resulted from an inflow of capital as foreign residents sought to obtain superior returns by investing in America.[15]

Although US officials were not worried about global payments imbalances, international agencies were. After the 1997 Asian crisis, the BIS and the IMF began voicing doubts about whether the US could sustain current-account deficits. Their language grew tougher when US fiscal and trade deficits soared in the new century.

To fight the war on terrorism the Bush administration pushed the budget deficit up to 3.6 percent of GDP in 2004, a major change from the four years of budget surpluses achieved under the Clinton administration and a Republican Congress. Meanwhile wages and salaries rose slowly, but consumer spending boomed, fueled by rising stock and home prices. Many home-owners took out second mortgages on homes to unlock equity and to support high-consumption lifestyles. Personal savings as a share of GDP fell from 2.4 to 0.4 percent in 2005. Household debt rose over 11 percent in 2003–5, the result of rapid increases in mortgage debt. This imbalance between spending and saving underscored the fragility of the economic recovery and helped to explain the rapid growth of imports.[16]

External imbalances

The global collapse of 2007–10 had multiple roots. One underlying cause involved chronic structural imbalances in a world of open financial markets and relaxed regulation. While these circumstances did not ignite the crisis, they accelerated its spread and exacerbated the collapse of business confidence.[17]

Much of the problem related to the world's largest economy, the US dollar, and its trade deficits. The US trade deficit in goods rose from $197.9 billion in 1997, the year of the Asian crisis, to $446.2 billion in 2000, $783.8 billion in 2005, and $839.5 billion in 2006, on the eve of the financial crisis. Deficits with Pacific Rim countries accounted for 43 percent of the deficit in 2006. Petroleum imports, which had risen from $54.9 billion in 1996 to $216.6 billion in 2006, represented another 25.8 percent. The broader CAD generally reflected the surging merchandise trade deficit. The CAD soared from $140.7 billion in 1997 to $802.6 billion in 2006, fueled by rising military and consumer spending, and higher energy prices for imports.[18]

Of course, one country's trade deficit is another's surplus. In this case Asia was the principal beneficiary of American consumerism, and over the decade after the 1997 regional economic crisis Asia became America's banker. In Asia export-led growth fueled an economic surge and a strong recovery from the 1997 regional crisis. So as not to become wards of the IMF in a future crisis, Asian governments resolved to build up large dollar reserves from exports. They succeeded in elevating their share of global GDP, and in raising per capita incomes. The resulting large current-account surpluses helped Asia build up huge cushions of foreign exchange reserves. In 1996 the five Asian countries most impacted by the 1997 crisis (Indonesia, Korea, Malaysia, the Philippines, and Korea) had foreign exchange reserves of only $132 billion. They all had CADs averaging 4.7 percent of GDP. A decade later in 2006 the five had $455 billion in reserves, and current account surpluses averaging 2.8 percent of GDP. China and India did even better. China increased its reserves tenfold from $107 billion in 1996 to $1,068 billion in 2006, while India raised reserves seven-fold – from $24.9 billion to $178 billion. In short, thanks to spendthrift consumers in high-income countries, developing nations in Asia were much better prepared for a financial tsunami than in 1997. But the combination of Asian saving and American spending created unsustainable imbalances that imperiled the global economy.[19]

As it turned out the surplus countries would continue to accumulate and by 2009 would be bankers to the world. By late 2010 world governments held $8.4 trillion in foreign exchange reserves, a substantial sum. China reported total reserves of $2,650 billion, Japan $1,070 billion, Russia $435 billion, Saudi Arabia $408 billion, and Taiwan $380.5 billion. Others with large reserves positions included Brazil, Hong Kong, India, and South Korea, all with more than $235 billion. In effect the surplus countries had become the new bankers of the world, lending to the rich countries money so that they could continue buying manufactures and oil.[20]

IMF data indicates that the surplus countries invested the vast majority of reserves (some 64 percent) in US bonds and other assets, helping to keep US interest rates low. In July 2010, the US Treasury reported that foreign residents held $4,065.8 billion of US Treasury securities, of which foreign governments held $2,726.5 billion. China owned the largest amount ($846.7 billion), followed by Japan ($821 billion), the United Kingdom

($374.3 billion), oil-exporting countries ($223.8 billion), Caribbean banking centers ($150.7 billion), Hong Kong ($135.2 billion), Russia ($130.9 billion), and Taiwan ($130.5 billion). Some of the British holdings may have come from oil-exporting nations.[21]

Although it had become the world's largest debtor, the US situation differed in one important respect from smaller debtor countries like Thailand (1997) and Argentina (2001). They had borrowed in foreign currencies from Western banks at 7 or 8 percent, instead of local banks at 15 percent. This was very attractive until the Thai baht depreciated against the dollar. Then borrowers could not meet their obligations. When the Thai baht plummeted from 26 to the US dollar in 1997 to over 50 baht per dollar in 1998, it cost a Thai borrower twice as much to make payments on a foreign loan. Many chose to default. One Thai entrepreneur whose real-estate business collapsed in the Asian crisis started selling sandwiches and sushi on the streets of Bangkok.

Unlike Thailand, the US was blessed by the fact that it could borrow in dollars and its overseas creditors generally preferred to hold dollars than some other currency. Thus there was an international market for America's debt. As it happened some exporting nations, such as Saudi Arabia and China, earned dollars by selling large quantities of petroleum and manufacturers to the US. Then they reinvested their dollar earnings in US debt, helping to keep interest rates down. In effect, they loaned dollars back to the US so that American consumers could continue to buy their exports. Chinese and other foreign reserves invested in US Treasuries, helping hold down long-term interest rates, and fueling the real-estate construction boom in the US that peaked in 2005.

This relationship was unique. One of the world's richest countries had become its largest debtor. When Britain managed the late nineteenth-century gold standard, it had run a trade deficit and exported capital to emerging countries like the US. In the twenty-first century the US ran a substantial, chronic trade deficit but borrowed capital from developing countries. The huge imbalances, the results of Asia and OPEC's current account surpluses, and the US's chronic deficits, led to large net capital flows from emerging market economies to the developed world. As Mervyn King, governor of the Bank of England, later said, these flows "provided the fuel which an inadequately designed regulatory system ignited to produce the financial firestorm that engulfed us all."[22]

Asia's persistent current account surpluses – the result of export-led growth – and America's recurring current-account deficits, brought about by profligate consumer spending and energy imports, presented a new version of an old problem. In the 1950s economist Robert Triffin had warned of the dollar dilemma. Once again growth in world monetary reserves depended, as it had under the Bretton Woods system, on the US running a current-account deficit. Beginning in 1982, the US had experienced a chronic current-account deficit – and the cumulative deficit approached $7.4 trillion by 2009.[23]

Given the huge imbalances, and the debtor role of the reserve currency country, it is not surprising that some creditor countries had second thoughts about holding so much of their foreign currency reserves in dollars. The dollar's share of total foreign currency reserves slipped from 73 percent in 2001 to 64 percent in 2007 (62% in mid-2010). The euro's share rose from 18 to 25 percent (26% in mid-2010). Even so, the dollar remained the world's most important currency for trade and finance. As a result the US continued to enjoy special privileges. The world needed the dollar to conduct business, but the persistent deficits raised concerns about Americans living beyond their means.[24]

The US was not the only country living beyond its means with an unsustainable current-account deficit. There were other consumers of last resort, among them the United Kingdom with cumulative CADs of $711 billion between 1980 and 2009. On a smaller scale, Spain, Greece, Portugal, Ireland, Iceland, Dubai, and Australia all spent more than they earned, and borrowed to sustain spending.[25]

Real estate excesses

The collapse of the US real-estate bubble in 2007 was the trigger for the global collapse. It too had a peculiar history. After the bubble in technology stocks burst in 2000, the Federal Reserve feared the dot.com crash would spill over into the overall economy. Under Greenspan's direction the central bank slashed interest rates. The average conventional 30-year fixed interest rate on home mortgages fell from 8.1 percent in 2000 to 5.86 percent in 2004. Cheap mortgage rates helped spur a real-estate construction boom, and lenders relaxed standards and qualified thousands of borrowers with sub-prime mortgages. From 2000 to 2007 the quantity of mortgage debt rose 115 percent from $6.8 trillion to $14.6 trillion.[26]

With 30-year mortgages generally available at about 6 percent or less, brokers hustled to find and qualify prospective home buyers. To sell condominiums in a West Palm Beach, Florida, complex, brokers offered prospective buyers no-money-down, no-closing-cost loans. Many of the buyers were first-time buyers, inexperienced with credit and unable to keep up payments. As the economy turned sour, 80 percent of those loans defaulted.[27]

In the United Kingdom a similar pattern occurred on a smaller scale. Aggressive lenders hooked large numbers on sub-prime loans and then, after housing values fell, buyers discovered they had insufficient equity to sell their homes and move.[28]

Sub-prime loans typically carried higher-than-market rates, sometime with onerous costs and penalties. Frequently lenders lured borrowers with low introductory rates that reset at higher rates after two or three years. In 2005, the peak year for sub-prime lending, one study showed that 55 percent of all sub-prime mortgages went to borrowers with credit scores high enough to qualify for conventional loans. Many chose sub-prime offerings because of hard-selling brokers or the attraction of quick approval with little paperwork. On average brokers collected 1.88 percent of the loan amount for a originating a sub-prime loan, but only 1.48 percent for conforming loans. As one mortgage lender told the press: "The market is paying me to do a no-income-verification loan more than it is paying me to do the full documentation loans. What would you do?" Greed thus led some brokers to misrepresentation and unethical conduct, duping borrowers.[29]

Along with lax lending standards and lender misconduct, governments in the US and Britain shared some of the blame. They assigned priority to expanding home-ownership among low-income people, and encouraged sub-prime lending to achieve that goal. Sub-prime lending enjoyed bipartisan support in the US. Elected officials pressured banks and others to make more home mortgage loans to sub-prime borrowers. In 2001 Senator Phil Gramm (R-TX), a key legislator on banking issues, said: "Some people look at sub-prime lending and see evil. ... I look at sub-prime lending and I see the American dream in action." He noted that his mother bought a home with a sub-prime loan. Under pressure from the Clinton administration, the Fannie Mae Corporation eased credit requirements on loans it would buy from banks to encourage lending to individuals with low and moderate income, particularly to minorities. Fannie Mae, a government corporation that purchased mortgages from lenders, encouraged "the most flexible underwriting criteria permitted."[30]

President Clinton's Secretary of Housing and Urban Development was Henry Cisneros, the first Hispanic to head a Cabinet-level agency. Eager to promote home-ownership for low-income families, Cisneros took steps to ease lending requirements. He allowed lenders to hire their own appraisers, and borrowers no longer had to show five years of stable income. After leaving government, he joined the board of Countrywide Financial, a firm that became the largest originator of sub-prime mortgage loans during the housing boom. One of the keys to Countrywide's success, its chief executive Angelo Mozilo admitted, was stretching the rules to qualify minority applicants. Lawsuits filed by state attorney-generals later alleged that Countrywide used misleading advertising and deceptive practices to trick customers into accepting loans that would lead to foreclosure. To conclude the litigation Bank of America, which bought out Countrywide, agreed to reduce principal and interest-rate payments for customers holding sub-prime loans, a settlement costing $8.8 billion. Under Mozilo's leadership, Countrywide had also sought to curry favor with regulators and lawmakers. It provided loans with special discounts to members of Congress and regulators with responsibilities in the housing area. Senator Chris Dodd (D-CN), the chair of the Senate Banking Committee and a frequent critic of predator lenders, was one beneficiary of Mozilo's largesse.[31]

In the late 1990s sub-prime loans were only 5 percent of all mortgage lending. Under Republican George W. Bush, elected president in 2000, sub-prime lending approached 30 percent in 2005. Bush shared Clinton's enthusiasm for boosting home-ownership, and continued the lenient approach to qualifying mortgage applicants. He set a goal of adding millions of minority home-owners (many of them Latino). In June 2002, Bush announced a target of having the federal government assist 5.5 million minority families to buy homes before the end of the decade. Bush signed legislation – the American Dream Downpayment Act of 2003 – helping 40,000 families with downpayment and closing costs. In doing so, he sought to end a home-ownership gap between Anglo America and black and Hispanic America. The home-ownership rate for minority families was 49 percent or less in 2003, compared to more than 75 percent for white, working families.

After the housing boom slowed in 2005, Warren Buffett succinctly summarized what was happening. He said that lenders happily made loans that borrowers couldn't repay, and borrowers just as happily signed up to meet those payments. Lenders and borrowers counted on a rise in home prices to make this otherwise impossible arrangement work. And, for a time, prices did rise. The median price of existing one-family homes climbed 51 percent between 2000 and 2006, fueled by easy credit. The consequences of this behavior would reverberate through the economy when the housing bubble burst.[32]

In the United Kingdom elected officials also promoted home-ownership to create a more stable society. Conservative Margaret Thatcher backed right-to-buy legislation in the 1980s to boost home-ownership among tenants in public housing projects at discounted prices. Prime Minister Tony Blair and the Labor government continued that policy. As a result many poor people acquired equity in their property, and home-ownership reached a plateau of about 71 percent in 2000. The press found that in Britain many sub-prime lenders had also flouted the rules on responsible lending, handing out loans to people on low incomes or with a checkered credit history. As further evidence of the globalization of finance, the largest British sub-prime lenders included subsidiaries of foreign firms GMAC, Merrill Lynch, and Deutsche Bank. The UK sub-prime market, however, was smaller than the one in the US, accounting for only 8 percent of lending in 2006 versus 20 percent in the US.[33]

Deteriorating credit standards

Deteriorating credit standards also helped bring on the financial crisis in which liquidity needed to sustain business transactions dried up. Among the problems were the widespread use of complex, new financial instruments, which few borrowers and lenders understood, and a growing tolerance for risk in lending.

Traditionally, banks and building societies had known their customers and kept home loans in their own portfolios. However, during the 1990s lenders, looking for new ways to expand profits, adopted the originate-to-distribute model. They learned how to bundle mortgages with others, and sell the resulting security as a collateralized debt obligation (CDO) to investors. With these complex, new instruments lenders succeeded in shifting the risk off their own books, while collecting fees for originating the loan. Banks then sold collateralized securities worldwide to investors looking for higher returns. As it turned out, the CDOs were so complex that not even ratings agencies knew their true value. Nor did customers eager for high returns understand the risks underlying such complex and opaque instruments. In the new interconnected world of finance, many of the customers lived in distant locations where there were large pools of savings – Australia, Germany, Japan, Norway, and many other locations.

The lure of quick profits led brokers and bankers to discount risk and mislead customers. In 2006, Merrill Lynch employees took home $5 billion in bonuses; 100 individuals received $1 million or more. The head of the bond division, who received a $350,000 salary, gained a $35 million bonus. Charles Prince, the CEO of Citigroup, said he was not concerned that problems with sub-prime loans would come back to haunt the industry.

"When the music stops, in terms of liquidity, things will be complicated. But as long as the music is playing, you've got to get up and dance."[34]

For decades those investing in debt had relied on qualitative assessments from conscientious independent rating agencies – Moody's, Standard and Poor's, and Fitch – to evaluate financial products. When one of these watch-dogs gave a security a top rating (such as Aaa), an investor could have confidence that the prospects for default were slight. However, in 2000 Moody's spun off from its parent Dun & Bradstreet and executives set out to establish a more business-friendly culture. Because issuers of securities paid for ratings, not investors as previously, the rating agencies competed for business and curried favor with investment banks. Executives report-edly pressured ratings analysts to be more profit-oriented, and even to manipulate ratings. Moody's, for example, raised its ratings on some of troubled lender Countrywide Financial's securities after it complained that Moody's assessment was too hard. Nor did the ratings agency exercise due diligence and examine the credit worthiness of individual mortgages pooled in a CDO. Rather they relied on mathematical models to determine risk, and stamped a label on the security. On the basis of that cursory rating pension funds, universities, municipalities, and institutional investors around the world made their purchases. In effect, as one former ratings agency executive acknowledged, the watchdogs had turned into lapdogs for investment banks.[35]

To cover risks inherent to mortgages, such as a default, bankruptcy, and credit downgrade, holders of CDOs bought credit default swaps (CDSs), essentially a derivative product intended to insure the CDO holder. These quickly became speculative assets. By 2007 the face value of credit default swaps was valued at $62 trillion, more than the GDP of the world ($54 trillion), according to the Congressional Research Service. CDS blurred the line with traditional insurance. They hedged risk but did not back it with sufficient capital to pay claims in case of default. In the absence of a supra-financial authority, regulation was spotty. The lines separating insurance companies, bank, and brokerages had blurred during the period of deregulation.[36]

A classic example involved insurance giant AIG, which came close to bankruptcy in September 2008 and received what would become a $182 billion bail-out from the US government. In return for the bridging loan, the government took a 79.9 percent equity stake. No simple insurance company, AIG was a big complicated company actively involved in insuring but also in derivatives. It offered insurance guarantees on derivative con-tracts and became a major player in the mortgage insurance business. A large reason for AIG's failure was its little-known financial products operation in London. It functioned in an environment involving "opulent pay, lax oversight, and blind faith in financial risk models. ..." AIG's financial products unit wrote some $500 billion in credit default swaps, insuring European and US banks against defaults on a variety of debt holdings. Because of AIG's double-A credit rating, it did not need to put up collateral to assure customers of its capacity to honor its obligations if necessary. It did not take steps to protect against the volatility that could bankrupt its business. Executives saw these contracts as comparable to catastrophe insurance for events that would not happen. As it turned out, much of the money received from the federal government (around $50 billion) went to customers such as Goldman Sachs, Merrill Lynch, and two French banks.[37]

Behind the new products and the securitization of risk were fundamental problems. Along with traditional flaws such as greed, loose regulation, easy monetary policy, and fraud, such as Bernard Madoff's Ponzi scheme, there were others: complexity and ignorance. Most bankers simply did not understand the complicated computer-based models that had been adapted from economics to measure credit risk. Even the IMF remarked approvingly in April 2006 that "the rapid growth of credit risk transfer instruments have enabled banks ... to outsource the warehousing of credit risk to a diverse range of investors. A wider dispersion of credit risk has 'derisked' the banking sector. ..." The IMF cited former Federal Reserve chairman Alan Greenspan's observation that "increasingly complex financial instruments have contributed to the development of a far more flexible, efficient, and hence resilient financial system" than existed several decades earlier. Thus, by turning their mortgages into bonds, banks found that they could make more loans with existing capital than previously, while complying with regulatory standards.[38]

More slicing and dicing meant more fees and higher bonuses for loan originators. Because most of these instruments were too specialized for the free market, they were valued using calculations from theoretical models. The boom in securitized loans continued until mid-2007 when sub-prime delinquencies rose, and accountants demanded that banks revalue these instruments downward.[39]

Several other factors contributed to increased risk in financial markets. For one thing the originate-to-distribute model for mortgages made mortgages easily available. Loan originators did not face penalties for mistakes, and buyers of debt obligations received little information about the quality of underling loans. They relied on ratings services. But the credit raters had conflicting interests. They received large fees for ratings and frequently turned a blind eye to underlying quality. The rating agencies had little experience with credit default swaps or with systematic risk. And regulators who accepted the conventional wisdom about efficient markets were disinclined to exercise vigorous oversight. There was little government regulation of those originating loans, and so rating services, such as Moody's, which prospered from large numbers of transactions with banks, could rate much of the securitized debt highly (Aaa).

Elected officials who nurtured the real-estate bubble also erred. Legislators authorized subsidies to first-time home buyers with little credit and pressured banks and lending organizations to ease standards in order to achieve higher rates of home-ownership. Legislators also failed to support vigorous supervision and regulation of financial markets.

The Collapse

Hindsight is often 20/20 in evaluating economic events; foresight seldom is. Early in 2007 a panel of investment analysts surveyed by *Barron's* stressed the global economy's underlying strength, despite serious problems in the US market. Few expected the party to end soon.

But, the bursting of the real-estate bubble in the US late 2006 and 2007, and the resulting sub-prime mortgage crisis, had heightened uncertainty in the world marketplace. Banks, insurance companies, investment houses, and individual consumers with large amounts of leverage debt were vulnerable to the downturn. As the shock reverberated, financial institutions sought to improve their capital ratio, by de-leveraging. That is, they had to sell assets and reduce lending.

By July and August 2007, the decline in the US real-estate market impacted several German regional banks. In September Britain experienced its first bank run in 150 years, forcing government intervention and, within a few months, nationalization. During the winter of 2008 there were a number of other high profile failures. In January 2008, UBS, a Swiss banking giant, announced $18 billion in write-downs from declines in US real estate. In March, to avoid a high-profile bankruptcy, the Federal Reserve managed the sale of investment bank Bear Stearns to JPMorgan Chase for a price about one-quarter of the original cost of Bear's Manhattan headquarters. The Federal Reserve also assumed $30 billion of Bear's liabilities. Bear Stearns, the bank praised by *Euromoney* in 2006 as the best investment bank in North America, had fallen victim to the sub-prime mortgage crisis.

Two of its hedge funds had invested heavily in securities backed by sub-prime mortgages.[40]

By mid-Spring 2008, three large financial service providers, Citi, Merrill Lynch, and UBS (Switzerland) had written down $53 billion in valuations. Another aggressive sub-prime lender, the Royal Bank of Scotland (RBS), announced heavy losses. It was led by the flamboyant Sir Fred Goodwin, dubbed "Fred the Shred." When IndyMac Bancorp imploded in April 2008, attention turned to other US regional lenders with exposure to mortgage financing, including Citizens, an RBS subsidiary. But RBS's major problem was an ambitious plan to take over ABN Amro, a Dutch lender, which stretched RBS's capital reserves to the limit.[41]

Collapse of Lehman Brothers

The incident that rocked Wall Street and helped turn the sub-prime crisis into a global panic was the bankruptcy of Lehman Brothers, a prestigious investment bank, in September 2008. It was the largest bankruptcy in US history at $639 billion. Lehman reported losses of $2.8 billion in its mort-gage business. This event proved a catalyst for a massive flight to safety and sell-off on world equity markets. Already in the process of de-leveraging, banks in high-income countries closed credit lines, repatriated funds, and reduced exposure to emerging markets. Over the next five weeks major stock markets plummeted. The Dow Jones industrial average fell 27%, and the FTSE 100 in London dropped 28%. In Asia, Tokyo's Nikkei 225 plunged 37%, while the Hang Seng in Hong Kong dived 35%. Meanwhile gold soared, rising 24% from $740.75 per ounce on September 11 to $918 on October 10.

Because of the many connections among world economies, the US decline rapidly spread outward. By early 2009 there was widespread concern about another Great Depression as stock markets dropped to new lows. By the end of March, 2009, the New York Stock Exchange had fallen 44.1% in dollar terms, as compared to a year earlier. The NASDAQ was down 29.6%, Tokyo 34.3%, London 31.4%, and the New York Stock Exchange in Europe 53.1%. Shanghai fell 28%, and Hong Kong 40%. Commodity prices also plummeted, with oil prices dropping 36.6% in 2009.

The catastrophic meltdown transformed Wall Street and world credit markets. Within a few months the five largest investment houses either changed hands (Bear Stearns sold to JPMorgan Chase, and Merrill Lynch to Bank of America), or entered bankruptcy (Lehman), or converted to bank holding companies (as Goldman Sachs, and Morgan Stanley) under federal supervision. And credit markets locked up, as financial institutions refused to lend money to one another. As Dominique Strauss-Kahn, the IMF's managing director, observed later: "With the collapse of Lehman Brothers, uncertainty turned to outright panic, and economic activity started to collapse. People raised the specter of another Great Depression, and these fears were not unfounded."[42]

In an era of open capital markets, many investors had borrowed in cheap markets, such as the US, and invested "hot money" in world markets with high growth rates seeking higher returns. Increasingly interconnected financial markets – with rapid communications and instantaneous money transfers – accelerated the spread of bad news and uncertainty. In the turmoil, hedge funds whose mathematicians asserted they could make money in rising or falling markets lost vast sums. Fear that seemingly secure companies might go bankrupt prompted credit markets to freeze, and interbank lending stalled. Nonetheless, some were surprised that a downturn in the housing market, affecting some $250 billion in mortgages, could cause cumulative output losses estimated at 20 times greater ($4,700 billion). David Smick, a financial analyst, explained the housing crisis was a "mere trigger for a collapse in trust of paper, followed by a deleveraging of the entire bloated-with-credit global financial system."[43]

Central and Eastern Europe

In 2007 and 2008 people far and wide – from the Arctic to Australia – experienced the pain as the financial system broke down. The global crisis hit emerging markets in Central and Eastern Europe severely. In the preceding two decades this region reoriented trade, integrated into the world economy, and became heavily dependent on foreign capital. Latvia, Estonia, and Lithuania borrowed heavily from global markets to achieve high growth rates. Others – Hungary, Ukraine, Bulgaria, Kazakhstan, and Kyrgyzstan – also had high levels of foreign debt and dependence on foreign investments. By 2008, it was estimated that 13 countries previously part of the Soviet Union had a collective foreign currency debt of $1 trillion. Much of that money had gone into real estate and consumption, not investment.[44]

Eager to achieve middle-class lifestyles, East European homeowners indulged in the "carry trade." They borrowed money in foreign currency to mortgage their homes. In Hungary, half of mortgages were estimated to be denominated in foreign currencies; in Poland, one-third; and in Latvia, perhaps 70 percent. One Hungarian businessman found he could borrow in Swiss francs at 5.75 percent, whereas an equivalent Hungarian mortgage would cost 14 percent. Engaging in the "carry trade" – the difference between interest rates in two countries – was risky business. If the borrower's currency fell, borrowers might default on mortgages and forfeit their property. West European banks, particularly Austrian and Italian banks, held most of the debt. Reports circulated that Austrian bank loans to Eastern Europe amounted to 70 percent of Austria's GDP.[45]

The situation in Eastern and Central Europe was critical, because debt needed to be rolled over as it matured. In an environment in which investors fled to safety and de-leveraged, rolling over debt proved extraordinarily difficult for countries with troubled finances. In 2008 Latvia ran an eye-popping CAD 22.9 percent of GDP and Bulgaria 21.4 percent. Countries in the region averaged CADs greater than 6 percent – unsustainable over the long term.[46]

As it was, financial institutions in high-income countries had substantial exposure to emerging markets – a total of $4.7 trillion. Of this, $1.6 trillion was to Central and Eastern Europe, $1.5 trillion to emerging Asia, and $1 trillion to Latin America. While US and Japanese banks were not over exposed to Eastern Europe, European and British banks were. Central and Eastern Europe accounted for 21 to 24 percent of total lending. As a consequence, the countries of Eastern and Central Europe had little choice but to seek emergency loans from the IMF to finance their deficits.[47]

Bernard Madoff

The financial crisis, which erupted in North America, impacted many other countries, underscoring the financial interdependence of economies and their vulnerabilities. A Ponzi fraud involving New York swindler Bernard Madoff illustrated these linkages. Madoff later pleaded guilty to felonies that allegedly defrauded investors of over $65 billion. As part of his scheme, Madoff paid investors abnormally high returns, doing so from money placed in his fund by later investors. His client list included European aristocrats, royalty, charities, celebrities, and universities. Investors included the Rothschild family and Liliane Bettencourt, founder of L'Oreal cosmetics empire and the world's richest woman. Madoff's feeder funds employed royalty like Prince Michael of Yugoslavia to solicit funds from other European royalty, such as the Prince of Wales. Some investors borrowed from major banks to place funds with Madoff. Spain's Santander and BBVA, Italy's UniCredit, France's BNP Paribas, Britain's HSBC and Royal Bank of Scotland, and Austria's Bank Medici, all admitted heavy losses in the Madoff scandal. So did Nomura Holdings of Japan. Banking giant HSBC acknowl-edged a potential exposure of $1 billion from loans made to funds investing in Madoff's scheme. Bank Medici, a private bank, disclosed a heavy expo-sure, $2.1 billion in client funds, while Spain's largest bank, Santander, may have lost $3.1 billion. Nomura, which lost $302 million to Madoff, also failed to make money in Icelandic banks and in an ill-timed purchase of Lehman Brothers overseas operations.

The Collapse Impacts Many Countries

Losses from the general financial collapse were not confined to wealthy clients and banks. Local governments, regional banks, and public pension funds took big hits. Financial casualties included charities, churches, and local councils in Australia, and regional banks in Germany. The state treas-ury of Maine experienced losses, as did homeowners in California and pension funds in many locations.

Norway

One sad situation involved six towns in the Arctic region of Norway. Following the advice of a broker in Oslo, local officials bought a package of collateralized-debt obligations packaged by New York's Citibank. For Narvik (population 18,512 and the site of a famous World War II naval battle) the investments amounted to one-quarter of its annual budget. And, when the bond market tanked, angry Norwegian investors found them-selves holding complex but worthless financial instruments.[48]

Great Britain

In Britain the collapse triggered the first bank run since 1866 – at Northern Rock bank in Newcastle, Britain's fifth largest mortgage lender. In September 2007 depositors queued outside branches of the bank demanding their money. They had heard Northern Rock had exposure to US sub-prime mortgages. Rumors had circulated that the bank needed a bail-out. Its risky business model involved borrowing money loaned to home buyers from international markets, and then selling mortgage-backed securities. The British government eventually provided guarantees to depositors, the Bank of England supplied loans to Northern Rock, and the government nationalized the bank. Eager to avoid another Northern Rock, Prime Minister Gordon Brown promoted a merger between Lloyds TSB and

HBOS, a dying rival. The takeover deal proved disastrous for shareholders in Lloyds.[49]

Germany

The seven German regional banks, or Landesbanken, were jointly owned by state governments and savings banks. Their mission was to provide state guarantees for regional business development. Protected by state guarantees, they set up structures to hold assets outside their balance sheets. Then they borrowed large sums in capital markets and invested in sub-prime products that offered high yields and had good credit ratings. When the credit crisis led to a downgrading of their sub-prime assets, two of the banks merged and state governments bailed out four others. All the Landesbanken ranked among the largest 15 German banks, and four held 23 percent of total assets among the top ten banks.[50]

Canada

Among the bigger casualties was Canada's largest pension fund, Caisse de depot et placement du Quebec. It lost $39.8 billion having taken oversized risks on complex derivatives and other untested financial instruments in an effort to boost its returns. Relying on mathematical models to manage risk that rested on only a few years of data, its managers had a false sense of security until the market meltdown taught them a hard lesson about risk. The models assumed that the economy was rational and efficient, and that fluctuations were highly predictable.[51]

Iceland

Another casualty was the country of Iceland. In 2008 the 300,000 residents of Iceland awakened to the volatility of international finance. During the go-go days of the early twenty-first-century boom Iceland metamorphosed from a country reliant on exports of cod fish to a global financial center. Incomes soared and thousands of Icelanders studied finance and tied their careers to new opportunities. But, when Iceland's three largest, deregulated, and over-leveraged banks crashed during a one-week period in October 2008, they had $100 billion in losses. Their failure contributed to an 85 percent collapse in the Icelandic stock market. The Icelandic krona depreciated more than 70 percent. Iceland's average income dropped from 160 percent of the US level in 2007 to 80 percent in 2008. Much-embarrassed

Icelanders found their country ridiculed in the world press as "Wall Street on the tundra." The collapse of Landsbanki, one of Iceland's private banks, hit 320,000 British and Dutch residents particularly hard. They had deposited large sums (some £4 billion) in high-interest, internet "Icesave" accounts administered by Landsbanki. The foreign depositors included charities, universities, and local governments. After Britain invoked anti-terrorist laws to freeze Iceland's assets and force compensation of foreign residents, the Icelandic government agreed to a settlement. It borrowed from the IMF and foreign governments, and assumed a debt equal to half the country's GDP in 2008. Iceland also agreed to join the European Union and to adopt the euro as its currency.[52]

Late in 2009, fast-food giant McDonald's announced the closure of its three restaurants in Iceland, indicating that the collapse of the krona would double the cost of imported ingredients used in making Big Mac burger. The decision to close the Golden Arches pushed Iceland to the perimeter of the global economy. Among European countries only Albania, Armenia, Bosnia, and Herzegovina lacked a McDonald's.

Global impact

The losses from the financial collapse worked through the financial system swiftly. The IMF estimated that bank write-downs and losses totaled $2.2 trillion from the start of the crisis through 2010. The largest were in the US ($885 billion), the euro area ($665 billion), and the UK ($455 billion). Asian banks, including Oceania, had much smaller losses, estimated at $2.3 billion.[53]

Given the interconnected nature of the global economy, it is not surprising that the financial collapse spread rapidly to other economic sectors, depressing growth, manufacturing output, commodity prices, trade, and employment. Real growth rates dropped sharply in major economies late in 2008, contracting 3.2% in advanced economies during 2009. In the US output declined 2.6%, in the European Union 4.1%, and in Japan 5.2%. In emerging and developing countries the rate of increase fell to 2.5% but remained positive, the IMF reported. The developing countries of Asia turned in 6.9% growth. In China and India, the world's two most populous countries, growth fell from double-digit levels (China 14.2%, India 9.9%) in 2007, but remained high by world standards. China grew 9.1% in 2009, while India managed 5.7% growth. The Middle East (2%) and sub-Saharan Africa (2.6%) experienced slower but positive growth. While these regions generally escaped the most severe consequences, Central and Eastern

European countries were especially vulnerable. They had relied on foreign credit to fuel rapid growth and when credit lines dried up they were unable to roll over their debts. Output in this region fell 3.6%, with the Russian economy contracting 7.9% in 2009. Latin American countries tied closely to the US economy, such as Mexico, experienced severe declines in output. In Mexico it dropped 6.5%. Dependent on foreign capital flows to fund growth, many of these countries had to draw down foreign exchange reserves to keep their currencies from falling against the dollar and increasing the difficulty of rolling over debts.[54]

Other data emphasize the breadth and depth of the economic collapse. In 2009 world trade fell sharply for the first time since World War II with the volume of trade in goods dropping 12.0%. The price of oil plummeted 36.3%, while nonfuel commodity prices fell 18.7% in 2009.[55]

According to the IMF, the recession left "gaping wounds" in labor markets with unemployment rising 30 million since 2007. Three-quarters of the increase occurred in high-income countries, notably in the US, the epicenter of the crisis, where unemployment climbed 7.5 million. In Spain, one of the most impacted countries, joblessness rose to 19.1 percent in 2010, up from 8.3 percent in 2007. Developing countries were not impacted so severely. The IMF reported that China lost 3 million jobs, Russia 1.9 million, Turkey 1.1 million, and Mexico about 900,000. Among developing nations the ones to experience the strongest negative effects were those highly integrated and dependent on foreign capital and merchandise markets. Turkey was dependent on the EU, and Mexico reliant on the US. Due to a drop in US demand for automobiles, televisions, and other products assembled south of the border, the Mexican economy contracted at its fastest pace since the 1930s. According to the IMF, the world's poorest countries – countries relatively insulated from tremors in the global economy – may have experienced a net increase in employment.[56]

International Organizations and Governments Respond

During the Great Depression efforts to achieve multilateral solutions failed. After Britain left the gold standard in September 1931, most countries followed and devalued. Twenty-three countries increased tariffs generally; 32 resorted to trade quotas and restrictions. The World Economic Conference, held in London in 1933 under the auspices of the League of Nations, sought to stabilize currencies, revive trade, ease debt problems, and restart the global economy. Attendees hoped to coordinate monetary and fiscal policies. But national differences were too great for agreement. Many commentators laid the blame for the conference's failure on President Franklin D. Roosevelt. He issued a pungent statement critical of attempts to promote currency stabilization before domestic recovery took hold. Other nations also preferred unilateral to coordinated approaches.[57]

As a result, governments generally acted independently to cushion their residents from the collapse of banking and industry. In the US the federal government erected high tariff barriers, devalued the dollar sharply, and engaged in Keynesian-style deficit spending to restore employment. The Roosevelt administration's gold- and silver-buying programs, designed to promote reflation, had the effect of attracting gold and silver from other countries and weakening their currencies. This beggar-thy-neighbor policy disadvantaged France, committed to the gold standard, and Mexico and China, which based their currencies on silver. The US government also sought to reform Wall Street and the banking sector with the Glass-Steagall Act, and to guarantee bank deposits. Buy-American legislation directed government agencies to procure domestically made products. In Germany, the National Socialist regime adopted public works and deficit-spending programs, but also exchange controls and barter to manipulate trade for national advantage. With growing state interference in the economy, Germany sharply boosted output and eliminated unemployment. In Great Britain policies were more orthodox. Government provided cheap money and protection to domestic industry, as well as imperial preferences to shape trade patterns, but there was no massive public employment program or state interference.[58]

Arguably, there was little alternative to unilateralism in the 1930s, as economic historian Charles Kindleberger later concluded. Britain was unable to continue its leading role as the lender and market of last resort. Politically, the US was not ready to assume that role until later in the 1930s. And the absence of reliable voice communications and fast travel via jet plane complicated efforts to coordinate actions.[59]

During the Great Recession of 2007–10, policy responses were better coordinated. Satellite communications and jet transportation enabled leaders to communicate easily and attend meetings. Moreover, there was a determination, and a capacity, to benefit from past mistakes. This time the watchwords were international cooperation and coordination. The vehicle for cooperative efforts was the new Group of Twenty (G-20), an informal forum of finance ministers and central bank governors founded in 1999 and expanded in the current crisis. The group designated itself the premier forum for international economic cooperation.

G-20 members accounted for 90 percent of world gross domestic product, 80 percent of world trade, and two-thirds of the world's population. Members included Argentina, Australia, Brazil, Canada, China, France, Germany, India, Indonesia, Italy, Japan, Mexico, Russia, Saudi Arabia, South Africa, South Korea, Turkey, the United Kingdom, and the United States, plus the European Union and the European Central Bank. Argentina's presence was curious given that country's long record of financial mistakes and defaults. Several significant financial centers – the Netherlands, Singapore, Spain, and Thailand – were not represented. Nor was there formal representation for some 2.6 billion people in 85 percent of the world's countries. But the G-20's membership did take into account long-term trends, such as the rise of Asia. Six members came from that region. Two other organizations had key roles in the process – the International Monetary Fund and a newly organized Financial Stability Board, created to assess the global financial systems' vulnerabilities and to implement strong regulatory, supervisory, and other policies to promote financial stability. In essence, members of the G-20 represented national financial authorities (central banks, regulatory and finance ministries), as well as international financial institutions. A secretariat at the Bank for International Settlements in Basel supported activities.[60]

Some commentators interpreted the emergence of the G-20 as evidence that the baton of economic leadership had passed again – first from Britain to the US during the Great Depression, and recently to an experimental forum espousing collective action. Martin Wolf, the insightful commentator of the *Financial Times,* explained the rise of the G-20 as a watershed in world history with economic power shifting away from the West.[61]

At a summit in Washington in November 2008, hosted by outgoing US president George W. Bush, the group initially expressed determination to work together to revive global economic growth and reform the world's financial systems. Members pledged strong and significant actions to stimulate economies, provide liquidity, strengthen the capital of financial institutions, protect savings and deposits, address regulatory deficiencies, unfreeze credit markets, and strengthen international financial institutions. Importantly, the ministers resolved to prevent the failure of any more financial institutions significant to the financial system, like Lehman Brothers.[62]

At the next meeting in London in April 2009, there was consensus in behalf of greater fiscal and monetary stimulus. The G-20 agreed to supply more money to the IMF and the multilateral development banks, to help emerging and developing countries cope with the crisis, and to provide

tighter financial regulations for banks, including higher capital requirements and closer supervision of rating agencies and hedge funds. The
London communiqué claimed the program involved $1.1 trillion in support
to restore credit, growth, and jobs in the world economy.

On the trade front, the G-20 meetings in Washington and London led
to commitments rejecting protectionism and WTO-inconsistent measures
to stimulate exports. They also reiterated a commitment to conclude the
Doha Round of multilateral trade negotiations that could boost the global
economy by at least $150 billion per annum, about two-tenths of 1 percent
of global GDP. This gesture was largely rhetoric, because public support
for trade agreements had cooled in high-income countries during the
recession.

In September 2009 the Obama administration hosted the G-20 in
Pittsburgh to assess progress and plan exit strategies from stimulus programs. As the world economy slowly began to revive, there were concerns
that stimulus programs might trigger inflation or, if suspended too quickly,
a double-dip recession. European leaders – including British Prime Minister
Gordon Brown, German Chancellor Angela Merkel, and French President
Nicolas Sarkozy – urged binding rules to regulate bank bonuses, while the
Obama administration emphasized the need for revised capital limits to
keep financial institutions from becoming highly leveraged.

Saying that the process of recovery and repair remained incomplete, the
G-20 leaders chose not to abandon stimulus activities. Instead, they focused
on reform issues – agreeing to a set of principles on restriction of bankers'
pay and on the need to elevate capital reserves that banks must hold against
financial losses. In addition, countries with large deficits, such as the US,
pledged to borrow less while major exporters, such as China and Germany,
promised to stimulate domestic consumption, so as to reduce global payments imbalances. G-20 members agreed that the IMF should review
domestic economic policies. Nonetheless, the agreement on broad principles did not involve an enforcement mechanism, or penalties, to restrict
national action.[63]

The next summit took place in Toronto in June 2010. With the sense of
urgency fading, world leaders reiterated lofty commitments to "ensure a
full return to growth with quality jobs, to reform and strengthen financial
systems, and to create strong, sustainable and balanced global growth."
They agreed to halve budget deficits by 2013 and to stabilize the ratio of
public debt to GDP by 2016, but took no specific steps to address fundamental global imbalances, involving China's chronic trade surpluses and
the America's chronic deficits.[64]

The G-20's approach to recovery reflected both Keynesian and monetarist thought. On the one hand, it involved heavy government spending (fiscal stimulus), the borrow-and-spend policies that Keynes championed during the Great Depression to stimulate spending and ease suffering. Most major countries boosted government spending, and many cut taxes as well.[65] The emphasis on a coordinated response also reflected Keynes' thinking. He, and his American counterpart Harry Dexter White, had foreseen at Bretton Woods the need for international cooperation to avert another Great Depression. Their efforts resulted in the Bretton Woods twins, the International Monetary Fund and the World Bank, two specialized agencies in the United Nations system. During the 2007–10 crisis, the IMF had a vital role as an emergency responder and policeman. It set fiscal stimulus targets and persuaded governments to meet those goals. The IMF took emergency steps to stabilize and support the monetary system, stimulate economies, and to encourage national actions to reform and regulate the financial system. In particular, it assisted the smaller countries of Central and Eastern Europe, and worked with the European Central Bank and national authorities to contain debt crises in Greece, Ireland, and other European countries. Meanwhile, the World Bank focused on helping developing and transition economies to mitigate and respond to the crisis, while continuing to fund long-term infrastructure and other development programs.

To contain the contagion and strengthen the financial sector, central banks and national governments took the lead. They lowered interest rates, expanded the money supply, recapitalized banks, and took other actions to restore confidence in credit markets. Governments of advanced and developing nations devised financial rescue packages for troubled businesses (such as General Motors), injected capital, restructured debt, and disposed of "toxic assets." The last were financial assets for which a market no longer existed. They also rescued financial institutions considered too large to fail (such as AIG and major banks) with government purchases of financial assets or nationalization.

In the US Congress and the Executive undertook a $700 billion Troubled Asset Relief Program (TARP) by which the Treasury invested in a number of banks, two auto companies (General Motors and Chrysler), and insurer AIG. These investments were in the form of preferred stocking paying quarterly dividends. In addition the Treasury and the FDIC initiated a Public Private Partnership Investment Program ($900 billion) to buy up "toxic assets" and help banks clean up their balance sheets.

Central banks played an essential role in the recovery process. Federal Reserve chairman Ben Bernanke, an economist who had studied the Great Depression era extensively, was well aware of Milton Friedman's criticism of prior Fed actions. Friedman had accused the depression-era Fed of failing to respond swiftly and effectively to circumstances. This time the Federal Reserve was pro-active. It made some $1.2 trillion in commitments to stabilize the financial sector. To keep the financial system operating, the Federal Reserve loaned money not only to big US banks and manufacturers like Citibank and General Motors but also to foreign banks and their subsidiaries. The latter included Barclays of the UK, UBS of Switzerland, BNP Paribas of France, and Sumitomo of Japan.[66]

To address the broader macroeconomic effects of the crisis, the International Monetary Fund had urged government to undertake fiscal stimulus programs amounting to 2 percent of global GDP. Governments responded with $2 trillion in stimulus packages. The US undertook a $787 billion stimulus package in February 2009, involving tax cuts, transfers to states, unemployment benefits, healthcare, education, and energy programs. As a result, the US budget deficit jumped from $642 billion in 2008 to $1.55 trillion in 2009 (up from -4.4 percent of GDP to -10.9 percent). In December 2008, the European Union and its member states undertook smaller stimulus programs costing $256 billion. While the specific measures varied, many included incentives for buying new automobiles. Japan approved some $406 billion in fiscal stimulus, involving tax cuts, subsidies for new cars, and grants to local governments. China embarked on a huge $586 billion domestic stimulus program intended to restore double-digit growth while reducing reliance on export markets.[67]

In addition to these initiatives, international institutions played an active role. Governments of the G-20 agreed to add $1.1 trillion to the resources of the International Monetary Fund, and to provide $250 billion to expand global trade, and $100 billion for multilateral banks. The International Monetary Fund assisted smaller countries, particularly those in Eastern and Central Europe. It provided $540 million to Armenia, $2.46 billion to Belarus, $25.1 billion to Hungary, $17.1 billion to Romania, $550.3 million to Serbia, and $16.4 billion to the Ukraine. Other beneficiaries included: Costa Rica ($735 million), El Salvador ($800 million), Guatemala ($935 million), Iceland ($2.1 billion), Mongolia ($229.2 million), Pakistan ($7.6 billion), and the Seychelles ($26.6 million). Countries with stronger fundamentals gained access to flexible credit lines, including Colombia ($10.5 billion), Mexico ($47 billion), and Poland ($20.5 billion).[68]

During 2010, the danger of sovereign defaults in Greece, Hungary, Ireland, Portugal, Spain, and other nations challenged the EU, the European Central Bank, and the IMF. The fear was that over-extended foreign banks – particularly in France, Germany, and Austria – could fail, setting off another global crisis in confidence and economic paralysis. The turmoil clouded prospects for global recovery and financial stability, and threatened the future of the euro.

By late 2010, the global economy appeared to be mending slowly. The OECD and the IMF voiced cautious optimism about prospects for sustained recovery despite the dangers of more financial turbulence. But the advanced economies were in bad shape. They had exploding public debt levels and faced major adjustments. The short-term fiscal stimulus measures had contained the crisis but raised government deficits to record levels and left a huge bill for taxpayers in the years ahead. In the United States, gross public debt was expected to climb from 62.1% of GDP in 2007 to 110.7% in 2015. In the euro area, gross debt was expected to rise from 65.9% in 2007 to 89.3% in 2015. For the UK the increase would be from 43.9% to 83.9%. In Japan, where government debt was already high as a consequence of a decade of deficit spending to address the market collapse of 1990, gross public debt was expected to climb from 187.7% in 2007 to an ear-popping 249.2% in 2015. The IMF wanted advanced economies to lower their debt levels to less than 60% of GDP.[69]

As a consequence, it appeared that most advanced countries must expect slow growth, high unemployment, and a protracted recovery. The IMF has projected that advanced countries would expand more slowly than before the crisis, with the US and the UK growing at about 2.5 percent over the medium term. Japan and the euro countries could expect even slower growth – in the 1.5 to 1.7 percent range.[70]

The bright spot in the global economy involved emerging and developing economies. Most had weathered the economic hurricane reasonably well and could expect to grow more rapidly (averaging 6 to 7% growth) in the medium term than before the crisis. The developing countries of Asia would lead the way, with GDP increasing between 8 and 9 percent annually. A World Bank study even predicted that developing economies might become the growth engine for the world. While growth in the rich countries had pulled the developing countries of Asia out of the 1997 Asian crisis, the shoe was now on the other foot. As a result of technology transfers and convergence, an expanding middle class, and growing trade among developing countries, many would become less dependent on the low-growth markets of high-income countries.[71]

Conclusion

In retrospect, the economic hurricane that shook the global economy during the period 2008 to 2010 did not shatter the international economy, as World War I and the Great Depression had done. Sensitive to past mistakes, world leaders took concerted action to stimulate economies with fiscal and monetary policies. Two deceased economists – John Maynard Keynes and Milton Friedman – laid the intellectual foundation for this response, demonstrating once again the enduring intellectual influence of defunct economists. However, the Great Recession of 2007–10 badly weakened the advanced countries at the epicenter of the crisis, and appeared to accelerate the rising influence of the developing world in global economic affairs. The crisis exposed flaws in the free-market model and spurred talk in the developing world of a new global order less dependent on the economic and financial health of high-income markets.

Chapter 10

The Underside of the Global Economy

Human trafficking and forced labor, sweatshops, unsafe products, and environmental destruction – all are contentious issues. When government and business leaders gather to celebrate market-opening policy initiatives, they are often overlooked. This chapter offers a window to the underside of the global economy. Here we encounter some of the human victims, the risks and dangers, and the harmful effects of loosely regulated globalization.

Forced Labor and Trafficking

One of the most sordid aspects of the global economy involves forced labor and human trafficking, a subject with deep roots in history. In ancient times the Greeks, Romans, and most other societies kept slaves, many of them captured in war. From the early sixteenth to the mid-nineteenth centuries, slave trade existed in the Atlantic region. About 11 million Africans were shipped from Africa to North and South America, until abolitionists persuaded governments to ban the slave trade in the mid-19th century. But forced labor and slavery have revived in contemporary times. More porous borders, improvements in transportation and communication, and the lack of economic opportunities in the world's poorest countries have given impetus to their revival. The ILO estimates that perhaps 12.3 million people worldwide are trapped in circumstances of forced labor, involving debt bondage, physical duress, or threats of violence, imprisonment, and deportation.[1]

The Contemporary Global Economy: A History Since 1980, First Edition. Alfred E. Eckes, Jr.
© 2011 Alfred E. Eckes, Jr. Published 2011 by Blackwell Publishing Ltd.

Forced labor may be imposed by governments for economic or other purposes, as in modern day Burma or North Korea. Or it may be linked to poverty and discrimination, as in much of sub-Saharan Africa, where the ILO says forced labor has received less attention than in other areas. Traditions of slavery in Niger have resulted in patterns of continuing dependency between descendants of slaves and former masters. Pygmies in the Congo, Gabon, and Cameroon are subject to forced labor. In the war-torn Congo, international mining companies have sourced minerals, such as coltran, from mining facilities using child and forced labor. Coltran, a shortened version of Columbite-tantalite, is one of the world's most prized materials, a key component of cell phones and computer chips. In the Congo, rebel groups have used forced labor involving children to extract this valuable resource, and then financed their warfare with profits from sales to the big mining companies.[2]

Forced labor may arise from clandestine smuggling and trafficking. Persons often employ smugglers as extra-legal travel agents to facilitate a border crossing. For instance, Chinese from coastal Fujian province have been known to pay as much as $50,000 to be smuggled into the US or Western Europe. In June 1993, ten Chinese died swimming to shore when a dilapidated steamer named the *Golden Venture* ran aground off the coast of New York. It had carried 286 illegal Chinese immigrants, who had paid Chinese gangsters for transportation to America, on a long voyage from Thailand. In June 2000, another 58 Chinese suffocated in an air-tight cargo container in Dover, England. Those illegals successfully reaching high-income destinations often remain deeply in debt to the smugglers to pay off their obligations.[3]

Traffickers frequently use violence and coercion, or deception, to exploit workers. This occurs between countries, and within larger countries such as China and India. The ILO has warned that with the deregulation of labor markets, outsourcing, and complex forms of subcontracting, forced labor abuse has penetrated the supply chains of large transnational companies.[4]

Of an estimated 12.3 million worldwide in some form of forced labor or bondage, the ILO said in 2005 that some 2.4 million persons were subjected to forced labor as a result of human trafficking. The highest number were in Asia (9.4 million) and Latin America and the Caribbean (1.3 million). At least 360,000 were in industrialized countries. The majority, some 56 percent of persons in forced labor, were females. The ILO estimated annual profits from human trafficking to be $32 billion or more, with profits outside the sex industry approaching $10.4 billion.[5]

Some writers claim that as many as 27 million people may be enslaved around the world. They are used to make basic commodities in the global marketplace. Brazilian steel, for instance, is produced with charcoal, the product of slave labor to cut down trees. Activists say that slaves harvest coffee, cocoa, sugar, beef, tomatoes, lettuce, apples, and other food products. They mine gold, tin, diamonds, and tantalum (used in cell phones and laptop computers), clothing, shoes, fireworks, and sporting goods.[6]

Within countries human trafficking is also widespread, most notably in the world's most populous countries, China and India. In China, a Chinese newspaper reported in 2008 that a forced labor network took thousands of children as young as nine years old from rural provinces to work in factories in the Pearl River Delta. Sold to factory owners, the children worked ten hours per day, seven days a week. Nongovernmental organizations say that tens of millions of Indians are subjected to forced and bonded labor, with children compelled to labor as factory workers.[7]

In African countries, such as Mozambique and Uganda, there is human trafficking of children and adults for the forcible removal of body parts. Witch doctors use body parts of live victims for medical concoctions ("muti") to heal illness or hurt enemies.[8] In Western medicine surgeons often transplant organs obtained from a flourishing black market that profits from organ donors in developing countries.

The need for kidney transplants, where demand far exceeds supply, is especially lucrative to criminals. While full data is lacking on the practice, anecdotal evidence suggests a flourishing trade, much of it illegal. In 2004, police broke up an international ring that arranged for Israelis to receive kidneys from impoverished Brazilians at a South African clinic. To circumvent Israeli laws, surgeons have performed kidney transplants from unrelated living donors in Estonia, Bulgaria, Turkey, Georgia, Russia, and Romania. Western journalists have produced numerous exposés of criminals recruiting the poor for organ donations, such as CBS correspondent Dan Rather's report on how desperate villagers from Moldova sold their kidneys for $3,000 in a market where impatient buyers spend up to $200,000 for a kidney. Much of the difference goes to rogue surgeons, criminal brokers, and corrupt officials. In China, prisoners are sometimes the involuntary donors of body parts. All of this has provoked a lively ethical debate among physicians, and awakened the interest of international police, and medical and labor authorities.[9]

Malaysia is one of the countries most tolerant of forced labor. There large numbers of poor but eager foreign workers who come to work from Indonesia, Nepal, Thailand, China, the Philippines, Bangladesh, and

Cambodia. Many face conditions of involuntary servitude. Reporting on the dark side of globalization in 2008, *Newsweek* found workers trapped in conditions resembling slavery. One much-publicized incident involved Local Technic Industry, a Malaysian company making cast-aluminum bodies for hard-disk drives used in brand-name computers. Job brokers lured guest workers from Bangladesh and other countries with false promises of high wages, and then charged high placement fees (as much as $3,600) for assembly-line jobs that yielded little income. The workers subsequently found themselves in a foreign country where they could not speak the language and had no identification documents, with a large debt burden.[10]

Debt bondage, where temporary workers are paid advances and then forced to pay off inflated charges, is also common in Latin American countries, particularly Brazil, Peru, and Argentina. The ILO has reported allegations of Bolivian men being trafficked to rural garment factories in Argentina. Their identity documents removed, the workers are locked in factories, and forced to work up to 17 hours per day.[11]

Remedies

As for solutions, international organizations and nongovernmental organizations strive to publicize conditions, improve data collection and research, and share knowledge about conditions. The UN and its affiliate agencies have taken an active role. In 2000, the UN adopted the Protocol to Prevent, Suppress and Punish Trafficking in Persons, especially Women and Children. It defines trafficking in persons and encourages a convergence of national approaches. In addition, the UN Office on Drugs and Crime (UNODC) sponsored a UN Global Initiative to Fight Human Trafficking in 2007. With financial support from Abu Dhabi, UNODC and several other agencies work with governments, business, academics, and others to combat human trafficking and assist the victims. The UN initiative also encourages national governments to strengthen laws and enforcement procedures, promote cooperation between sender and destination countries, and strengthen workers' and business alliances against forced labor and trafficking.[12]

In the US Congress passed the Trafficking Victims Protection Act of 2000, which requires annual reports ranking countries on government efforts to prevent trafficking, enforce laws, and protect victims. Countries with the worst records are placed in Tier 3 – which in 2010 included Burma, Cuba, the Dominican Republic, Eritrea, Iran, Kuwait, Mauritania, North Korea, Papua New Guinea, Saudi Arabia, Sudan, and Zimbabwe. The

United Nations, and its affiliate organizations, particularly the World Health Organization (WHO), the ILO, the International Organization for Migration, the Global Commission on International Migration, and UN Office on Drugs and Crime (UNODC) have assigned priority to the issue.[13]

Organized Crime

In recent years police and law enforcement agencies have given renewed attention to international aspects of organized crime. For criminals, the fall of the Berlin Wall and the collapse of the Soviet Union were the most important economic developments of modern times, creating new opportunities for gangs to exploit. Like legitimate businesses, criminals source from one continent, move products across others, and market in third continents. Using established banking, trade, and communications networks (including financial centers, shipping containers, and the internet) the underworld smuggles people and products vast distances to their destinations. In past generations organized crime often involved a hierarchical gang determined to control criminal activity in an area – such as bootlegging in Chicago during Prohibition. In the twenty-first century it may be a loosely structured, flexible organization. In it three or more persons work in concert over a period of time to profit and conduct serious illegal activities. Among the most egregious activities (and the estimated value of the annual activities to end users) are trafficking in persons for sexual exploitation ($3 billion). Other remunerative criminal activities include the smuggling migrants from Latin America to North America or from Africa to Europe ($6 billion). Then there is drug smuggling. Trafficking in cocaine from the Andes region of South America to North America and Europe is valued at $72 billion. Trafficking in heroin from Afghanistan to Russia and Europe is estimated at $33 billion. Other illicit activities include trading in counterfeit goods from Asia to Europe ($8.2 billion) and identity theft ($1 billion). International criminal activity also involves child pornography, gun smuggling, maritime piracy, and environmental resource trafficking, including poaching of large species, such as rhinos, and illegally harvested timber in Southeast Asia.[14]

Sweatshops

The international media have long delighted in turning the spotlight of publicity on sweatshops, where workers toil long hours for miserly wages in uncomfortable or unsafe facilities. Sweatshops may involve forced labor, slavery, and debt bondage. They typically are found in the textiles, apparel, footwear, toy, and electronics industries. In these industries employers need large numbers of low-skilled workers for sewing or assembly-line operations. Because of the intense competition, obtaining a contract often depends on a seller slicing a few pennies off cost per unit. Thus, businesses often attempt to save money on air conditioning, or safety equipment, and require long hours and unpaid overtime from workers. Instances of abuse are widespread, and occur on all continents, even in the largest cities of high-income countries.

Clandestine workshops employing immigrants in sub-standard conditions have been discovered in the US and a number of European countries. In 1995, the media exposed a clothing enterprise in El Monte, California, where 72 illegal Thai women worked in slave-like conditions, stitching brand-name clothes. Paid $0.69 per hour, they worked from dawn until midnight to pay off inflated debts for transportation to the US. At night they were locked up, and threatened with harm if they tried to escape.[15]

In the apparel industries of New York and Los Angeles sweatshops are not unknown. In 2008 New York authorities uncovered a factory in Queens where 100 Chinese immigrants worked seven days a week at wages far below the state's minimum wage. State officials found the factory paid sweatshop wages, kept fake records, and told workers to lie about wages and working conditions. In Saipan, a US commonwealth, the media found in 1998 more than 50,000 female immigrants from China, the Philippines, Bangladesh, and Thailand. They labored in slavery-like conditions, working 15 hours a day, seven days a week, to repay exorbitant hiring fees. They worked in garment factories owned by Chinese and Koreans that ignored US laws and enjoyed political support from US lawmakers. The latter received substantial political contributions from lobbyist Jack Abramoff, who subsequently served jail time for corrupting public officials. The garments contained "Made in USA" labels, and sold under Calvin Klein, Ralph Lauren, J.C. Penny, and Tommy Hilfiger brand names. Eventually, improved federal enforcement of immigration laws, and class-action law suits alleging labor violations, brought down the garment factories and forced them to move elsewhere.[16]

Sweatshops, like moles in backyards, pop up regularly in the global economy, despite vigorous regulatory efforts. In labor-intensive industries with low profit margins, ethically challenged entrepreneurs constantly scour the world for cheap labor and lax regulations.

The ILO has reported clusters of clandestine sweatshops in the Netherlands, the Chinese quarter of Paris, Belgium, southern Italy, and the United Kingdom. In these illegal immigrants copied and pirated well-known brand names, and specialized in the rapid turnover of small orders. In London, immigration officials raided a sweatshop making clothes for a high street chain with illegal workers from China, Turkey, and Vietnam. Activists have also uncovered sweatshop-type activities involving immigrants in Australia and Canada who operate as home workers. Australian and New Zealand businesses ran garment sweatshops in nearby Fiji in the South Pacific. In South Africa, a Chinese-owned factory making mascots for the World Cup 2010 competition shut down production amidst allegations of sweatshop conditions involving teenage workers on 13-hour shifts.[17]

Some of the worst working conditions are in low-income developing countries, such as Bangladesh, Cambodia, and Vietnam. In Bangladesh, the garment workers federation says there have been 33 major factory fires since 1990, killing more than 400 workers. In 2,000 factory fires over this period, 5,000 workers were injured. Critics blame lack of health and safety inspections, the absence of fire escapes and extinguishers, the practice of locking factory exits, and inadequate fire-protection services. They demand reforms as well as a $71 per month living wage, and more effective enforcement of laws relating to hours of work, overtime, health, and safety. In export-processing zones, where an estimated two million workers make clothes for export, trade unions complain that lowly paid workers are denied the right to engage in union activities. Police have broken up protests with batons and tear gas.[18]

In Cambodia, the low wages and working conditions have produced periodic clashes between management and labor unions. Gunmen have killed several labor leaders attempting to organize garment workers. Union organizers complain about complicity among the police, courts, and management to break strikes, dismiss union organizers, and disperse worker protests.[19]

Vietnam, like other low-income countries, seeks to attract foreign investment and factories to set up residence and provide jobs. With some of the lowest wages it has lured garment and footwear jobs from China, Korea, and Taiwan. By the mid-1990s Taiwanese and Japanese investors were swarming into Vietnam, attracted by wage costs 35 percent below Chinese levels and six-day work weeks. Nike was one of the first US firms to test the waters in Vietnam, and soon encountered controversy when the CBS program "48 Hours" exposed the sweatshop labor practices of its contractors in 1996. CBS reported that Nike's contract employees were making less than Vietnam's minimum wage, and worked 500 or more hours of overtime per year, far above the 200 hours authorized in Vietnam's labor law. CBS also found a boot-camp assembly system in which workers were physically abused and humiliated for mistakes.[20]

Forced by media and public opinion to demonstrate social responsibility, Nike set up a monitoring system that graded each of its suppliers. In 2005 it openly acknowledged that employees worked more than 60 hours per week in more than half of its factories, and that wages were below the legal minimum in 25 percent of its factories. Among its Asian factories many restricted access to toilets and drinking water during the day. Four years later Nike, which relies on some 618 factories in 46 countries with more than 820,000 contract employees, over 90 percent them in Asia, reported some improvement. It said that 365 of its factories were compliant with standards, but that 25 percent of rated facilities did not comply with Nike monitoring criteria. Blaming the global recession for having a "devastating impact" on worker welfare, Nike acknowledged that many of its contract employees had seen their incomes decline. Overtime work was often unavailable, and some factories had eliminated optional worker benefits to control costs.[21]

How well did monitoring and compliance efforts work? One former sweatshop inspector acknowledged that employers frequently coached employees and that the success of such efforts depended on whether the company commissioning the inspection sincerely desired to improve the situation. He cited toymaker Mattel and Nike for running exemplary programs. But some activists say that corporate-sponsored monitoring is not as effective as government regulation and free labor unions.[22]

In defense of sweatshops

Human rights activists and labor unions in advanced countries often decry working conditions in low-income countries. But people in those countries with limited opportunities often line up at factory gates seeking "sweatshop jobs." When Nike withdrew orders from an Indonesian subcontractor in 2002 because of a sub-par performance, 3,000 workers took to the streets to protest. Despite the low wages and working conditions, the workers wanted their jobs back.[23]

Those who dare to defend sweatshops often make the point that low-wage jobs are better than no jobs. *New York Times* columnist Nicholas Kristof, who has editorialized on third-world famines, genocide, and sex trafficking, rails against the do-gooders who attempt to improve wages and working conditions in the apparel industry. He argues that these jobs are better than crime, prostitution, or picking through garbage. Indeed, for many people sweat-shop jobs bring an upward leap in living standards. He recalls a young Indonesian woman who hopes that her son can get such a job when he is older. A Cambodian woman, he writes, thinks the idea of being exploited in a garment factory six days a week for $2 a day is a "dream" compared to earning the equivalent of 75 cents working all day in the boiling sun.[24]

Many academic economists agree, arguing that sweatshops "are an integral part of economic well-being," as Ohio University economist Richard Vedder put it. He noted that every developed nation made a transition from an agricultural economy to an industrial one. The sweatshops of yesterday produced prosperity for subsequent generations, and allowed workers and their families to improve their living standards. Nobel laureate economist Paul Krugman has criticized activists for trying to raise wages in poor countries. He claims that third-world export industries can't exist "unless they are allowed to sell goods produced under conditions that Westerners find appalling, by workers who receive very low wages."[25]

As late as spring 2010, images of sweatshop labor continued to attract Western media coverage. Pictures appeared in the world press of teenagers at a KYE factory in Guangdong, China, slumped over their desks from exhaustion while working grueling 15-hour shifts in 86-degree heat, six or seven days a week. They made Microsoft mice and Xbox controllers. News stories about the incident cited the complaint of one worker: "We are like prisoners ... It seems like we live only to work. We do not work to live." Several weeks later the media reported a spate of worker suicides at a factory town in Shenzhen, China, near Hong Kong. There Foxconn, a Taiwanese-owned subcontractor, operated factories for Apple, Dell, HP, Nintendo, and Sony. Foxconn is the world's largest contract electronics maker making, among other products, the Apple iPhone. Some 420,000 people live and work in the facility, a giant industrial park with dormitories and 15 manufacturing buildings for different customers. The typical monthly salary is about $131, but most of the workers put in many extra hours of overtime. They have little social life. Many of the young migrant women working in the facility said the only alternative to working the lines is street walking, or prostitution. Under pressure from the media, Foxconn announced a 65 percent pay raise for its factories in Shenzhen.[26]

Even the state-controlled Chinese media began to cover criticism of foreign-owned factories. By the spring of 2010 there was mounting evidence of worker discontent with low wages and poor working conditions in China where inflation was shrinking paychecks. Honda motor cars of Japan suffered a series of crippling strikes among its suppliers that resulted in wage increases of 24 to 32 percent. Reports of the labor strikes against foreign-owned firms appeared with little censorship in the state media, leading to the interpretation that the Chinese government was accepting the need to change its low-cost, export-driven manufacturing model toward a model driven by domestic demand. And indeed wages for migrant workers were rising, the result of increases in minimum wages and tighter job markets. Wages for migrant workers reportedly rose 19 percent in 2008 and 16 percent in 2009, according to Cai Fang, an economist with the Chinese Academy of Social Sciences. With higher wages Chinese consumers could buy more goods, and pressure for political change might abate. More sustainable growth might also boost China's imports and reduce its huge current-account surplus, some commentators thought.[27]

By early June the Chinese Communist party had barred press coverage of strikes, apparently fearful that unrest among migrant workers might spread through China. Whether the Chinese example would also energize workers in other low-income countries, like Vietnam and Bangladesh, was a future story. But it was evident that greater awareness of working conditions and living standards in the outside world, brought about by the global spread of information and improved communications technologies, was having a dramatic impact on the global economy.[28]

Health and Safety and the Global Economy

During the first decade of the twenty-first century natural disasters, terrorism, disease, and hazardous products presented new challenges to the integrity of global transportation and information networks. While national economies benefitted from the abundance of affordable products available in a relatively open global system, they also experienced increased vulnerability. In 2010 volcanic eruptions in Iceland disrupted air travel and cargo shipments in the North Atlantic region, and underscored the fragility of global supply chains. With air freight grounded, warehouses full, and stockpiles of finished goods in factories, retailers encountered a six-week disruption to supply chains. Producers of perishable products, such as the Kenya fresh-cut flower industry, lost millions of dollars in shipments. International airlines reported $1.7 billion in losses. While most goods travel by sea, valuable items often travel by air. Because of the disruption to air-cargo shipments, Japanese automaker Nissan had to close production lines at factories in Japan when pneumatic sensors from Ireland did not arrive on time.[29]

Both air and ocean shipping have presented inviting targets for terrorists. After attacks on New York, London, Madrid, and Mumbai, many nations awakened to these dangers. The trading world worried those standard steel shipping containers might transport harm as well as value to citizens and consumers around the world. The standard 20- or 40-foot nondescript container had the capacity to carry electronics, shoes, apparel, or weapons of mass destruction – perhaps all in the same big box.

In the contemporary global economy the box container is ubiquitous. On a typical day 1.3 million containers are loaded and unloaded at ports around the world. Huge wide-bodied ships can unload as many as 14,500 TEU (20-foot equivalent) containers in less than a day. These metal boxes carried some 60 percent of seaborne trade. The remainder moves in tankers and bulk ships, which transport oil and gas, coal and grain, automobiles and heavy equipment.

Containers travel through a complex transportation mosaic with more than 700 ports. Of the 486.8 million standard containers loaded or unloaded in ports during 2008, 115 million (28.7%) passed through China and Hong Kong. Six of these ports rank among the world's top ten. Singapore, the world's largest single port, handled another 30 million containers (6.1%), while Japan loaded and unloaded another 18.8 million (3.9%). South Korea accounted for 17.8 million (3.7%). The US handled 40.3 million (8.3%), the euro area 74 million (15.2%), and the United Kingdom 7.1 million (1.4%). Stated differently, every minute of every day 926 containers on average are being loaded or unloaded somewhere in the world.[30]

Large multinational corporations – and especially retailers – depend on the integrity and timeliness of container deliveries to support their business models. Through electronic tags and GSM monitoring they know where every container is at any point in time. It is a big task, made simpler with new technology. In 2007, giant retailers Wal-Mart imported 720,000 containers into the US. Its rival, Target, received 435,000. Home Depot unloaded 365,300, and K-Mart 248,600.[31] But, containers also arrive at ports from remote locations where security is poor.

As a result, officials responsible for security have a demanding task in countries targeted by terrorists. In September 2001, when terrorists struck New York and Washington, DC, the US Customs Service had resources sufficient to inspect physically less than 2 percent of the sea containers entering the US. Careful physical inspection of a single container by two inspectors could take all day and delay a shipment with perishable contents for a day or more.

The emergence of the terrorist threat to transportation routes forced authorities in a number of countries to contemplate nightmare scenarios. One of the most worrisome involved weapons of mass destruction (WMD). If terrorists sneaked a nuclear weapon, or other weapons of mass destruction, into a container full of textiles or televisions, and succeeded in slipping it through customs, they might cause hundreds of thousands of casualties. Such a catastrophic event would bring shipping to a halt, disrupt global supply chains, cause economic havoc, and bring crippling lawsuits against the shipper and importer. Studies have estimated the costs of a WMD attack on a US port as costing from $58 billion to $1 trillion.[32]

Nor were these issues of concern only to residents of high-income countries. In November 2008 Pakistani terrorists assaulted Mumbai, India's largest city and a major seaport, with small arms, killing 173 people. The episode heightened India's sensitivity to container security issues, and its vulnerability to nuclear terrorism.[33]

In the aftermath of 9/11 the US took the lead in promoting container security. Congress decreed that all containers entering the US must have tamper-proof high security seals by 2008 and be scanned by 2012. Under the Container Security Initiative, Congress ordered customs officers to inspect by July 2012 100 percent of all US-bound cargo containers at foreign seaports before being placed on a vessel. They were instructed to scan all containers for radiation and nuclear weapons – a giant task since the US received containers from 611 foreign ports in 2008.

Shippers and some foreign governments found the enhanced-security idea unworkable. Shippers complained that the extra security measures were a giant mistake. They predicted increased port congestion and huge costs for suppliers, shippers, and consumers. The World Customs Organization, an international association of government customs officials, unanimously expressed concern in June 2008. It approved a resolution saying that implementation of the 100 percent scanning approach would be detrimental to world trade and could result in unreasonable delays, port congestion, and international trade difficulties. Many foreign governments viewed the mandate as a unilateral initiative, and an impractical one fraught with technical and operational difficulties. A European Commission analysis claimed the scanning mandate would create excessive costs (estimated as an investment of $581 million in scanning and radiation equipment and an annual expenditure of $270 million in operating costs), with "no proven security benefit." Subsequently, the Obama administration bowed to pressure and delayed implementation of 100 percent scanning. It looked for more acceptable options based on a risk-based assessment.[34]

In addition to nuclear terrorism, cyber terrorism posed another unprecedented threat to a world reliant on global networking and information flows. As a threat to economic and national security, the cyber menace was largely invisible to the general public but very real to specialists. Cyber terrorists did not need proximity to their target, as did physical attackers. Both state-sponsored and freelance hackers can operate from distant corners of the world, and route incursions through anonymous or third-party computers. Intelligence officials have said that a coordinated attack from a remote location could disrupt critical infrastructure, such as electrical power grids, transportation networks, and the banking system, creating potentially as much damage as nuclear weapons.[35]

Increasing imports of harmful products – including food, toys, and medicines – also presented challenges for national regulatory authorities in the era of global supply chains. With globalization consumers now enjoy seasonal food products all year round. But increased imports from developing countries with lax environmental and regulatory standards present special concerns those responsible for food safety. The US imports 15 percent of its food supply, including 80 percent of seafood and 60 percent of fresh fruits and vegetables from 150 countries. The EU is a net importer of food products, relying heavily on Brazil for cereals and meats, Norway, China, and Vietnam for seafood, Thailand, China and Turkey for vegetables, and Thailand and China for fruits and nuts.

In the US, the Food and Drug Administration (FDA) shares responsibility for food safety with Homeland Security and the Department of Agriculture (USDA). FDA oversees about 80 percent of the food supply including dairy products, fruits, seafood, and vegetables. Customs and Border Protection (CBP) in the Department of Homeland Security has some responsibilities for inspection and coordinating with FDA, while the USDA takes charge of imported meat and poultry safety.

According to the Government Accountability Office, FDA has resources to examine physically only about 1 percent of imported food, but is developing a predictive risk system to improve targeted screening. From 2001 to 2008, FDA conducted 1,186 inspections of foreign food facilities, but only 46 in China during that period.

With manufacturers sourcing more and more ingredients in China, and other developing countries, product safety concerns have emerged. Chinese products accounted for more than 60 percent of the dangerous consumer products notified through the EU's rapid alert system (RAPEX) in 2009.

The number of notifications has quadrupled (to 1,993) since 2004 as China became the largest exporter of toys to the EU. In the US the Consumer Product Safety Commission announced 473 recalls in 2007, a peak year, and 82 percent involved imports, many from China.

A series of products ranging from baby food and children's toys to pet food and toothpaste were discovered to contain poisonous substances. In 2008 European regulators found the toxic chemical melamine in baby food and soy bean meal imported from China, and banned those imports. Food safety experts said children could become ill if they ate more than a bar of chocolate per day made with the melamine-laden Chinese milk powder. US regulators ordered the recall of children's toys coated with lead paint, and toothpaste containing a harmful chemical (diethylene glycol, or DEG), and called public attention to corrosive drywall in construction.[36]

Seafood is another item of concern. Seventy percent of the world's farmed fish comes from China. Chinese fish farmers have mixed illegal veterinary drugs and pesticides into fish food, and importing nations have concluded that these contain poisonous and carcinogenic residues posing health threats to consumers. As a result, regulators in the European Union and Japan banned Chinese seafood, and US officials have rejected shipments.[37]

US and EU regulators want to block dangerous products at the source, but have had difficulty obtaining full cooperation from Chinese authorities. Nonetheless, regulators strive to educate producers on health and safety requirements. They seek to improve cooperation and exchanges of information among officials in exporting and importing countries, and to strengthen inspection procedures at the border.

China is not the only supplying country with product problems. The problem is that the rapidly growing global supply chain simply has overwhelmed the resources of regulatory authorities to cope with the flood of imports. With low prices driving the supply chain, unscrupulous producers have financial incentives to scrimp on product quality. This is what the US Consumer Product Safety Commission discovered in an investigation of harmful toys from China. In an intensely competitive environment, toy suppliers resorted to paint with high lead levels because this paint sold at one-third the price. Similar problems have also emerged in India, Malaysia, and Singapore. In China, while safety standards are reportedly high – indeed, sometimes higher than in the United States – enforcement is lax.[38]

One problem in inspecting foreign food imports are commitments in free-trade agreements and WTO obligations. These pledge non-discrimination and "national treatment" for imports, and effectively bar the US from inspecting imported foods at a greater rate than domestic foods. Thus the US is obliged to rely on private inspectors to certify the safety of food imports. The US Department of Agriculture found that private inspectors used to certify Chinese organic farms had conflicts of interest.[39]

Environment and the Global Economy

Another contentious issue involves the relationship between the global economy and environmental protection. This debate has many focal points – including climate change, pollution, and environmental destruction. Over the last generation a series of incidents in the interconnected global economy have elevated public interest in environmental issues. Disasters such as the 1989 Exxon Valez oil spill in Prince William Sound Alaska, and BP's recent catastrophic deep-water oil well explosion in the Gulf of Mexico, both polluted the oceans and harmed wildlife. In Europe a 1986 accident at the Chernobyl nuclear power plant in the Ukraine sent a plume of radio-active fallout over much of the continent. Environmental activists have warned about the destruction of Amazon rain forests to make way for cattle ranches needed to supply the world's hunger for hamburgers. They have called attention to illegal logging in Indonesian forests. Both increase greenhouse gas (GHG) emissions and reportedly promote global warming. Also, in an Oscar-winning documentary film, former US Vice President Albert Gore predicted a 20-foot rise in sea levels, flooding New York and Miami, and leaving millions homeless.

On the one hand, environmentalists tend to associate expanded economic activity with environmental damage. Many doubt that greater wealth will bring improvements. They note that the free-market pricing system, the basis of most international trade, does not reflect the full costs of environmental damage. They believe that national governments instinctively strive to protect national industries against "costly" environmental demands, thus the only effective solution involves a strong system of rules at the national and international levels.[40]

On the other hand, economists and defenders of the WTO's multilateral trading system have a different perspective. They argue that trade creates wealth and benefits humankind. From this perspective, expanding trade (a 32-fold increase in volume since 1950) is deemed beneficial to the environment. It promotes efficiency and less-wasteful use of natural resources, improves access to environmentally friendly technologies, and creates wealth that can be used for environmental improvements. Officials of the

WTO observe that people with higher living standards tend to be among the strongest proponents of environmental protection.[41]

Trade advocates express concerned that national governments may use environmental rationalizations as loopholes to protect national industries and to avoid their WTO obligations. They assign primacy to the rules of the multilateral trading system. But in response to rising public concern about environmental harm, WTO officials have softened their defense. They emphasize that the WTO's founding charter contains a commitment to optimal use of the world's resources in accordance with the objective of sustainable development. In the absence of a post-Kyoto multilateral climate-change agreement, such as was proposed for the Copenhagen Summit of 2009, WTO officials are reluctant make definitive pronouncements about whether specific national steps to reduce greenhouse gases comply with WTO rules.[42]

Critics of the WTO and free-trade agreements, like NAFTA, complain that these agreements trump legitimate environmental concerns. For example, NAFTA contains a controversial Chapter 11, which assigns higher priority to investors' rights than to protection of the environment. Private parties enjoy the right to sue governments before secret tribunals to challenge actions involving waste management, regulation of pollutants, and land-use planning if these mitigate the terms of the agreement.

Environmentalists also complain that the WTO's dispute-settlement process allows governments to challenge other government's trade restrictions. Dispute settlement rulings can thus weaken domestic environmental laws. Environmental advocates say that in 1995 cases involving reformulated gasoline, Venezuela and Brazil successfully challenged US Environmental Protection Agency regulations on use of additives to reduce emissions. The complainants argued successfully that US rules discriminated against foreign producers, a violation of GATT's national-treatment provision, and a founding legal principle of the WTO.

Another high-profile case in 1996 involved turtles drowning in shrimp nets. The US sought to ban imported shrimp from countries without sea turtle protections, but several Asian nations filed a complaint with the WTO. The dispute panel decided against the US, effectively ordering it to change its environmental protection regulations or pay penalties.

However, in two more recent cases involving asbestos and tires, the dispute settlement panels affirmed that WTO rules allow an appropriate balance between the right of WTO members to regulate to achieve legitimate policy objectives, and the rights of other members to nondiscriminatory trade. Like court proceedings generally, dispute settlement cases are fair, but costly and time-consuming. They are thus an inefficient way to make public policy.[43]

The conflict between international economic and environmental priorities is an important aspect of the contemporary debate over climate change. For much of the last generation many have worried that climate change threatened the global economic system. Interestingly, in the mid-1970s climatologists spoke about a different kind of climate change, a new "Ice Age." The climatologists interpreted a series of harsh winters as ominous signs of a dramatic change in weather patterns that could portend a drastic decline in world food production. A CIA report suggested that cooling would upset the world's political balance, with India and China facing famine conditions and becoming more and more dependent on imports from the North American breadbasket. The prestigious National Science Foundation even construed declining temperatures as the beginning of "the next glacial age." But by the 1980s temperatures began to warm up, and scientists discovered evidence of a different trend – global warming.[44]

Within the international community the global-warming thesis gained traction. The Intergovernmental Panel on Climate Change (IPCC), established in 1988 by UN agencies, issued a series of alarming assessments. They appeared to link human activities to increasing atmospheric concentrations of greenhouses gases resulting in higher temperatures on the Earth's surface. A fourth assessment, issued in 2007, stated that warming of the climate system was "unequivocal," and attributed the increase in global average temperatures since the mid-twentieth century to GHG concentrations. It warned that past and future carbon dioxide emissions would contribute to global warming and rising sea levels for more than a millennium. For its warning of possibly disastrous consequences for mankind, IPCC shared the 2007 Nobel Peace Prize with former US Vice President Albert Gore.

The IPCC's conclusions have shaped multilateral diplomatic efforts under UN auspices to stabilize and reduce GHG concentrations. The Framework Convention on Climate Change negotiated at the 1992 Earth Summit in Rio de Janeiro is a non-binding treaty in which 192 countries committed to reducing emission levels. The Kyoto Protocol of 1997 set binding obligations for developed countries to reduce greenhouse emission levels by an average of 7 percent below 1990 levels by 2012. The US did not subscribe, nor did developing countries, such as China and India. The latter thought the limitations penalized emerging industrial countries unfairly and would restrict their growth.

Eager to counteract global warming, European nations have taken the lead in efforts to reduce carbon emissions. In January 2008 the European

Commission released a climate strategy intended to cut greenhouse-gas emissions by 20 percent by 2020. The strategy involved auctioning carbon-emission certificates. Because there was a fear that European industry might simply close factories and move to countries without strong environmental laws ("leakage"), the strategy sought to address traded goods. France and Germany proposed a tax on carbon-intensive imports to offset competition from countries with weaker carbon protections, such as China and India. Britain and the United States expressed concerns about this approach, and its compatibility with obligations to the WTO. The US Trade Representative has said that climate or the environment should not be used as an excuse to close markets. Similarly a number of developing countries have denounced carbon tariffs as protectionist.[45]

At a meeting in Copenhagen, Denmark, in December 2009, European leaders sought to win support for an ambitious agreement to reduce GHG emissions in the post-2012 period, but that conference foundered. Governments did not agree on a binding program for long-term action. Among the obstacles were sharp differences between developed and developing countries over how to implement a reduction. Also there was concern that a climate agreement might increase business uncertainty and delay economic recovery from the global recession. Seven months later at the G-20 Summit in Toronto, world leaders softened talk about cutting global temperatures, and substituted vague pledges to do their best on climate change issues. In the view of outside observers, steps to prevent global warming were losing public appeal. Leaders in Australia, Great Britain, France, Spain, and Italy found the public increasingly skeptical about global warming and opposed to carbon taxes. Public opinion polls in the Britain, Germany, and the US showed a dramatic fall in the number of people who believed climate change is man-made.[46]

Part of the explanation for declining public support for efforts to reduce GHG emissions may involve scandals involving the IPCC and climate researchers. Small errors in recent IPCC reports and an episode in which hackers accessed the e-mail of climatologists at a prominent British research center sharpened public doubts. The e-mails appeared to show that East Anglia climate researchers worked assiduously to keep diverging views out of IPCC reports and leading journals. They appeared to hide data of recent global temperature decreases that might influence public understanding of the climate-change debate. Later, several public reviews sharply criticized the IPCC's procedures and lack of transparency, but did not challenge the scientific consensus in behalf of global warming.[47]

In the aftermath of the failed Copenhagen summit some international officials look to another conference, scheduled for South Africa in December 2011. By then the global recession may have eased, and the mistakes of climate researchers may have been forgotten, permitting renewed efforts to forge a new multilateral climate-change protocol.

Conclusion

This chapter shows that the contemporary global economy involves far more than complex issues of efficiency, growth, income distribution, development, and trade balances. It also touches the human and legal rights of individuals, the health and safety of society, and environmental protection. Open borders have expanded opportunities for criminals and drug dealers, and have challenged regulators responsible for health, food, and product safety. The quest for growth and economic efficiency at times appears to raise conflicts between regimes, such as the WTO, intended to promote trade, and parallel efforts to reduce greenhouse gases and protect the environment. It underscores the problems of governance in a world of nation-states with common and also conflicting interests.

Chapter 11

Epilogue

Sweeping economic transformations and turmoil characterized the 30-year period from 1980 to 2010. The long battle between the state and the market seemed over in 1989 when the Berlin Wall came crashing down, signaling the end of the Cold War. Adam Smith and his free-market followers had apparently won. Karl Marx and the supporters of socialism were relegated to the dustbin of history. Governments proceeded to deregulate industries, open markets, and privatize state-owned enterprises. Trade agreements, such as the Uruguay Round WTO agreement, NAFTA, Mercosur, and the European Union, removed border barriers and opened markets, expanding business opportunities. Meanwhile, new information and communications technologies – such as personal computers, cell phones, and the internet – integrated markets and reduced transaction costs. In the 15 years from 1990 to 2005, a half billion workers entered the world's labor force to produce goods for export. Manufacturing, service, and research jobs migrated from high-income countries to Asian countries with lower labor costs.[1]

In this turbo-charged environment, finance enjoyed a long and powerful run. The bulls charged as the London FTSE 100 stock average soared from 509 at the beginning of 1980 to a 1999 peak of 6930, before closing December 2010 at 5900. It was a rollercoaster ride, but the small investor who bought a basket of stocks at the beginning reaped 1,059 percent gains. Similarly, those who bought the Dow Jones industrials in early January 1980 at the 825 level watched in amazement as their portfolios rocketed to 14,165 in October 2007, before closing December 2010 at 11,578, an increase of 1303

The Contemporary Global Economy: A History Since 1980, First Edition. Alfred E. Eckes, Jr.
© 2011 Alfred E. Eckes, Jr. Published 2011 by Blackwell Publishing Ltd.

percent. In constant dollars the gain was about 430 percent. Around the world rising markets lifted millions of people and improved lives.

There were many tangible improvements. As noted in Chapter 1, residents of most countries achieved longer life-spans. Life expectancy rose seven years on average in high-income countries and ten years in least-developed countries. The literacy rate in the developing world rose over 10 percentage points. GDP per capita, one of the best indicators of personal incomes, climbed 60 percent in constant dollars from 1980 to 2009. In developing countries, it jumped 104 percent. As a result, millions of new consumers entered the market for televisions, cell phones, computers, software, motorized transportation, and other items. Improvement in lives and living conditions were most apparent in East Asia where growth rates advanced sometimes at double-digit rates, less obvious in sub-Saharan Africa where conflict, corruption, and poverty delayed meaningful development.

But turmoil and market volatility were also present. For economists these disruptions presented few surprises. Economists have long associated dislocations with progress. Joseph A. Schumpeter the prominent Austrian economist of the early-twentieth century had written that "economic progress, in capitalist society, means turmoil." He popularized the term "creative destruction," to describe the transformations associated with new innovations.[2]

Many industrial workers and family farmers in high-income countries found nothing creative or equitable about the destruction of their jobs and the transfer of work opportunities to low-wage countries. They perceived that globalization and free trade benefited the rich and well-heeled at the expense of the working classes. Millions of them saw open markets and globalization threatening their livelihoods, and the well-being of their families and communities. Many protested, sometimes violently, sometimes democratically. They opposed free-trade agreements, boycotted foreign products, and embraced protectionist remedies. While self-interest is always a powerful motivation to action, they were not alone. Citizen activists used massive anti-globalization rallies, such as the 1999 Seattle WTO protests, to call attention to a variety of labor, health and safety, and environmental concerns. These included human trafficking, forced labor, sweatshops, unsafe products and foods, and pollution. Police and national security specialists also expressed concerns about terrorists and organized crime exploiting opportunities in a world without border controls.

A case in point involved violence in Mexico. Supporters of NAFTA had claimed that approval of the free-trade agreement would create jobs, slow emigration, and bind a prosperous and stable Mexico to the North American market. Instead, 20 years later drug gangs challenged the stability of the

Mexican state. As they battled to control a much-expanded flow of drugs and migrants to the US and Canada, they gunned down public officials who stood in their way. Open borders and closer international connections thus created opportunities for criminal elements, as well as law-abiding citizens.

For some bears, the pessimists who had foreseen hard times, the financial collapse of 2007–10 seemed inevitable. It confirmed the dangers of easy money and loosely regulated markets in a world economy dominated by finance capitalism. A collapsing real-estate bubble in the US spread rapidly to the far corners of the world, igniting fears of contagion. Lacking confidence, markets locked up, banks stopped lending, and businesses laid off workers. While some of the victims had made imprudent investments, others were bystanders hit in the collapse.

As this book goes to press, governments and central banks have apparently arrested the economic decline. During the fire-fighting phase many authorities cut taxes, increased government spending, expanded money supplies, and lowered interest rates. They also intervened to rescue some politically powerful manufacturing and financial corporations deemed too large to fail. In the US production revived in 2010 as exports of industrial supplies and capital goods rebounded. Financial markets experienced a limited recovery. Substantial uncertainty remains. Real estate remains depressed, and home buyers with good credit find mortgages difficult to obtain. Joblessness remains high. In Europe the economic situation is especially worrisome. Debt-ridden Greece and Ireland have accepted bail-outs and severe austerity to avoid sovereign defaults. There is concern that the ECB and the EU may lack sufficient resources and resolve to keep financial contagion from spreading. If Portugal and Spain succumb, the eurozone could splinter, jeopardizing the future of European integration. Another concern is that the continuation of Keynesian stimulus measures and low interest rates could ignite inflation and speculative bubbles. Some with longer-term perspectives warn that bloated government deficits to deal with immediate problems in many high-income countries could jeopardize longer-term fiscal solvency and growth. The strait jacket of rising debt could constrain government responses to future problems – natural disasters, economic crises, environmental degradation, and wars – and limit resources for health and pension entitlements to support aging populations.

Reforming Finance

Efforts to reform the international financial system and to address underlying causes of the recent economic calamity limped along in 2010. In the

US, the epicenter of the eruption, Congress did pass a major financial reform measure in July. The 2,319 page law had an ambitious title: "Dodd-Frank Wall Street Reform and Consumer Protection Act." Dodd-Frank, named for Senator Chris Dodd (D-CN) and Representative Barney Frank (D-MA), asserted the responsibility of the federal government to prop up failing financial institutions. It extended Federal Deposit Insurance Corporation oversight to a broader range of financial institutions. Regulators gained authority to break up too-big-to-fail companies, if needed for financial stability. Other provisions sought to give regulators more information about hedge funds and shadow banking, and to improve the performance of credit rating agencies. The act established a Bureau of Consumer Financial Protection in the Federal Reserve to address some of the problems that appeared in the housing market, regulatory gaps involving mortgage finance companies, payday lenders, and credit-card issuers.

Another important provision limited the ability of commercial banks and affiliated companies to invest in hedge funds or private equity funds, or to engage in trade unrelated to customer needs. Former Federal Reserve chairman Paul Volcker had recommended the latter provision. It represented a partial return to Glass-Steagall restrictions enacted in 1933.

While Dodd-Frank promised sweeping reforms, it avoided some issues and left key decisions over implementation to regulators and rule-makers. Dodd-Frank did nothing to restrain the political impulses that led members of Congress to press financial administrators to ease credit standards and qualify low-income individuals for home mortgages. Among the important areas left to regulators was the problem of too-big-to-fail institutions. These are financial institutions so large and interconnected that government must bail them out to avoid systemic collapse, no matter what risks and bad decisions the banks and financial institutions made. Dodd-Frank established a complex and cumbersome process requiring agreement from multiple regulatory authorities. Whether it is workable in times of crisis remains to be tested. The passage of Dodd-Frank, with its wide scope for regulatory interpretation and rule-making, gives renewed life to the regulatory state and rule by lawyers. As noted in Chapter 5, James Landis gave impetus to this approach during the Great Depression.

Elsewhere, enthusiasm for financial-sector reform appeared to slow in 2010. On Wall Street and in the City of London banks recovered profitability, and resumed hiring. Bonuses in financial institutions moved back to dizzying heights. Nonetheless, international financial institutions reiterated the call for action. In its 2010 annual report the BIS warned that banks remained vulnerable. It insisted that efforts to restructure and strengthen the financial system should continue. The IMF expressed concern about the exposure of banks to the sovereign debt of certain countries facing difficulties, such as Greece, Spain, and Portugal.[3]

From Basel, the Financial Stability Board reported regularly to the G-20 on efforts to develop and implement strong banking regulatory policies. The Basel Committee on Bank Supervision oversaw negotiations to fix certain regulatory problems, including capital requirements for the largest banks and financial firms. The overall goal was to lessen systemic risk and build up capital buffers so as to provide greater resilience to shocks. After deliberations involving banking supervisors from 27 countries, the committee recommended a new leverage ratio. But, in deference to hard-pressed European banks, the committee agreed to delay compliance until 2018. Britain and the US had wanted more extensive and timely reforms to restore confidence to the financial sector. European banks with exposure to risky sovereign debt in Mediterranean countries insisted on additional time to improve the quantity and quality of capital holdings. Subsequently, some US banking officials complained that politically and financially powerful institutions had persuaded regulatory authorities to back off efforts to tighten capital requirements.[4]

Addressing Imbalances

On another underlying cause of the financial crisis – global imbalances – there was little progress and considerable turmoil. Both the IMF and the BIS warned that persistent and large current-account surpluses and deficits were unsustainable, and dangerous to the global economy. But China and the US, the two most culpable, continued to generate huge external imbalances. In October 2010 the IMF projected China's current account surplus would grow from $297 billion in 2009 to $778.2 billion in 2015. It anticipated the US deficit would climb from $378.4 billion in 2009 to $601.7 billion in 2015. Little had changed since the crisis began to unfold in 2007. As before, China viewed export-led growth as an instrument to mitigate internal unrest and to create jobs for peasants. To facilitate exports it maintained an artificially low exchange-rate, and invested export earnings in foreign bonds and financial instruments. With interest rates remaining low, consumers in the US and other high-income countries continued to purchase inexpensive imports on credit. Officials in both surplus and deficit countries seemed reluctant to upset the delicate relationships, despite growing pressures to do so.[5]

As a result, the great transfer of wealth from the advanced countries of the Atlantic region to Asia and the developing world proceeded. Between 1997 and 2009 the US ran cumulative current account deficits aggregating $6,484 billion. Several other major economies also lived beyond their means with chronic current-account deficits. Australia's cumulative deficit was $385.3 billion, Spain's $747.5 billion, and the United Kingdom's $500.9 billion. Meanwhile the countries of southern and eastern Asia, including Japan, accumulated surpluses of $4,787.7 billion. Russia gained another $635.3 billion.[6]

What could be done to restore balance? The IMF and other international agencies counseled the need to expand domestic consumer demand for goods in China, and to boost savings and restrain consumption in deficit countries. They also attached importance to exchange-rate adjustments. However, Beijing resisted international pressure to cease exchange-rate intervention and to allow market forces to revalue the Chinese currency, steps that would make exports more expensive. China apparently feared that domestic demand could not substitute for export orders, and the result might be unemployment and social unrest. It resolved not to yield to international pressure.

In the US, election-year pressure grew to retaliate unilaterally against Chinese currency manipulation. Critics claimed that China's currency manipulation stole 2.5 million manufacturing jobs. In late September the US House of Representatives passed a bill on a 348–79 vote allowing the US to levy tariffs on countries that undervalue their currencies. Big multinational firms seeking to maintain good relations with the Chinese regime lobbied vigorously against sanctions.[7]

On the Chinese side there were also signs of frustration. Fearful that inflation and depreciation of the dollar would shrink the value of its US bond holdings, China began to diversify its holdings, buying Japanese, Korean, and even European debt. While signaling displeasure, the Chinese appeared reluctant to make a precipitous move. A decision to dump their holdings of American bonds could unsettle markets, exaggerate losses and, in a worst-case scenario, disrupt the global economy. Instead China chose to diversify its holdings and demonstrate its muscle. It encouraged state-owned enterprises to bid for oil, gas, copper, and other critical materials around the world. In sub-Saharan Africa, Latin America, and Australia Chinese investors pursued their version of "dollar diplomacy." They cultivated new friends with dollars and purchased strategic assets. In one area where China could exert effective leverage, it did so. It controls over 97 percent of the world's supply of rare earths used in high-technology products. When Japan seized a fishing-boat captain in disputed waters, China embargoed rare earth shipments. To critics, like economist Paul Krugman, this behavior indicated a rogue superpower determined to get its way.[8]

Meanwhile, fears mounted in October 2010 of currency warfare involving the US, the EU, and China. Talk of further quantitative easing by the Federal Reserve drove the dollar down sharply in exchange markets. To spur the domestic economy and reduce unemployment, the Federal Reserve proposed to buy more long-term bonds, a step that effectively involved printing money. Currency markets anticipated that a resulting outflow of dollars might bid up currencies and assets in developing-world markets. Some countries acquiesced to stronger currencies, others used the occasion to build up reserves, and still others imposed controls on capital flows. South Korea intervened to cheapen its currency and keep exports competitive.

The resulting currency turmoil as nations acted unilaterally to advance national interests invited invidious comparisons to the Great Depression when nations had also acted unilaterally with disastrous results for the international economy. A malignant scenario involved a competitive cycle of currency interventions and capital controls, which could disrupt global trade and payments. In a benign outcome China would permit greater exchange rate flexibility, and let market forces facilitate global rebalancing.

Redistributing Power in the Global Economy

Behind the continuing flow of wealth and jobs to Asia in the period 1980 to 2010 was the overarching reality that cost arbitrage shaped the contours of the contemporary global economy. In a world without effective borders, work of all types moved easily to locations with the lowest costs. With the world's population expected to rise and hundreds of millions of people entering the global workforce over the next decades, labor arbitrage was expected to expand. This trend would likely benefit Brazil, China, India, Mexico, the Philippines, and Thailand – countries with high-quality, productive workers – and hamper high-cost economies in Western Europe, Japan, and North America. In the latter group high-cost employees may continue to face job displacement and retraining issues.[9]

The emerging power and influence of the so-called BRIC countries (Brazil, Russia, India, and China) underscored a fundamental transition in the global economy. The four rising powers were only developing countries but they were rich in potential. They represented 42% of the world's population, and generated 24% of world GDP in 2009, up from 12.9% in 1990. By mid-2010 the four BRICs had nearly $3.5 trillion in monetary reserves, 72% more than Canada, the US, Japan, the euro area, and the UK combined ($2.04 trillion). Except for Russia, the BRICs had avoided serious distress during the 2007–10 recession. The IMF expected them to grow much faster than the high-income countries for years to come. Brazil and Russia might grow in the 4 to 4.5% range annually, while China and India would grow twice as fast – near 10%. GDP per capita was expected to rise nearly four to five times faster in emerging economies than in high-income OECD countries.[10]

In a rosy scenario, the developing countries thus could become the new engines of growth for the global economy. Assuming continued growth, and no world war or large-scale catastrophe, millions of people might escape poverty over the next decade. The global middle class could expand by 1.8 billion people to 3.2 billion by 2020. Some 40 percent of the world's population might acquire middle-class status. In addition to supplying manufactured goods and services, these expanding economies could become major exporters of capital and skilled workers. Their expanding markets could also help to reboot the global economy, providing new export opportunities for the advanced countries.[11]

Because the collapse of global finance in 2007–10 tarnished the free-market model associated with Anglo-American economic leadership, a new model could emerge in the decade ahead. Among the emerging BRIC giants there is interest in creating a new international reserve currency to supplant the dollar. There is also enthusiasm for state-owned enterprises, an indication that emerging nations may use the power of the state to advance national champions and restrain foreign competitors. Rather than adhering to Western norms of open markets and financial integration, the BRICs seem eager to preserve national freedom of action and to advance their own regional and development ambitions. Another group of developing countries – including Indonesia, Nigeria, South Africa, Turkey, and perhaps Vietnam – could join their ranks. Higher growth-rates among developing countries generally could create opportunities for an expansion of trade among middle-income developing countries. In Southeast and East Asia regional integration may offer an alternative for reliance on export markets in Europe, Japan, and the US.

But, while the emerging powers are likely to take a more prominent role in the global economy of the mid-twenty-first century, the US, the eurozone, Japan, and the UK will remain powerful. With 12 percent of the world's population, they generate 44 percent of world GDP and 45 percent of world merchandise exports.

The prospects for some other regions remain cloudy. Sub-Saharan Africa could fall farther behind. The region has a long history of civil conflict, corruption, and instability. Africa lacks infrastructure and has challenging demographics, with high birth rates and a bulge of youth entering job markets. While elites might benefit from surging demand for petroleum and other natural resources, the windfall profits are more likely to sustain entrenched regimes than to promote national development. In Latin America, except for Brazil and a few smaller countries, the region is not expected to match the high growth and economic competitiveness of Asia. The future of the Middle East in the global economy is even more uncertain, because of political tensions, civil unrest, and terrorism. China and India, which rely on the Middle East for energy imports, can be expected to exert more influence in that area, as American involvement recedes.

Eastern and Central Europe enjoyed higher living standards for two decades before the global recession, but were hit harder than any other region in the world, according to World Bank analysts. Having lived beyond its means with heavy dependence on foreign loans, this region faces the challenge of adjustment. It must increase savings and tackle a host of new problems, including an aging population and the need to boost the region's productivity in order to compete in an interconnected global economy.[12]

Finally, demographic trends will contribute importantly to longer-term transformations in the global economy. An increase of 1.1 billion persons between 2010 and 2025 may place pressure on the world's energy, food, and water resources. High population growth likely will have the greatest impact on Asia, Africa, and Latin America. However, high-income countries in Western Europe and Japan with aging, or declining, populations may struggle to maintain living standards and preserve social services and medical care for an aging citizenry. Because the US has a higher birth rate and is more open to immigration, it may experience fewer strains. With population soaring in disadvantaged nations, and population contracting or holding steady in privileged areas, there is likely to be an increase in the number of migrants seeking better opportunities abroad.

The generation from 1980 to 2010 witnessed far-reaching changes, as the drivers of globalization transformed the world, opening markets, bringing people closer together, and improving livelihoods. In this complex process technological innovations and transfers played key roles, as did demo-graphic, political, and economic factors. It should not be forgotten that volatility and dislocations accompanied this progress, severely impacting and disrupting many lives while improving opportunities for others. In the generation ahead, the pace of change is not likely to slacken nor is the turmoil.

Notes

Chapter 1

1. Zoellick 2008.
2. OECD, *Growing Unequal?*, 2008.
3. Keynes 1920: chapter II.
4. World Bank, *WDI*.
5. World Bank, *WDI*; Maddison 2010; Capgemini, *World Wealth Report*, 2010.
6. World Bank, *WDI*.
7. UNDESA 2004: vii–viii; UNDESA 2008; Moch 2003: 147–60, 161–97; Panayi 2009.
8. ILO 2004: 8–9.
9. UNDESA 2008; MPI 2010.
10. Pylynskyi 2009.
11. MPI 2010.
12. World Bank, *WDI*.
13. World Bank, *WDI*.
14. World Bank, *WDI*.
15. World Bank, *WDI*; Wilson and Dragusanu 2008.
16. "Investors … ," 1998.
17. World Bank, *WDI*.
18. World Bank, *WDI*.
19. World Bank 1993.
20. Klein and Cukier 2009; World Bank, *WDI*; OECD, *StatExtracts* 2010; IMF, *WEO*, April 2010; UKDMO, *Quarterly Report* (various issues); US Treasury, *Treasury Bulletin* (various issues).
21. World Bank, *WDI*.
22. USCIA, *World Factbook*.

The Contemporary Global Economy: A History Since 1980, First Edition. Alfred E. Eckes, Jr.
© 2011 Alfred E. Eckes, Jr. Published 2011 by Blackwell Publishing Ltd.

23. World Bank, *WDI*.
24. UNCTAD, *WIR 2010*: Annex Table 7; UNCTAD, *WIR 2007*: 47.
25. World Bank, *WDI*.
26. World Bank, *WDI*.
27. UN, *Millennium* 2009: 9; Canuto and Giugale 2010: 388.
28. Eckes 2007: 417–21.
29. Eckes and Zeiler 2003: 157–8; ATA, "Annual Results;" UNWTO, "International Tourism Receipts 2009."
30. ATA, "Annual Results."
31. Levinson 2006.
32. ITU, ICT Statistics.
33. ITU, ICT Statistics.
34. Eckes and Zeiler 2003: 203.

Chapter 2

1. Chanda 2007; Hopkins 2002; Headrick and Griset, 2001: 543–78.
2. Findlay and O'Rourke 2007: 382–407.
3. Cassis 2006: 81–3; Eichengreen 2008: 34–42.
4. Obstfeld and Taylor 2004: 29, 52–60; James 2001: 10–25.
5. Engel 2007.
6. Maddison 2010. Because World Bank data for this period is unavailable, we rely extensively on Maddison's estimates, based on constant 2000 dollars and purchasing price parities. For details see Maddison's "Explanatory Background Note on Historical Statistics," www.ggdc.net/maddison/.
7. Findlay and O'Rourke 2007: 414–24; Stone 1977.
8. Maddison 2006: 32.
9. Smith 2003: 103; Findlay and O'Rourke 2007: 409; Michie 2006: 130–2.
10. Angell 1911: vii; Ferguson 1999: 411; "Mr. Churchill … ," 1911; Mahan 1912.
11. Maddison 2010.
12. Ferguson 2005.
13. Eckes and Zeiler 2003: 44–5.
14. Berend 2006.
15. Kindleberger 1973; James 2001; Cassis 2006, 182.
16. Michie 2006: 187; Wigmore 1985.
17. Smith 2003: 105–42; Michie 2006: 176–89; Bernanke, November 8, 2002.
18. Yergin and Stanislaw, 1998: 22–38.
19. Reinhart and Rogoff 2009; Bordo, Goldin, and White 1998; USBoC 1975, 2: 1104.
20. Moggridge 1982.
21. Greasley and Oxley 2002; Rothermund 1996: 82–6.
22. Nanto and Takagi 1985: 372–3; Rothermund 1996: 77–8, 115–19; Singer 1983.
23. Duranty 1931; Duranty 1932.
24. Findlay and O'Rourke, 2007: 430–72.
25. Reinhart and Rogoff, 2009: 96.

26. Eckes, 1979: 123–4.
27. Findlay and O'Rourke 2007: 479–88; Yergin and Stanislaw 1998: 67–91.
28. Findlay and O'Rourke 2007: 19–45.
29. Eckes 1975: 207–8.
30. Findlay and O'Rourke 2007: 479–88; Yergin and Stanislaw 1998: 67–91.
31. Maddison 2006: 24.
32. Maddison 2010.
33. Maddison 2010.
34. USBoC data, www.census.gov/statab/hist/HS-31.pdf and www.census.gov/compendia/statab/2010/tables/10s0708.pdf.
35. Maddison 2010.
36. Maddison 2010.
37. USBoC 2010; USBoC data, www.census.gov/statab/hist/HS-31.pdf and www.census.gov/compendia/statab/2010/tables/10s0708.pdf.

Chapter 3

1. WTO Database, http://stat.wto.org, accessed September 2010.
2. *Economist*, 1984; Sullivan 1984.
3. Khanna 2008: 3–9; OECD, *StatExtracts*; *Economist* 2004a; Reuters 2009.
4. Ash 2010.
5. Jackson 2009; Pinder 2009.
6. Dinan 2009.
7. Dinan 2009.
8. Dinan 2009; Owen 1988.
9. Flockton 2009.
10. Flockton, 2009; Eichengreen 2007.
11. WTO, *ITS* 2009: 34; WTO, *TP* 2009: 175.
12. Maddison 2010.
13. *Fortune* 2010.
14. WTO, *ITS* 2010: 14.
15. WTO, *TP* 2010.
16. Champion, Slater, and Mollenkamp 2009; Ahamed 2009; EU-Russia 2009.
17. WTO, *TP* 2010; Eurostat.
18. UNCTAD, *WIR* 2010: 172.
19. Ibarra and Koncz, 2009: 32–4.
20. IMF, COFER.
21. Gonzalez-Paramo 2009; ECB 2010: 66.
22. WEF, Global Competitiveness Index, 2010–11.
23. WTO, *ITS* 2010: 10.
24. WEF, Global Competitiveness Index 2010–11; World Bank, *WDI*.
25. World Bank, *WDI*.
26. Ramo 1999; Woodward 2000.
27. Mishel, Bernstein, and Shierholz 2008: 2, 7–8, 14.

28. Mishel, Bernstein, and Shierholz 2008: 365.
29. Guidolin and La Jeunesse 2007; OECD, *FB* 2009.
30. WTO Statistical Database, http://stat.wto.org/, accessed September 2010.
31. OECD *FB* 2009; USBEA 2010b; WTO, *TP* 2009: 177.
32. WTO, *TP* 2010.
33. d'Aquino 1992.
34. Laver 1985.
35. Laver 1985; Salter 1986.
36. WTO, *TP* 2010.
37. Angus Reid Global Monitor 2008; 2009.
38. World Bank, *WDI*; WEF, Global Competitiveness Index 2010–11; WTO, *TP* 2010; Pomfret 2010a.
39. Waite 2004.
40. World Bank, *WDI*; WTO, *TP* 2010.
41. WTO, *TP* 2010.
42. WTO, TP *2010.*
43. World Bank, *WDI*; *Economist* 2007.

Chapter 4

1. O'Neill 2001.
2. O'Neill and Stupnytska 2009.
3. World Bank, "How We Classify Countries."
4. World Bank 1993.
5. Moore 2010.
6. World Bank, *WDI*; World Bank, *GEP* 2009: 4–5, 58; WTO, *ITS* 2010: 14; WTO *TP* 2010.
7. World Bank 2010.
8. Fingleton 2008.
9. Enright, Hoffmann, and Wood 2010; McGregor 2010.
10. *Fortune* 2010.
11. Halper 2010.
12. Lee 2010.
13. WTO, *TP* 2010.
14. World Bank, *WDI*.
15. World Bank, *WDI*; WEF, Global Competitiveness Index 2010/2011.
16. International Contractors Association of Korea (accessed 2010).
17. OECD, *EO* (November 2009): 192; WTO, *TP* 2010.
18. OECD 2009: 227.
19. WTO, *TP* 2010; USTR 2009.
20. WTO, *TP* 2010.
21. Central Bank of the Republic of China 2010.
22. Rickards 2009.
23. WTO, *ITS* 2010: 28; Klein and Cukier 2009: 8.

24. World Bank, *WDI*.
25. Clifford and Engardio 2000: 209.
26. WTO, *TP* 2010: 82; World Bank, *WDI*.
27. WTO, *TP* 2010: 106.
28. Maddison 2010; World Bank, *WDI*; TI 2009.
29. WTO, *TP* 2010.
30. *The Edge Malaysia* 2010; Maddison 2010.
31. Canuto and Giugale 2010: 387.
32. WTO, *TP* 2010.
33. Cimoli, Dosi, and Stiglitz 2009: 297–8.
34. Panagariya 2008.
35. WTO, *TP* 2010.
36. WTO, *TP* 2010.
37. Maddison 2010; World Bank, *WDI*; Khanna 2008: 132–6.
38. WTO, *TP* 2010; USBoC, "Foreign Trade Statistics."
39. WEF, Global Competitiveness Index 2010–2011.
40. WTO, *ITS* 2010: 26.
41. WTO, *TP* 2010; USTR 2010.
42. WTO, *TP* 2010.
43. World Bank, *WDI*; WEF 2010–11.
44. Khanna 2008: 36–7.
45. World Bank, *WDI*; WTO, *TP* 2010.
46. WTO, *TP* 2010.
47. Canuto and Giugale 2010: 377.
48. WTO, *TP* 2010; USCIA 2010.
49. WTO, *TP* 2010.
50. Canuto and Giugale 2010: 327; WEF 2009a: 97.
51. WEF, Global Competitiveness Index 2010/2011; TI 2009.
52. World Bank, *WDI*; Maddison 2010.
53. World Bank, *WDI*.
54. World Bank, *WDI*.
55. Wonacott 2010.
56. Aldcroft 2001.
57. Randoux 2009.
58. Katkakrosnar 2007.
59. World Bank, *WDI*.
60. Roland Jackson 2009; IMF 2009; Canuto and Giugale 2010: 353.
61. Wedel 1998; Hoffman 2003.
62. Abdelal 2007: 159.
63. USEIA 2008; USCIA, *WF* 2010.
64. WTO, *TP* 2010.
65. *Economist* 2009; Budrys 2010.
66. World Bank, *WDI*; Kramer 2008.
67. World Bank, *WDI*.

Chapter 5

1. Keynes 1936: 383.
2. Thatcher 2002: 415; Smith 1937: 13.
3. Smith 1937: 14.
4. Smith 1937: 4–5, 423; Samuels, Biddle, and Davis 2007: 113.
5. Smith 1937: 461; Ross 1995: 275.
6. Smith 1937: 431–9.
7. Anderson, Shughart, and Tollison 1985.
8. Reinert and Reinert 2005: 14–15; Smith 1937: 347–52, 431.
9. Smith 1937: 128; Thatcher 2002: 412–66; Klaus 2006.
10. Samuels, Biddle, and Davis 2007: 432–35.
11. Irwin 1996: 102.
12. Reinert 2007; Chang 2008: 47–8.
13. Zachariah 2004: 34; Szporluk 1988; Metzler 2006: 98–130.
14. Dutt 2005: 107–11, 120.
15. Toye and Toye 2004: 126–33; Saad-Filho 2005: 128–45; Dosman 2008: 246–9.
16. Sachs and Warner 1995: I:17–19; Chang 2002: 3–6; Fallows 1994: 179.
17. Roncaglia 2005: 244–75; Marx 1848; Marx and Engels 1848.
18. Yergin and Stanislaw 1998: 11–12; Hobson 1902; Lenin 1916.
19. Chang 2003: 23–4.
20. Zachariah 2004; Herring 1999.
21. Tignor 2006: 179–80.
22. Woo-Cumings 1999: 1–31; Chang 2008: 26–31.
23. Roncaglia 2005: 30.
24. McCraw 1984: 212–16.
25. Goodwin 2003: 610–11.
26. Skidelsky 1994.
27. Mitchell 1993: 656, 753.
28. Thatcher 1993: 12–13.
29. Shleifer 2009: 123–35.
30. Skinner, Anderson, and Anderson 2001: 254.
31. Greenspan 2007: 40, 52–3, 208, 375–6.
32. Andrews 2008.
33. Fox 2009: 107.
34. Fox 2009: 24, 94.
35. Fox 2009: 197; Stiglitz 2010: 238–74.
36. Lipton and Labaton 2008.
37. Wedel 1998.
38. Wayne 1989.
39. Williamson 2002.
40. Toye and Toye 2004: 266–7; Krueger 1997.
41. Stiglitz 2002.

42. Stiglitz 2010; Cimoli, Dosi, and Stiglitz 2009; Galbraith 2008.
43. Stiglitz 2002.
44. Halper 2010.
45. Galbraith 2008: 14.
46. Krugman 1987; 2007; 2010a.
47. Toffler 1980; 1990.
48. Naisbitt 1982.
49. Wriston 1982b: 92–5; Wriston 1997: 172–82.
50. Drucker 1977; 1980: 95–100; 1986: 789.
51. Drucker 1986: 783–4.
52. Mettler 1981.
53. Roach 1987.
54. Halsall 2009.
55. Ohmae 1989a: 153; 1985.
56. Dearlove and Crainer 2005.
57. *Economist* 1990: 53.
58. Magaziner and Reich 1982.
59. Thurow 1985; McKenzie 1991.
60. Hughes 2005: 278.
61. Bergmann 2005.

Chapter 6

1. Brinkman 2004.
2. WTO, *WTR* 2008: 28–40.
3. WTO, *ITS* 2009; Findlay and O'Rourke 2007: 515.
4. World Bank, WDI.
5. WTO, *ITS* 2007: 4.
6. WTO, *ITS* 2010: 181, 189.
7. Drucker 1977.
8. Engardio, Bernstein and Kripalani 2003.
9. *Financial Times* 2009: 16.
10. WTO, *ITS* 2007: 3.
11. WTO, *ITS* 2010: 174.
12. WTO, *WTR* 2008: 17.
13. Fukuyama 1992; Friedman 1999.
14. Findlay and O'Rourke 2007: 498.
15. WTO, *WTR* 2008: 18.
16. WTO, *WTR 2008*: 87–8.
17. WTO, *WTR* 2007: 207–9.
18. WTO, *WTR* 2008: 76.
19. WTO, *WTR* 2008: 81–3.
20. WTO 2001.
21. ICC 2001.

22. Srinivasan 2007: 1039–41.
23. Van Damme 2008.
24. WTO, "Dispute Settlement," 2010.
25. Eckes in press.
26. Choi 2007.
27. WTO. Available online at http://rtais.wto.org/.
28. Eckes 1995: 98–9.
29. Murray and Belkin 2010.
30. *Africa News* 2009a; *Africa News* 2009b.
31. Ahearn 2005.
32. Council of Canadians 2010.
33. Hufbauer and Schott 2007.
34. Hufbauer and Schott 2007.
35. *Agence France Press* 2009.
36. Zalewski 2010.
37. Lamont and Hille 2010.
38. *Agence France Press* 2008.
39. *Korea Times* 2010.
40. Klom 2003: 351–8.

Chapter 7

1. Stone 1989; Ohmae 1989b: 145.
2. UNCTAD, *WIR* 2009: 19.
3. UNCTAD, *WIR* 1992: 1, 183; *WIR* 2009: 17, 247–54; WIR 2010: Annex Table 26, http://www.unctad.org/ (accessed October 2010).
4. UNCTAD, WIR 2010: 17, Annex Table 26.
5. UNCTAD, *WIR* 2009: 22.
6. UNCTAD, *WIR* 2009.
7. *Fortune*, 2010; Bremmer 2010; UNCTAD, *WIR* 2009: 20.
8. Atkey 2007; Corcoran 2010; White 2009; Yeates 2009.
9. USBEA 2008; Eales 1981; Wilkins 1974: 285–324; Brinkley 2003: 601–2.
10. Shapiro 1973; Schacht 1970.
11. Servan-Schreiber 1968.
12. Wilkins 1974: 335–6; Gavin 2004; James 1996.
13. Kaletsky 1984.
14. UN General Assembly 1974.
15. Bales, Gogel, and Henry 1980; *Globe and Mail* 1979; Lewis 1979; BIS, *AR* 1980.
16. UNCTAD, *HoS* 2009.
17. Vogel 1979.
18. Badaracco and Yoffie 1983.
19. Feldstein 1983.
20. Young 1985: 34.
21. Hughes 2005: 166.

22. Hughes 2005: 327–75.
23. Walters and Monsen 1983.
24. Eckes 1995: 199.
25. USBoC, *SA* 1982: 837; 1992 : 401.
26. *Public Papers* 1987: 476–78.
27. Mirza, Sparkes, and Buckley 1996: 42.
28. Simon and Button 1990.
29. Cohen 1998; Page 1981: 27–8.
30. *The Times* 2006.
31. *Economist* 1979: 61.
32. Stone 1989.
33. Housego 1984: 1:1; *Financial Times* 1985; Quinlan 2003: 9.
34. ICC 1999.
35. Kohut and Wike 2008.
36. Steingraber 1996.
37. Welch 1983: 549.
38. Smith 1998.
39. Levitt 1983.
40. Brouthers, McCray, and Wilkinson 1999; Dibenedetto 2008.
41. Brooks 2002.
42. Eckes 2009a: 262.
43. Ohmae 1993; Reynolds 1989; Uchitelle 1989.
44. *Asia Pulse* 2005; Talbott 1992.
45. Friedman 2005; Florida 2005.
46. Rugman and Verbeke 2008.
47. Palmisano 2006.
48. Lohr, July 5, 2007: 1.
49. *Economist* 2004b.
50. UNCTAD, *WIR* 2001: 24–6.
51. UNCTAD, *WIR* 2005: 205, 216.
52. UNCTAD, *WIR* 2004: xxvi.
53. Tappin and Cave 2009.
54. Zeng and Williamson 2003.
55. Karabell 2009.

Chapter 8

1. BIS, *AR* 2009: 3.
2. Kindleberger 1996; Reinhart and Rogoff 2009: xxvi; Gorton 2010: 30–1; Cipolla 1982: 5–9.
3. Seligman 2003; US Senate Banking Committee 1999.
4. Michie 2006: 232–3; Schooner and Taylor 1998–9: 595; Reinhart and Rogoff 2009: 205; Eichengreen 2003: 17.
5. Eckes 1975: 162.

6. Cassis 2006: 201.
7. Kapur, Lewis, and Webb 1997: I:100; Cassis 2006: 220–7.
8. UNCTAD, *HoS* 2009.
9. Eichengreen 2008: 104–12.
10. Triffin 1960.
11. Schwartz 2003: 70, 93.
12. Shultz 1995: 4.
13. Eckes 1975: 248–50.
14. Friedman 1962: 56–74; http://nobelprize.org/nobel_prizes/economics/laureates/.
15. Fox 2009; http://nobelprize.org/nobel_prizes/economics/laureates/.
16. BIS, *AR* 1987: 86, 88.
17. Rickards 2008; Reinhart and Rogoff 2009: xxvii–xxviii.
18. Ebenstein 2001: 290–6.
19. Thatcher 1993: 12; Friedman 1979.
20. Zweig 1996: 388.
21. Abdelal 2007: 2; BIS, *AR* 2007: 87.
22. Fortson 2006; *Economist* 2006.
23. Ashton 2009.
24. Burns 1987; BIS, *AR* 1987; *Globe and Mail* 1997.
25. Michie 2006: 296.
26. Cassis 2006: 238–41.
27. Wriston 1980.
28. BIS, *AR* 1981: 51–3.
29. Mayer 1998: 87–95.
30. Heimann 1980; Calomiris 2000: 337; Thomson and Stepanczuk 2007.
31. Heimann 1980.
32. Zweig 1996: 40–4; Walter Wriston 1982a.
33. Kaufman 2000: 263; BIS, *AR* 1977: 101–3; James 1996: 320–1.
34. BIS, *AR* 1980: 8; BIS, *AR* 1981: 108–10.
35. Zweig 1996: 853–7; Lissakers 1991; Kunz 1997: 275–81; James 1996: 374–401.
36. Michie 2006: 298; IFSL 2009.
37. *Economist* 1988.
38. Cassis 2006: 268; Berger 1990.
39. Cassis 2006: 268–70.
40. Leigh 1998.
41. Weiss 2008.
42. UNCTAD, *WIR* 2008: 216; IFSL 2009; BIS, *AR* 1990: 208–9; BIS, *AR* 2009: 5; UNCTAD, *FDISTAT 2010*; BIS 2008: 1–10.
43. UNCTAD, *HoS* 2010.
44. Abdelal 2007: 12–17.
45. IMF, *Independent Evaluation* 2005: 3; IMF, *AR* 1996: 26; IMF, *AR* 2007: 39, 59–60, 79, 86. In 2010 IMF economists would change their advice to emerging market economies and state that capital controls are "justified as part of the policy toolkit to manage inflows." Ostry, Ghosh, and Habermeier 2010: 5.
46. UNCTAD, *HoS* 2008.

47. UNCTAD, *HoS* 2008.
48. BIS, *AR* 1998: 122, 128.
49. Clifford and Engardio 2000; BIS, *AR* 1998: 128.

Chapter 9

1. Abdelal 2007: 2; BIS, *AR* 2007: 87; BIS, *AR* 2008: 3–4; Greenspan 2007: 5–10.
2. WFE.
3. Schwartz, Leyden, and Hyatt 1999; Bianco 1998; *Business Week* 2001; Glassman and Hassett 1999; Kadlec 1999.
4. Hershey 1999.
5. Ferguson 2005; Ferguson 1999: 411–12; Chernow 1990: 183.
6. Friedman 1996; Friedman 1999: 195–7.
7. *Economist* 2000b; 2000a.
8. BIS, *AR* 1999: 100–1.
9. *Washington Post* 2008; Tett 2009: 74–5; Lipton 2008; Hirsh 2010: 202–4.
10. BIS, *AR* 1999: 6; BIS, *AR* 2000: 143; BIS, *AR* 2001: 149–50.
11. IMF, *GFSR* (March 2002): 34–9; IMF, *AR* 2000: 23–4; IMF, *AR* 2001: 14–15.
12. Kaufman 2000: vi, 298–301.
13. Buffett 2002: 13–15; 2003: 15.
14. Greenspan 2007: 178.
15. BIS, *AR* 2006: 66; USFRBSF 2009; Greenspan 2007: 346–7; Woodward 2000; *Economist* 2002.
16. US *Economic Report 2009*: Table B-79; USFRBG 2009.
17. Jickling 2010.
18. USBoC, "Foreign-Trade."
19. World Bank, *WDI*.
20. IMF, COFER, July 2010.
21. IMF, COFER, July 2010; US Treasury 2010.
22. King 2009.
23. OECD, *StatExtracts* 2010; Eckes 2009b: 6–7.
24. IMF, COFER, July 2010.
25. OECD, *StatExtracts* 2010; Roubini and Mihm 2010.
26. US *Economic Report 2009*: Table B-76; USBoC, *Statistical Abstract 2008*: Table 1166.
27. El Boghdady and Keating 2009.
28. *Observer* 2009.
29. Bajaj and Haughney 2007.
30. Lipton and Labaton 2008; Holmes 1999.
31. Streitfeld and Morgenson 2008; Norberg 2009: 31; *Wall Street Journal* 2008.
32. Buffett 2008: 11; USBoC, *Statistical Abstract* 2008: Table 942.
33. Poulter 2007; Black 2007; Evans-Pritchard 2007.
34. Nakamoto and Wighton 2007.
35. Hall 2009; Morgenson 2008b; Norberg 2009: 58–65.
36. Nanto 2010: 34.

37. Morgenson 2008a; 2009.
38. IMF, *GFSR* (April 2006); Tett 2009; Greenspan 2005.
39. Mollenkamp and Ng 2007: A1.
40. Cohan 2009: 321–30.
41. Mollenkamp and Ng 2007; Elder and Hume 2008: 40; Davies, Tett, and Thallarsen 2008.
42. Sorkin 2009; Strauss-Kahn 2009.
43. Blanchard 2009; Smick 2009.
44. Evans-Pritchard 2009; Canuto and Giugale 2010: 21.
45. Karmin and Perry 2007: A1; Ahamed 2009.
46. Nanto 2010: 41.
47. Nanto 2010: 42.
48. Cody 2009; Landler 2007.
49. Carer and Tighe 2007.
50. Zimmermann and Schafer 2009; Norberg 2009: 45–6.
51. Marotte and Seguin 2009.
52. Lewis 2009; Jonsson 2009; Ward 2009.
53. IMF, *GFSR* October 2010: 12; IMF, *GFSR* April 2010: 13.
54. World Bank, *WDI*; Nanto 2010: 44; IMF, *WEO* (April 2010): 2; IMF, *WEO* (October 2010): 177, 181.
55. World Bank, *WDI*; World Bank, *GEP*, Summer 2010; IMF, *WEO* (October 2010), 210.
56. OECD, *EO* (May 2010); IMF 2010: 15, 37, 44.
57. Aldcroft 2001: 73–4; James 2001: 129–33; Kindleberger 1973: 199–231.
58. Aldcroft 2001: 78–92.
59. Eichengreen 1995: 351–3; Kindleberger 1973: 28.
60. Financial Stability Board 2010.
61. Sachs 2009; Wolf 2009.
62. Wolf 2009.
63. Shin and Eilperin 2009.
64. http://www.g20.org/pub_communiques.aspx/.
65. OECD, *Factbook*, "Composition of Fiscal Packages."
66. Nanto 2010; Chan and McGinty 2010.
67. USCBO 2010: Tables F-1, F-2; Nanto 2010: 39.
68. IMF, *WEO* (October 2010): 209; Nanto 2010: 86–8.
69. IMF, *WEO* Database (October 2010), http://www.imf.org/ (accessed October 2010).
70. IMF, *WEO* (October 2010): 196, 210.
71. IMF, *WEO* (October 2010): 196, 210.

Chapter 10

1. ILO 2009: 1.
2. USDoS 2010; ILO 2009: 15–16; Essick 2001.

3. Liu 1993; Gladwell 1993; Reid 2000.
4. ILO 2009: 11.
5. ILO 2009: 1.
6. Bales 2009; USDoS 2010; UNODC 2010; Essick 2001.
7. USDoS 2009: 104–5; Reeves 2003.
8. USDoS 2010: 244, 333; South Africa, National Prosecuting Authority 2010.
9. Friedlaender 2002; Interlandi 2009; Rather 2010.
10. USDoS 2009: 197–9; Wehrfritz, Kinetz, and Kent 2008.
11. ILO 2009: 20.
12. UNODC 2009.
13. USDoS 2010: 49.
14. UNODC 2010; Interpol 2008.
15. Noble 1995.
16. ILO 2000; Lin 1998; Wang and Goodridge 2009.
17. Greenhouse 2008; *Scottish Daily Record* 2009; ILO 2000; White 1996; *New Zealand Herald* 2005; 2010.
18. *Right Vision News* 2010; ICFTU 2006b.
19. ICFTU 2006a.
20. Wehrfritz 2005; Baskin 1996.
21. Teather 2005; Nike 2007–9: 44, 56.
22. Frank 2008; Esbenshade 2004.
23. Associated Press Worldstream 2002.
24. Kristof 2004; 1998.
25. Brill 1999; Krugman 2001.
26. Hull and Sorrell 2010; Foster 2010; Chinadaily.com.cn 2010.
27. Bradsher, June 10, 2010; *Thai Press* 2010.
28. Tam and Lau 2010.
29. Morrell 2010; Gross 2010.
30. World Bank, *WDI*.
31. McCormack 2010.
32. USGAO 2009.
33. Joshi 2010.
34. Biesecker 2008; *Inside US Trade* 2010.
35. Goldsmith 2010.
36. Ma 2008.
37. Barboza 2007a.
38. Barboza 2007b.
39. Public Citizen 2007; Neuman and Barboza 2010.
40. United Nations Environment Program 2005: 4–5.
41. Yerxa 2010.
42. *Inside US Trade* 2009.
43. Yerxa 2010.
44. Power 1976; Gwynne 1975: 64; Schlesinger 2003.
45. Stokes 2008.

46. Solomon 2010: 19.
47. *Economist* 2010; Theil and Mascarenhas 2010.

Chapter 11

1. Greenspan 2010.
2. Schumpeter 1947: 32.
3. Elliott, Teather, and Treanor 2010; BIS, *AR* 2010: 3; IMF, *GFSR* (July 2010).
4. Braithwaite 2010: 1; Hoenig 2010.
5. IMF, *AR 2009*: 9; BIS, AR 2009: xiii; IMF, *WEO* (October 2010), http://www.imf. org (accessed October 2010).
6. IMF, *WEO* 2010.
7. US–China Business Council.
8. IMF, *WEO* (October 2010), http://www.imf.org (accessed October 2010); Krugman 2010b.
9. Bryan 2010; USNIC 2004.
10. IMF, *Principal*, 2010.
11. Kharas 2010: 27.
12. Canuto and Giugale 2010: 351–63.

Suggestions for Further Reading

Chapter 1: Introduction

Cudahy, Brian J. *Box Boats: How Container Ships Changed the World* (New York: Fordham University Press, 2006).

Dierikx, Marc. *Clipping the Clouds: How Air Travel Changed the World* (Westport, CN: Praeger, 2008).

Eckes, Alfred E., Jr. "Globalization," in *A Companion to International History 1900–2001*, ed. Gordon Martel (Oxford: Wiley-Blackwell, 2007), 408–21.

Engel, Jeffrey A. "A Shrinking World," in *A Companion to International History 1900–2001*, ed. Gordon Martel (Oxford: Wiley-Blackwell, 2007), 52–64.

Maddison, Angus. *Statistical Revisions*. www.ggdc.net/Maddison/.

Maddison, Angus. *The World Economy* (Paris: OECD, 2006).

OECD. *Stats*. http://stats.oecd.org/index.aspx.

UNCTAD. *Handbook of Statistics*. www.unctad.org/.

World Bank. *World Development Indicators*. www.worldbank.org/.

Chapter 2: The Global Economy before 1980

Chanda, Nayan. *Bound Together: How Traders, Preachers, Adventurers, and Warriors Shaped Globalization* (New Haven: Yale University Press, 2007).

Eckes, Alfred E., Jr., and Thomas Zeiler. *Globalization and the American Century* (New York: Cambridge University Press, 2003).

Findlay, Ronald, and Kevin H. O'Rourke. *Power and Plenty* (Princeton, NJ: Princeton University Press, 2007).

Foreman-Peck, James. *A History of the World Economy* (2nd edn., Reading, MA: Pearson Education, 1995).

Hopkins, A. G., ed. *Globalization in World History* (New York: Norton, 2002).

Kenwood, A. G., and A. L. Lougheed. *The Growth of the International Economy 1820–2000* (4th edn., London: Routledge, 1999).

Rothermund, Dietmar. *The Global Impact of the Great Depression 1929–1939* (New York: Routledge, 1996).

Chapter 3: The Rich Nations

Berend, Ivan T. *An Economic History of Twentieth-Century Europe* (Cambridge, UK: Cambridge University Press, 2006).

Eckes, Alfred E., Jr. "Europe and Economic Globalization Since 1945," in *A Companion to Europe since 1945*, ed. Klaus Larres (Oxford: Wiley-Blackwell, 2009), 249–69.

Flockton, Christopher. "European Integration since Maastricht," in *A Companion to Europe since 1945*, ed. Klaus Larres (Oxford: Wiley-Blackwell, 2009), 270–301.

King, Stephen D. *Losing Control: The Emerging Threats to Western Prosperity* (New Haven, CN: Yale University Press, 2010).

Chapter 4: The Developing World

Chang, Ha-Joon. *Bad Samaritans: The Myth of Free Trade and the Secret History of Capitalism* (New York: Bloomsbury Press, 2008).

Fingleton, Eamonn. *In the Jaws of the Dragon* (New York: St. Martin's, 2008).

Khanna, Parag. *The Second World: How Emerging Powers Are Redefining Global Competition in the Twenty-first Century* (New York: Random House, 2008).

Panagariya, Arvind. *India: The Emerging Giant* (New York: Oxford University Press, 2008).

Shenkar, Oded. *The Chinese Century* (Saddle River, NJ: Pearson, 2005).

Chapter 5: Thinking about the Global Economy

Chang, Ha-Joon. *Kicking Away the Ladder: Development Strategy in Historical Perspective* (London: Anthem Press, 2002).

Fox, Justin. *The Myth of the Rational Market* (New York: HarperCollins, 2009).

Friedman, Milton, and Rose D. *Two Lucky People: Memoirs* (Chicago: University of Chicago Press, 1998).

Greenspan, Alan. *The Age of Turbulence* (New York: Penguin, 2007).

Hughes, Kent H. *Building the Next American Century* (Washington, DC: Woodrow Wilson Center, 2005).

Roncaglia, Alessandro. *The Wealth of Ideas: A History of Economic Thought* (New York: Cambridge University Press, 2005).

Skidelsky, Robert. *Keynes: The Return of the Master* (New York: Public Affairs, 2009)

Toye, John, and Richard Toye. *The UN and Global Political Economy* (Bloomington, IN: Indiana University Press, 2004).

Wedel, Janine R. *Collision and Collusion: The Strange Case of Western Aid to Eastern Europe 1989–1998* (New York: St. Martin's, 1998).

Wolf, Martin. *Why Globalization Works* (New Haven: Yale University Press, 2004).

Yergin, Daniel, and Joseph Stanislaw. *The Commanding Heights* (New York: Simon and Schuster, 1998).

Zweig, Philip L. *Walter Wriston, Citibank, and the Rise and Fall of American Financial Supremacy* (New York: Crown, 1996).

Chapter 6: International Trade

Barton, John H., Judith L. Goldstein, Timothy E. Josling, and Richard H. Steinberg. *The Evolution of the Trade Regime* (Princeton, NJ: Princeton University Press, 2006).

Eckes, Alfred E., Jr. *US Trade Issues* (Santa Barbara, CA: ABC Clio, 2009).

Lovett, William A., Alfred E. Eckes, Jr., and Richard L. Brinkman. *US Trade Policy: History, Theory and the WTO* (2nd edn., Armonk, NY: M.E. Sharpe, 2004).

Van Den Bossche, Peter. *The Law and Policy of the World Trade Organization* (2nd edn., New York: Cambridge University Press, 2008).

Chapter 7: Global Business

Drucker, Peter F. *Managing in Turbulent Times* (New York: HarperCollins, 1980).

Jones, Geoffrey. *Multinationals and Global Capitalism* (New York: Oxford University Press, 2005).

Ohmae, Kenichi. *Triad Power: The Coming Shape of Global Competition* (New York: Free Press, 1985).

Porter, Michael. *The Competitive Advantage of Nations* (New York: Free Press, 1990).

Chapter 8: Internationalization of Finance

Cassis, Youssef. *Capitals of Capital* (New York: Cambridge University Press, 2006).

Eichengreen, Barry. *Globalizing Capital* (2nd edn., Princeton, NJ: Princeton University Press, 2008).

Mayer, Martin. *The Bankers* (New York: Plume, 1998).

Michie, Ranald C. *The Global Securities Market* (New York: Oxford University Press, 2006).

Reinhart, Carmen M., and Kenneth S. Rogoff. *This Time is Different* (Princeton, NJ: Princeton University Press, 2009).

Chapter 9: The Global Financial Crisis of 2007–10

Hirsh, Michael. *Capital Offense* (New York: John Wiley, 2010).
Krugman, Paul. *The Return of Depression Economics* (New York: Norton, 2009).
Jonsson, Asgeir. *Why Iceland?* (New York: McGraw-Hill, 2009).
Nanto, Dick K. *The Global Financial Crisis* (Washington, DC: CRS Report for Congress, February 4, 2010).
Roubini, Nouriel. *Crisis Economics* (New York: Penguin, 2010).
Stiglitz, Joseph E. *Free Fall* (New York: Norton, 2010).
Tett, Gillian. *Fool's Gold* (New York: Free Press, 2009).

Chapter 10: The Underside of the Global Economy

Bales, Kevin. *Ending Slavery* (Berkeley: University of California Press, 2007).
International Labor Organization. *The Costs of Coercion* (Geneva: ILO, 2009).
Kimball, Ann Marie. *Risky Trade: Infectious Disease in the Era of Global Trade* (London: Ashgate, 2006).
United Nations Office on Drugs and Crime. *The Globalization of Crime* (Vienna: UNODC, 2010). Available online at www.unctad.org/.

Chapter 11: Epilogue

Bremmer, Ian. *The End of the Free Market* (New York: Portfolio, 2010).
Cohen, Stephen S., and J. Bradford DeLong. *The End of Influence* (New York: Perseus, 2010).
Halper, Stefan. *The Beijing Consensus* (New York: Basic Books, 2010).
Rajan, Raghuram G. *Fault Lines* (Princeton, NJ: Princeton University Press, 2010).

References

Abdelal, Rawi. 2007. *Capital Rules* (Cambridge, MA: Harvard University Press).

Africa News. 2009a. "Ghana: Was Country Blindfolded into the Interim EPAs?" (Jun. 19).

Africa News. 2009b. "Namibia: What Are Economic Partnership Agreements?" (Apr. 17).

Agence France Press. 2008. "S. Korea's Lee Apologises, Urges MPs to Pass US Free Trade Pact" (May 22).

Agence France Press. 2009. "S. Korean MPs Approve Free Trade Pact with India" (Nov. 6).

Ahamed, Liaquat. 2009. "Subprime Europe," *New York Times* (Mar. 8).

Ahearn, Raymond. 2005. *Japan's Free Trade Agreement Program* (CRS Report for Congress, Aug. 22). Available online at www.nationalaglawcenter.org/crs/.

Aldcroft, Derek. 2001. *The European Economy 1914–2000* (4th edn., London: Routledge).

Anderson, Garry M., William F. Shughart II, and Robert D. Tollison. 1985. "It's True! Adam Smith Was a Bureaucrat," *Wall Street Journal* (Aug. 26).

Andrews, Edmund L. 2008. "Greenspan Concedes Flaws in Deregulatory Approach," *New York Times* (Oct. 24).

Angell, Norman. 1911. *The Great Illusion* (repr. New York: Garland, 1972).

Angus Reid Global Monitor. 2008. "Canadians Think US Benefits Most from NAFTA" (Mar. 12).

Angus Reid Global Monitor. 2009. "Canadians Want Free Trade Deal with India" (Dec. 1).

Ash, Timothy Garton. 2010. "Europe Is Sleepwalking to Decline," *The Guardian* (May 19).

Ashton, John. 2009. "On Top of the World," *Sunday Times* (Oct. 11).

Asia Pulse. 2005. "Cisco Plans Expansion in Chinese Market" (Jun. 17).

Associated Press Worldstream. 2002. "Nike Workers Protest Cutbacks in Production" (Aug. 20).

ATA. "Annual Results," www.airlines.org/. Accessed Jul. 2010.

The Contemporary Global Economy: A History Since 1980, First Edition. Alfred E. Eckes, Jr.
© 2011 Alfred E. Eckes, Jr. Published 2011 by Blackwell Publishing Ltd.

Atkey, Ron. 2007. "Putting National Security to the Test," *Globe and Mail* (Canada) (Oct. 15), A17.

Badaracco, Joseph L., Jr., and David B. Yoffie. 1983. "'Industrial Policy': It Can't Happen Here," *Harvard Business Review* 61:6 (Nov./Dec.), 97–105.

Baines, Dudley. 1995. *Emigration from Europe 1815–1930* (Cambridge, UK: Cambridge University Press).

Bajaj, Vikas, and Christine Haughney. 2007. "More People With Weak Credit Are Defaulting on Mortgages," *New York Times* (Jan. 26), 1.

Bales, Carter F., Donald J. Gogel, and James S. Henry. 1980. "The Environment for Business in the 1980s," *McKinsey Quarterly* (Winter).

Bales, Kevin. 2007. *Ending Slavery* (Berkeley: University of California Press).

Bales, Kevin. 2009. "Winning the Fight: Eradicating Slavery in the Modern Age," *Harvard International Review* (Spring), 4–17.

Barboza, David. 2007a. "China's Seafood Industry: Dirty Water, Dangerous Fish," *New York Times* (Dec. 15), 1.

Barboza, David. 2007b. "Why Lead in Toy Paint?" *New York Times* (Sept. 11), 1.

Baskin, Roberta. 1996. "Controversy Surrounds Nike as Exclusive Investigation Reveals Abuse of Workers in Foreign Countries and Very Low Wages," *48 Hours* (Oct. 17). Accessed Jun. 2010 at LexisNexis Academic.

Bender, Daniel E., and Richard A. Greenwald, eds. 2003. *Sweatshop USA* (New York: Routledge).

Berend, Ivan T. 2006. *An Economic History of Twentieth-Century Europe* (Cambridge, UK: Cambridge University Press).

Berger, Michael. 1990. "Values Soar Out of Reach on Japanese Real Estate Market," *San Francisco Chronicle* (Nov. 24), A13.

Bergmann, Barbara R. 2005. "State of Economics: Needs Lots of Work," *Annals of the American Academy of Political and Social Science* 600 (Jul.), 52–67.

Bernanke, Ben S. 2002. "Remarks" (Nov. 8) Chicago, Illinois. Accessible at www.federalreserve.gov/.

Bernard, Andrew B., J. Bradford Jensen, Stephen J. Redding, and Peter K. Schott. 2007. "Firms in International Trade," *Journal of Economic Perspectives* 21, no. 3 (Summer), 105–30.

Bianco, Anthony. 1998. "The Prophet of Wall Street," *Business Week* (Jun. 1), 124.

Biesecker, Calvin. 2008. "GAO, WCO Outline Challenges to Scanning All US Bound Cargo Containers," *Defense Daily* (Jun. 18).

BIS. 1930–. *Annual Report (AR)* (Basel).

BIS. 2008. *Financial Globalization and Emerging Market Capital Flows* (BIS Papers No. 44) (Basel: BIS, Dec.).

Black, David. 2007. "UK Sub-Prime Lender Victoria Goes into Administration," *Glasgow Herald* (Sept. 11), 32.

Blanchard, Olivier. 2009. "The Crisis: Basic Mechanisms, and Appropriate Policies," *IMF Working Paper* WP/09/80.

Bordo, Michael D., Claudia Goldin, and Eugene N. White, eds. 1998. *The Defining Moment: The Great Depression and the American Economy in the Twentieth Century* (*Chicago*: University of Chicago Press).

Bowe, John. 2008. *Nobodies* (New York: Random House).

Bradsher, Keith. 2010. "A Labor Movement Stirs in China," *New York Times* (Jun. 10).

Braithwaite, Tom. 2010. "Basel Standards Committee Is 'Succumbing' to Bank Lobbying," *Financial Times* (Jul. 20).

Bremmer, Ian. 2010. *The End of the Free Market* (New York: Portfolio).

Brill, Marta. 1999. "Prof Says Sweatshop Labor Aids Economies in U. Michigan Lecture," *University Wire* (Nov. 11).

Brinkley, Douglas. 2003. *Wheels for the World* (New York: Viking).

Brinkman, Richard L. 2004. "Free Trade: Static Comparative Advantage," in William A. Lovett, Alfred E. Eckes, Jr., and Richard L. Brinkman, *US Trade Policy: History, Theory and the WTO* (2nd edn., Armonk, NY: M.E. Sharpe), 96–100.

Brooks, Rick. 2002. "Buying Jobs: How Big Incentives Won Alabama a Piece of the Auto Industry," *Wall Street Journal* (Apr. 3), A1.

Brouthers, Lance Eliot, John P. McCray, and Timothy P. Wilkinson. 1999. "Maquiladoras: Entrepreneurial Experimentation to Global Competitiveness," *Business Horizons* (Mar./Apr.), 37–43.

Bryan, Lowell. 2010. "Globalization's Critical Imbalances," *McKinsey Quarterly* 3:57–68.

Budrys, Aleksandras. 2010. "Russia to Set Up Food Sector Protectionism – Lobby," Reuters News (Feb. 18).

Buffett, Warren. 2002 and 2003. Berkshire Hathaway "Shareholder Letter". Accessed Oct. 2009 at www.berkshirehathaway.com/letters/.

Burns, John F. 1987. "Canada Opens Markets' Doors," *New York Times* (Jan. 13).

Business Week. 2001. "Dear Abby, You Goofed" (Sept. 10).

Calomiris, Charles W. 2000. "Universal Banking "American-Style," in Charles W. Calomiris, ed., *US Bank Deregulation in Historical Perspective* (New York: Cambridge University Press), 337.

Canuto, Otaviano, and Marcelo Giugale, eds. 2010. *Day After Tomorrow: A Handbook on the Future of Economic Policy in the Developing World* (Washington, DC: World Bank).

Capgemini SA and Merrill Lynch & Co. 2010. *World Wealth Report* (Jun.), www.us. capgemini.com/worldwealthreport09/. Accessed Jun. 2010.

Carer, Gabriel, and Chris Tighe. 2007. "Savers Queue to Move Their Money," *Financial Times* (Sept. 18), 2.

Cassis, Youssef. 2006. *Capitals of Capital* (Cambridge, UK: Cambridge University Press).

Central Bank of the Republic of China (Taiwan). "International Investment Position." Available online at www.cbc.gov.tw/.

Champion, Marc, Joanna Slater, and Carrick Mollenkamp. 2009. "Banks Reel on Eastern Europe's Bad News," *Wall Street Journal* (Feb. 18).

Chan, Sewell, and Jo Craven McGinty. 2010. "In Crisis, Fed Opened Vault Wide for U.S. and World, Data Shows," *New York Times* (Dec. 2), 1.

Chanda, Nayan. 2007. *Bound Together: How Traders, Preachers, Adventurers, and Warriors Shaped Globalization* (New Haven: Yale University Press).

Chandler, Lester V. 1958. *Benjamin Strong: Central Banker* (Washington, DC: Brookings).

Chang, Ha-Joon. 2002. *Kicking Away the Ladder: Development Strategy in Historical Perspective* (London: Anthem Press).

Chang, Ha-Joon. 2003. *Globalization, Economic Development, and the Role of the State* (New York: Zed Books).

Chang, Ha-Joon. 2008. *Bad Samaritans: The Myth of Free Trade and the Secret History of Capitalism* (New York: Bloomsbury Press).

Chernow, Ron. 1990. *The House of Morgan* (New York: Simon and Schuster).

Chinadaily.com.cn. 2010. "Suicides at Foxconn Reveal Woes" (May 26). Accessed Jun. 2010 at LexisNexis Academic.

Choi, Won-Mog. 2007. "To Comply or Not to Comply? Non-Implementation Problems in the WTO Dispute Settlement System." *Journal of World Trade* 41 (5): 1043–71.

Cimoli, Mario, Giovanni Dosi, and Joseph E. Stiglitz, eds. 2009. *Industrial Policy and Development* (New York: Oxford University Press).

Cipolla, Carlo. 1982. *The Monetary Policy of Fourteenth-Century Florence* (Berkeley: University of California Press).

Clifford, Mark L., and Peter Engardio. 2000. *Meltdown: Asia's Boom, Bust, and Beyond* (New York: Prentice-Hall).

CNN Moneyweek. 1998. "Investors Brace for Statement Shock; Executive Cabinet Calls Out for Support" (Dec. 13).

Cody, Edward. 2009. "Norwegian Hamlets Seek Wall Street Amends," *Washington Post* (Aug. 25).

Cohan, William D. 2009. *House of Cards* (New York: Doubleday).

Cohen, Stephen D. 1998. "Limits to Friendship: Why the US and the European Union Have Been Unable to Devise a Common Trade Strategy Toward Japan," *International Trade Journal* (Jun. 1), 198.

Cohen, Stephen S., and J. Bradford DeLong. 2010. *The End of Influence* (New York: Perseus).

Constantine, Gus. 2009. "Congo, A Country That's Broken," *Washington Times* (Sept. 8), 3.

Corcoran, Terence. 2010. "The Rise of Global Statism," *Financial Post* (Apr. 12).

Council of Canadians. 2010. "Open Civil Society Declaration on a Proposed Comprehensive Economic and Trade Agreement between Canada and the European Union." Available online at http://canadians.org/.

Craig, Susanne, and Kara Scannell. 2010. "Goldman Settles its Battle with SEC," *Wall Street Journal* (Jul. 16), A1.

d'Aquino, Thomas. 1992. "Suicide or Renaissance? Canada at the Crossroads," *Vital Speeches of the Day* (Mar. 31), 537–9.

Davies, Paul J., Gillian Tett, and Peter Thallarsen. 2008. "Untimely Gamble on ABN Amro Is the Root Cause of RBS Woes," *Financial Times* (Apr. 23).

Dearlove, Des, and Stuart Crainer. 2005. "Porter Thinks His Way to the Top," *The Times* (London) (Dec. 1), 5.

Dibenedetto, Bill. 2008. "Maqs Are Back," *Journal of Commerce* (Oct. 13), 22.

Dierikx, Marc. 2008. *Clipping the Clouds: How Air Travel Changed the World* (Westport, CN: Praeger).

Dinan, Desmond. 2009. "European Integration: From the Common Market to the Single Market," in Klaus Larres, ed., *A Companion to Europe Since 1945* (Oxford: Wiley-Blackwell), 133–50.

Dosman, Edgar J. 2008. *The Life and Times of Raul Prebisch, 1901–1986* (Montreal & Kingston: McGill-Queen's University Press).

Drucker, Peter. 1977. "The Rise of Production Sharing," *Wall Street Journal* (Mar. 15), 22.

Drucker, Peter F. 1980. *Managing in Turbulent Times* (New York: HarperCollins).

Drucker, Peter F. 1986. "The Changed World Economy," *Foreign Affairs* 64:4 (Spring), 768–91.

Dunlap, Albert J., and Bob Andelman. 1997. *Mean Business: How I Save Bad Companies and Make Good Companies Great* (New York: Times Books).

Duranty, Walter. 1931. "Russia Also Hit by World Crisis," *New York Times* (Apr. 3), 12.

Duranty, Walter. 1932. "Soviet in 16th Year; Calm and Hopeful," *New York Times* (Nov. 13), E4.

Dutt, Amitava K. 2005. "International Trade in Early Development Economics," in *Development Economics* (New York: Zed Books), edited by KS Jomo and Erik S. Reinert, 107–11, 120.

Eales, Roy. 1981. "Challenge in Reverse: Foreign Investment in America," *McKinsey Quarterly* (Winter), 53.

Ebenstein, Alan. 2001. *Hayek's Journey: The Mind of Friedrich Hayek* (New York: Palgrave Macmillan).

ECB. 2010. *Financial Stability Review* (Frankfurt: ECB, Jun.).

Eckes, Alfred E., Jr. 1975. *A Search for Solvency: Bretton Woods and the International Monetary System, 1941–1971* (Austin: University of Texas Press).

Eckes, Alfred E., Jr. 1979. *The US and the Global Struggle for Minerals* (Austin: University of Texas Press).

Eckes, Alfred E., Jr. 1995. *Opening America's Market* (Chapel Hill, NC: University of North Carolina Press).

Eckes, Alfred E., Jr. 2004. "US Trade History," in William A. Lovett, Alfred E. Eckes, Jr., and Richard L. Brinkman, *US Trade Policy: History, Theory and the WTO* (2nd edn., Armonk, NY: M.E. Sharpe), 36–92.

Eckes, Alfred E., Jr. 2007. "*Globalization*," in Gordon Martel, ed., *A Companion to International History 1900–2001* (Oxford: Wiley-Blackwell), 408–21.

Eckes, Alfred E., Jr. 2009a. "Europe and Economic Globalization Since 1945," in Klaus Larres, ed., *A Companion to Europe Since 1945* (Oxford: Wiley-Blackwell), 249–69.

Eckes, Alfred E., Jr. 2009b. *US Trade Issues* (Santa Barbara, CA: ABC Clio).

Eckes, Alfred E., Jr. In press. "Administration of Trade Policy," in Mordechai Kreinin and Michael Plummer, *Oxford Handbook of International Commercial Policy* (New York: Oxford University Press).

Eckes, Alfred E., Jr., and Thomas Zeiler. 2003. *Globalization and the American Century* (New York: Cambridge University Press).

Economist. 1979. "EEC and Japan: Answering Injury with Insult" (Apr. 7), 61.

Economist. 1984. "The Old World's New Fears" (Nov. 24), 93.

Economist. 1988. "Pity Those Poor Japanese" (Dec. 24), 48.

Economist. 1990. "Porter v. Ohmae" (Aug. 4), 53.

Economist. 2000a. "A Hard Landing" (Dec. 9).

Economist. 2000b. "A Tale of Two Debtors" (Jan. 20).

Economist. 2002. "The O'Neill Doctrine" (Apr. 27).

Economist. 2004a. "A Golden Age?" (Feb. 28).

Economist. 2004b. "Sweating for Fashion" (Mar. 6).

Economist. 2006. "Capital City: London as a Financial Center" (Oct. 21).

Economist. 2007. "No Country Is an Island" (Dec. 1).

Economist. 2009. "Gasping for Gas" (Jan. 7), 53.

Economist. 2010. "Science Behind Closed Doors" (Jul. 10).

Eden, Lorraine, and Stefanie Lenway. 2001. "Introduction to the Symposium Multinationals: The Janus Face of Globalization," *Journal of International Business Studies* 32:3, 383–400.

Edge Malaysia. 2010. "Vietnam: Asia's Next Growth Story" (Mar. 29).

Eichengreen, Barry. 1995. *Golden Fetters* (New York: Oxford University Press).

Eichengreen, Barry. 2003. *Capital Flows and Crises* (Cambridge, MA: MIT Press), 17.

Eichengreen, Barry. 2007. *The European Economy Since 1945* (Princeton, NJ: Princeton University Press).

Eichengreen, Barry. 2008. *Globalizing Capital* (Princeton, NJ: Princeton University Press).

El Boghdady, Dina, and Dan Keating. 2009. "The Next Hit: Quick Defaults; More FHA-Backed Mortgages Go Bad Without a Single Payment," *The Washington Post* (Mar. 8), A1.

Elder, Bryce, and Neil Hume. 2008. "RBS Suffers 7% Fall as Fears Rise Over its US Subsidiaries," *Financial Times* (Jul. 16), 40.

Elliott, Larry, David Teather, and Jill Treanor. 2010. "The Survivor," *The Observer* (Aug. 8).

Engardio, Pete, Aaron Bernstein, and Manjeet Kripalani. 2003. "The New Global Job Shift," *Business Week* (Feb. 3), 50.

Engel, Jeffrey A. 2007. "A Shrinking World," in Gordon Martel, ed., *A Companion to International History 1900–2001* (Oxford: Wiley-Blackwell), 52–64.

Enright, Michael J., W. John Hoffmann, and Peter Wood. 2010. "Get Ready, Here China Inc. Comes," *Wall Street Journal* (Feb. 24).

Esbenshade, Jill. 2004. *Monitoring Sweatshops* (Philadelphia, PA: Temple University Press).

Essick, Kristi. 2001. "Guns, Money and Cell Phones," *Industry Standard Magazine* (Jun. 11).

Estevadeordal, Antoni, Matthew Shearer, and Kati Suominen. 2007. "Multilateralizing RTAs in the Americas: State of Play and Ways Forward." Paper presented at the conference on Multilateralising Regionalism, Geneva, Sept. 10–12. Available online at www.wto.org/.

European Round Table of Industrialists. See www.ert.be/home.aspx.

Eurostat. 2008. *Food: From Farm to Fork Statistics.* Available online at http://epp.eurostat. ec.europa.eu.

EU-Russia Energy Dialogue. 2009. *Tenth Progress Report* (Nov.), http://ec.europa.eu/ energy/international/bilateral_cooperation/russia/doc/reports/progress10_en.pdf.

Evans-Pritchard, Ambrose. 2007. "Subprime Lenders Slammed by FSA," *Daily Telegraph* (London) (Jul. 5), 2.

Evans-Pritchard, Ambrose. 2009. "Currencies Crumble on Debt Crisis Fears," *Daily Telegraph* (London) (Feb. 17).

Fallows, James. 1994. *Looking at the Sun* (New York: Pantheon).

Feldstein, Martin. 1983. "Is Industrial Policy the Answer?" *Vital Speeches of the Day*, 122–6.

Ferguson, Niall. 1999. *The House of Rothschild, 1849–1999* (New York: Viking).

Ferguson, Niall. 2003. *Empire* (New York: Basic Books).

Ferguson, Niall. 2005. "Sinking Globalization," *Foreign Affairs* 84 (Mar./Apr.), 64–77.

Financial Stability Board. "History." Accessed Jul. 2010 at www.financialstabilityboard.org/about/history.htm.

Financial Times. 1985. "Multinationals May Leave 'if Europe Does Not Unite'" (Apr. 25), I:1.

Financial Times. 2009. "Deadline Clouds Boeing's Horizon" (Nov. 19), 16.

Findlay, Ronald, and Kevin O' Rourke. 2007. *Power and Plenty* (Princeton, NJ: Princeton University Press).

Fingleton, Eamonn. 2008. *In the Jaws of the Dragon* (New York: St. Martin's).

Flockton, Christopher. 2009. "European Integration Since Maastricht," in Klaus Larres, ed., *A Companion to Europe Since 1945* (Oxford: Wiley-Blackwell), 270–301.

Florida, Richard. 2005. "The World Is Spiky," *Atlantic Monthly* (Oct.), 48–50.

Fortson, Danny. 2006. "The Day Big Bang Blasted the Old Boys into Oblivion," *The Independent*, Oct. 29, 6.

Fortune. 2010. *Global 500*. Accessed Jul. 2010 at http://money.cnn.com/magazines/fortune/global500/2010/full_list/.

Foster, Peter. 2010. "Xbox Factory 'Using Teenage Slave Labor'," *Daily Telegraph* (London) (Apr. 17), 16.

Fox, Justin. 2009. *The Myth of the Rational Market* (New York: HarperCollins).

Frank, T. A. 2008. "Confessions of a Sweatshop Inspector," *Washington Monthly* (Apr.).

Friedlaender, Michael M. 2002. "The Right to Sell or Buy a Kidney: Are We Failing Our Patients?" *Lancet* (Mar. 16), 971–3.

Friedman, Milton. 1962. *Capitalism and Freedom* (Chicago: University of Chicago Press).

Friedman, Milton. 1979. "Hooray for Margaret Thatcher," *Newsweek* (Jul. 9), 56.

Friedman, Milton, and Rose D. Friedman. 1998. *Two Lucky People: Memoirs* (Chicago: University of Chicago Press).

Friedman, Thomas L. 1996. "Foreign Affairs Big Mac I," *New York Times* (Dec. 8).

Friedman, Thomas L. 1999. *The Lexus and the Olive Tree* (New York: Farrar, Straus & Giroux).

Friedman, Thomas L. 2005. *The World Is Flat* (New York: Farrar, Straus and Giroux).

Fukuyama, Francis. 1992. *The End of History and the Last Man* (New York: Free Press).

Galbraith, James K. 2008. *The Predator State* (New York: Free Press).

Gavin, Francis J. 2004. *Gold, Dollars, & Power: The Politics of International Monetary Relations, 1958–1971* (Chapel Hill: University of North Carolina).

Giles, Chris. 2009. "Taxpayers Face a Generation of Pain," *Financial Times* (Nov. 25).

Gladwell, Malcolm. 1993. "US Policy Seen Encouraging Wave of Chinese Immigration," *Washington Post* (Jun. 13), A25.

Glassman, James K., and Kevin Hassett. 1999. *Dow 36,000* (New York: Three Rivers Press).

Global Commission on International Migration (GCIM). 2005. *Migration in an Interconnected World* (Geneva: GCIM).

Globe and Mail (Canada). 1979. "Governments Can't Do Much, IMF Says Economic Forecast Bleak" (Sept. 17).

Globe and Mail. 1997. "Domestic Giants, Global Pip-squeaks" (Jun. 28).

Goldsmith, Jack. 2010. "The New Vulnerability," *The New Republic* (Jun. 24), 21.

Gonzalez-Paramo, Jose Manuel. 2009. "Fiscal Policy and the Financial Crisis" (Sept. 4). Accessed Feb. 2010 at www.ecb.int/press.

Goodwin, Craufurd D. W. 2003. "Economics and Economists in the Policy Process," in Warren J. Samuels, Jeff E. Biddle, and John B. Davis, eds., *A Companion to The History of Economic Thought* (Oxford: Wiley-Blackwell), 610–11.

Gorton, Gary B. 2010. *Slapped by the Invisible Hand: The Panic of 2007* (New York: Oxford University Press, 2010).

Graham, Frederick. 1949. "New Planes Will Cut Flying Time This Spring," *New York Times* (Mar. 6), 27.

Gramm, Phil. 2002. *Congressional Record* (Jul. 10), S6553.

Greasley, David, and Les Oxley. 2002. "Regime Shift and Fast Recovery on the Periphery: New Zealand in the 1930s," *Economic History Review* 55:4 (Nov.), 697–720.

Greenhouse, Steven. 2008. "Apparel Factory Workers Were Cheated, State Says," *New York Times* (Jul. 24), 2.

Greenspan, Alan. 2005. "Economic Flexibility," remarks before the National Italian American Foundation, Washington (Oct. 12). Accessed at www.federalreserve.gov/.

Greenspan, Alan. 2007. *The Age of Turbulence* (New York: Penguin).

Greenspan, Alan. 2010. "Overseas Savings Glut Kept Long Term Rates Low," Testimony to US Financial Crisis Inquiry Commission (Apr. 7), www.fcic.gov/hearings/.

Gross, Daniel. 2010. "The Days the Earth Stood Still," *Newsweek* (May 3), 46.

Guidolin, Massimo, and Elizabeth A. La Jeunesse. 2007. "The Decline in the US Personal Saving Rate: Is it Real and Is it a Puzzle?" *Federal Reserve Bank of St. Louis Review* (Nov./Dec.) 89(6), 491–514.

Gwynne, Peter. 1975. "The Cooling World," *Newsweek* (Apr. 28), 64.

Hall, Kevin G. 2009. "How Moody's Sold its Ratings – And Sold Out Investors," *McClatchy Newspapers* (Oct. 18).

Halper, Stefan. 2010. *The Beijing Consensus* (New York: Basic Books).

Halsall, Robert. 2009. "The Discourse of Corporate Cosmopolitanism," *British Journal of Management* 20, S138.

Hari, Johann. 2003. "Hypocrisy and the IMF," *The Independent* (Nov. 9).

Headrick, Daniel R., and Pascal Griset. 2001. "Submarine Telegraph Cables: Business and Politics, 1838–1939," *Business History Review* 75:3 (Autumn), 543–78.

Heimann, John G. 1980. "Deposit-Taking Institutions Can Widen Traditional Role if Freed of Restrictions," *American Banker* (May 2).

Herring, Ronald J. 1999. "Embedded Particularism: India's Failed Developmental State," in Meredith Woo-Cumings, ed., *The Developmental State* (Ithaca: Cornell University Press), 306–34.

Hershey, Robert, Jr. 1999. "Down and Out on Wall Street," *The New York Times* (Dec. 26), 3:1.

Hirsh, Michael. 2010. *Capital Offense* (Hoboken, NJ: John Wiley).

Hobson, J. A. 1902. *Imperialism* (New York: J. Pott).

Hoenig, Thomas A. 2010. "Hard Choices," Federal Reserve Bank of Kansas City (Aug. 13), www.kc.frb.org/.

Hoffman, David E. 2003. *The Oligarchs: Wealth and Power in the New Russia* (New York: Public Affairs).

Holmes, Steven A. 1999. "Fannie Mae Eases Credit to Aid Mortgage Lending," *New York Times* (Sept. 30).

Hopkins, A. G., ed. 2002. *Globalization in World History* (New York: Norton).

Housego, David. 1984. "European Business 'Must Link to Face Outside Competition'," *Financial Times* (Sept. 27), I:1.

Huber, Jurgen. 1981. "The Practice of GATT in Examining Regional Arrangements under Article XXIV," *Journal of Common Markets Studies* 19:3 (Mar.), 281–98.

Hufbauer, Gary Clyde, and Jeffrey J. Schott. 2007. "Multilateralizing Regionalism: Fitting Asia-Pacific Agreements into the WTO System," Geneva: WTO (Sept. 10–12). Available online at www.wto.org.

Hughes, Kent H. 2005. *Building the Next American Century* (Washington: Woodrow Wilson Center Press).

Hull, Liz, and Lee Sorrell. 2010. "The Image Microsoft Doesn't Want You to See," *Daily Mail On-Line* (London) (Apr. 18).

Ibarra, Marilyn, and Jennifer Koncz. 2009. "Direct Investment Positions for 2008," *Survey of Current Business* (Jul.), 32–4.

ICC. 1999. Commission on Trade and Investment, "World Business Priorities for a New Round of Multilateral Trade Negotiations" (Jun. 21). Accessed at www.iccwbo.org/.

ICC. 2001. "World Business and the Multilateral Trading System" (Nov.). Available online at www.iccwbo.org/.

ICFTU. 2006a. "Cambodia: Annual Survey of Violations of Trade Union Rights." Accessed Jun. 2010 at www.icftu.org/.

ICFTU. 2006b. "Internationally-Recognized Core Labor Standards in Bangladesh" (Sept.).

IFSL. 2009. "London Maintains Leading Role in International Equity Trading Despite Market Volatility in 2008" (Jun. 15), www.ifsl.org.uk/.

ILO. 2000. *Labor Practices in the Footwear, Leather, Textiles and Clothing Industries* (Geneva: ILO).

ILO. 2004. *Towards a Fair Deal for Migrant Workers in the Global Economy* (Geneva: ILO), 8–9.

ILO. 2009. *The Costs of Coercion* (Geneva: ILO).

IMF. "Currency Composition of Official Foreign Exchange Reserves (COFER)." Accessed Jul. 2010, at www.imf.org/.

IMF. 1947–present. *Annual Report (AR).*

IMF. 1980–present. *World Economic Outlook (WEO).* (Washington, DC: IMF).

IMF. 2002–present. *Global Financial Stability Report (GFSR).* (Washington, DC: IMF).

IMF. 2005. Independent Evaluation Office, *The IMF's Approach to Capital Account Liberalization* (Washington, DC: IMF).

IMF. 2009. "The IMF's Role in Helping Protect the Most Vulnerable in the Global Crisis," IMF, Oct. 29. Accessed online at www.imf.org/.

IMF. 2010. *The Human Cost of Recessions* (Washington, DC: IMF).

IMF. 2010. *Principal Global Indicators* (Aug. 20), www.imf.org/.

IOM. 2005. *World Migration Report* (Geneva: IOM).

Inside US Trade. 2009. "Lamy Sees Room for Climate Change Border Measures Under WTO Rules" (Jul. 3).

Inside US Trade. 2010. "EU Report: Scanning Mandate Would Create High Costs, Divert Security" (Feb. 26).

Interlandi, Jeneen. 2009. "Not Just Urban Legend," *Newsweek* (Jan. 19), 41.

International Contractors Association of Korea. "Current Status of Overseas Construction." Accessed Feb. 2010 at www.icak.or.kr/eng/kciw/kciw_01.php.

Interpol. 2008. *2008 Annual Report* (Paris: Interpol).

Irwin, Douglas A. 1996. *Against the Tide: An Intellectual History of Free Trade* (Princeton: Princeton University Press).

ITU. ICT Statistics. www.itu.int/. Accessed Jul. 2010.

Jackson, Ian. 2009. "Economic Developments in Western and Eastern Europe Since 1945," in Klaus Larres, ed., *A Companion to Europe Since 1945* (Oxford: Wiley-Blackwell), 95–112.

Jackson, Roland. 2009. "Eastern Europe Faces Depression Without Bailouts: Analysts," *Agence France Press* (Mar. 26).

James, Harold. 1996. *International Monetary Cooperation Since Bretton Woods* (New York: Oxford University Press).

James, Harold. 2001. *The End of Globalization* (Cambridge, MA: Harvard University Press).

Jickling, Mark. 2010. *Causes of the Financial Crisis* (Washington, DC: Congressional Research Service, Apr. 9). Accessed at www.crs.gov/.

Johnson, Simon, and James Kwak. 2010. *13 Bankers* (New York: Random House).

Jonquieres, Guy de. 2006. "Global Trade: Outlook for Agreements Nears Moment of Truth," *Financial Times* (Jan. 25).

Jonsson, Asgeir. 2009. *Why Iceland?* (New York: McGraw-Hill).

Joshi, Manoj. 2010. "India Is High on the Hit List," *Mail Today* (India), Apr. 13.

Kadlec, Charles W. 1999. *Dow 100,000* (Englewood Cliffs, NJ: Prentice Hall).

Kaletsky, Anatole. 1984. "Jobs: What Europe Can Learn from America," *Financial Times* (Feb. 13), 18.

Kapur, Devesh, John P. Lewis, and Richard Webb. 1997. *The World Bank: Its First Half Century* (Washington, DC: Brookings).

Karabell, Zachary. 2009. "What's Good For IBM . . . Is as Good as it Gets for America," *Newsweek* (Aug. 31).

Karmin, Craig, and Joellen Perry. 2007. "Trading Up: Homeowners Abroad Take Currency Gamble in Loans," *Wall Street Journal* (May 29), A1.

Katkakrosnar, Pat. 2007. "Flocking to 'the Detroit of the East'," *Financial Times* (Dec. 17), 15.

Kaufman, Henry. 2000. *On Money and Markets: A Wall Street Memoir* (New York: McGraw-Hill).

Khanna, Parag. 2008. *The Second World: How Emerging Powers Are Redefining Global Competition in the Twenty-First Century* (New York: Random House).

Kharas, Homi. 2010. "The Emerging Middle Class in Developing Countries," OECD Development Centre, Working Paper No. 285 (Jan.).

Keynes, John Maynard. 1920. *The Economic Consequences of the Peace* (New York: Harcourt, Brace and Howe).

Keynes, John Maynard. 1936. *The General Theory of Employment, Interest, and Money* (New York: Harcourt, Brace).

Kimball, Ann Marie. 2006. *Risky Trade: Infectious Disease in the Era of Global Trade* (London: Ashgate).

Kindleberger, Charles P. 1973. *The World in Depression* (Berkeley: University of California Press).

Kindleberger, Charles P. 1996. *Manias, Panics, and Crashes* (3rd edn., New York: John Wiley).

King, Mervyn. 2009. "Speech to Scottish Business Organizations," Edinburgh, Scotland (Oct. 20). Accessed Oct. 2009 at www.bankofengland.co.uk/publications/speeches/2009/speech406.pdf.

King, Stephen D. 2010. *Losing Control: The Emerging Threats to Western Prosperity* (New Haven, CN: Yale University Press).

Klaus, Vaclav. 2006. "The Threats to Liberty in the 21st Century" (May 6). Available online at www.klaus.cz/.

Klein, Brian P., and Kenneth Neil Cukier. 2009. "Tamed Tigers, Distressed Dragon Subtitle: How Export-Led Growth Derailed Asia's Economies," *Foreign Affairs* 88:4 (Jul./Aug.), 8–16.

Klom, Andy. 2003. "Mercosur and Brazil: A European Perspective," *International Affairs* 79(2): 351–68.

Kohut, Andrew, and Richard Wike. 2008. "Assessing Globalization," *Harvard International Review* 30:1 (Spring), 70–4.

Korea Times. 2010. "From Cottage Industry to Global Export Powerhouse in 60 Years" (Apr. 9).

Kovacheva, V., and D. Vogel. 2009. "The Size of the Irregular Foreign Resident Population in the European Union in 2002, 2005 and 2008," Hamburg Institute of International Economics, Working Paper No. 4.

Kramer, Andrew E. 2008. "Empires Built on Debt Start to Crumble," *New York Times* (Oct. 18), 1.

Kristof, Nicholas D. 1998. "Asia's Crisis Upsets Rising Effort to Confront Blight of Sweatshops," *New York Times* (Jun. 15), 1.

Kristof, Nicholas D. 2004. "Antitrade Democrats Fail the World's Poorest," *International Herald Tribune* (Jan. 15), 6.

Krueger, Anne O. 1997. "Trade Policy and Economic Development: How We Learn," *American Economic Review* 87:1 (Mar.), 1–22.

Krugman, Paul. 1987. "Is Free Trade Passé?" *Journal of Economic Perspectives* 1:2 (Fall), 131.

Krugman, Paul. 2001. "Reckonings; Hearts and Heads," *New York Times* (Apr. 22), 17.

Krugman, Paul. 2007. "Trouble with Trade," *New York Times* (Dec. 28), 23.

Krugman, Paul. 2010a. "Chinese New Year," *New York Times* (Jan. 1), 29.

Krugman, Paul. 2010b. "Rare and Foolish," *New York Times* (Oct. 18), 35.

Kunz, Diane B. 1997. *Butter and Guns* (New York: Free Press), 275–81.

Kwong, Robin. 2009. "China Eyes a Bridge to the World through Hong Kong," *Financial Times* (Jul. 29).

Lamont, James, and Kathrin Hille. 2010. "China Offers to Accelerate Trade Talks with India," *Financial Times* (Apr. 3).

Landler, Mark. 2007. "US Credit Crisis Adds to Gloom of Arctic Norway's Long Night," *New York Times* (Dec. 2).

Laquer, Walter. 2007. *The Last Days of Europe* (New York: St. Martin's).

Laver, Ross. 1985. "Free Trade," *Maclean's* (Sept. 16), 24.

Lee, B. J. 2010. "Selling South Korea: Lee Myung-bak Wants to Move His Country to the Center of the World," *Newsweek* (Feb. 8).

Leigh, David. 1998. "Billions Hidden Offshore," *Guardian* (London) (Sept. 26), 1.

Leitner, Kara, and Simon Lester. 2008. "WTO Dispute Settlement 1995–2007: A Statistical Analysis." *Journal of International Economic Law* 11 (1) (Feb.), 180–1, 192.

Lenin, Vladimir Ilyich. 1916. *Imperialism, the Highest Stage of Capitalism.* Available online at www.marxists.org/archive/lenin/works/1916/imp-hsc/index.htm.

Levinson, Marc. 2006. *The Box* (Princeton, NJ: Princeton University Press).

Levitt, Theodore. 1983. "The Globalization of Markets," *Harvard Business Review* 61:3 (May-Jun.).

Lewis, Michael. 2009. "Wall Street on the Tundra," *Vanity Fair* (Apr.).

Lewis, Paul. 1979. "O.E.C.D. Outlook Is Gloomy," *New York Times* (Dec. 20).

Lin, Jennifer. 1998. "Your Pricey Clothing Is Their Low-Pay Work," *Philadelphia Enquirer* (Feb. 8), A1.

Lipton, Eric. 2008. "Gramm and the 'Enron Loophole'," *New York Times* (Nov. 17).

Lipton, Eric, and Stephen Labaton. 2008. "Deregulator Looks Back, Unswayed," *New York Times* (Nov. 16).

Lissakers, Karin. 1991. *Banks, Borrowers, and the Establishment* (New York: Basic Books).

Liu, Melinda. 1993. "The New Slave Trade," *Newsweek* (Jun. 21), 34.

Lohr, Stephen. 2007. "A Smarter Way to Outsource," *New York Times* (Jul. 5), 1.

Lovett, William A., Alfred E. Eckes, Jr., and Richard L. Brinkman. 2004. *US Trade Policy: History, Theory and the WTO* (2nd edn., Armonk, NY: M. E. Sharpe).

Ma, Josephine. 2008. "Scandal Will Stoke Fears of 'Made in China' Label," *South China Morning Post* (Sept. 13), 4.

Maddison, Angus. 2006. *The World Economy* (Paris: OECD, Development Center Studies).

Maddison, Angus. 2010. "Statistics on World Population, GDP and Per Capita GDP, 1–2008 AD," www.ggdc.net/Maddison. Accessed Jul. 2010.

Magaziner, Ira, and Robert Reich. 1982. *Minding America's Business: The Decline and Rise of the American Economy* (New York: Vintage Books).

Magee, Gary B., and Andrew S. Thompson. 2006. "'Lines of Credit, Debts of Obligation': Migrant Remittances to Britain, c. 1875–1913," *Economic History Review* LIX, 3, 539–77.

Mahan, Rear-Admiral A. T. 1912. "The Great Illusion," *North American Review* 195 (Mar.), 319.

Marotte, Bertrand, and Rheal Seguin. 2009. "Down 25%," *Globe and Mail* (Feb. 26), B1.

Marx, Karl. 1848. "On the Question of Free Trade" (Jan. 9). Available online at www.marxists.org/archive/marx/works/1848/01/09ft.htm#marx.

Marx, Karl, and Frederick Engels. 1848. *The Communist Manifesto*. Available online at www.anu.edu.au/polsci/marx/classics/manifesto.html.

Mayer, Martin. 1998. *The Bankers* (New York: Plume).

McCormack, Richard. 2010. "Made in the USA: The Plight of American Manufacturing," *American Prospect* 21:1 (Jan./Feb.), A2.

McCraw, Thomas K. 1984. *Prophets of Regulation* (Cambridge, MA: Belknap Press of Harvard University Press).

McGregor, James. 2010. "Red Flags over China's Trade Policies," *Washington Post* (May 14).

McKenzie, Richard B. 1991. "The First and Second Reich: The Taming of an Industrial-Policy Advocate," *Cato Journal* 11:1 (Spring/Summer).

Meadows, Donella H., Dennis L. Meadows, Jorgen Randers, and William W. Behrens, III. 1972. *The Limits to Growth* (New York: Universe Books).

Mettler, Ruben F. 1981. "Make Trade, Not War!" *Industry Week* (Aug. 10), 13.

Metzler, Mark. 2006. "The Cosmopolitanism of National Economics: Friedrich List in a Japanese Mirror," in A. G. Hopkins, ed., *Global History: Interactions between the Universal and the Local* (New York: Palgrave Macmillan), 98–130.

Michie, Ranald C. 2006. *The Global Securities Market* (New York: Oxford University Press).

Mirza, Hafiz, John R. Sparkes, and Peter J. Buckley. 1996. "Contrasting Perspectives on American and European Direct Investment in Japan," *Business Economics* 31:1 (Jan.), 42.

Mishel, Lawrence, Jared Bernstein, and Heidi Shierholz. 2008. *The State of Working America 2008/2009* (Washington: Economic Policy Institute).

Mitchell, B. R. 1993. *International Historical Statistics: The Americas, 1750–1988* (New York: Stockton Press), 656, 753.

Moch, Leslie Page. 2003. *Moving Europeans: Migration in Western Europe Since 1650* (2nd edn., Bloomington, IN: Indiana University Press).

Moggridge, Arnold, ed. 1982. *The Collected Writings of John Maynard Keynes: Activities 1931–1939* (New York: Macmillan), XXI: 236–7.

Mollenkamp, Carrick, and Serena Ng. 2007. "Wall Street Wizardry Amplified Credit Crisis," *Wall Street Journal* (Dec. 27), A1.

Moore, Malcolm. 2010. "Two More Suicide Bids at Apple Factory," *Daily Telegraph* (London) (May 27).

Morgan, Lee L. 1977. "Opportunities for Mutual Action," *California Management Review* 19:4 (Summer), 91–3.

Morgenson, Gretchen. 2008a. "Behind Biggest Insurer's Crisis, A Blind Eye to a Web of Risk," *New York Times* (Sept. 28), 1.

Morgenson, Gretchen. 2008b. "Debt Watchdogs: Tamed or Caught Napping?" *New York Times* (Dec. 7), 1.

Morgenson, Gretchen. 2009. "A.I.G., Where Taxpayers' Dollars Go to Die," *New York Times* (Mar. 8), 1.

Morrell, Liz. 2010. "Supply Chain – Up in Smoke," *Retail Week* (Apr. 30).

MPI. "MPI Data Hub," www.migrationinformation.org. Accessed Jul. 2010.

Murray, Sara, and Douglas Belkin. 2010. "Americans Sour on Trade," *Wall Street Journal* (Oct. 2), 1.

Naisbitt, John. 1982. "Restructuring America," *US News* (Dec. 27), 49.

Nakamoto, Michiyo, and David Wighton. 2007. "Bullish Citigroup Is 'Still Dancing' to the Beat of the Buy-Out Boom," *Financial Times* (Jul. 10), 1.

Nanto, Dick K. 2010. *The Global Financial Crisis* (Washington: CRS Report for Congress, Feb. 4).

Nanto, Dick K., and Shinji Takagi. 1985. "Korekiyo Takahashi and Japan's Recovery from the Great Depression," *American Economic Review* 72:2 (Papers and Proceedings) (May), 372–3.

Neuman, William, and David Barboza. 2010. "U.S. Drops Inspector of Food in China," *New York Times* (Jun. 14).

New Zealand Herald. 2005. "Sweatshops Close to Home" (Jul. 29).

New Zealand Herald. 2010. "'Sweatshop' Claim Halts World Cup Toy Production" (Mar. 10).

Nike. 2007–9. *Corporate Responsibility Report, 2007–2009*, 44, 56. Accessed Jun. 2010 at www.nikebiz.com/responsibility/.

Noble, Kenneth B. 1995. "Thai Workers Are Set Free in California," *New York Times* (Aug. 4), 1.

Norberg, Johan. 2009. *Financial Fiasco* (Washington, DC: Cato Institute).

Observer. 2009. "Millions Trapped by Equity Failings" (Aug. 16), 12.

Obstfeld, Maurice, and Alan M. Taylor. 2004. *Global Capital Markets* (Cambridge, UK: Cambridge University Press).

OECD. 1997–present. *Economic Outlook (EO)*.

OECD. 2002. *International Mobility of the Highly Skilled* (Paris: OECD).

OECD. 2005–present. *Factbook (FB)* (Paris: OECD). Accessible online at www.oecdili-brary.org/.

OECD. 2008. *Growing Unequal?* (Paris: OECD).

OECD. 2009. *Agricultural Policies in OECD Countries* (Paris: OECD).

OECD. 2010. *StatExtracts* (Paris: OECD). Accessed Jul. 2010 at http://stats.oecd/index.aspx.

Ohmae, Kenichi. 1985. *Triad Power: The Coming Shape of Global Competition* (New York: Free Press).

Ohmae, Kenichi. 1989a. "Managing in a Borderless World," *Harvard Business Review* 67:3 (May/Jun.), 152–61.

Ohmae, Kenichi. 1989b. "Planting for a Global Harvest," *Harvard Business Review* 67:4 (Jul./Aug.), 136–45.

Ohmae, Kenichi. 1993. "The Rise of the Region State," *Foreign Affairs* 72:2 (Spring), 78–87.

O'Neill, Jim. 2001. "Building Better Global Economic BRICs" (Goldman Sachs: Global Economics Paper No: 66, Nov. 30), www.gs.com. Accessed Sept. 2010.

O'Neill, Jim, and Anna Stupnytska. 2009. "The Long-Term Outlook for the BRICs and N-11 Post Crisis" (Goldman Sachs: Global Economics Paper No: 192, Dec. 4), https://360.gs.com. Accessed Sept. 2010.

Ostry, Jonathan, Atish R. Ghosh, and Karl Habermeier. 2010. "Capital Inflows: The Role of Controls," International Monetary Fund Research Department (Feb. 19), 5. Available online at www.imf.org.

Owen, Richard. 1988. "Europe 'Is on Course' for 1992," *The Times* (London) (Jun. 29).

Paddock, William, and Paul Paddock. 1967. *Famine – 1975!* (Boston: Little, Brown).

Page, S. A. B. 1981. "The Revival of Protectionism and its Consequences for Europe," *Journal of Common Market Studies* 20:1 (Sept.), 27–8.

Palmisano, Samuel J. 2006. "The Globally Integrated Enterprise," *Foreign Affairs* 85:3 (May/Jun.), 127.

Panagariya, Arvind. 2008. *India: The Emerging Giant* (New York: Oxford University Press).

Panayi, Panikos. 2009. "Postwar Europe: A Continent Built on Migration," in Klaus Larres, ed., *A Companion to Europe Since 1945* (Oxford: Wiley-Blackwell), 433–49.

Paulson, Henry M. 2010. *On the Brink* (New York: Business Plus).

Pinder, John. 2009. "Federalism and the Beginnings of European Union," in Klaus Larres, ed., *A Companion to Europe Since 1945* (Oxford: Wiley-Blackwell), 25–44.

Pomfret, John. 2010a. "Australia Welcomes China's Investment, if Not its Influence," *Washington Post* (Feb. 14), A-1.

Pomfret, John. 2010b. "China's Industrial Policy Is Bigger Concern than Yuan, US Executives Say," *Washington Post* (May 7), A24.

Porter, Michael. 1990. *The Competitive Advantage of Nations* (New York: Free Press).

Poulter, Sean. 2007. "Britain's Own Subprime Crisis 'Is Underway'," *Daily Mail* (Dec. 2).

Power, Jonathan. 1976. "The Deterioration of the World's Weather," *Washington Post* (Oct. 11).

Public Citizen, Global Trade Watch. 2007 (Jul.). *Trade Deficit in Food Safety.* http://www.citizen.org/documents/FoodSafetyReportFinal.pdf.

Public Papers of the Presidents: Ronald Reagan. 1987. (Washington: GPO), 476–8.

Pylynskyi, Yaroslav. 2009. "Migration Processes in the Contemporary World," *Problems of Economic Transition* 52:7 (Nov.), 83.

Quinlan, Joseph P. 2003. *Drifting Apart or Growing Together?* (Washington, DC: Center for Transatlantic Relations).

Rajan, Raghuram G. 2010. *Fault Lines* (Princeton, NJ: Princeton University Press).

Ramo, Joshua Cooper. 1999. "The Three Marketeers," *Time* 153 (6) (Feb. 15).

Randoux, Fabrice. 2009. "Neighborhood Policy: EU Launches Eastern Partnership to Stabilize Six Ex-Soviet States," *Europolitique* (May 19).

Rather, Dan. 2010. "Kidney Pirates," *Dan Rather Reports* (Apr. 27). Accessed Jun. 2010 via LexisNexis Academic.

Reeves, Phil. 2003. "Scandal of Silk Industry Where Child Slaves Work Seven Days a Week," *The Independent* (London) (Jan. 24).

Reid, Tim. 2000. "58 Die in Lorry Ride to Hope," *The Times* (London) (Jun. 20).

Reich, Robert. 1982. "Making Industrial Policy," *Foreign Affairs* 60:4 (Spring), 852–81.

Reinert, Erik S. 2007. *How Rich Countries Got Rich ... and Why Poor Countries Stay Poor* (New York: Carroll & Graf).

Reinert, Erik S., and Sophus A. Reinert. 2005. "Mercantilism and Economic Development," in K. S. Jomo and E. S. Reinert, eds., *The Origins of Development Economics* (New York: Zed Books).

Reinhart, Carmen, and Kenneth S. Rogoff. 2009. *This Time Is Different* (Princeton, NJ: Princeton University Press).

Rennie, David. 2006. "McDonald's Condemned for EU Staff 'McPassport'," *Daily Telegraph* (London), Sept. 13, 17.

Reuters. 2009. "US European Bank Writedowns, Credit Losses" (Nov. 5).

Reynolds, Larry. 1989. "Has Globalization Hurt America?" *Management Review* (Sept.), 16–17.

Rickards, James G. 2008. "A Mountain, Overlooked; How Risk Models Failed Wall St. And Washington," *Washington Post* (Oct. 2).

Rickards, Jane. 2009. "Over Protest, Taiwan Moves Toward Free Trade with China," *Washington Post* (Dec. 23), A10.

Right Vision News. 2010. "Bangladesh: Why Must We Live with Fire Hazards?" (Mar. 10).

Roach, Alfred J. 1987. "Caribbean Offers a Golden Opportunity," *Industry Week* (Mar. 9), 14.

Robinson, Richard D. 1981. "Background Concepts and Philosophy of International Business from World War II to the Present," *Journal of International Business Studies* 12:1 (Spring/Summer), 13–21.

Roncaglia, Alessandro. 2005. *The Wealth of Ideas: A History of Economic Thought* (New York: Cambridge University Press).

Rose, Andrew. 2004. "Do WTO Members Have More Liberal Trade Policy?" *Journal of International Economics* 63:2 (Jul.), 209–35.

Rosen, Ellen Israel. 2002. *Making Sweatshops* (Berkeley, CA: University of California Press).

Ross, Ian Simpson. 1995. *The Life of Adam Smith* (Oxford: Clarendon Press).

Rothermund, Dietmar. 1996. *The Global Impact of the Great Depression 1929–1939* (New York: Routledge).

Roubini, Nouriel, and Stephen Mihm. 2010. *Crisis Economics* (New York: Penguin).

Rugman, Alan M., and Alain Verbeke. 2008. "A Regional Solution to the Strategy and Structure of Multinationals," *European Management Journal* 26, 305–13.

Saad-Filho, Alfredo. 2005. "The Rise and Decline of Latin American Structuralism and Dependency Theory," in K. S. Jomo and E. S. Reinert, eds., *The Origins of Development Economics* (New York: Zed Books), 128–45.

Sachs, Jeffrey. 2009. "America Has Passed on the Baton," *Financial Times* (Sept. 30), 1.

Sachs, Jeffrey, and Andrew Warner. 1995. "Economic Reform and the Process of Global Integration," *Brookings Papers on Economic Activity* I:1–118.

Salter, Michael. 1986. "The Pitch for an Open Trade Policy," *Maclean's* (Mar. 24), 41.

Samuels, Warren J., Jeff E. Biddle, and John B. Davis, eds. 2007. *The History of Economic Thought* (Oxford: Wiley-Blackwell).

Schacht, Henry B. 1970. "Living with Change in the Seventies," *Management Review* (Nov.), 29.

Schlesinger, James R. 2003. "Climate Change: The Science Isn't Settled," *Washington Post* (Jul. 7).

Schooner, Heidi Mandanis, and Michael Taylor. 1998–9. "Convergence and Competition: The Case of Bank Regulation in Britain and the United States," *Michigan Journal of International Law* 4, 595.

Schumpeter, Joseph. 1947. *Capitalism, Socialism, and Democracy* (2nd edn., New York: Harper).

Schwartz, Peter, Peter Leyden, and Joel Hyatt. 1999. *The Long Boom* (Cambridge, MA: Perseus).

Schwartz, Thomas Alan. 2003. *Lyndon Johnson and Europe* (Cambridge, MA: Harvard University Press).

Scottish Daily Record. 2009. "Swoop on Sweatshop" (Sept. 19).

Seligman, Joel. 2003. *The Transformation of Wall Street: A History of the Securities and Exchange Commission and Modern Corporate Finance* (New York: Aspen).

Servan-Schreiber, Jean-Jacques. 1968. *The American Challenge* (New York: Atheneum).

Shapiro, Irving S. 1973. "One-World Economics," *Vital Speeches of the Day* (Oct. 15), 18–22.

Shenkar, Oded. 2005. *The Chinese Century* (Saddle River, NJ: Pearson).

Shin, Annys, and Julliet Eilperin. 2009. "G-20 Grabs a Bigger Role in the Global Economy," *Washington Post* (Sept. 27), A01.

Shleifer, Andrei. 2009. "The Age of Milton Friedman," *Journal of Economic Literature* 47:1, 123–35.

Shultz, George P. 1995. "Economics in Action: Ideas, Institutions, Policies," *American Economic Review* 85:2 Papers and Proceedings (May), 4.

Simon, R., and G. Button. 1990. ""What I Learned in the Eighties," *Forbes* 145:1 (Jan. 8), 100–10.

Singer, Morris. 1983. "Ataturk's Economic Legacy," *Middle Eastern Studies* 19:3 (Jul.), 301–11.

Sito, Peggy. 2010. "State Enterprises Moving in on Global Real Estate," *South China Morning Post* (Mar. 15), 3.

Skidelsky Robert. 1994. *John Maynard Keynes: The Economist as Savior, 1920–1937* (London: Penguin).

Skidelsky, Robert. 2009. *Keynes: The Return of the Master* (New York: Public Affairs).

Skinner, Kiron K., Annelise Anderson, and Martin Anderson, eds. 2001. *Reagan in His Own Hand* (New York: Free Press).

Smick, David. 2009. "Now What? How We Got into Today's Mess and Where We Go From Here," *The Weekly Standard* (Jul. 24).

Smith, Adam. 1937. *The Wealth of Nations* (New York: Modern Library).

Smith, B. Mark. 2003. *A History of the Global Stock Market* (Chicago: University of Chicago Press).

Smith, Hedrick. 1998. *Surviving the Bottom Line* (Jan. 17) (Films for the Humanities & Sciences VHS ISBN: 978-0-7365-9870-5).

Solomon, Lawrence. 2010. "Catastrophism Collapses," *Financial Post* (Canada) (Jul. 3), 19.

Sommer, Nolan B. 1977. "The Challenges Facing the Multinational Corporation," *Vital Speeches of the Day* (Nov. 15), 85–9.

Sorkin, Andrew Ross. 2009. *Too Big to Fail* (New York: Viking).

South Africa, National Prosecuting Authority. 2010. *Tsireledzani: Understanding the Dimensions of Human Trafficking in Southern Africa* (Mar.). Accessed online Jun. 2010 at www.hsrc.ac.za/Document-3562.phtml.

Srinivasan, T. N. 2007. "The Dispute Settlement Mechanism of the WTO: A Brief History and an Evaluation from Economic, Contractarian and Legal Perspectives," *The World Economy*, 1039–41.

Steingraber, Fred G. 1996. "The New Business Realities of the Twenty-First Century," *Business Horizons* (Nov./Dec.), 1–5.

Stiglitz, Joseph E. 2002. *Globalization And Its Discontents* (New York: W. W. Norton).

Stiglitz, Joseph. 2010. *Free Fall* (New York: W. W. Norton).

Stokes, Bruce. 2008. "Going Green in Trade Policy," *National Journal* (Feb. 9).

Stone, Irving. 1977. "British Direct and Portfolio Investment in Latin America before 1914," *Journal of Economic History* 37:3 (Sept.), 690–722.

Stone, Nan. 1989. "The Globalization of Europe: An Interview with Wisse Dekker," *Harvard Business Review* 67:3 (May/Jun), 90–5.

Strauss-Kahn, Dominique. 2009. "Economic Stability, Economic Cooperation, and Peace–The Role of the IMF," address in Oslo (Oct. 23). Accessed Nov. 2009 at www.imf.org/external/np/speeches/2009/102309.htm.

Streitfeld, David, and Gretchen Morgenson. 2008. "Building Flaw American Dreams," *New York Times* (Oct. 19), 1.

Sullivan, Scott. 1984. "The Decline of Europe," *Newsweek* (Apr. 9), 44.

Szporluk, Roman. 1988. *Communism & Nationalism: Karl Marx versus Friedrich List* (New York: Oxford University Press).

Talbott, Strobe. 1992. "America Abroad: The Birth of the Global Nation," *Time* (Jul. 20), 70.

Tam, Fiona, and Mimi Lau. 2010. "Shutters Slammed on Reporting of Strikes at Factories," *South China Morning Post* (Jun. 12), 1.

Tappin, Steve, and Andrew Cave. 2009. "Hard Globalization," *Business Strategy Review* (Spring), 35–7.

Teather, David. 2005. "Nike Lists Abuses at Asian Factories," *The Guardian* (London) (Apr. 14), 17.

Tett, Gillian. 2009. *Fool's Gold* (New York: Free Press).

Thai Press. 2010. "China Companies Warned of Increasing Labor Costs in China" (Jun. 14). Accessed via LexisNexis Academic.

Thatcher, Margaret. 1993. *The Downing Street Years* (New York: HarperCollins).

Thatcher, Margaret. 2002. *Statecraft: Strategies for a Changing World* (London: HarperCollins).

Theil, Stefan, and Alan Mascarenhas. 2010. "A Green Retreat," *Newsweek* (Jul. 19).

Times (London). 1911. "Mr. Churchill on Free Trade and Peace" (Apr. 8), 6.

Times (London). 2006. "Sir Roy Denman" (Apr. 19), 60.

Thomson, James, and Cara Stepanczuk. 2007. "Foreign Banks in the United States," *Economic Trends* (Cleveland: Federal Reserve Bank of Cleveland, Aug. 6), www.clevelandfed.org/research/trends/2007/0807/.

Thurow, Lester C. 1985. *The Zero-Sum Solution* (New York: Simon and Schuster).

TI. 2009. *Corruption Perceptions Index 2009* (Berlin, Germany: TI).

Tignor, Robert L. 2006. *W. Arthur Lewis and the Birth of Development Economics* (Princeton, NJ: Princeton University Press).

Toffler, Alvin. 1980. *The Third Wave* (New York: Bantam Books).

Toffler, Alvin. 1990. *Power Shift* (New York: Bantam Books).

Toye, John, and Richard Toye. 2004. *The UN and Global Political Economy* (Bloomington, IN: Indiana University Press).

Trentmann, Frank. 2007. *Free Trade Nation* (Oxford: Oxford University Press).

Triffin, Robert. 1960. *Gold and the Dollar Crisis* (New Haven: Yale University Press).

Uchitelle, Louis. 1989. "US Businesses Loosen Link to Mother Country," *New York Times* (May 21).

United Kingdom Debt Management Office, *Quarterly Report* (various issues), www.dmo.gov.uk/. Accessed Jul. 2010.

UNCTAD. 1991–. *World Investment Report (WIR) (annual).* Available online at www.unctad.org/.

UNCTAD. 2009. *Handbook of Statistics 2009 (HoS).* Available online at www.unctad.org/.

UNCTAD. 2010. *FDISTAT 2010.* Available online at www.unctad.org/.

UNDESA. 2004. *World Economic and Social Survey 2004: International Migration* (New York: UN).

UNDESA. *World Population Prospects: The 2008 Revision Population Database.* Accessed Mar. 2010 at http://esa.un.org/unpp.

United Nations. 2009. *The Millennium Development Goals Report* (New York: UN).

United Nations Environment Program. 2005. *Environment and Trade: A Handbook* (2nd edn., Geneva: UN Environment Program).

United Nations, General Assembly. 1974. "Declaration on the Establishment of a New International Economic Order" (May 1). Available online at www.un-documents.net/s6r3201.htm.

UNODC. 2009. *The Global Report on Trafficking in Persons* (Vienna: UNODC). Available online at www.unodc.org/.

UNODC. 2010. *The Globalization of Crime* (Vienna: UNODC). Available online at http://www.unctad.org/.

UNWTO. 2010. "International Tourism Receipts 2009" (Apr.). Accessed Jul. 2010 at www.unwto.org/.

USBEA. 2010a. "International Investment Position." Accessed Jul. 2010 at www.bea.gov/international/datatables/.

USBEA. 2010b. "US International Transactions Accounts Data." Accessed Jul. 2010 at http://www.bea.gov/international/bp_web/.

USBoC. "Foreign Trade Statistics," www.census.gov/.

USBoC. 1878–present. *Statistical Abstract of the United States (SA) (annual)*, www. census.gov/.

USCBO. 2010. *Budget and Economic Outlook* (Washington, DC: GPO, Jan.). Accessed Jul. 2010 at www.cbo.gov/.

US–China Business Council, www.uschina.org/.

USCIA. *World Factbook (WF)*. Available online at www.cia.gov/.

USDoS. 2001–. *Trafficking in Persons Report (TIPR)*. Available online at www.state. gov/g/tip/rls/tiprpt/.

US Economic Report of the President (Washington, DC: annual).

USEIA. 2008. *Country Analysis Briefs: Russia* (May). Available online at www.eia.doe. gov.

USFRBG. 2009. "Flow of Funds Accounts" (Sept. 17). Accessed Dec. 2009 at www.fed-eralreserve.gov/.

USFRBSF. 2009. "US Household Deleveraging and Future Consumption Growth," *FRBSF Economic Letter* (May 15).

USGAO. 2009. *Supply Chain Security* (GAO-10-12) (Washington, DC: GAO, Oct. 30).

USNIC. 2004. *Mapping the Global Future* (Washington: GPO, Dec.).

US Senate Banking Committee. 1999. "Gramm's Statement at Signing Ceremony for Gramm-Leach-Bliley Act" (Nov. 12). Available online at http://banking.senate.gov/public/.

USTR. 1985–. *National Trade Estimate Report on Foreign Trade Barriers (NTERFTB)*. Available online at www.ustr.gov.

US Treasury. 2010. "Major Foreign Holders of Treasury Securities" (Jul. 16), www.treas. gov/tic/mfhhis01.txt.

US Treasury. *Treasury Bulletin* (various issues). Available online at www.fms.treas.gov/ bulletin/index.html. Accessed Jul. 2010.

Van Damme, Isabelle. 2008. "Seventh Annual WTO Conference: an Overview," *Journal of International Economic Law* 11:1, 155–65.

Vogel, Ezra F. 1979. *Japan as Number One* (Cambridge, MA: Harvard University Press).

Waite, James. 2004. "Reducing the Cost of Distance: Technological Change and the Globalization of New Zealand, 1960–2000," *Global Economy Journal* 4:1, Article 5.

Wall Street Journal. 2008. "Dodd and Countrywide" (Oct. 10).

Walters, Kenneth D., and R. Joseph Monsen. 1983. "Nationalization Trends in European Industry," *McKinsey Quarterly* (Spring), 51–69.

Wang, Chun Yu, and Walt F. J. Goodridge. 2009. *Chicken Feathers and Garlic Skin: Diary of a Chinese Garment factory Girl on Saipan* (New York: Passion Profit Company).

Ward, Andrew. 2009. "McDonald's Pulls Out of Iceland," *Financial Times* (Oct. 26).

Washington Post. 2008. "How They Saw it, What They Said" (Oct. 15), A08.

Wayne, Leslie. 1989. "A Doctor for Struggling Economies," *New York Times* (Oct. 1).

Wedel, Janine R. 1998. *Collision and Collusion: The Strange Case of Western Aid to Eastern Europe 1989–1998* (New York: St. Martin's).

Wehrfritz, George. 2005. "Vietnam Revs Up," *Newsweek* (Nov. 28), 43.

Wehrfritz, George, Erika Kinetz, and Jonathan Kent. 2008. "Lured into Bondage," *Newsweek* (Mar. 24).

Weiss, Martin A. 2008. *Sovereign Wealth Funds: Background and Policy Issues for Congress* (CRS Report for Congress, RL34336) (Sept. 3).

Welch, John F. 1983. "The New Competitiveness: Can it Survive the Recovery?" *Vital Speeches of the Day* (Jul. 1), 549.

WEF. 2009a. *The Africa Competitiveness Report 2009* (Geneva: WEF). Accessed Jul. 2010 at www.weforum.org/.

WEF. 2009b. *The Travel & Tourism Competitiveness Report 2009* (Geneva: WEF).

WEF. 2010–11."The Global Competitiveness Index 2010–2011 Rankings," at www.weforum.org/.

WFE. "Statistics: Time Series." Available online at http://world-exchanges.org/.

White, Nancy J. 1996. "Home Sweat Home," *Toronto Star* (Sept. 1), F1.

White, Lawrence. 2009. "Investment Banking: China Buys into Raw Materials," *Euromoney* (Mar.).

Wigmore, Barrie A. 1985. *The Crash and its Aftermath: A History of Securities Markets in the United States, 1929–1933* (Westport, CT: Greenwood Press).

Wilkins, Mira. 1974. *The Maturing of Multinational Enterprise: American Business Abroad from 1914 to 1970* (Cambridge, MA: Harvard University Press).

Williamson, John. 2002. "Did the Washington Consensus Fail?" speech (Nov. 6). Accessed Jun. 2009 at www.iie.com/publications/papers/paper.cfm?researchid=488.

Wilson, Dominic, and Raluca Dragusanu. 2008. "The Expanding Middle: The Exploding World Middle Class and Falling Global Inequality" (Goldman Sachs: Global Economics Paper No: 170, Jul.).

Wolf, Martin. 2004. *Why Globalization Works* (New Haven: Yale University Press).

Wolf, Martin. 2009. "The West No Longer Holds All the Cards," *Financial Times* (Sept. 24).

Wonacott, Peter. 2010. "World Cup Lends South Africa Confidence to Unite Continent," *Wall Street Journal* (Jul. 18).

Woo-Cumings, Meredith, ed. 1999. *The Developmental State* (Ithaca: Cornell University Press).

Woodward, Bob. 2000. *Maestro: Alan Greenspan and the American Boom* (New York: Simon & Schuster).

World Bank. 1978–present. *World Development Report (WDR)*.

World Bank. 1993. *East Asian Miracle* (New York: Oxford University Press).

World Bank. 1998–. *Global Economic Prospects (GEP)*. Available online at http://web.worldbank.org.

World Bank. 2009. *Migration and Remittance Trends 2009* (World Bank, Nov. 3).

World Bank. 2010. "Foreign Direct Investment – the China Story" (Jul. 17), www.worldbank.org. Accessed Oct. 2010.

World Bank. "How We Classify Countries," http://data.worldbank.org/. Accessed Sept. 2010.

World Bank. *World Development Indicators (WDI)*. Available online at http://ddp-ext.worldbank.org.

WTO. 1998–. *International Trade Statistics (ITS)*. Available online at www.wto.org/english/res_e/statis_e.

WTO. 2001. "Ministerial Declaration" (Nov. 14). Available online at www.wto.org/.

WTO. 2003–. *World Trade Report (WTR)*. Available online at www.wto.org/english/res_e/r eser_e/wtr_e.

WTO. 2005–. *Trade Profiles (TP)*. Available online at www.wto.org/english/res_e/reser_e/trade_profiles_e.htm.

WTO. "Dispute Settlement," Available online at www.wto.org/english/tratop_e/disp_e/.

Wriston, Walter. 1980. "Technology, Inflation Render Fortress Banking Untenable," *The American Banker* (May 2).

Wriston, Walter. 1982a. "Banking Against Disaster," *New York Times* (Sept. 14), A27.

Wriston, Walter. 1982b. "The Information Society," *Vital Speeches of the Day* (Nov. 15), 92–5.

Wriston, Walter. 1997. "Bits, Bytes, and Diplomacy," *Foreign Affairs* 76:5, 172–82.

Yeates, Clancy. 2009. "Brakes Put on Chinese Investment," *The Age* (Melbourne, Australia) (Sept. 25), 1.

Yergin, Daniel, and Joseph Stanislaw. 1998. *The Commanding Heights* (New York: Simon and Schuster).

Yerxa, Rufus. 2010. "Speech to the United Kingdom Public Interest Environmental Law Conference in London" (Mar. 26). Available online at www.wto.org/english/news_e/news10_e/envir_26mar10_e.htm.

Young, John A. 1985. "Global Competition: The New Reality," *California Management Review* 27:3 (Spring), 34.

Zachariah, Benjamin. 2004. *Nehru* (London: Routledge).

Zacher, Mark W., and Tania J. Keefe. 2008. *The Politics of Global Health Governance*. (New York: Palgrave Macmillan).

Zalewski, Jan. 2010. "EU, India Discuss Free Trade Agreement," *Global Insight* (Jan. 28).

Zeng, Ming, and Peter J. Williamson. 2003. "The Hidden Dragons," *Harvard Business Review* (Oct.), 92.

Zimmermann, Klaus, and Dorothea Schafer. 2009. "Germany Must Waste No Time in Reforming its Banks," *Financial Times* (Jul. 23), 9.

Zoellick, Robert. 2008. "Modernizing Multilateralism and Markets" (Washington: Peterson Institute for International Economics, Oct. 6). Available online at www.piie.com/events/event_detail.cfm?EventID=86.

Zweig, Philip L. 1996. *Walter Wriston, Citibank, and the Rise and Fall of American Financial Supremacy* (New York: Crown).

Index

The Contemporary Global Economy: A History Since 1980, First Edition. Alfred E. Eckes, Jr.
© 2011 Alfred E. Eckes, Jr. Published 2011 by Blackwell Publishing Ltd.